How to Sell to the CIO and CISO

First Edition

An insider's guide to building trust and gaining executive buy-in

David J. Gee

<packt>

How to Sell to the CIO and CISO

First Edition

The author acknowledges the use of cutting-edge AI with the sole aim of enhancing the language and clarity within the book, thereby ensuring a smooth reading experience. It's important to note that the content itself has been crafted by the author and edited by a professional publishing team.

Portfolio Director: Vijin Boricha
Senior Portfolio Manager: Rahul Nair
Program Manager: Ankita Thakur
Content Engineer: Rebecca Youé
Technical Editor: Nithik Cheruvakodan
Copy Editor: Rebecca Youé
Indexer: Rekha Nair
Proofreader: Rebecca Youé
Production Designer: Prashant Ghare
Growth Lead: Ankita Thakur

First published: July 2026
Production reference: 2100826
Published by Packt Publishing Ltd.
Grosvenor House
11 St Paul's Square
Birmingham
B3 1RB, UK.

ISBN 978-1-80730-079-1
`www.packtpub.com`

For Anna – three books, three years, and still smiling. Love you.

For my amazing family – Nathan, Amber, Jeremy, Sabrina, Samson, Virginia, Azalea and Harrison. You had me at hello. You are the whole point (I love you all).

My appreciation to the amazing team that helped me with this book. The technical reviewers (Tanya, Fred, and Jimmy) and the many CIO, CISO, champions, analyst and vendors. In total there were 55+ friends that provided their insights as quotations and I'm grateful for their willingness to share their wisdom. Finally, the great team at Packt – Dhruv, Rahul, Rebecca, Ankita, and Gandhali for their expertise and ability to deliver!

In the AI era, your greatest competitive advantage is still the creativity and curiosity that only a human heart can hold. For that reason, my future plans include writing a series of children's tech, cyber and AI books with the creative talents of my two grandkids Azalea (Azzy) and Harrison (Harry).

Watch out world for that collaboration!

David J. Gee

Foreword

Every CISO I know carries two burdens at once: the operational burden of keeping the organization safe today, and the strategic burden of moving it somewhere better tomorrow. Early in my career, I believed the first burden was the job. Thirty years and five executive seats later, I've come to understand that the second burden is the job. Security that only defends what already exists is playing a finite game. Security that drives change is playing the long game. I've spent much of my career, and most of my writing, trying to convince my peers that this second game is the one worth mastering, what I call the infinite game.

That distinction is why this book matters.

A CISO's strategic agenda is only as strong as the coalition behind it. You can have the right roadmap, the right risk model, and a board-approved budget, and still watch initiatives stall in committee, in Procurement, or in the quiet resistance of a business unit that doesn't yet see why anything needs to change. Positive change inside a large organization is never a solo act. It is a partnership between the CISO, and the internal champions scattered across Engineering, Legal, Finance, and the business who are willing to put their own credibility behind an idea before it's proven. Those champions are how a strategic agenda becomes an operational reality. And more often than most people admit, the right vendor, brought in at the right moment by the right champion, is what turns a stalled initiative into a shipped one.

This is exactly where most vendor relationships fail CISOs, and where this book succeeds. It treats the vendor relationship not as a transaction to be survived, but as a lever for the change the CISO is already trying to drive. That is a harder thing to teach than a sales technique, because it requires understanding both sides of the table: what the CISO is actually accountable for, and what a vendor needs to demonstrate before a CISO, and the champions standing behind that CISO, will bet their program, their team, and their credibility on that vendor's product.

I've had the unusual experience of sitting on both sides of that table. I've built and led security and technology programs as a CISO, CIO, and CSO across federal government, municipal government, telecommunications, global investment, and technology carrying the budget, hiring the team, and answering to the board for the outcome. I've also stood on the vendor side, as a Field CISO representing a security company to the very peer group I once sat among, trying to earn the kind of trust I used to demand from vendors calling on me. That dual vantage point changed how I think about the CISO-vendor relationship. From the operations side, you learn to spot the vendor who is selling a feature versus the vendor who understands your mission. From the vendor side, you learn how much of a lasting relationship is really built before the pitch ever happens, through patience, listening, and showing up with something useful instead of something to sell.

What both seats taught me is this: the CISOs and vendors who build relationships that last are the ones who treat trust as the product, and the sale as the byproduct. The internal champion is the person willing to stake their own reputation on that trust being real. The vendor's job is to earn it before asking for it. The CISO's job is to protect the champions who take that risk on the vendor's behalf.

This book, by David Gee, gives you a rare, practical map for building that kind of relationship from both directions. Whether you are a CISO trying to build the coalition that will carry your strategic agenda forward, or a vendor trying to become the partner a CISO trusts enough to champion internally, the principles in these pages will serve you well.

Read it as a playbook, but treat it as a relationship guide. In both cybersecurity and technology, as in the infinite game, the partnerships you build are the only advantage that compounds.

Gary Hayslip, CISSP

CISO | CIO | CSO | Field CISO

Author, CISO Executive Intelligence series

San Diego, California

Foreword

Ideas are easy. Creating lasting change in complex organisations is hard.

The paradox of modern technology leadership is that while CIOs and CISOs desperately need new ideas, the sheer volume of ideas competing for their attention makes it harder than ever to identify the ones that matter.

This book is for the internal champions and partners who understand that success is not measured by being heard, but by helping leaders turn the right ideas into meaningful outcomes.

Gerard Florian

Former ANZ Bank Group Executive & CIO

Foreword

I am thrilled to have the opportunity to introduce David's latest work, though I will confess that my qualifications for doing so have nothing to do with technology.

I am not a CIO. I am not a CISO. I have never sat in a board risk committee or evaluated a vendor's AI governance framework.

What I have done is sit in the next room, watching David labor over every word. There was a quiet intensity to it, the unmistakable energy of someone working through a problem that matters deeply.

And that is what I can speak to.

I know from David's own career that driving change has always been his north star. It is not something he just talks about, it is something he has lived and at times fought for. That experience shapes every page of his book.

And he deeply cares about developing the next generation of leaders to drive that change.

At its heart, this book is his attempt to make this whole process better. To give vendors the language, frameworks, and honesty required to show up differently. But perhaps more importantly, it challenges the internal champions (architects and advocates) within enterprises to step forward with confidence.

I may not understand every argument in these pages. But I understand why he wrote them.

Anna Gee

Contributors

About the author

David J. Gee is a grandfather, a father, and a Buddhist. A third-generation Australian born Chinese who grew up in Darwin in the Northern Territory, he is the proud son of David and Cindy Gee. He brings to everything he does a perspective shaped by culture, family, and a quiet but persistent belief that how we do things matters as much as what we do.

His professional career has been extensive and international, spanning roles as a CIO, CISO, and Risk Executive before transitioning into his current work as a Board Risk Advisor, Keynote Speaker, and Non-Executive Director. He is someone who has not just observed the technology leadership landscape from the outside, but has lived inside it at the highest levels, across multiple industries and geographies.

This third book continues that journey of service to the technology leadership community, turning his attention this time to the relationship between technology leaders and the vendors who want to earn their trust.

He can be found at `linkedin.com/in/davidjordangee`.

About the reviewers

Fred Stute has operated in CISO, CIO, and CA roles internationally at insurers, service providers, and standards organizations. He has presented at industry forums extolling the criticality of security and cloud design, having also been active in contributing to the initial Salesforce.com Technical Architect certification program. He has contributed to start-ups delivering cloud services and artificial intelligence in the provision of health services and insurance. When not in front of a computer, he can be found clocking kilometers on a gravel bike and enjoying time with his family.

Jimmy Wong is a global cybersecurity executive with 15+ years leading enterprise security, risk governance, cyber crisis management, and executive engagement across regulated financial services environments in APAC. He has a proven track record of owning major enterprise cyber capabilities and transformation programs end-to-end, from threat detection through board reporting, while building high-performing teams and sustained security cultures.

In recent years, he has focused on developing next-generation cyber leadership, strategy frameworks, third-party risk management, and technology regulatory change. He holds a first-class honors master's degree in executive IT Management from the University of Melbourne, completed during the COVID lockdown, and is a Graduate of the Australian Institute of Company Directors (GAICD). He is the current President of the ISC2 Melbourne chapter.

Tanya Graham is a seasoned technology and transformation executive with deep experience leading technology, digital, data, and cyber portfolios in complex, high-stakes environments. As a CIO who has navigated major organizational change, vendor partnerships, and enterprise-wide technology decisions, she has firsthand experience of exactly what it takes to capture the attention of a technology executive, build genuine trust, and turn that into a productive long-term partnership.

Tanya is able to draw on real-world executive insight into the priorities, pressures, and decision-making rhythms of CIOs and CISOs, offering a grounded perspective on what truly resonates with technology leaders and why, and equally what doesn't work.

Table of Contents

Preface

In the beautiful medieval city of Florence, Italy, stands the 17-foot-tall statue of David. This magnificent tribute to the biblical hero looks alive. If you stand close enough, you can almost feel the blood flowing through the veins in his arms and muscular legs.

Decades ago, before everyone carried a camera phone, I came as a visitor and could simply stand in awe of this masterpiece and reflect on the workmanship. But this incredible artistry hides a messy history.

Michelangelo was the third artist to work on the statue. Two earlier artisans started the project but quit. They believed the giant block of marble was too flawed to use. The stone sat abandoned for 26 years. Then, a 26-year-old Michelangelo took over the ruined block and carved a miracle:

P.1 – Michelangelo's David (By Jörg Bittner Unna, CC BY 3.0 (https://creativecommons.org/licenses/by/3.0/deed.en) via Wikimedia)

Today, every CIO and CISO faces a similar challenge. They want to build a legacy. Yet, they must build it on top of a messy, flawed technology stack—their flawed block of marble. CIO and CISO executive leaders have the vision to create something great; however, they cannot do it alone. They need true partners to make the magic happen.

Unfortunately, no one would call the current sales process a masterpiece. Most people use much uglier words to describe how vendors and tech leaders interact today. Leaders do not need aggressive vendors; they need an internal champion to help them find true artisans to help them carve the marble.

This book is a guide to fixing the broken sales process. It offers a fresh approach to vendor relationships. It will help you help CIOs and CISOs turn their flawed technology stack into a masterpiece.

> **Note**
>
> Great partnerships rely on deep trust to unlock true potential.
>
> With that trust, you can sculpt your legacy together.

This book is your guide to seeing the world through the eyes of the CIO and CISO. The insights that follow are drawn from my own experience on both sides of the table; as the executive being sold to, and as the advisor who has done the selling, and they are offered with the honesty that only comes from having lived the consequences of getting this relationship right.

> **Note**
>
> When I was a younger leader, I was once told by a colleague that *I could sell anything to anyone.* At the time I was a Director at EY, and selling IT consulting, and I was speaking to Hussein Rifai, a peer who later in life became a successful chairman of a large iconic Australian listed company.

In this book I will share what the CIO and CISO look for beyond the demo, how to empower internal champions to fight for your solution when you are not in the room, and how to earn the kind of credibility that survives a difficult conversation that could have gone either way. I will also share tips on how to navigate the political landscape that surrounds every significant buying decision and how to position your solution within the strategic frameworks that CIOs and CISOs use to weigh risk, assess fit, and decide who deserves their trust.

Trust, I have learnt, is not built through polished presentations or persuasive proposals but by solving problems that matter and by showing up the same way, regardless of if the deal is years away.

This book is a guide to fixing the broken process that has made vendor relationships more transactional, and less valuable than they should be. It offers a fresh approach, one that takes the full journey seriously, from the first cold approach to the moment a customer becomes an advocate.

Who this book is for

This book is for vendors who want to sell to CIOs and CISOs, and for the internal champions that support them.

Whether you represent a package (an integrated platform) or a best of breed solution, you will learn how to shift every conversation away from features and toward outcomes, anchoring your value to the metrics that matter to the board rather than the capabilities that impress the architecture team.

This book will also encourage internal champions to drive strategic initiatives with confidence and clarity, but I will be honest about where the risks are and where your credibility is most exposed.

What this book covers

Chapter 1, How to Sell to the CIO and CISO, sets the foundation by exploring how CIOs and CISOs prioritise competing demands, make decisions under pressure, and evaluate the vendors who are asking for their time. Establishing the mindset shift that the rest of the book depends on, from vendor who pitches to partner who understands. The focus is on business acumen and the ability to speak the language of outcomes rather than features. The vendor who cannot do both will struggle to apply anything that comes after this chapter.

Chapter 2, How to Partner with the CIO and CISO, goes into CIO and CISO personas, including what drives them, and what threatens them. It also covers how they respond to the "carrots" of opportunity and the "sticks" of consequence that shape their decision making every day. The chapter closes with an honest examination of C-Suite churn, exploring why the short tenure of these roles can open doors for vendors willing to build relationships early, and why the vendors who understand that every incoming executive arrives with a mandate to prove themselves and a window of openness to new ideas that closes faster than expected.

Chapter 3, Contacting the C-Suite, tackles the most fundamental challenge in enterprise sales: getting in front of the CIO and CISO. Continuous outreach and generic digital approaches do more damage than most vendors realize. I will also make the case that the internal champion who builds credibility and partners with the vendor is key.

Chapter 4, Why Identifying (or Becoming) the Internal Champion is a Career Accelerant, focusses on how the internal champion is the most powerful accelerant. Their credibility inside the organization will always carry more weight than any external pitch vendors can deliver. I also discuss the career opportunity for the champion, which is real and significant, but so is the risk.

Chapter 5, Your Preparation, explores how most vendors arrive underprepared with a generic pitch. AI has given every vendor access to the same research tools, which means showing up informed is no longer a differentiator but a baseline expectation. The vendor who arrives with genuine insight is the one who stands out.

Chapter 6, Walking Into the Office of the CIO and CISO, shows you that getting into the room is just the beginning. This chapter is about the soft skills that carry the meeting, including: executive presence, active listening, and emotional intelligence. The vendor who walks out of a first meeting having sharpened the CIO and CISO's thinking has earned the invitation to come back.

Chapter 7 Deep Dive Into the CIO and CISO Perspective, exposes how the CIO and CISO actually think; not the polished version they present to the board, but the permanent tension they navigate every day, between the "F1" speed that executives demand and the fragile legacy infrastructure that makes that speed genuinely dangerous.

Chapter 8, Stepping Into the Shoes of the Architect, establishes why the architect is often the most consequential relationship a vendor can build below the C-suite. Converting them from gatekeeper to champion creates the most powerful form of internal advocacy available. The architect champion who feels respected and genuinely understood will do more for a vendor's chances of success than any executive sponsor, because they carry both the technical credibility to validate the solution and the organizational credibility to make others believe it.

Chapter 9, Gap Analysis, explores where real trust is built. Vendors who arrive for the gap analysis having done their own honest internal assessment, disclose weaknesses proactively, and frame gaps in terms of workarounds and roadmap timelines will always outperform those who try to hide problems.

Chapter 10, Navigating the Maze of Politics, confronts the reality that political friction is the hidden killer of deals that are technically sound and commercially justified. As a vendor, you are largely blind to it, which makes your internal champion essential, because they are your only reliable window into organizational dynamics.

Chapter 11, The Value of Research Analysts and Advisors, explains that analysts provide independent political insulation to defend technology choices upward to boards and CFOs. The evaluation is only half the job though, and making it easy for the executive to defend their choice with credible third-party support is the other half.

Chapter 12, Proof Positive, covers the proof of concept (POC) and proof of value (POV) stage—the most structured and highest stakes phase of the entire sales cycle. This is a dress rehearsal for the partnership itself, where how your team behaves under pressure, responds to queries, and handles gaps honestly is being evaluated as carefully as the product performance. The winner of a POC or POV is not always the objectively best solution.

Chapter 13, Packages vs. Best of Breed Solutions (vs. AI), explores the package vs. best of breed debate. This is a question that has never been fully resolved and that the AI era is now making significantly more complex. The most important question this chapter leaves every vendor with is simple: do you know where your solution sits in the CIO and CISO's strategic, core, or essential classification, and can you articulate why it belongs there?

Chapter 14, Selling into a Major Transformation, covers the scenario where your solution gets absorbed into a major enterprise transformation. This is where the rules of engagement change completely, and the Chief Transformation Officer (CTO) emerges as a new buyer who speaks only in board-visible business outcomes.

Chapter 15, When Ownership is Unclear, confronts one of the most common and frustrating deal-killers in enterprise sales: an unclear ownership. This is a dynamic that is almost always invisible from the outside, but where projects become orphans, budgets get reallocated, and champions lose their ability to drive decisions.

Chapter 16, Let's Go for Lunch, explores why a simple lunch invitation carries far more political and relationship weight than most vendors appreciate. If the timing is wrong, you are pitching it to the wrong persona, or framing it as a celebration rather than a working session, you can damage trust that took months to build. We look at what the safest approaches to take are, while still investing in building trust.

Chapter 17, Show Your Bench Strength, explains that the people behind the product often become the deciding factor in sales decisions. You must build relationships deliberately and early at every level, because introducing yourself to a critical stakeholder in the middle of a crisis is poor timing.

Chapter 18, Business Case Approval, explores the business case approval stage. This is the moment the sale moves beyond the CIO and CISO's control into a web of Chief Financial Officer (CFO) scrutiny, board politics, and competing budgets. The vendor who prepares the CIO and CISO for multiple rounds of challenge will always be more trusted.

Chapter 19, The Procurement Playbook, explores the complex dynamics between technology leaders and procurement teams during the buying journey. Procurement operates independently with genuine veto power, and their incentives are structurally misaligned with the CIO and CISO's priority of implementation speed.

Chapter 20, Contracting, explores the contracting stage. This is one of the most frustrating phases of any technology process because it shifts control away from the vendor, the CIO, and the CISO and into the hands of legal teams who operate by entirely different rules. The vendors who move through Legal fastest are the ones who arrive prepared.

Chapter 21, Building a Partnership of Trust, proposes that trust is not a milestone to be reached at contract signing. Instead, this is a currency that compounds through consistent behavior across transparency, reliability, commitment, and alignment, and depletes the moment your conduct falls short. The vendor-champion relationship is the connective tissue that holds the partnership together. A genuine win-win requires both parties to prioritize the long-term relationship over short-term gain.

Chapter 22, Book of Secrets, brings together candid wisdom from CIOs, CISOs, vendors, and advisors on what genuinely works. This chapter provides, from the community, the clearest picture of what separates the vendors who earn lasting trust from the ones who are remembered only for what they got wrong. What emerges consistently is that successful vendors shift from transactional selling to genuine partnership by doing deep research, speaking the language of business outcomes, helping executives navigate internal politics and showing up with commitment from the first interaction.

Chapter 23, How to Be an MVP, argues that the most valuable player (MVP) vendor status is not a commercial milestone but a career-long distinction. This is earned through sustained trust and repeated performance that makes the CIO and CISO look good across their professional lives. This trust survives role changes, organizational shifts, and the inevitable moments of difficulty.

To get the most out of this book

I'd suggest taking the traditional approach of starting at the beginning of this book; however, I'm aware that each reader will come with a different set of expectations and perhaps also a very specific learning objective.

More than 55 CIOs, CISOs, internal champions, vendors, and analysts have contributed their insights and perspectives to these pages, sharing their experiences, their hard-won lessons and candid observations. Some readers will perhaps personally know one or two of the CIOs, CISOs, vendors, champions, analysts or other leaders who have contributed a quotation; hence, they may want to begin with them.

Most of all, enjoy the read, however you read the book. Reflect on the relevance of the material to your own journey and how you can make the sales process better.

Finally, please do connect with me on LinkedIn (`https://www.linkedin.com/in/davidjordangee/`) and share your feedback and any questions about the book with me.

Best regards,

David J. Gee

Download the color images

Your purchase includes a color, DRM-free PDF copy of this book, ideal for viewing color images, screenshots, and diagrams. Refer to the *Free benefits with your book section* at the end of the *Preface* to unlock your PDF copy.

Conventions used

There are a number of text conventions used throughout this book.

Bold: Indicates a new term, an important word, or words that you see onscreen. For instance, words in menus or dialogue boxes appear in **bold**. For example, " A CISO might report to the CIO (focusing on partnership), the CEO (prioritizing visibility), the **Chief Financial Officer** (CFO) or General Counsel (emphasizing compliance)."

> Note
>
> **Important notes**
>
> Appear like this.

> Tip
>
> Tips appear like this.

Get in touch

Feedback from our readers is always welcome.

General feedback: If you have questions about any aspect of this book, email us at `customercare@packtpub.com` and mention the book title in the subject of your message.

Errata: Although we have taken every care to ensure the accuracy of our content, mistakes do happen. If you have found a mistake in this book, we would be grateful if you would report this to us. Please visit `www.packtpub.com/support/errata` and fill in the form. All valid errata will be timely updated on GitHub: `https://github.com/PacktPublishing/How-to-Sell-to-the-CIO-and-CISO`

Piracy: If you come across any illegal copies of our works in any form on the internet, we would be grateful if you would provide us with the location address or website name. Please contact us at `copyright@packt.com` with a link to the material.

If you are interested in becoming an author: If there is a topic that you have expertise in and you are interested in either writing or contributing to a book, please visit `authors.packtpub.com`.

Share your thoughts

Once you've read *How to Sell to the CIO and CISO*, we'd love to hear your thoughts! Scan the QR code below to go straight to the Amazon review page for this book and share your feedback.

https://packt.link/r/180730079X

Your review is important to us and the tech community and will help us make sure we're delivering excellent quality content.

Free benefits with your book

This book comes with free benefits to support your learning. Activate them now for instant access (see the *How to unlock* section for instructions).

Here's a quick overview of what you can instantly unlock with your purchase:

DRM-Free PDF Version

Download DRM-free PDF and ePub copies of this book.

7-Day Packt Library Access

Get 7-day unlimited access to 8,000+ books and videos. No credit card required.

Available for first-time Packt+ trial users only.

Next-Gen Reader Access

Read this book on Packt Reader with progress sync, dark mode and note-taking.

How to unlock

Scan the QR code (or go to `packtpub.com/unlock`). Search for this book by name, confirm the edition, and then follow the steps on the page.

UNLOCK NOW

Note: Keep your invoice handy. Purchases made directly from Packt don't require one.

Part 1 (First Base)

Recognition and Building Credibility

In this first part of the book, you'll develop a solid foundation in recognizing opportunity and building credibility with the most influential technology leaders in any organization. I will share with you my insights into how CIOs and CISOs actually allocate their attention and why unsolicited outreach almost always fails, then dive into how to read their personas, motivations, and career stages to craft an approach that lands.

You will learn from my advice how to get in the room through warm introductions, intelligent jostling, and champion-led internal pull. Once inside, you'll discover how to read the room in the first sixty seconds, listen your way to insight, and handle objections without becoming defensive. You will also discover why identifying and nurturing internal champions, those rare leaders who self-select through their own mindset, skills, and behaviors, can be the single greatest accelerant to your success. By the end of this part, you'll have the confidence and the language to walk into the office of a CIO or CISO, earn their trust, and position both yourself and your champions for visibility and impact at board level.

This part of the book includes the following chapters:

- *Chapter 5, Your Preparation*
- *Chapter 6, Walking Into the Office of the CIO and CISO*

1

How to Sell to the CIO and CISO

I've written this book as the current sales process is significantly flawed; however, this process is a strategic lifeline that the CIO and CISO are highly dependent on to be able to successfully reinvent their enterprises.

This book talks about this sales process and provides insights on how to do this better. How the CIO and CISO think and operate is somewhat of a mystery to many who have never held this position. I've had the privilege of being a CIO and CISO for over 25 years. My intention with this book is to provide insights into their thought process using my own experience on this topic. My own perspective is also supplemented with quotations from peer CIOs, CISOs, architects, champions (those who help drive change within the enterprise). I've also reached out to vendors, procurement, research analysts, and advisors to add from their vantage point how they see this process.

In essence, what I've attempted to do is evaluate the entire process and highlight what the exceptional trusted vendors do. This is through lived experience with perspectives from all sides of the table.

This first chapter provides an overview of how CIOs and CISOs are currently prioritizing this activity, when there is significant vendor "noise" trying hard to gain attention for their solution. The problem is that most vendors do not understand the strategic intent of the CIO and CISO. Without this absolute clarity on their priorities, selling to them becomes a very inexact science.

The classic expression "selling sand in a desert", implies that a great salesperson can persuade anyone to buy anything, even if they already have it in abundance. This is akin to selling to the CIO and CISO. They have an abundance of options; it is truly a buyer's market, and they are spoiled for choice.

CIOs and CISOs are surrounded every day by "sand", in their case "technology". They usually have too much technology already and are inundated with pitches from vendors and consultants to add more to the stack. This abundance of technology leads to duplicate, outdated, and poorly maintained systems that become increasingly difficult to keep current and serviceable.

More technology does not make your organization more resilient or efficient. For CIOs, these aging technologies drive up maintenance and support costs, while for CISOs they introduce additional security risks, such as unpatched vulnerabilities, unsupported software, and increased exposure to cyber threats.

The average CIO and CISO will often prefer to consolidate platforms rather than add new ones. They want to standardize their environments and whenever possible, retire older systems. Hence selling any new products and/or services to the CIO and CISO is always going to be difficult and the CIO and CISO are far more likely to say "no" than "yes" to a new pitch.

When coaching any CIO or CISO, I often focus on strategic decision-making, which is about making hard choices. When I reflect on the career of the aspiring CIO and CISO, I notice they often make strong career progress by saying "yes" and getting great results. These leaders often come from program and project delivery and are acknowledged as having a "can do" attitude. At some early point in the career of the CIO and CISO, however, they realize they will be overrun if they continue to say "yes". At this point, they start to rewire their brain to say "no".

It is against this backdrop that you enter the dialogue wanting to sell your product and/or service to the CIO and CISO.

This chapter contains the following topics:

- Vendor noise
- Selling is both complex and complicated
- How to sell to the CIO and CISO – from the outside-in

Note

Download the PDF version of this book

Your purchase includes a DRM-free PDF copy of this book and a range of exclusive benefits. To unlock everything, follow the *Free benefits with your book* section in the *Preface*.

Vendor noise

CIOs and CISOs are often rewarded for performing their role strategically to enable business growth by providing a stable operating platform. Because of this, these roles significantly influence critical technology and security decisions. As a result, they are literally inundated with sales outreach via email, mobile phones, and even deliveries to their office and home.

> Note
>
> *"It was the best of times, it was the worst of times, it was the age of wisdom, it was the age of foolishness, it was the epoch of belief, it was the epoch of incredulity..."*
>
> *This Dickens' quote from his 1859 classic novel,* A Tale of Two Cities, *neatly sums up the experience CIOs have with our vendor community. There can be wonderfully successful experiences. Equally, they can be nightmares you long to awake from. Both legacies can outlive the decision makers and have enduring impacts on CIOs, vendors and their respective networks.*
>
> *Trust is often ephemeral, fleeting and transitory. This begs the question: how can trust be formed, given buyers often see the goal being to extract as much value as possible from the client and transfer that wealth to the sell side?*
>
> **John Sutherland – Chief Digital Information Officer, Calvary Health Care**

There is a "catch-22" here as well. The CIO and CISO risk their strategic progress if they do not engage with the possible opportunity that innovation can provide. However, by being open to this engagement, they also receive a significant amount of irrelevant and useless information about products and services that are of no interest.

As a former CIO and CISO, I also desperately wanted to be aware of new and emerging technologies. But unfortunately, the signal-to-noise ratio with the extent of vendors pushing new products to engage was counterproductive in my experience. The number of valuable connections was usually less than a handful each month compared to a high volume of vendor-attempted contacts and outreach. The following figure illustrates the sheer volume of outreach a typical executive faces, and how little of it actually breaks through as a strategic opportunity:

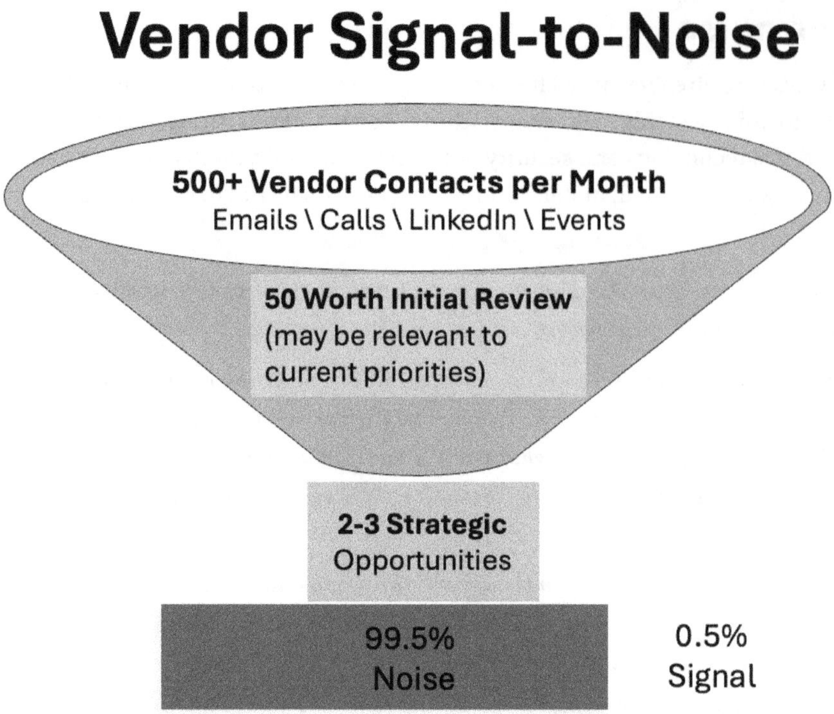

Figure 1.1 - Vendor noise outweighs signal

I've personally noticed that the ratio of valuable insights to promotional content "noise" is why the whole sales process gets so much bad press. The CIO and CISO become increasingly cynical of these attempts to connect.

There is another "noisy" dynamic worth naming directly - when every vendor arrives leading with the same theme as whatever is currently moving on the Gartner® Hype Curve™. The cumulative effect, in my opinion, is noise rather than persuasion. And noise, at sufficient volume, produces only one outcome: a CIO or CISO who has learned to stop listening before the pitch is finished.

In response to this "noise", the CIO and CISO have turned to occasional industry events. However, these too have changed. What were once select, paid technology events have morphed into many free events where clearly the attendees are the product being sold. CIOs and CISOs are therefore very selective about the events they attend, and the ones they attend will usually be related to a business or technology challenge at the time or a strategic area being explored.

> **Note**
>
> *If you want time with a CISO, show that you're part of the solution and you're not approaching them to just make a sale. Guess what? CISOs don't achieve their position by being stupid. They're quite smart. Not only do they know a lot about security and their business, but they are also highly sensitive to BS. There are some CISOs who will jump for every steak dinner or golf outing you throw their way, but most who are simply trying to be good at their job will politely decline. Make your first outreach on their terms. Learn something about them, their business, and their needs. I rarely see salespeople do basic open-source intelligence (OSINT) to figure that out. The information is there. You just have to do the work. And now with AI, it should be able to do a lot of that work for you.*
>
> **David Spark – Producer, Managing Editor, Co-Host at the CISO Series**

Alternatively, the CIO and CISO will turn to independent analysts such as Gartner®, Forrester®, IDC, IT-Harvest and Frost & Sullivan for guidance. We'll look at these in *Chapter 11*.

Every CIO and CISO will have a mental model of vendor engagement that looks like the following example:

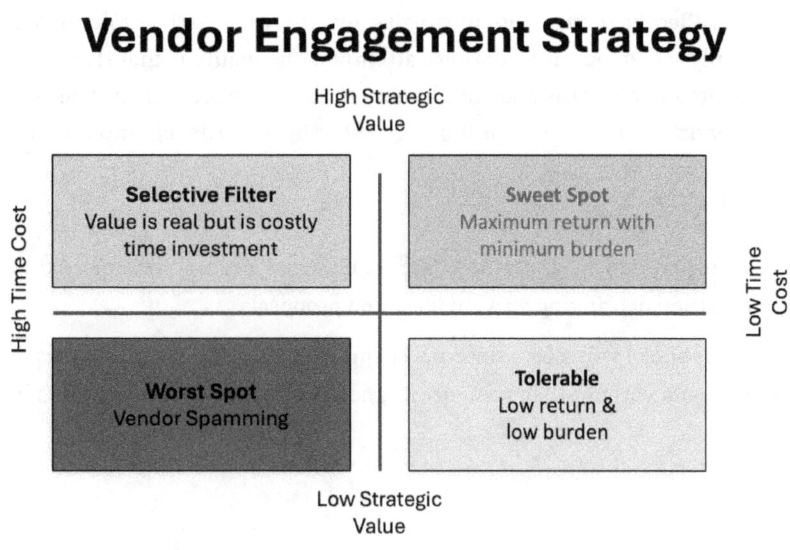

Figure 1.2 - Making the personal choice of vendor engagement

This matrix maps the vendor landscape through the lens that matters most to a CIO or CISO—how much strategic value an interaction delivers against how much time it costs. I'd argue that the goal is simple: move every vendor relationship toward the top right and eliminate everything that lives in the bottom left.

> Note
>
> *Show up prepared and document the process. Most procurement processes are similar, but the first step is to document the steps to understand what they are, how long each is expected to take, whether there is a specific owner, and, finally, the inputs/outputs of each step. Beyond that, show up prepared with the required information for each step ready for the customer.*
>
> **Dan Wheatley – Vice President of Sales, Gravwell**

They must make the choice between higher or lower engagement, then try to avoid being either overwhelmed or missing a golden opportunity.

Note that each of these executives can likely only devote a few hours per week to this task of evaluating potential vendors. Based on my own experience as a CIO and CISO, I would put this at around 2 hours per week. This then amounts to 8 hours per month. These 480 minutes a month then divided by, say, 500 contact points gives the CIO and CISO about 57 seconds per attempted contact. Clearly, they are unable to give any attention to that volume. This means that they will simply screen out most of these attempts. The reality is that they will try to ignore any unsolicited phone calls and emails, not because they are rude but because they simply lack bandwidth. This math helps illustrate why the "internal champion" is so critical to this equation.

> Note
>
> To be successful in driving change, the CIO and CISO need internal champions to support the mission of bringing forward ideas and proposals.
>
> Throughout this book I will refer to internal champions. They form a critical part of this overall process, and without their presence it is nearly impossible for a vendor to have a successful sale.

Now, on top of the time pressure for the CIO and CISO, to make matters even worse, we are not talking about simple consumable products like a toothbrush, here. These are complex technologies.

Selling is both complex and complicated

The marketplace is both a very complex and complicated place. By "complex" I mean that as CIO and CISO we are adding a new product or solution to what we already have connected to our environment and needing these interconnected systems to work well together.

At the same time, our enterprises are "complicated"; they are often not well documented and hard to understand. Things may work, or work to a degree, but it's difficult to know how an enterprise operates as a whole (or even sometimes in parts). This is what you have to think about when you are trying to sell a new idea for a product or service. There is inertia not to upset the status quo.

If the enterprise itself does not have a clear understanding of the current architecture and inventory of their existing systems, your sale into this environment may also be hampered. Indeed, you may never be able to access some of these system details. There will be incomplete information and data that are not shared with you.

To succeed, you must understand the hidden parts of the equation. Here are a few examples of things to consider:

- What CIOs/CISOs think during vendor presentations vs. what they say
- How champions get burned out or become strong advocates
- What the internal politics are that buyers navigate that sellers never see
- What the role of consultants and other advisors is

How high are the stakes?

When you look at any enterprise or government institution, the spending on technology and cyber can very often be significant line items. The global data at time of writing shows this spending to be more than $5.75 trillion dollars (`https://www.statista.com/statistics/203935/overall-it-spending-worldwide/`). There is also a velocity to this with a 9.3% increase from the prior year—if you drill down on these numbers, you can see explosive growth with AI and Cybersecurity leading to this acceleration.

This spend at a company level varies by industry. Affordability becomes a key factor of spending on technology, as a percentage of revenue, which then becomes a metric that you can compare between industries. (See `https://meriplex.com/it-budget-benchmarks-by-industry/`).

There will always be a natural magnetic draw into the higher spending industries where the CIO and the CISO have larger annual budgets. The difficult question we will want to explore is how much of this is discretionary and can be invested in a new project – that is often a known unknown. Also note that some of this budget can be allocated, or sit inside a business budget line item, so it is influenced by, but not directly controlled by, the CIO and CISO.

Selling as the game of baseball

While my own sporting background is in Rugby and Basketball, I've often admired the strategic battle at the heart of baseball, whether watching the NY Yankees or the Hanshin Tigers in Japan. Even without being a massive fan of the sport, the parallels to the business world are striking.

Selling to a CIO or CISO is a game of patience and strategy, much like baseball. You don't win by swinging at every pitch or trying to hit a home run on your first attempt. Success comes from reading the environment, understanding the "pitcher," and waiting for the right moment to make your move. This level of discipline is essential when building a relationship with a senior executive.

A baseball game has innings, and similarly the sales process has different stages - discovery, qualification, proof of concept, business case approval, and then finally securing the sale. This is both a team game and an individual challenge. Reaching first base means that you have identified a business problem that the CIO and CISO care about. At this point you have gained recognition and are starting to build credibility with the CIO and CISO.

In second base, your solution starts to be seriously considered. You are in the process of developing your relationship with the CIO and CISO, and there is a budget that is perhaps not yet approved but is being earmarked for future consideration. The result is that you have problem validation and are starting to build trust.

In the third base, you have managed to navigate the fielders—legal, procurement, etc.—and are then en-route to the final negotiation to get a home run. The solution proposed has been validated.

Finally, there is home base, when you have achieved your objective and have a closed deal and the beginnings of what could be a partnership.

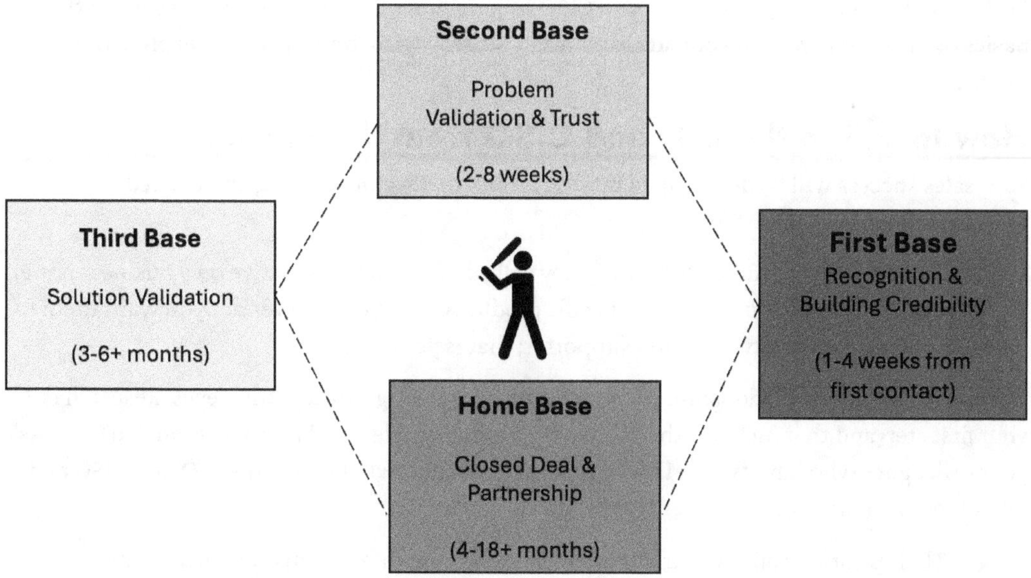

Figure 1.3 - The baseball analogy for selling to the CIO and CISO

I've added some average durations for each base in the preceding diagram but note that the timing of these will depend upon the complexity of the location and the culture that exists in terms of decision making. I'd expect that in Japan, for example, these timings will usually exceed those in the USA.

At the risk of sounding corny, I can say that in sales you "strike out" more than you hit the ball and you will often not get three attempts to make a run. The CIO and CISO are experienced ball players and frankly have seen every pitch possible. It is likely not possible to surprise them with a novel and innovative approach that wins them over.

There will be the grind of "working the singles" to get yourself to first base and have internal champions on your side who help you navigate all bases till you reach home base. Without their help, your endeavor has limited chances of success. In baseball, one star pitcher cannot win the game alone, and nor can one salesperson.

I've also observed that baseball has a concept of playing small ball and not swinging for the rafters but instead making a sacrificial "bunt" (a bunt is a strategic baseball hit where the batter lightly taps the ball into the infield rather than taking a full swing). The analogy here is that a tech vendor can get themselves into a small pilot and under the radar faster than trying to go straight for a big contract. A pilot may be possible on second base as you try to have your solution validated.

Both baseball and selling to the CIO and CISO require practice, preparation, and getting the basics right. Selling from the outside is not easy. So, stay with me and we will explore this further.

How to sell to the CIO and CISO from the outside

Your sales success will be determined by your ability to develop a strong and trusted relationship with a CIO and/or CISO.

You will know you have succeeded when they call you for your perspective on a business issue, even if it has nothing to do with your specific product or service. As a vendor you want them to become your strongest advocate and supporter; that is your goal!

To reach this level of relationship, you must start by thinking through their eyes. Research is your first step and that includes their LinkedIn profile, articles, and interviews on YouTube. Ask your colleagues who have worked with them, for instance, what drives the CIO and CISO and what their primary objectives are. Try these as a starting set:

- Their priorities and the strategic contexts they operate in. This can include the following:
    - What challenges or initiatives did they focus on most when you spoke?
    - What industry trends or role-specific opportunities seem to excite them?
    - What immediate pain points or specific problems are they actively trying to solve right now?
- Communication style:
    - How do they prefer to communicate? (e.g., data-driven, relationship-focused, or strategic?)
    - What level of detail do they prefer—high-level vision or technical specifics?
    - Are the CIO and CISO more interested in business outcomes or technical architecture?
- Decision-making:
    - Are they a decisive leader, or do they prefer to involve a wider team? Who do they trust for advice?
    - What specific evidence or proof points has resonated with them in the past?

Remember, your goal here is to understand not just what the CIO and CISO care about, but why and how they think about problems. This will help you frame your approach to increase your chance that this resonates with their specific current and emerging priorities. Since all humans can change their views, this analysis is ongoing, not static.

What is on their mind?

Your first task is to learn to speak their language (literally and figuratively). What is critical here is that you start to build up your understanding of their priorities and demonstrate business acumen. Let me break that down for you.

What are the CIO's and CISO's priorities?

This refers to their long list of key strategic priorities, including things they really care about, what their stakeholders care about, and what homework regulators have given them. Discerning the relative weighting and order of these is your first assignment. Their team can provide a perspective on this, and sometimes this list of priorities is documented and shared with management.

Exercise caution here; these documented priorities are just table stakes. Some of these priorities may indeed be tied to their bonus package, but that does not mean that these are their only priorities. Every leader has their own pet projects and things that they always have wanted to do but haven't had the opportunity. CIO and CISO will often speak about these "pets" with a glint in their eye, and your tricky task is to work out when this is of personal high interest but not yet approved. Then, you can determine the background history of this topic, for instance, what risk mitigation you can assist them with through your own network or recent case studies that may be related to this to assist their deliberation.

There are also the emerging priorities that are not documented or approved but are in line for next year or the following planning cycle. This is the "sweet spot" because these ideas are not fully formulated but are on their radar to research and understand more extensively. These emerging priorities are often highly confidential, and there may be no approved business case. That business case is likely being built, and they are looking for benchmarks and stories of how other leading enterprises have tackled similar problems. When your product or service is aligned to a new emerging priority, then you have struck gold and you are lucky.

> **Note**
>
> This can be what is referred to as a "Blue Ocean Strategy" (as termed by Professor W. Chan Kim and Professor Renée Mauborgne in 2004, both professors at INSEAD). This is a space where the market is uncontested and your value proposition is unique.
>
> This is the polar opposite of a "red ocean," where you are constantly fighting for market share with other competitors (`https://hbr.org/2004/10/blue-ocean-strategy`).

At this stage many CIOs and CISOs will be curious about the topic but hesitant to disclose their internal thoughts to someone they don't yet trust. Your goal is to encourage this exploration phase by providing enough value to earn that trust, helping them move the idea toward a formal initiative.

In reality, your position as a vendor usually sits somewhere on a spectrum. The following matrix helps you classify these opportunities by determining the "Priority Status" and then where the CIO and CISO are in this process:

Priority Status	**No Market Solutions**	**Market Solution exists**	**Planned or in progress**
Emerging Priority **(0–12 months awareness)**	**Sweet Spot** Early mover advantage, you can shape requirements	**Staple** Fast follower, differentiated	**Sour (unripe)** Displacement play (risky)
Active Priority **(Currently working on)**	**Sweet Spot** An urgent need, budget available	**Staple** Competitive displacement possible	**Rotten (Waste)** Timing is poor, move on to next client
Established Priority **(12–18 months old)**	**Salty** Gap in market or they're struggling	**Sour** Satisfied or locked in	**Rotten (Legacy)** Only engage if current is failing; move on

Table 1.1 - Priority Decision Matrix

This priority status matrix can be used as a guide to understand how IT departments narrow down a list of projects for final execution. Their top 10 priority list is indeed the approved strategic projects; however, these include both active and established priorities, so for the vendor and champion this may be too late.

Most of the time you are working in the middle of the matrix where a market solution already exists, thus in the eyes of the customer you are a "staple" product. You may think of your offering as special, but you are in the "red ocean" and there is competition with many others.

If your product or solution is currently a "medium" or "low" priority, then it may be best not to invest your time. However, don't burn your bridges with the CIO and CISO before moving on to the next target beyond them. An occasional, low-pressure check-in with industry stories where other enterprises have moved your product/service into a high priority and made good progress can keep you on the executive's radar for future roles or new initiatives.

> **Note**
>
> This reminds me of a savvy real estate agent. I own a lovely waterfront apartment that is tenanted out, yet I get a call every few months from the agent just to share intel on recent local sales. My apartment is not for sale, but the agent is investing in a future "sweet spot", to create an early mover advantage by proving that she has her hand on the pulse of the market. When I eventually decide to sell, she will be the first person I call.

In short, my advice is that you try to understand where your product/service fits in the CIO and CISO's top 10 list of priorities. Remember that all items on the list may not be approved. To break this down further, you should understand which of these programs are their personal pet projects, which are their key stakeholders', and which are regulatory compliance driven.

> **Note**
>
> *It is all about what they have on their agenda to solve, not what is on yours. If you have something that is not a priority, and you think they should add to their priority list, it often needs to be at the expense of something else. They will do it if you give them context to what it means in their world and how you will make them successful, sometimes you will need to accept that the timing is wrong and ask permission to reconnect at an agreed time in the future.*
>
> **Yigal Elstein – Chief Revenue Officer, Checkmarx**

In my experience, while every CIO and CISO prioritizes differently, they are all ultimately trying to achieve a trifecta of benefits:

- Deliver value while reducing major risk to the business
- Deliver positive Customer experience
- Meet regulatory requirements

> **Note**
>
> Note that a "trifecta" is a horse racing bet where you pick first, second, and third place. When I was 18 years old, my mother (Cindy Gee) won $25,000 by picking a horse race, so while I don't gamble, I always fondly remember this labelling.

While it is possible that one project may tick more than one of these boxes, you will want to be able to align your strategy to what gives you all these benefits and in the right sequence.

Now that we understand their priorities, let's look at the second key point I made about business acumen.

How do I demonstrate my business acumen?

When you are a tech or cybersecurity professional selling products or services to CIOs and CISOs, you can differentiate yourself by thinking the way they do by developing your business acumen. This means that your expertise should extend beyond the features of your tech products and services to an understanding of the executive's reality.

The CIO and CISO have busy, stressful roles, and they are under constant time pressure to deliver and ensure operational resilience. You are trying to sell your product and/or service into what is an already crowded schedule.

Here's an example of a typical day for a CIO. When you make contact, it is likely that their mind is already overloaded with at least 5-6 of these issues:

Figure 1.4 - A day in the life of a CIO

Similarly, here is what a day in the life of a CISO might look like:

Figure 1.5 - A day in the life of a CISO

Unfortunately, the diary of the CISO is probably even busier and therefore even less open to taking an additional meeting.

To differentiate yourself, you must demonstrate an understanding of the broader aspects of their role, their budget pressures, evolving organizational dynamics, and the specific risk landscape of their industry, including benchmarking exercises. And finally, a rough idea of how they are measured for their success. While this last point is often harder to ascertain, gaining this insight will help you align your message perfectly.

Understanding the budget situation

Normally, overall budget spend is confidential. Your internal contacts may be willing to share the year-on-year budget cuts or percentage increases. However, you may be able to gain a broad understanding from this of centralized versus departmental budget spend, plus a rough idea of the breakdown of operating expense vs. capital.

It is strategically important to understand if your proposed product or service is replacing an existing product, in which case there is an existing budget bucket to start with, or is in a new category and therefore there is no budget line item for it. When there is an incumbent, you will be roughly aware of their solution costing but understand that cost per seat and site licenses may be subject to some changes as human headcount reduces and AI agents increase.

Know that while the CIO and CISO may be the budget owners or indeed the budget sponsors, they are often not close to the breakdown of the numbers. They will leave this to their teams' feedback, which can sometimes be reduced to a simple claim that "this product or service is expensive". This is often an "apples and oranges" comparison, and you must be prepared to defend your value in these competitive situations.

The importance of trust

True success comes by really understanding your target, in this case the CIO or CISO. It must start with understanding their environment and what they have in place, then what their current and emerging priorities are.

We all start from a base of zero with usually no strong current relationship – how, then, do we start to build this understanding of what their stated priorities are, and which ones they really care about?

This is a new relationship; it is dynamic, and you will build trust over time. All the questions that you have about their strategic priorities, current environment, budget constraints, etc., are part of the jigsaw puzzle you'll need to assemble.

> **Note**
>
> *Across four decades working alongside CXOs, and boards throughout Asia Pacific, one constant has remained: technology decisions do not start with products — they start with trust. What has changed is the environment in which trust is tested. We have moved from relatively contained IT estates to highly interconnected digital ecosystems where resilience depends on third parties, integrated platforms, and continuous control assurance.*
>
> *Earlier in my career, enterprise selling was activity-driven — access was created through reach. CRM digitised that model, but it was still volume-based. Today, in cyber and IT, access is earned through relevance to a defined risk and the ability to deliver measurable outcomes within real operating constraints. The leaders I advise are not measured by what they deploy; they are measured by what they can prove to boards and regulators — sustained service, effective controls, and predictable recovery.*
>
> *This shift changes every stage of engagement. Buying signals are outcome-based. Disengagement occurs when a solution does not move a named control objective. Shortlists are built on operational credibility, peer outcomes, and time-to-value. Proof is defined by incident performance and audit-ready evidence. Advisor trust is earned through execution reality, not positioning.*
>
> *CIO and CISO priorities have converged around organisational resilience — service continuity, recoverability, and defensible risk posture. The ecosystem is consolidating toward vendors who can integrate into existing operating models, reduce complexity, and remain accountable beyond the transaction, particularly during incidents and audit cycles.*
>
> *In this resilience-driven market, technology enables the outcome but trust determines the decision. People buy from people they trust to help them succeed on their worst day.*
>
> **Sam Ghebranious – Director, Axcelerate / Senior Advisor, Frost & Sullivan**

The more you can gain trust, the faster you will be able to learn about these clues and gain the information required to sell effectively into their enterprise.

So, what do you need to be able to partner with the CIO and CISO? That's my next chapter and through that, I will help you be ready to tackle how to build this relationship with them when they already have more technology than they want.

Summary

In this chapter, we have explored the CIO and CISO as primary leaders in the sales process, whether you are selling from the "outside in" as a vendor or from the "inside up" as an internal champion. Of course, as a vendor you will want to cultivate champions that help you to sell inside up and support their mission; these are therefore not separate processes but interlinked and interdependent.

I have explored how CIOs and CISOs operate in a state of technology overload—they receive constant vendor noise, prefer platform consolidation over new additions, and have rewired themselves to default to "no."

There is no doubt that fundamentally selling solutions to executive-level buyers is challenging and complex. Selling to them requires a deep understanding of their stated, emerging, and personal priorities, framed through business acumen rather than product features.

I also introduced the baseball metaphor which will act as an anchor for the sales process across this book. Patience, incremental base progression, and internal champions are essential as home runs rarely come on the first pitch.

The key learnings from this chapter are:

- **Signal-to-noise problem** – CIOs/CISOs have only ~2 hours/week for vendor engagement; unsolicited outreach is largely ignored, making the internal champion critical.
- **Priority mapping matters** – differentiate between stated priorities, personal "pet projects," and *emerging* priorities (the sweet spot where budget is forming and the field is less crowded). Align your solution to where the buyer sits across priority status and market maturity; avoid "rotten" and "sour" quadrants in the Priority Decision Matrix.
- **Business acumen over product pitch** – understand their budget dynamics, organizational politics, risk landscape, and how they're measured.
- **Trust is the currency** – long-term relationships outperform transactional ones; relevance to *their* agenda, not yours, is what earns access.

2

How to Partner with the CIO and CISO

Knowing that CIOs and CISOs have a default answer of "no", you must play the long game, building a relationship over many months or even years. In their current technology architecture, adding a solution often requires them to deduct one first by retiring an existing product or solution, and this requires trust.

While partnering with the CIO and CISO is your goal, this may not be the CIO or CISO's goal, at least initially. A partnership is earned over time, particularly once you are onboarded and they realize your product or service is strategically important to their success.

This chapter will give you context by exploring the mindset of the CIO and CISO, building a partnership with these executives, and providing you with a starting point. These learnings will help you to speak to them in their language, navigate their politics, and understand what they regard as their "carrots and sticks". We will also examine specific executive personas and, finally, how to build lasting trust with each of them.

In short, the key topics we will cover in this chapter are:

- Speaking their language
- Understand what keeps them in the job
- Organizational politics
- CIO and CISO – personas that matter
- Classifying vendors

Note

Involve the technology leadership in your sales process as early as possible. When you do an end run around CIOs and CTOs to sell directly to department and business unit heads, you create confusion and delay. At some point, the tech and security execs will have to weigh in.

Martha Heller – CEO, Heller (former CIO)

Speaking their language

The CIO and CISO are strategic executives measured on outcomes, not features; pitching your product roadmap to this audience is therefore the fastest way to lose them. Standard sales training often gets this exactly backward, leading with capability when it should be leading with curiosity.

It is more valuable to explore what your target wishes he or she could stop doing. That single but subtle shift, from pitching to listening, is what separates a transactional vendor from one who earns a seat at the strategic table.

Here are five examples of questions you could ask:

- What is a critical manual process that you wish were automated?
- What percentage of your budget is BAU vs. innovation?
- What tech processes require more effort without delivering proportional benefits?
- Is there any specific alert fatigue in your environment you wish was fixed?
- If you could use a magic wand to make a change happen now, what would that be?

The idea is to understand the CIO/CISO's pain points. This discovery process allows you to learn what the CIO and CISO care about, even though it may not be directly related to an immediate sale. By prioritizing their needs, you earn the trust required for a long-term partnership (after all, every leader wants to stay in their job). This leads to our next section: what keeps the CIO and CISO in their job?

Understand what keeps them in the job

It is a universally known truth that a CIO is mostly valued for delivering digital innovation and data analytics with speed. However, they are also measured on system availability, cost optimization, and business enablement. When the CIO is well aligned with stakeholders and management, they ensure that prioritized projects are delivered.

On the other hand, CISO is measured primarily by their ability to reduce cyber risk exposure, maintain compliance, and prevent breaches. They are also expected to manage the security uplift program within budget.

As a vendor of a product or solution, you must move past features and frame what you deliver in terms that help these executives be successful with their key metrics. Here is an example of a good framing: "We improve your recovery time from ransomware from *X* days and hours to *Y* days and hours, significantly reducing potential downtime costs."

> Note
>
> *When I did the CISO Manifesto article that I put up on LinkedIn, I listed about 16 things that CISOs don't like from salespeople. I've talked with CISOs and it really annoys many of them because they feel salespeople just want to come on in and just get the purchase order:*
>
> *1. How about you come in and get to know me as a person?*
>
> *2. How about you come in and we kind of get a relationship going here?*
>
> *3. How about you spend some time understanding what I'm trying to build.*
>
> **Gary Hayslip – CISO, Halcyon.ai, Board Director and Investor**

It is worth being aware that both the CIO and CISO roles can be short-lived, perhaps just 2-4 years of service (for example, see `https://www.cio.com/article/4153245/bad-cios-are-good-for-the-business.html`). In my view, this is due to the high-stress nature of these roles and the fact that these roles are increasingly being asked to take on further responsibility. Consequently, you must demonstrate benefits that accrue in the short term, rather than just promising medium- and long-term gains. This bias for results may indeed color their preferences for products and solutions that deliver quick visible wins for their own performance review.

To find these quick wins, you must do your homework first. For example, rather than asking the CIO to explain their entire tech stack, ask them to clarify the gaps in the research you have conducted. For instance, there may be some external enterprise news you have seen that highlights recent initiatives.

You also need to ensure you have a deep understanding of the specific regulations that they must comply with.

Politics is rarely something the CIO or CISO seeks out, but it is inescapable at the level that they operate. Every significant technology decision land inside an organizational context that is shaped by competing priorities and competing agendas. As a vendor, developing an awareness of these dynamics is essential for navigating the sales process effectively. I provide some context as to how this impacts their thinking in the next section.

Organizational politics

The CIO and CISO may have different bosses and competing priorities, which dictate how they weigh specific initiatives. A CISO might report to the CIO (focusing on partnership), the CEO (prioritizing visibility), the **Chief Financial Officer** (**CFO**) or General Counsel (emphasizing compliance), or the **Chief Operating Officer** (**COO**) (valuing operational stability). Recently, I have seen that some CISOs have begun reporting to the **Chief Risk Officer** (**CRO**) to maintain independence from IT pressures.

A COO, for instance, is interested in the impact of business operational growth being supported and will look for benchmarks and case studies that demonstrate this strength. Conversely, a CFO focuses on cost-benefit analysis, to compare your project against requests from the other departments.

These political forces may be difficult to understand from the outside. You must work with your internal champion to get an understanding of what ammunition is needed to sell your solution internally. This does not mean you engage with politics; rather you are being maze-savvy, navigating the corridors to get to the right outcome. I will discuss politics further in *Chapter 10*.

> Note
>
> *Having a relationship and getting to know them, you start learning where CISOs are at in that cycle. A lot of times you end up talking to one of their peers and gain more insight into the challenges they are facing to better understand if you can partner with them or not. Sometimes it's just not the right time and you have to be ok with that.*
>
> *Sometimes they just don't want to speak to you right now. That's ok, you find your champions, those that do want to work with you, those that you can do projects with right now, and then they say good things about you and through that feedback from peers, reluctant CISOs, hopefully, come around and want to speak with you.*
>
> **Gary Hayslip – CISO, Halcyon.ai, Board Director and Investor**

In most enterprises, technology and cybersecurity budgets may be funded at the expense of other departments. There can be resistance from the COO and CFO with the concern that IT and cybersecurity spending have hard-to-measure returns and are always escalating new budget requests compared to other departments.

While this internal friction is not your direct problem, it heavily impacts your own ability to close the sale. Therefore, you must understand the resistance your targets face and where feasible, provide data and reference stories to help facilitate their business case.

Talking about risk and value in business terms

Risk management is a crucial component of how enterprises manage their daily operations. In my opinion, the worst mistake you can make is leading with product and services features when selling, rather than linking your solution to how it reduces critical risks. For instance, if you can frame security investments as "buying down risk" to acceptable levels, then this is speaking their language. Once you have framed it this way, then you can talk about the features.

Talking about value is harder because it means different things to different people in different organizations at different moments. The CFO's definition of value is not the same as the CIO's definition, which is not the CISO's definition. And even within a single organization, what counted as value last year may not count this year if the strategic priorities have shifted.

Similarly, you will get to the point of speaking about a "pilot", proof of concept (POC), or proof of value (POV). Each of these activities is designed to reduce the actual risk of buying a new product by first testing this in a trial run. The CIO and CISO may not really care too much about the strict definition of these processes as they often see this as a step toward an end, but getting this language correct is vital to being able to set clear expectations with them:

POC **(Proof of concept)**	A proof of concept is a non-production test designed to validate whether a solution performs as claimed within a narrowly defined scope. It typically runs over 3-8 weeks and is governed by success criteria agreed between the vendor and the technology team before the exercise begins.
POV **(Proof of value)**	Using real data and use cases, this is an exercise to measure outcomes to see if it creates value as expected. There may be some limited integration with production systems with this. POVs often take around 2-4 weeks.
Pilot	We deploy for real with a limited set of users for a set period of 1-6 months. This may be one department or geographical area with success criteria.

Table 2.1 - POC vs POV vs Pilot

Clearly what you don't want is to do a POC, then be asked to do a POV and then a pilot (after that there is, of course, contracting and procurement to tackle). To avoid this, use your relationships with executive stakeholders, your champion, to move straight to a pilot, if you can. (In *Chapter 3*, we will explore how to develop these internal champions.) In *Chapter 12*, we will dive deeper into how to successfully navigate these validation exercises. There are often many different company and personal agendas that will be encountered.

As you want to partner with the CIO and CISO, there is a simple question to ask that helps you understand if the problem your solution addresses is known and accepted or just emerging. The simple acid test is to ask if this addresses a high-rated issue on the risk register. If a risk does not appear on the risk register, the risk committee is unlikely to pay much attention to it. Hence, you must draw a link between a critical risk that has already been identified and not addressed, and then to how your product or service can address this gap. Ideally, your conversation should be a dialogue rather than a direct pitch. You also want to position yourself not as merely a vendor but as someone who is helping the CIO/CISO think through a problem that they care about. You may also share what you have seen other enterprises or industries do that have worked well for them. In short, you are sharing market intelligence as a valuable currency. While it is true that you are delaying your product or service pitch by doing this, when you do come to a point where you discuss your offering, you will have earned the right to be direct.

> **Tip**
>
> Here is one approach to try: *If this is not one of your top 5 priorities in the next 18 months, then I will stop talking to you about this.*
>
> This is a high-risk move, and you need to be ready for their answer. Speaking as a former CIO and CISO, this approach would be immediately appreciated. The honesty and respect for their bandwidth constraints is felt and what you are also doing is creating a moment of clarity that they would value. This can set a positive tone for conversations going forward.

Carrots and sticks

Does the CIO and CISO see your product as an approach to avoid being hit by the regulator "stick" or is there an incentive ("a carrot") that improves the customer experience, and that several C-Suite executives are excited about wanting to support? When it comes to incentives vs punishment, which of these is more important to the CIO and CISO? In this section I will talk about how this is subtly different to these two executives.

Note

Most CIOs and CISOs want to leave behind a positive reputation and legacy. This thinking is usually in the back of their minds, although it can get lost in the haze of everyday activities and stress.

In this context, carrots can be tokens that help the CIO and CISO achieve internal and perhaps even an external promotion. This means that they not only keep their job but may also be rewarded for successful implementation.

From my experience the CIO cares about cost optimization and operational excellence, but these are table stakes. Being exceptional at keeping the lights on generates no political capital and earns no extra credit in the boardroom.

What genuinely motivates the CIO is the ability to drive change, to be the executive who led the digital or AI transformation that the board credits as a strategic turning point.

The vendor who connects their solution to that transformation agenda is speaking to what matters; a vendor who leads with cost savings is speaking to what is merely expected.

Note

This is where vendors lose deals by treating (security buyers) as one persona. The CIO lens is continuity, recoverability, integration burden, cost to run, vendor stability. And the CISO lens: control effectiveness, audit defensibility, incident readiness, board narrative. Where vendors fail is selling the CIO on (security posture) without quantifying operational cost. And selling the CISO on (platform vision) without showing control evidence and incident impact. If you can't help both leaders and tell the same story, you create internal friction.

Sam Ghebranious – Director, Axcelerate / Senior Advisor, Frost & Sullivan

The CIO will be more favorable to some larger, more strategic "carrots"—these provide this leader with more personal incentive.

Figure 2.1 shows how most CIOs will evaluate key benefits:

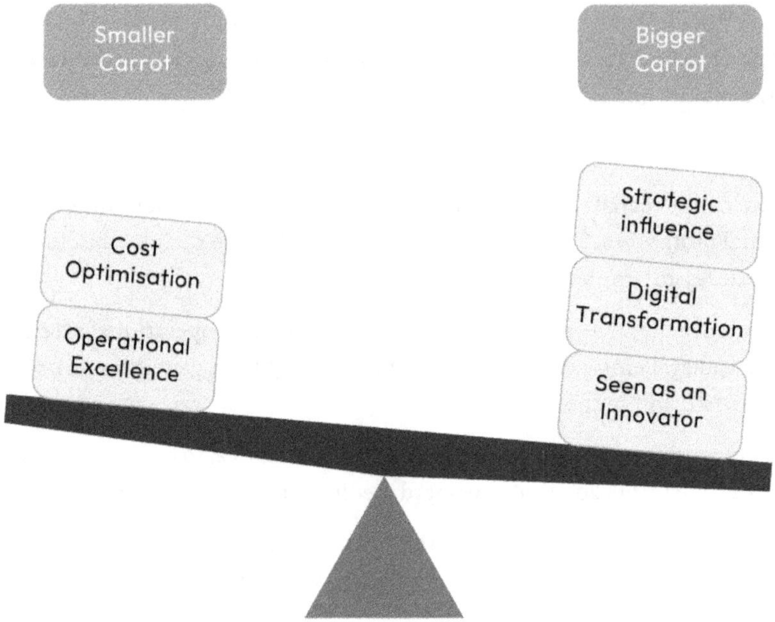

Figure 2.1 - What the CIO sees as real "carrots"

From my experience the "bigger carrots" are the more challenging and dynamic changes that the CIO will want to be seen driving. This does not mean they do not care about operational excellence and cost optimization, but that typically they will be recognized for delivering the "bigger carrots".

The perspective of the CISO, while often reporting to the CIO, is very different from the CIO. *Figure 2.3* displays the typical CISO view of "carrots"; the CISO is often less concerned about industry recognition and business growth (although this is shifting, though):

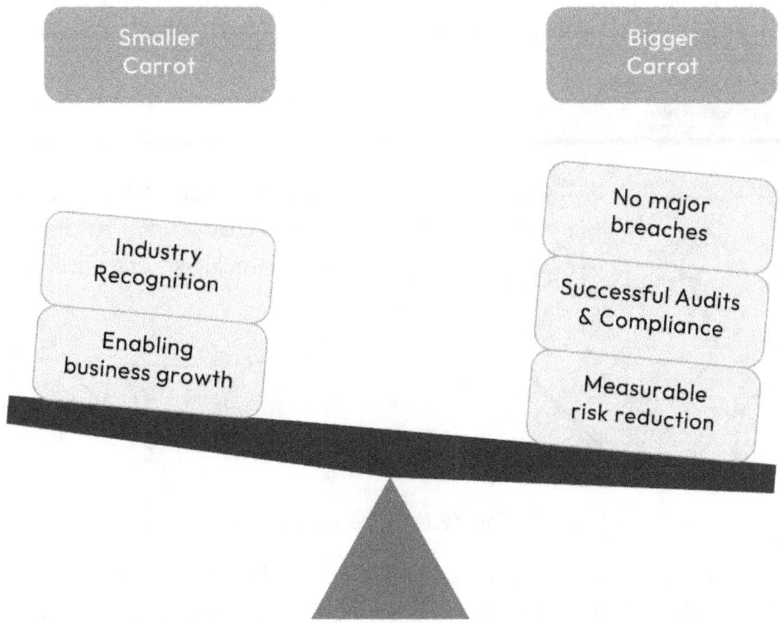

Figure 2.2 - What the CISO sees as real "carrots"

An average CISO will want to avoid bad outcomes such as a poor audit result, major cyber breach etc. These instances can result in their compensation such as bonus being impacted (carrot) but also may eventuate with a "stick" that they are hit with, such as being fired. One can argue that each of the CISO "carrots" are indeed "sticks" dressed up to look like a carrot.

Avoiding the pain (sticks)

The threat of being "hit with a stick" can range from losing one's bonus to losing one's job. CIOs and CISOs often see examples of this with their peers who have been punished. So, when approaching CIOs and CISOs with your great new idea, think of the disincentives that they will be considering. These are the individual "sticks" that they will feel could be their punishment if they fail.

A classic stick is when they have a compliance pain point. These may be old or referred to as "aged" audit or regulatory issues but can also be new emerging issues that have been identified after an incident or a near-miss. For example, an issue with an end-of-life critical system which is no longer operational and able to be patched. If this happens, then it could be front page news, and the incident would attract fines from regulators.

Let's return to the CIO here. As CIO, I was always rewarded for keeping the business operating and humming along to make revenue and faced extraordinary pressure when systems were not available and there was downtime of customer-facing systems. Management and the board want to see the CIO be a key driver of transformation and digital uplift.

Figure 2.3 - CIO perspective

To complicate matters the CIO must also address the "build vs buy" decision. The CIO will at times consider building a new tool rather than spending operating expense or capital expenditure. There can be ego involved and perhaps a perception that they can execute faster and thus gain credibility by a small agile project. The current trend is to "buy" most of the standard solutions, and only "build" where there is a competitive advantage.

The CIO does not want to be seen as hindering the business. If this occurs, then they risk losing part of their job scope and overall authority. While you will be focusing on the positive benefits of your product or service, the CIO will hear you, but inside their head there are other voices speaking:

- My legacy systems may well break if I add one more thing
- My team is already overloaded with projects
- I don't want my career legacy to be that I made the business fail
- How will my key stakeholders react to this proposal?

The CIO mostly fears the negative operational and financial impact of this change not working as expected. Often the CIO (and CISO) are dealing with considerable technical debt from historical legacy. This tech debt can't be ignored and is on the minds of the CIO whenever they consider any new project. Incidents often occur when new systems integrate with old legacy. The CIO must make a trade-off to accept risks that are known but are accepted with no immediate action to mitigate them.

> **Tip**
>
> The key thing you can do, as a vendor, is to provide them, where feasible, with case studies of other sites that are a close mirror image of this enterprise.

Now, let's discuss the CISO.

CISOs have an overarching thought that they are the "protector." They must protect the enterprise from attacks but also protect their own livelihood. They want to avoid being on duty when the enterprise is breached.

Figure 2.4 - CISO perspective

The CISO truly fears regulatory compliance (stick); they recognize that if there is a major breach, then there may be front page headlines followed by regulator fines, class actions, and damaged enterprise reputations.

These negative factors can overwhelm CISO and lead to inaction. Their primary focus is protecting the enterprise from risk; they do this 24x7 and often on weekends; they are constantly weighing the level of risk and wanting to be more comfortable with it. However, while the CISO will never talk openly about reducing risk to protect themselves, this is a secondary focus.

The professional liability stick that can "hit" the CISO is very real, and the concern that their Director and Officer's (D&O) Insurance as an employee may be insufficient to cover a major breach is often present. This means that the CISO is very motivated to make decisions that are well-documented and defensible.

Their inner voice will be playing questions like these at full volume:

- Is my attack surface larger with this new product?
- Does this add more complexity to my environment that makes defense harder?
- How much risk does this take off the table?
- Are these benefits greater than the additional risk exposure?

You need a sound understanding of their state of regulatory readiness for regulations and standards that apply to their industry (GDPR, Privacy Act, HIPAA, PCI-DSS, SOC 2, etc.). Also, where feasible, frame your solution in terms of helping them be compliant. (For example, the continuous monitoring of LLMs for model drift will ensure ongoing compliance with the EU AI Act for their loan book.) There are always new regulations that are emerging and will be a concern for the CISO.

CYA (cover your assets) documentation

To help the decision-making process, the CIO and CISO will want some evidence that they have made documented and defensible decisions. As a vendor you should consider providing them some "cover your assets" documents. This may include risk assessments that have highlighted and recommended specific threats that were called out as emerging and requiring additional action.

What one CISO or CIO will require in terms of coverage depends on their own personal risk profile and where they are in their career in terms of longevity in the role and expectations for change in that status. Personally, in these roles I focused on fixing the issue rather than documenting them. Having a sense of how much your CIO and CISO are willing to take a risk versus seeking a safer route really matters in terms of how to pitch them and be aligned with their expectations. We all have different risk profiles; many are more constrained by risks and less entrepreneurially minded.

The CIO and CISO will always prefer a safe choice by an industry leader rather than an unproven newbie. Forrester®, Gartner®, and other independent advisor reports can provide this specific content. Blue chip customer reference reports and industry benchmarks can also be strong proof.

I'd add that the best proof is to proceed with a POC. The POC process provides great evidence of how a product or service is a good selection. A detailed implementation plan with risk mitigation strategies documented also demonstrates that worst case scenarios have been considered.

These approaches can help the more typically risk adverse CIO and CISO to get more comfortable with planning. (In the next section I refer to this CIO and CISO persona as the "Risk" CIO and CISO). Your key focus should be on de-risking the change with a POC with clear success criteria, a pilot before a rollout, and rollback plans when implementation has hiccups. In addition, proof points such as respected peer adoption of this technology gives them a shield to defend their position and gain upwards approval.

I've illustrated the two opposite CIO and CISO risk tolerance approaches in the following continuum:

Figure 2.5 - Risk continuum

On this risk continuum, at one end is the risk-averse CIO/CISO and at the other end is the transformation CIO/CISO (willing to take more risks to achieve the outcomes).

The Transformation CIO or CISO, on the right side of this figure, is extremely rare, and is on a mission to deliver accelerated change. You must connect the outcome from your solution to their transformation roadmap. They often are leaders that are very concerned about their legacy and what they can deliver that makes a significant contribution. Thus, you'll need to join the dots on how your product or service helps with their game changing plans. There is no need to oversell, as they are usually quick study that wants to move fast.

Let's explore CIO and CISO personas further.

CIOs and CISOs - Personas that matter

Every CIO and CISO is different, but we can classify them into a few broad personas. Having a rough sense of each leader's persona will help you adapt your approach to best influence their decisions.

I'll note that this is not an exact science, but you can ask two key questions to plot them into a simple 2x2 grid:

- Are they strategically (external) or operationally (internal) oriented?
- Is their focus on business growth or stability?

This same approach works for both the CIO and CISO roles. Their key focus areas just have some differences.

CIOs

The primary focus for CIOs is on business value, and this provides you clues as to where they will want to invest their budgets (scope), and why they say yes.

A 2x2 grid for the CIO personas would look like this:

	Growth focus	**Stability focus**
Strategic	Transformation CIO	Risk CIO
Operational	Business CIO	Operational CIO

Table 2.2 - How to classify CIO personas

Strategically focused CIOs will prefer to invest in new digital products and innovation to drive business revenue, while the operationally focused CIO prefers upgrading technically to make the environment more automated and stable. On the other hand, CIOs that have an orientation to stability will value compliance more than new tools to support business growth and their behavior will tend to reflect this natural bias.

The following table provides further analysis of the four personas identified in the preceding matrix:

Persona	Primary Motivation
Transformation CIO 	*Seeks Innovation and Growth* Is motivated to help drive revenue, create new business models, and achieve market leadership.
Operational CIO 	*Seeks Efficiency and Cost Control* The focus is on streamlining existing processes, standardizing tech stacks, and maximizing uptime and reliability.
Risk CIO 	*Seeks Business Stability and Compliance* Wants to protect the company's financial and reputational standing. Often influenced by recent breaches or regulatory pressure.
Business CIO 	*Seeks Influence and Alignment* Focus is on building consensus, managing stakeholder relationships, and ensuring the IT budget aligns perfectly with executive goals.

Table 2.3 - CIO personas

Try to classify the CIOs that you work with (or for) and see how you can do a draft categorization. Remember there are no right or wrong answers. You can present this as a "confidential" strategy exercise to your trusted colleagues, who can compare their assessment with your draft.

It is likely that many CIOs will naturally want to see themselves as "Transformation CIOs", as this is what every board and management team wants to have on their side, but the reality is that this is likely to be a small percentage of the total, as I noted earlier. My observation is that this is about 15-20%.

> **Note**
>
> Gartner® Research uses some different labels, but their survey of 2,400 CIOs were classified into three personas (`https://www.gartner.com/en/newsroom/press-releases/2023-10-17-gartner-survey-of-over-2400-cios-reveals-that-45-percent-of-cios-are-driving-a-shift-to-co-ownership-of-digital-leadership`) in this way:
>
> - Operator 55%
> - Explorers 33%
> - Franchiser 12%
>
> The "Franchiser" is aligned to the "Transformation CIO" persona that I've used.
>
> These ratios provide a good benchmark to sense check your own distribution assessment. Note that there may be a natural bias against labelling someone as an Operational CIO ("Operator") as this is seen as business as usual (BAU) (hence less bullish on investing in new technology products and services).

After classifying each CIO, next you should focus on the best approach to pitch to them. In the following table, I have provided some guidance on how each CIO thinks and then how to pitch them. Give this a try and keep checking for evidence that your "draft" persona classifications are correct:

Persona	**How to pitch to each CIO**
Transformation CIO 	**CIO Outlook** Likes cutting-edge solutions and is comfortable with high-reward risk **Vendor Pitch** Focus on revenue growth, new markets, and product innovation differentiation. Support this lead with case studies showing a competitive advantage.
Operational CIO 	**CIO Outlook** Only works with tech that is proven and reliable. **Vendor Pitch** Provide clear ROI benefits (cost savings or efficiency metrics), for instance, TCO, Automation %, etc.
Risk CIO 	**CIO Outlook** Favors solutions that offer comprehensive monitoring, governance, and regulatory compliance. **Vendor Pitch** Use words like "governance" and "defensibility." Strong focus on audit readiness and evidence for compliance metrics.

Persona	How to pitch to each CIO
Business CIO 	**CIO Outlook** Focuses on back-office systems and wants to drive success to earn influence with stakeholders. **Vendor Pitch** Focus on executive stakeholders and cross-departmental benefits.

Table 2.4 - How to pitch for each CIO persona

Using this approach, you may initially assess a CIO as a Business CIO, then as you test this with your pitch, you may have to re-assess to Transformation CIO. Active listening is crucial and you should allow some level of agility in your approach. Note that recent incidents, board meetings, budget cycles, and time of year can influence many CIOs' perspectives, so do consider these data points.

The position that a CIO or CISO occupies on this continuum is not fixed. Leaders adapt their persona to the needs of the enterprise; a transformation-minded CIO will shift toward caution following a significant incident, and a risk-averse CISO may be pushed toward bold action when the board demands acceleration. Context shapes behavior.

But beneath that visible adaptability, every CIO and CISO has a natural style they will gravitate toward when the pressure eases. This is their default setting, the instinct they return to when nobody is forcing them in a particular direction. Some are fundamentally wired for control and compliance. Others like me are restless without a transformation agenda on the table.

CISOs

Now let's turn and evaluate the personas for CISOs. These leaders are focused on risk management and security posture as the two primary priorities. The CISO classification table has a marked difference in that the role has more of a time-based urgency factor; it is more strategic vs. tactical. Every CISO must deal with incidents and urgent issues, and the key here is to identify the natural comfort zone for that leader. Similarly, all CISOs care about threats and compliance; it just depends on where they tend to focus their attention. Here is the 2x2 grid for the CISO personas:

	Threat focus	**Compliance focus**
Strategic	Transformation CISO	Business CISO
Tactical	Risk CISO	Operational CISO

Table 2.5 - How to classify CISO personas

In some cases, your assessment of the CISO focus may be influenced by the current environment. For instance, if there are many demanding board and management leaders then this may force CISO to operate in compliance mode following a major breach or regulatory incident. The very best CISOs can act like chameleons and change their form as required by the situation, but as I've mentioned, every leader has a natural preference that they will fall back on.

In the following table is an overview of each of the CISO personas and what their primary motivators are:

Persona	**Primary Motivation**
Transformation CISO 	*Drives the Strategic Cyber Roadmap* This CISO cares about setting a vision and building cyber architecture and enterprise resilience. They look ahead at what needs to be built and have a strong focus on sequencing this remediation.

Persona	Primary Motivation
Risk CISO 	*Seeks Strong Compliance* Focus on being compliant with regulations and all audit findings. Loves governance, framework, and policies. Documents carefully to ensure that there is strong evidence they can share if needed.
Business CISO 	*Right-sized Cyber Governance* Focus is on doing more with less. They manage budgets closely and ensure controls are right-sized and not over-invested. They work closely with all stakeholders to keep everyone as happy as possible.
Operational CISO 	*Runs a tight ship* They have a focus on protecting against all new threats and strong leadership when there is an incident that can impact the enterprise; they lead from the front.

Table 2.6 - CISO Personas

Now that we have identified our CISO persona and motivation, what is the best approach to sell to them? How should you tailor your message, with relevant proof points and engagement so that it resonates? The following table provides some examples of each CISO persona and how to pitch them:

Persona	How to pitch to each CISO
Transformation CISO 	**Outlook** This CISO accepts that risk is a necessary part of doing business. They focus on balancing protection with agility while reducing risk for the board. **Vendor pitch** You must talk about strategic roadmap alignment with platform consolidation. The CISO likes to hear about automation and transitioning to a long-term vision.
Risk CISO 	**Outlook** They focus on ensuring they pass audits and regulatory compliance. They want to keep the board happy by maintaining a low-risk profile and demonstrating clear management of risk. **Vendor pitch** Show them the data and how it allows them to be more compliant, and how it maps to NIST (National Institute of Standards and Technology). How does your product provide evidence that can be valuable in demonstrating progress and positive outcomes?
Business CISO 	**Outlook** These CISOs care about being fiscally responsible, so tell them why you help them be more cost-effective. **Vendor pitch** Be sure to frame your product or service as a safe investment that will reduce resourcing demand, including how this integrates well with their current technology stack and reduces the total cost of ownership (TCO).

Persona	How to pitch to each CISO
Operational CISO 	**Outlook** These focus on being strong at threat detection, rapid response, and insightful threat intelligence. **Vendor pitch** Talk to them about how your product or service provides great visibility of cyber threats, with a strong message around the metrics that help them manage operations efficiently.

Table 2.7 - Examples of CISO personas

> **Note**
>
> Note, having both leaders with the same persona type in the same enterprise at the same time is rare.

If your product or service represents "leading edge innovation" then this is the sweet spot for the Transformation CIO and the Transformation CISO.

Alternatively, if your product or service is strong on compliance then the Risk and Business CIO and the Risk and Business CISO are a perfect match for your offer. Finally in the case that this is an integrated package pitch, that may have a lower TCO, that will particularly appeal to the Operational CIO\CISO and Business CIO\CISO.

You will usually have a CIO and CISO combination that is diverse, so you must carefully consider how to approach them; this is all about trying to understand what their common ground is.

Finding common ground

This is going to be a real test, as you want to be able to appeal to more than one persona, so there may be some conflicting objectives. But if we boil this down, then regardless of the combination of CIO and CISO, they will have some views that they are 100% aligned to.

I'd add the following as a starting point:

- They both want to look good in front of the board
- They both do not want to be breached
- They both want a positive outcome

So then how do you start to speak and tailor your message to them? Instead of taking absolute positions, you will want to position your product and service as being able to address both of their requirements. For example, this new tool improves the digital customer experience *and* reduces the cybersecurity risk.

One approach to supplement this is to develop champions within both the CIO and CISO teams. If these internal champions see that their career development is aligned with the new developments, they will be excited to support your initiatives.

Identifying champions does not necessarily mean you select them based on hierarchical positional power, but of course that helps. You must pay attention in meetings to figure out and listen to their language; here are some positive and negative examples to watch out for:

Positive Signals	**Negative Signals**
They share internal context you would not otherwise know or be aware of	They talk about current solutions being good and not requiring changes
They bring colleagues to follow-up meetings	They are not available for follow-ups
They are keen to pilot or be involved in a POC	They are passive and not keen to learn more
They ask about the implementation	They focus on edge cases

Table 2.8 - Positive and Negative Signals

I go into champion identification in more depth in later chapters.

While you are working so hard to build a relationship and a level of trust, at the same time you should remain cognizant that the CIO and CISO do change roles routinely every few years.

The impact of C-suite churn

Does churn at the top matter? Clearly this is disruptive to your relationship and can mean that priorities can shift dramatically. This can be a double-edged sword though and be beneficial as well as harmful.

The sales cycles for a large enterprise product can be more than 12 to 24 months when attached to large-scale transformation, and between this and 1 year for a new platform. This churn can mean that the stakeholder you have been working with now provides you with an additional access point in their new enterprise.

Then the new CIO, who you may already know from the sales process, might want to brand themselves with some quick wins. If this person is one of your internal champions, then you have a head start. Thus, your own career hedge against CIO and CISO churn is that you don't put all your eggs in one basket. Seek to build a few strategic relationships with different stakeholders. There is also the reality that the new CIO can inherit the positive outcomes that your change can deliver. Either way your investment in building multiple relationships can ensure that your influence is maintained when churn occurs.

There are clues that you can gather to be able to have that sixth sense of when an executive is about to leave. I've seen this multiple times in my career and my hit rate for predicting someone is about to leave is about 75% success. Usually, the clues are in the language that they use when they speak to you (for example, talking about their legacy and all the great things they have been able to achieve), but there are other cookie crumbs to be aware of too.

I noted earlier in this chapter that the industry average for turnover of CIO and CISO is between 2-4 years, with CIOs tending at the higher end of that range.

Now, once the CIO or CISO has been in their role for 3 years, then I'd say you will need to be watching the overall environment. When there is a change of their direct supervisor, this can trigger a shift in their role in the next 12-18 months, as the new incumbent may want to move in their own leader that they believe in and consider to be loyal.

At other times, I've had requests to meet with other CISOs or CIOs who are curious about my experience working at *ABC* or *XYZ*. In another example, I was being interviewed by a Group CIO for a CTO role and was just convinced by the lack of energy and drive in their behavior, and the fact that the IT strategy had not been updated, that this CIO was about to leave. (I was correct and they did leave within 4-5 months).

When this leader is also less available and misses your regular catchups that can be a sign, but as these roles are very busy this is not a very accurate metric.

At the macro level, when there are mergers and acquisitions or budget cutbacks in the company this can also trigger the passive search to commence for a new role. Then of course if you have developed strong trust relationships with your internal contacts, this may be something they disclose to you in confidence.

To delve into the perspective of a CIO and a CISO, they want to have "trusted advisor relationships" and many of them will be open to vendors acting in this capacity, but they will be skeptical as most of them are inundated with many vendors wanting to sell to them and vendors are incentivized to meet their target quotas. The average CIO and CISO will have very few trusted advisors; those they do have are likely to be their peers in other firms. In a roundabout way the trust you build with the CIO and CISO will result in them recommending you to their peers if they find you are worth speaking to.

This is very dynamic and of course all trust tokens can be lost in a few moments of inappropriate engagement, however.

Classifying vendors

In my experience, most vendors are noise; they are present in the market but are not yet earning meaningful engagement.

I've classified different vendor types in the following table in accordance with how the CIO and CISO will view them:

Level	Vendor label	Attributes
0	Noise	*This vendor is a commodity, and I took a meeting with them by mistake*
1	Known Quantity	*I know this company and will take the meeting if* my *schedule allows*
2	Credible Vendor	*I rate your product and you talk straight to me*
3	Preferred Vendor	*I'm happy to talk to you as you have helped me*
4	Strategic Vendor	*I ask your opinion on things outside of your product scope*
5	Trusted Advisor	*You have earned my full trust*

Table 2.9 - Different levels of vendors

Most productive vendor relationships I have worked with operate at level 2 or 3. These are good, functional relationships; they are vendors who deliver reliably, communicate well, and add genuine value, but have not yet earned the deeper trust that defines a strategic partnership. Reaching Level 4 is rare, and it should be. In my experience it takes one of two things:

- A defining moment where the vendor stepped up under real pressure, resolving a critical issue or saving a significant transformation
- Or a sustained period of Level 3 engagement over at least three years of consistently positive delivery

You cannot shortcut your way to Level 4. It is earned slowly and lost quickly. For most vendor relationships, achieving and maintaining Level 3 is a great place to target as an objective. Not every vendor needs to be a strategic partner, but every vendor should be aspiring to move up, not settling for where they are.

Level 5 is rarified, and you reach this stage only when there is a very strong level of trust. Both parties can speak plainly, and the engagement can be more informal.

The premise of best practices in selling comes from practitioners like Neil Rackham who wrote *Spin Selling*. His finding is that "successful selling in major sales is about creative problem-solving rather than persuasion, with the salesperson becoming more important than the product."

CIOs and CISOs want vendors to:

- Understand customer needs deeply through structured questioning
- Position themselves as a consultant rather than a pusher of products
- Build long-term relationships based on understanding our problems
- Allow them to tell you their needs rather than being told what they need

> Note
>
> *Trusted vendors talk in consequences, while marketing-only vendors talk in categories. So, when a vendor arrives and they already understand the likely pain:*
>
> *They can name the customer's likely pressure points (regulatory, audit, ransomware, tooling sprawl, staffing limits)*
>
> *They test for maturity early (runs with what you have)*
>
> *They lead with an outcome (detection, recovery)*
>
> *They are comfortable saying "We're not the right fit"*
>
> **Sam Ghebranious – Director, Axcelerate / Senior Advisor, Frost & Sullivan**

You don't ever want to be seen as "noise" but instead your sweet spot is to be seen as a "preferred or strategic" vendor. Even the most trusted advisor will not try to sell sand in the desert. When you are selling products or services that are not serving the customer's interest, then you are a vendor and not a partner. Don't then be surprised if the relationship does not work!

I do appreciate that it is hard to walk away from a deal, when you are not sure if this is the right solution. That requires an extreme level of integrity and playing the long game. The real winners in sales play this long game with a sense of urgency across their portfolio on some tactical revenue to survive the short-term quota pressure.

The long game is all about building that trust with your relationships, developing your internal champions and positioning your company. The short game is when you close your sale with a contract.

In the next chapter I turn to a key question: how do you get in front of the CIO and CISO in the first place? It sounds simple. It is not. Getting the attention of an executive who receives hundreds of unsolicited approaches a month, who has a filter built from years of being pitched to, and who has less than a minute to decide whether you are worth their time, is tricky. I believe the market rewards those who have done the work and show up with something worth saying.

Summary

In this chapter, we explored partnering with CIOs and CISOs and how this requires playing a long game—building genuine trust over months or years by understanding their internal pressures, political environment, and career motivations rather than leading with product features.

Talk to them in business terms by understanding what they regard as "carrots and sticks." You should also tailor your approach to the specific persona of the executive.

The overarching goal is to move from a level of "noise" to "preferred" or "strategic vendor," becoming a consultant who solves real problems—not a salesperson pitching features.

These are the key learnings from this chapter:

- **Lead with discovery, not pitch** – ask what they wish they could *stop* doing.
- **Know their "carrots and sticks"** – CIOs are driven by transformation and business enablement; CISOs by compliance, defensibility, and breach avoidance. These are distinct and require tailored messaging.
- **Categorize your target into one of the CIO & CISO personas** – Transformation, Operational, Risk, and Business. Misreading the persona is one of the most common reasons deals stall.
- **CYA documentation matters** – risk-averse CIOs/CISOs need defensible evidence (POC results, peer benchmarks, Gartner/ Forrester /IDC reports) to get internal approval; help them build that case.
- **Skip the POC treadmill if you can** – the goal is to move directly to a time-bound pilot with a senior champion (POC → POV → Pilot sequentially can be a deal killer).
- **C-suite churn is an opportunity** – build relationships across multiple stakeholders. A departing CIO/CISO becomes a new access point, and their successor often wants quick wins.

3

Contacting the C-Suite

The CIO and CISO operate in a challenging and dynamic environment where work/life balance is often out of natural equilibrium. It is against this backdrop that they have vendors approach them to hopefully commence a dialogue that will lead to a sale. This is a critical first step for you, but it can very quickly end if you manage this dialogue poorly or if it comes at an inappropriate time.

We have established that the CIO and CISO are your targets, but how on earth do you gain access to these executives? They are already drowning in vendor pitches, and their default answer is "no". When I was a CIO and CISO, I received unexpected phone calls, emails, faxes, letters, invitations, and even drop-in meetings. I could usually tell from the first few seconds of contact that I should close it as soon as possible.

In this chapter I will explore how to best contact the CIO and CISO, including how to use connections to facilitate this introduction, and then how to start to build this relationship. Given the stress and strains of a day in the life of a CIO and CISO, this requires some good judgment on your part and a little luck. I've looked at this broadly and you will see that this chapter covers five distinct approaches that you can use.

The key topics we'll cover in this chapter are:

- Spamming the CIO and CISO
- Starting outreach
- How to cold call the CIO or CISO

- A warm introduction to the CIO or CISO
- The art of "jostle"
- Vendor hosted events and junkets
- Finding and nurturing a champion
- Combining the jostle and champion approaches
- Daring to be different
- Final thoughts on contacting C-suite

Note

Download the PDF version of this book

Your purchase includes a DRM-free PDF copy of this book and a range of exclusive benefits. To unlock everything, follow the *Free benefits with your book* section in the *Preface.*

Spamming the CIO and CISO

I'd like to start with worst practices and highlight what must be avoided when you are looking at contacting the CIO and CISO. In my personal experiences as a CIO and CISO, I received 100-300 vendor outreaches on average each week. This degree of attempted contact naturally created a degree of frustration; it can feel like this never stops.

An average CIO and CISO day is already filled with demands that exceed their attention span. Then there are, of course, board meetings, travel, and other executive governance sessions that will require preparation and in-person attendance.

The truth is that while this is part and parcel of the CIO and CISO's role, they often dislike spam the most; it is seen as wasting their time with little payback in terms of benefit. The following table highlights the volume of spam that CIOs and CISOs can receive on a weekly basis. Note these are my own estimates based on my experience and from talking to colleagues.

Emails 	80-200, with the majority arriving on Tuesday and Wednesday

LinkedIn	20–40 new connection requests
Phone	10-30 calls and voicemails, which their executive assistant (EA) will often screen
Dinners	3-4 invites for lunch or dinner with vendors
Events	2-3 tech and cyber events, such as industry conferences (Gartner®, RSA, etc.)

Table 3.1 - Weekly volume of spam received by CIO and CISO

My own way of managing this "noise" was that I would typically have a blanket response of "no" to each of these communications. This differed slightly for dinner and event invitations, but these would usually only be considered when the dinner or event had an attractive topic or an industry speaker who had an opinion that I personally rated.

As these dinners and event invitations often come from known vendors, if I was interested, I started to form a more positive opinion of them, with a degree of previous relationship at play if they then approached me later.

> **Note**
>
> Since I would also expect to receive more invitations the next day, I didn't want to sit on these responses. If this was an attractive event, then I would RSVP more or less immediately.

On the other hand, emails, phone calls, and LinkedIn are all commonly considered the worst of spam channels. Direct phone contact, given the already busy schedules of CIOs and CISOs, means that you are nearly 100% likely to call them when they are already in a meeting and trying to concentrate.

The overall impact of this spam approach, when this is replicated by many from your company, is simple: there will be direct brand damage to your company, with the CIO and CISO having their trust eroded by this barrage of attempted connections. While you may be thinking that your own company has been judicious in making this contact, consider the cumulative effect of the entire industry adopting these approaches.

> **Note**
>
> *The net effect of being excessively aggressive on these channels is that the CIO and CISO community will also share their frustration with fellow peers, which may result in a formal or informal blacklisting of your brand. As a result, your goodwill is lost, and you will be excluded from their consideration as you are perceived as a bad partner to work with. A lot of times, that's what ends up happening in the CISO community - we're on Slack channels together, we are going to events and staying at an Airbnb together. We talk about technologies and vendors we trust.*
>
> **Gary Hayslip – CISO, Halcyon.ai, Board Director and Investor**

Starting outreach

You may follow a framework similar to this when establishing organizations to target with your solution:

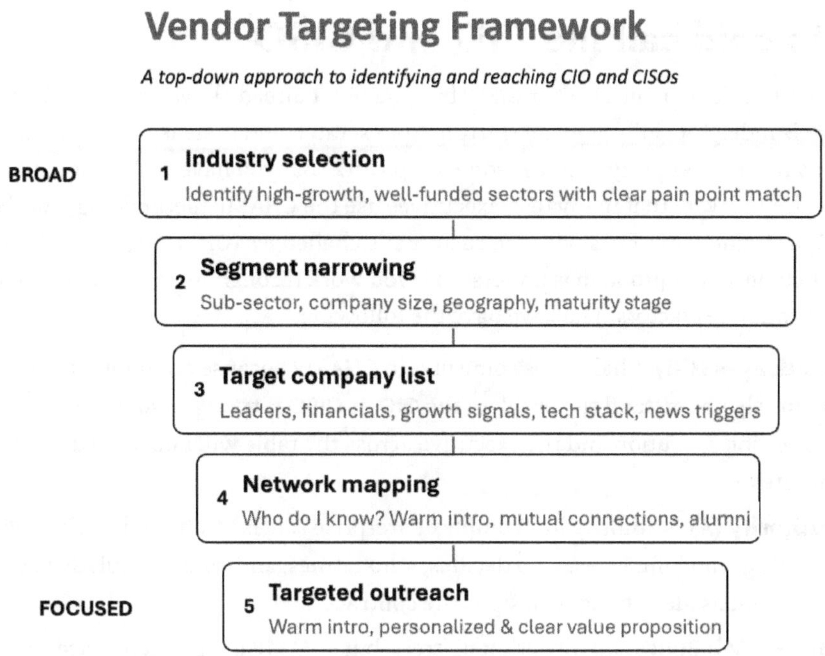

Figure 3.1 - Overview of vendor targeting approach

By this point you may have already conducted steps 1 to 3. For many vendors, some of these steps will be part of an overall go-to-market (GTM) strategy and there will be little room for negotiation. This chapter will cover steps 4 and 5.

> **Note**
>
> *Effective engagement often starts long before direct contact. Thought leadership through industry forums, research, webinars, and peer references helps establish credibility and relevance. By the time a vendor reaches out, there should already be clarity on the problem they solve and the outcomes they enable.*
>
> **Sunil Varkey – CISO, Hexaware Technologies(Former HSBC CISO)**

This top-down approach is ideal; however, this assumes that you have network coverage that is relevant. The reality is that there will always be gaps where access to the C-Suite and even leaders within the enterprises selected are concerned. I will therefore start with coverage of cold calling.

How to cold call the CIO and CISO

So, you want to call or email a CIO or CISO, but you don't already have any relationship with them. That is indeed "cold"—you are starting from scratch and there is no judgment or expectation from either party. There is some prep work that you have to do first in identifying your call list. I'm aware that many tech executives use the CHAMP methodology for this analysis. This framework starts with the customer's challenges (CH) rather than the vendor's agenda. Then once that problem is understood, you work through Authority (A), Money (M) and Prioritization (P) factors. Thus, we have the following:

- **Challenges (CH)**: Challenges come first in CHAMP because a vendor who does not genuinely understand the problem the CIO or CISO is trying to solve has no business presenting a solution and the executive across the table will know it within the first five minutes
- **Authority (A)**: Authority in a complex enterprise sale is rarely held by a single person; mapping who influences, who decides, who ratifies, and who can quietly veto is as important as identifying who signs the contract
- **Money (M)**: Budget qualification matters, but CHAMP deliberately places it third because the money conversation is most productive after the value of solving the problem has been established
- **Prioritization (P)**: Even when the challenge is real, the authority is clear, and the budget exists, a deal will stall if the problem is not urgent enough to act on now which is why understanding where your solution sits in the queue of everything else competing for the CIO and CISO's attention is important

Once you have the CIO or CISO's email or mobile phone number, know that you invariably will likely catch them when they are already in a meeting and not interested in any interruptions. Understand that this approach is highly likely to fail. I'd estimate from my own experience that the cold call works only 5% of the time.

Why is this? well, there are a few reasons:

- The EA has likely been specifically trained to filter any vendors
- Their inbox may have filters and file external emails into different folders
- Their chat channels are reserved for known connections

Note

Your phone rings. A number that you don't know.

Yep, your screening, that's really failed you, right?

What do you do? Do you pick up the vendor and its blah, blah, then. Just hang up.

If it pops up and I don't know who it is, I just let it go to voicemail.

Gary Hayslip – CISO, Halcyon.ai, Board Director and Investor

There are times when I personally have received a cold phone call, and I've decided to answer it, sometimes out of curiosity or mistaken identity of the caller. In those cases, I have said, *you have caught me between meetings, and I have literally 5 minutes, after which I will have to hang up.* I have had many examples of this kind of interaction, and most don't end well. I recognize that 3-5 minutes is not a long time, but if you are able to succinctly and precisely introduce why you are calling, then you may earn the right to have a longer discussion.

Note

When I receive a cold call directly to my mobile phone from a telephone marketer claiming to represent a big tech firm and get asked questions such as "How are you doing today? Am I speaking to Ong Siau Wah Alvin" (and the person would read out my full name and often mispronounce my Chinese name to my amusement. My preferred name is simply "Alvin Ong")'. "Are you currently the Chief Information Officer of Khoo Teck Puat Hospital?" (caller's CRM database is outdated, as the caller refers to my previous company), then I would immediately tell the caller that I am busy and hang up the phone. This type of cold call has happened so many times and is such a waste of our precious time.

Alvin Ong – Former Nanyang Technological University CIO

Having myself received many calls that sound just like someone is reading a script, it is most off-putting and will be a call that is terminated with very little ceremony. While I'm aware that this is that person's job, it comes across as a complete waste of my time. Moreover, the brand damage that this does to your company and solution can be long-lasting. Here is an example of what has worked to get my attention as a CIO and CISO, and perhaps also a follow-up:

Step	Timing	Example Run Sheet
The Problem	*30 seconds*	We work with CIOs and CISOs in financial services who are struggling with *(specific pain points you face)*. Based on your role at ABC, I thought this might be relevant to you.
<Pause>	*2 seconds*	Short pause to see if there's any reaction, but don't wait.
The Value	*60 seconds*	We help organizations like yours with *(specific outcome)*. Share a brief, relevant customer story with measurable results. This usually helps make your case.
The Ask	*30 seconds*	I'm not trying to sell you anything today. I have two questions that would help me understand if this is even relevant to you. *(Ask two pointed questions about their current challenges)*
Listening	*Time remaining*	Based on their affirmative answers to the problem being relevant, you may suggest a follow-up 30-minute conversation with their team to dive deeper.

Table 3.2 - Your 5-minute intro pitch to a CIO or CISO

Does your cold call sound like that? It may be the case that the fact that someone answered feels like a total surprise, which results in you launching into a spiel and failing to listen for any clues.

We all understand that the cold call, by nature, has an extremely low probability of success, but what has surprised me is that when callers do get through, they often lack a polished enough approach to earn a follow-up meeting. The approach I have suggested in the preceding table works because in 5 minutes, you have demonstrated that you:

- Respect their time
- Done your homework
- Discuss outcomes, not product features
- Engaged in a dialogue rather than just listing the details of your product

This approach is not guaranteed to work, but it can give you a chance for a follow-up meeting without damaging your own brand and your company's.

> **Tip**
>
> If the CIO or CISO does not respond positively, then best practice is not to keep going. I'd suggest you stop and regroup to work out your next step.

> **Note**
>
> *What is frustrating is I've got a work phone and a personal phone. And somehow (I was told by the callers that they got the list from a marketing group from LinkedIn data), people got a lot of our numbers. And so, I get calls 24 hours a day on my personal devices and emails.*
>
> **Scott Collary – Group CIO, Westpac Group**

What works even better than the cold call is when there is a warm introduction from someone in your target CIO or CISO's network that they trust.

A warm introduction to the CIO or CISO

Warm introductions are far more effective than a cold call. A warm introduction is a personal referral from a trusted mutual contact that opens a door on your behalf, with borrowed credibility significantly increasing the likelihood that meeting a CIO and/or CISO actually happens. CIOs and CISOs are more likely to accept an introduction to you in this way as a favor to their peers and colleagues; they may consider this a personal obligation from the network.

In my experience, warm introductions via peer networks succeed roughly 10–20% of the time; this is better than cold calling but clearly not always a winner. Of course, this depends on the strength of the relationship of the leader doing the introduction.

Personally, I get asked to provide introductions every few days. I have complete strangers ask me this on LinkedIn, then acquaintances via email or chat messaging, and peers over coffee. You can also find connections through networking at industry events, where CIOs and CISOs gather.

I've also served as an advisory board member, and such associations provide a more formalized mechanism for leveraging board member networks.

Note

Best is having someone they know, and trust/respect introduce you, someone on their team that can drive change associated with your technology, a business partner that has credibility with the CxO, someone in common in your network.

Yigal Elstein – Chief Revenue Officer, Checkmarx

A warm introduction is the overwhelmingly popular choice that all C-Suites will prefer.

The following table outlines the main sources for a warm introduction:

Source	**Why influential?**	**Advice**
Peer Network	A personal peer network is most trusted as they fully understand the executive's role.	Consider these options: • CIO and CISO peers • Colleagues worked with in their past role • Industry connections from associations,
Advisors	Industry advisors tend to be well trusted, although this is based upon the strength of an ongoing relationship and, in some cases, a retainer.	Look for Advisors that they work with: • Bain, McKinsey, BCG, Gartner, Forrester, etc. • Board Member & Non-executive director • FS-ISAC and other industry contacts

Source	Why influential?	Advice
Internal Champions	These are colleagues that work either for the CIO or CISO already, or in adjacent teams. As such, there will likely already be a relationship.	Seek out in your network: • Prior client now moved to their company • A direct report and is trusted- • A peer in a different department

Table 3.3 - Warm Introductions

Once you have identified potential facilitators, bear in mind that there are two key factors to consider before making your request.

First, you must have earned the right for an introduction from experience in working with them and doing exceptional work, being considered at least a "Preferred Vendor" by them. This really does take time, and there are no shortcuts, unless you are ready to operate unsustainably.

Second, most leaders will be reluctant to abuse this trust with their peers, and there is a natural limit on how many times they can make a warm introduction.

> **Note**
>
> I've always thought of introductions as spending a "token," which raises the question: what's in it for me? My network is built on trust, and if I'm careless about where I place that trust, its value depreciates.
>
> These tokens function like a bank account, with each introduction acting as a debit or credit. Every time I make an introduction, the CIO and CISO I'm speaking to mentally reconcile whether it was a good or poor use of their time.
>
> A good introduction is a deposit into my account: the CIO or CISO sees value in the meeting, and my own reputation is reinforced as someone with a strong network. Conversely, a bad introduction is a withdrawal: it damages my account and, in this case, my own personal brand.

Good introductions create mutual benefit, such as new insights or opportunities for both sides. Bad ones offer little reciprocal value. Repeating poor introductions also erodes the introducer's social trust capital. If this pattern continues, they lose the right to expect their network to respond, and their network will conclude that they are wasting their time.

The same principle applies to trusted advisors: they are reluctant to spend their tokens unless they see a return benefit.

> Note
>
> *There is no 100% right answer. Obviously, referrals get an easier glide path to a meeting. But even if it is a cold outreach, the manner in which they do contact is paramount. For example, if on a LinkedIn message, just taking some time to explain who they are and why they want to meet up.*
>
> **Paul O'Rourke – former CISO, CRO and BCG Global Cyber Leader**

Allow me to explain why the warm introduction is such a great approach. From my own personal experience, the introducer's hard-earned credibility with the CIO or CISO is extended to the vendor, creating a starting position of borrowed trust that no email or LinkedIn message can replicate.

> Note
>
> The double opt-in principle is what makes that transfer of trust legitimate, confirming that both sides want the introduction before it happens. The introducer protects their own reputation, and the executive's time is respected. You then enter the conversation knowing the door was opened willingly rather than pushed.

Let's now explore in more detail how to navigate peer relationships when it comes to a warm introduction. I'd argue that peer warm introductions carry a category of trust that no other prospecting method can match when one CIO or CISO recommends a vendor to another.

Strengths of peer relationships

From the interviews I conducted for this book, peers have been cited as the most effective "warm" channel for a vendor to gain that first initial meeting. Here are a few of these inputs:

> Note
>
> *Referrals from peers (not more senior people who are disconnected from the issues at hand) are often useful because relationships are often based on a network of trust – especially in national and cyber security. In today's age we can't afford to waste time going down rabbit warrens. But ultimately, they would need to demonstrate their capability to us. I don't just take someone else's word for it.*
>
> **Dr Maria Milosavljevic – former ANZ Bank CISO**

> **Note**
>
> *Warm introductions, referrals, or context-aware outreach are always more effective than cold sales calls. Senior leaders respond to value and insight, not volume and persistence.*
>
> **Sunil Varkey – CISO, Hexaware Technologies (Former HSBC CISO)**

> **Note**
>
> *Referrals or trusted introductions always win—ideally from another CISO or a peer I respect. Cold emails rarely work—in my opinion, it's a waste of time. LinkedIn is a lot of spam now, but I will look if the message is short, relevant, and human. If it looks like a copy-paste from a sales template, I ignore it. Build some trust with me as a peer and good advisor, and then you can talk about the product.*
>
> **Adam Palmer – CISO, First Hawaiian Bank**

The peers' network arguably contains the strongest relationships to our CIO and CISO, but how can you classify the strength of these links? What are the clues to watch out for?

From my experience in working as an advisor, I'm often asked to provide a list of my key industry contacts, but what is most important is the depth of the relationship, which I classify from being inner circle level (we are friends and are quite close) through to a baseline level (I know your name) (see *Figure 3.2*).

The value of the warm introduction is commensurate with the relationship's maturity. Earlier I noted that a warm introduction can work on average 10-20% of the time. However, I'd argue that the probability of traction is significantly higher if your warm introduction is from the CIO or CISO's inner circle.

The warm introduction hierarchy is best understood as a pyramid and the closer to the top you can operate, the more powerful the trust transfer becomes:

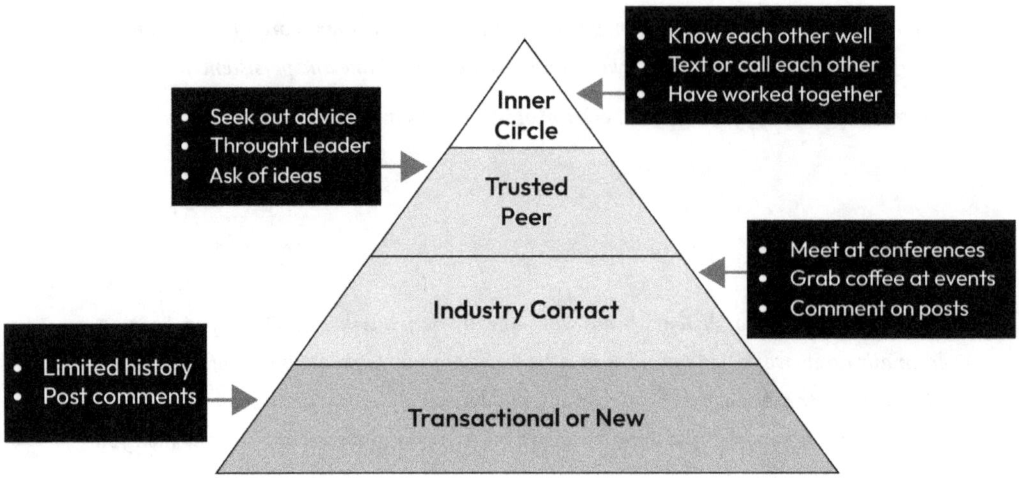

Figure 3.2 - Strength of the peer relationship

At the apex of this pyramid sits the inner circle, the board member who has the CIO's ear or a former colleague who has earned a decade of trust. A warm introduction from this level carries a weight that is qualitatively different from anything below it.

Below this is the warm introduction from the trusted peer. The trusted peer is someone who has walked the same path as the CIO or CISO and speaks from experience rather than commercial interest. Their recommendation carries credibility because the CIO or CISO receiving it knows instinctively that it was given freely and honestly.

Next is the industry contact, whose value is breadth where the trusted peer's value is depth. An industry contact can open many doors with consistent and reliable credibility, making them a different kind of asset in the vendor's relationship portfolio.

The transactional or new relationship sits at the base of the pyramid; a warm introduction from these sources is least effective. A warm introduction is directly targeted, and this approach is one that is respected by the CIO and CISO. In this next section, I will explore another approach I've seen work: when you find the CIO and CISO in a more relaxed mood and more receptive to new ideas.

The art of "jostle"

"Jostle" is a word I've heard described as when you accidentally run into someone else on the dance floor. To my mind, this word aptly represents the act of maneuvering yourself to get someone's attention, but with a degree of tactfulness. How can you innocently but purposefully be at the same coffee shop or event that gets you a few moments of a CIO or CISO's time, without them thinking that this was a setup?

I have limited data, but my own estimate is that jostling in the vendor-CIO/CISO context also has a 10-20% chance of success, but I believe this depends on the actual event. For instance, at a closed industry roundtable, the CIO and CISO will usually arrive in networking mode, and their guard is more down. The key here is that you want this to feel like just a coincidence and that you both serendipitously met at this time and place. Your goal is to make this seem completely natural rather than manipulative in any way.

In all honesty, as a CIO and CISO, I've seen forms of stalking that occur on LinkedIn and at public conferences. Having said that, I've personally seen that when someone has either just posted or made a keynote speech, there are some natural approaches that you can try to engage with them, and typically, their guard is down as they are in engagement mode. Let's discuss jostling via bumping into a CIO or CISO at an event vs seeking them out on LinkedIn. In truth, you might want to do both, combining these efforts.

Bumping into the CIO or CISO at an event

The advantage of an in-person event is that the CIO or CISO is likely to have assigned the day to the event, rather than business meetings. Mutual connections can be an opportunistic way to join a discussion with them. When you do talk to them, there is an opportunity to build rapport; you can watch their body language.

You also need to be spatially aware of who else is queuing to speak with them and decide on the timing of when to introduce yourself, bearing in mind when the sessions start again.

> Note
>
> *Let's be honest, a buyer's inbox is a graveyard of feature-dump emails. What actually works is visibility and empathy. Digital outreach is fine, but in-person conversations at industry events consistently yield better results. It strips away the sales script and allows for an actual human conversation about risk.*
>
> **Jayant Dave – CISO, Check Point Software**

If you read the room and their body language – they are relaxed and not rushing back to the office – then it is an ideal time for that "accidental" and incidental meeting. While you know this encounter is planned, you want the CIO or CISO to be unaware of your true objective.

So, you have your moment to approach. What should you say and what should you not say? Well, you must do your homework rather than being impulsive:

Preparation	Approach
Homework 	*David, I'm Susan, and I understand that your team is working on* ABC *as a priority to meet transformation/compliance. We just concluded a similar project at* XYZ. *How is your effort tracking?*
No Prep 	*David, I'm Susan, and I'm doing work on large-scale transformation change management for a few large enterprises. Where does your team focus right now?*

Table 3.4 - Bumping into a CIO or CISO with and without preparation

You should not directly pitch your product or ask for time to demo it; their guard will be up in an instant at that approach.

> **Note**
>
> You may know their background well, but it is likely that you are not yet on their radar.

Having a basic understanding of their pain points is essential. Your objective is to ensure that the CIO or CISO walks away thinking they are okay with talking further with you later. They may be interested in your case study, or in some cases, may already be aware of it and want to hear more.

Seeking CIO and CISO on LinkedIn

The LinkedIn platform can be a powerful research tool, but in my experience, the effectiveness in terms of securing a meeting through it is low. The platform offers significant scale, and LinkedIn Sales Navigator provides additional tools, but none of it is magic.

As I mentioned earlier, CIOs and CISOs are literally bombarded on LinkedIn. Your special message is in effect "noise" to them, as it is competing with many other vendors, recruiters, and connection requests. If your touchpoint lacks relevance and looks templated, then it will be ignored or just deleted without being read.

> **Tip**
>
> Don't send a CIO or CISO a blank connection request.

> **Note**
>
> *On LinkedIn, I get people that reach out all the time, and so I do a little bit of diligence on them to take a look at who they are and what their technology does. There are things that I look for to see if the request to connect is a bot, fake account, phishing, etc. I find I spend a lot of time just blocking requests.*
>
> **Gary Hayslip – CISO, Halcyon.ai, Board Director and Investor**

The reality is that because CIOs and CISOs receive too many connection requests, their first impression may be one of suspicion—what does this person want?

> **Note**
>
> *If the CIO or CISO has just posted, that's your opportunity to engage with them by making a comment on their post, or reposting and tagging them in an engaging manner. Bear in mind that many CIOs and CISOs only occasionally operate on this platform however, and/or have a measured presence. Your attempts to engage them, even in this way, may not be welcomed. Some of them start off innocuous like - I just want to follow you and, you know, see what you say on LinkedIn or whatever. And if you respond, within 30 seconds, you get the sales pitch and "I'm going to call you, next Tuesday or Wednesday's a good day for me", you know, kind of thing. That not a great way to start a conversation; not unexpected anymore but not great.*
>
> **Scott Collary – Group CIO, Westpac Group**

> **Tip**
>
> The "jostle" can be an effective approach to start a dialogue with a CIO or CISO but remember that too much repetition in this regard risks it feeling like you are stalking them.

To differentiate yourself from the crowd, be sure to be seen as adding value. Here are a few ideas to consider:

- Ask a thoughtful follow-up question
- Add a new insight or your own experience
- Be professional and do not "write a novel"
- Avoid any sales pitch

Let's take an example of dialogue that you may choose to approach a target CIO or CISO via LinkedIn, with the view that this can lead to a meeting with them. The CIO or CISO writes a post, and you are not connected, but you decide to make a comment:

LinkedIn Post	How a CIO or CISO may react
Love your ABC *post, can we meet for coffee to discuss?*	This will feel salesy. A CIO or CISO will most likely ignore the comment and not react either way.
Agree with some of your insights, David; however, I also have some different perspective on ABC *that I've seen from my own personal experience*	This post is more likely to engage a CIO or CISO intellectually, provided that you are offering a different perspective that they may not have considered.

Table 3.5 - LinkedIn comment examples

In my view, using too much flattery feels disingenuous and does not have the positive impact that you are aiming for. The fact is, it will feel as if you are trying too hard.

Note

Cold emails and LinkedIn messages are acceptable, but responses should not be expected. I collect propositions for future needs. Personal relationships become relevant only later, once trust and credibility need to be verified.

Franco Marconcini – Group CISO, Electrolux Professional

Taking the time to genuinely engage with executives will bring engagement that can help provide you access after your "accidental bump." Remember you don't want them to feel that this is a jostle; instead, you want the CIO or CISO to think to themself that this was a useful chance encounter, and they gained a new insight to consider for their thinking. There is a real subtlety to these scenarios.

Let's now turn to a planned event that you, as a vendor, are creating or sponsoring, to get face to face with CIOs and CISOs. You want to create an environment conducive to engaging them.

Vendor hosted events and junkets

There are vendor-hosted events with many different names and formats. Vendor-hosted events are based on the planning assumption of sharing thought leadership and industry insights. The hospitality is incidental to the event.

On the other hand, a "junket", is where the hospitality is the main attraction with some networking and little content. The word "junket" is commonly used to refer to trips taken and paid for by someone else. These could be events in fancy restaurants or even a harbor cruise in a beautiful setting.

> Note
>
> I was invited to many meetings of both types as a CIO and CISO. For those I attended, I was always careful to disclose these within the policy requirements of my enterprise.
>
> I never wanted to have any perception of impropriety, and I never wanted to carry the weight of ethical uncertainty into a vendor relationship. The moment a CIO or CISO accepts hospitality that sits outside their enterprise's declared policy even once, even modestly, they have handed the vendor something they should never have.

Some vendors will use a private industry breakfast or lunch event for this purpose and invite several CIOs and CISOs (among other peers of theirs) to a session. In these cases, CIOs and CISOs will often attend because one of their inner circle or trusted colleagues is also coming.

A major focus for you will be on getting these executives to the table where they can relax with their industry peers, while you have an opportunity to introduce some relevant thinking and concepts to them.

For the CIO and CISO, these events can be amusing, but they also must disclose them for compliance reasons. This can be a barrier to excessive junket frills.

Most important is that you don't sell at the sessions; this will only drive away C-Suite from accepting your invitations again in the future. Best practice is to make these engaging, thought-provoking sessions, without the sell.

> Note
>
> *Very clearly an opportunity for them to engage with each other and their peers, then that's where they will always get the value.... We are so firm on making sure that it's about them.*

> *It's knowing your audience and listening to your audience and giving your audience a chance to talk with each other. If they all walk out thinking that's what's happened, then I think that was a good use of their time.*
>
> **Matt Boon – Senior Director, Strategic Research, Adapt**

Invitations for these events are either an email that arrives in your inbox or a phone call that is received. CIOs and CISOs often recognize these and may put these interruptions aside. The invitations that are accepted have the right combination of elements that first make timing for the event possible and secondly, are of sufficient interest for them to invest the time required to attend.

CIOs and CISOs generally get invited to more events than they could possibly attend and do their role properly. This then becomes a trade-off; they want to try to participate and stay in touch with the industry network but also begrudge receiving too many invitations.

What goes through the mind of the CIO and CISO when thinking about attending these events? I'd say it generally goes like this, and in this order, building up cumulatively to a decision:

Order	Consideration	Thought process
1		My schedule allows me to attend.
2		I have no board meeting or critical meeting just before or after.
3		The topic being discussed is relevant and interesting to me.

Order	Consideration	Thought process
4		Some trusted peers are also attending.
5		The venue is interesting and the location is easy to get to.
6		The food is good at that venue.

Table 3.6 - Deciding whether to attend an event or not

Note that #4 is key as CIOs and CISOs work within a challenging environment with often no one to talk to about their issues except for their peers. Obviously, no CIO or CISO will openly admit or talk about very sensitive issues, however.

> **Tip**
>
> Getting executives to engage at these events sometimes depends on the skill of the moderator to set the tone and share stories from their own experience.

I've seen both sides as a CIO and CISO attending the event, and more recently, as an advisor who moderates these sessions for vendors. I've seen these dynamics myself. Tech and cyber vendors want to create an environment that facilitates these conversations, knowing how valued they are by the CIO and CISO audience.

Often, the CIO and CISO that you really want to get time with are not available at the time you set for the event, or they can't get past #1 or #2 from the decision tree.

Tip

There is usually a high cost for these sponsored events, and invariably, the CIO and CISO work on crises and incidents that can also block their attendance at the last minute.

Now, allow me to discuss the most compelling approach: engaging a champion. These are the people you invite to these junket events if you cannot get into the CIO or CISO's diary. The champion is a critical asset that you will want to develop, and their value to you, as a product or service vendor, is immeasurable.

How do you identify and nurture these leaders? That is exactly what I will cover next (I'll go into this further later in the book).

Finding and nurturing a champion

Bruce Lee is well known as a martial arts master, an icon who is famous and revered. Yet it is not well understood that the movies he made were only from 1971-73; his film career was short but incredibly impactful. Bruce did not need a decade to forge his name as an "icon"; he was able to create significant impact in a short period of time.

This is exactly what you want from your champion. Having an internal champion on side is more powerful than any "jostle"; ideally, this is someone who you know and trusted from past positive experiences. However, it is likely that you will always be identifying and developing new champions to help gain a foothold within companies. I've been a champion of many new products and solutions myself. The champion may or may not be a direct report of the CIO or CISO (obviously, immediate reporting is better).

This contact can be a leader whom you can easily get a coffee with and seek their advice on the best approaches to consider in selling to the CIO or CISO. Note that the champion does not need to be of high hierarchical rank however, but they must be influential and have strong credibility. Usually, the best champions have been in their role for some time, thus have influence beyond what may normally be expected in their position. The key, though, is that they have the ear of the CIO and CISO and are leaders who are trusted by them.

Note

The best champions are often found within their immediate teams or among those dealing with daily operational issues.

Dr Maria Milosavljevic – former ANZ Bank CISO

You also want them to be naturally engaging with the CIO and CISO in their everyday work, in meetings, roadmap strategies, or budget planning. In the best cases, they can also develop into being an advocate for you, when they have a direct interest in the product or service you are selling, for their own career success.

This highlights how critical it is to pick the right champion for you. The following table lists some key attributes for a champion, to allow you to compare some different candidates. Note that there are personal, positional, and other attributes that make up a great champion. I've ordered the items in the following table in order of priority and decreasing criticality within each area:

Personal Attributes	Positional Attributes	Other Attributes
Credibility and positive track record	Organizational influence	Budget owner/influencer
Aligned motivation to drive this change	Access to CIO/CISO	Project Owner
Politically savvy	Decision maker	Governance Committee member
Strong communication skills	Tenure and stability	Stakeholder management

Table 3.7 - How to pick your champion

In my experience, personal and positional attributes are the most important criteria. Note that this table is a means to an end and just a way to help you identify the ideal internal champion to work with. The discussions required to find good synergies depend on how the vendor and champion engage.

This framework can help you get a short list of potential champions. However, there is more to this in terms of observing behaviors, and this is covered in *Chapter 4*.

Champions are not hired. They are found, cultivated, and earned through the quality of the relationship you are willing to invest in. The real determinant of a successful champion relationship is how the vendor and champion engage with each other, the quality of the conversations had and the degree to which each party genuinely serves the other's interests.

I should note that it is also important that the candidates for the role of the champion are not too junior – enthusiasm and technical know-how are important, but they may have limited opportunity to voice their views. Also, be very careful not to select a champion who just wants to pad their CV with experience with your product or service.

> **Note**
>
> During the interviews I conducted for this book, Yigal Elstein provided me with the most direct advice on selecting a champion, whom he calls a "change agent":
>
> *Look for alignment with executive vision*
>
> (He shared a success story where his team found a champion who wanted to fix specific security concerns that aligned perfectly with what the CISO wanted to achieve in the coming year)
>
> *Utilise them to build the agenda*
>
> (Yigal stressed that it is always better to have a champion take the vendor to the executive and help build the agenda for the meeting to ensure it focuses on the right priorities)
>
> *Target those who drive change*
>
> (Yigal's point here is that the best introduction is often through someone on the executive's own team who is empowered to drive change associated with your technology)
>
> **Yigal Elstein – Chief Revenue Officer, Checkmarx**

These attributes will help you identify a champion, but when you are new to an account and don't know anyone, then where do you start? This requires some detective work to seek out the candidates that have the attributes I've mentioned. Also see how they are engaged with their own network, perhaps with someone who is your champion at another enterprise? I will discuss champion identification further in *Chapter 4*.

You may want to use the jostle approach to initially engage your champion. From there, cultivating a champion will take more than a few lunches and coffees. They value having insider information about industry trends and recent incidents, and this can help them to build even more influence within their organizations. These champions must be nurtured over time; it is naïve to try to create an effective connection overnight with the strength of your offering.

With a champion on your side, you are then back to the warm introduction approach.

Combining the jostle and champion approaches

The jostle approach, combined with using a champion (for a warm introduction and beyond), is the ideal approach to establishing a connection with a CIO or CISO. You want to use both tools to succeed.

My advice is to think of your strategy as two forces working in concert: a jostle - an external force pulling you into the CIO and CISO's world through reputation and peer endorsement, and an internal (champion) force driving conviction from within through a champion who genuinely believes in the outcome. While your champion creates internal pull, you should expect that this internal force will also meet some resistance, this will probably be lower however than if you were approaching the CIO or CISO cold, as the champion will have a level of credibility. The following is an illustration of these two forces and illustrates how the dynamics can play out:

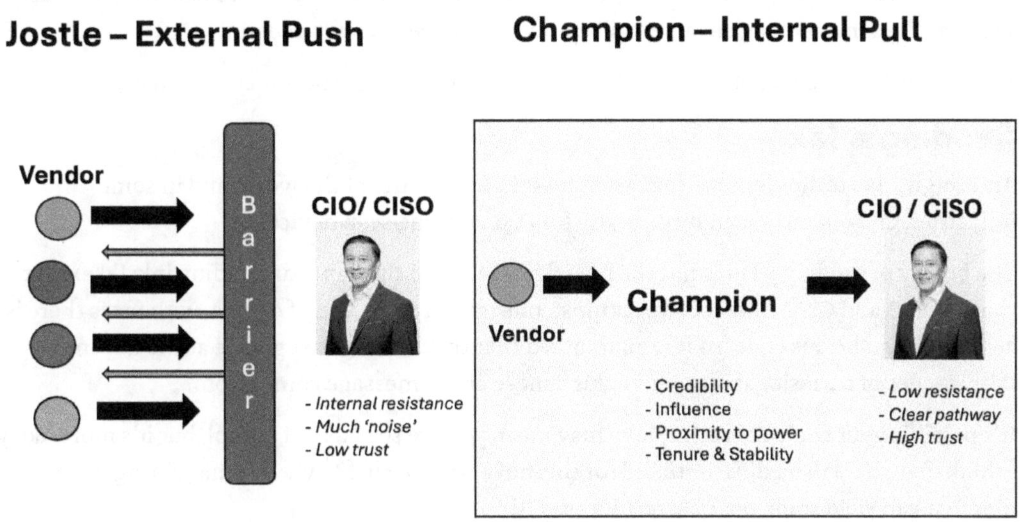

Figure 3.3 - The jostle versus champion approach

Combining both a "jostle" and champion approach is a potential winning strategy that helps you stand out among the noise. Moreover, this is one that can feel acceptable to the CIO and CISO.

Daring to be different

Making initial contact with CIOs and CISOs is often the most dreaded part of the sales process. This is also dreaded by CIOs and CISOs, as many are not that naturally interested in meeting new people, particularly vendors.

How can you change this equation? You can dare to be different. Let me share a few examples.

Sending a letter

Yes, you heard me correctly: send a printed (A4 or letter page) letter with a real signature. I can nearly guarantee due to curiosity that the Executive Assistant (EA) will open this and will likely put it on the CIO/CISO's desk, as this rarely ever occurs nowadays.

> **Tip**
>
> I've seen this approach enhanced by including a small chocolate with the letter—a little KitKat (have a break!) will bring a smile to any hardened CIO and CISO's EA.

When I commenced my CI-ISAC Australia Ambassador pro-bono role, I wrote personal (paper) letters to tier-1 bank and insurance CIOs and CISOs in Australia and followed these up with emails to check if they got a chance to review my letter. Nearly all letters reached their desks, whereas the same message in an email would likely have been filtered out.

Restrict the letter to just one page. A letter with too many pages becomes junk mail.

Sending a fax

Amazingly, this technology still exists, at least in some parts of the world and in some industries, and operates usually as multi-functional print/scan devices.

The beauty of sending a fax is not the nostalgic feeling of the paper and fading ink; I'd expect that the CIO and CISO only receive, at most, one fax per year. And of course, with faxes there is zero fear of malicious code, so it is guaranteed that they will at least glance at the document with a sense of curiosity about where this time-warped message comes from.

It's possible your choice of technology may mean you are seen as old school, but it's more likely I think that you will be differentiated for this novel approach. My view is that daring to be different can yield some positive results – try it!

Participating in peer forums or professional body events

While the C-Suite receive honestly too many invitations to industry events, peer forums and industry body involvement are attractive to the CIO and CISO for the purpose of networking with their peers, and when feasible, to simply relax; they also may want to get a respected colleague's opinion on a new product. These sessions can be hard to fit into their schedules but are seen as desirable when feasible.

These industry events are usually vendor free in terms of sponsorship; however, this does not mean that vendors are prohibited from being members and joining the events. Being involved in the industry in this way can be advantageous and, therefore, a worthy investment of your time. I've seen several partners in the ecosystem embed themselves into these events to the point that no one sees them as being there to sell. For instance, a cyber recruiter became ISACA Vice President and has seen numerous tech vendors also heavily engaged with the community.

> Note
>
> *For vendors to build long-term credibility, they should participate in peer forums, such as councils and industry events, to position themselves as strategic partners.*
>
> **Linus Lai – Group Vice President, IDC**

Final thoughts on contacting C-suite

The same purchasing authority that makes CIOs and CISOs strategically important also makes them the most spammed audience in enterprise sales and the cumulative effect of that attention is a default of scepticism.

There is a common saying that CIOs and CISOs often repeat: *I don't buy products from my inbox, but I buy products from my network's recommendations.*

Be brave and take my word for it, as someone who has been both the party reaching out and the party receiving excessive requests and messages from vendors, that being introduced by a peer or trusted colleague remains the best approach to contacting C-suite.

What most vendors fail to appreciate is the capacity for CIOs and CISOs to remember which vendors treated them with respect and which ones treated them as a target. And this memory travels with them across every organization they lead. Vendors who play the long game, who show up with integrity even when there is no immediate opportunity, and who treat every interaction as a deposit in a trust account that may not pay out for years, are those who become partners.

> Note
>
> For this book, as well as my previous book, I wanted to get candid insights and contributions from other CIOs and CISOs. When I did my own cold calling for this via LinkedIn, email, etc., this was hit or miss in terms of getting a response. Yes, these leaders assumed I was just spamming them, and in some cases my message was ignored.

However, when I contacted them via an introduction from another CIO or CISO (for this book), the success ratio improved from around 10% to 75-80%! Therefore, know that I have practiced what I am preaching!

Summary

In this chapter, I explored how the current model of bombarding CIOs and CISOs with messages and cold calls doesn't work well. CIOs and CISOs can receive 100–300 vendor outreaches per week, making unsolicited contact almost certain to fail. The dreaded cold call works roughly 5% of the time, while warm peer introductions achieve 10–20% success rates, climbing to 75–80% when the CIO or CISO has a strong relationship with the introducer.

A winning strategy combines these elements: a deliberate "jostle" (engineering serendipitous encounters at events or via LinkedIn) and cultivating an internal champion who creates pull from inside the organization (and provides a warm introduction).

The key learnings from this chapter are:

- **Warm introductions are the gold standard** – but treat them as tokens. Every bad introduction erodes your introducer's trust capital and their future willingness to refer again.
- **Continuous spamming causes lasting brand damage** – aggressive outreach doesn't just fail, it can get you blacklisted. Remember CIOs and CISOs share their frustrations with peers.
- **The "jostle" is a skill** – the goal is targeting the C-Suite, leaving them walking away thinking it was a useful chance encounter, not a sales ambush.
- **LinkedIn is overused and underperforming** – comment on CIO and CISO posts with genuine insight rather than sending connection requests. Flattery is often ignored, while a contrarian perspective may earn engagement.
- **Champions create internal pull** – prioritize credibility over access to the CIO/CISO. A champion with the CIO or CISO's ear but a weak reputation inside the organization is a liability.
- **Dare to be different** – a physical letter or fax cuts through digital noise almost every time.

4

Why Identifying (or Becoming) the Internal Champion is a Career Accelerant

One of the career lessons that I learned in my very first enterprise-wide transformation at Pioneer International is that, in most cases, large-scale technology change is driven by a number of inspired internal champions. These leaders have the courage and fortitude to take great personal career risks to drive the organization forward. The CIO and CISO simply most likely do not have the bandwidth to commit to this task personally, while they may want to. Rather, they are looking for leaders who are willing to step up and drive this on their behalf. (This may sometimes be a formal invitation, but usually, from my own experience, this is self-initiated by those with the "champion DNA," or by those striving to be champions themselves).

Internal champions are vital to both your success and the success of the enterprise. Champions help you prepare to speak with the CIO and CISO, giving you invaluable additional context. They also have a relationship with the CIO and CISO already—the internal champion is generally a leader that is trusted by the executive. The role they play to drive change is fundamentally impacted by the degree of trust that they have at the start of their engagement.

When it comes to their enterprise, there is a high risk that the enterprise stagnates and cannot be truly innovative or address new cyber threats that are being detected without the work of internal champions. I know from my own experience in these roles that having many change agents creates momentum that overcomes the friction that many enterprises inherently face.

I was just 33 years old when I had my first chance to be an internal champion. The CIO had just departed from the role, and I stepped into the leadership role to drive my first transformation.

My personal learnings from this period were instrumental for my own career in the opportunities for personal growth that this allowed.

In this chapter I explain "champion DNA," and how to identify an internal champion to help you make a successful sale. For those who may be interested themselves in taking on a champion role, I will cover the career-accelerating benefits of doing this but also provide some words of warning. I'd like to dedicate this chapter to all aspiring internal champions who want to drive change.

The key topics this chapter will cover are:

- The importance of internal champions
- Understanding champion DNA
- How to find internal champions
- Becoming an internal champion yourself

> Note
>
> *CISOs, like most managers, trust their employees before they trust a salesperson they've never met. That's all you need to know.*
>
> **David Spark – Producer, Managing Editor, Co-Host at the CISO Series**

The importance of internal champions

I have learned from my CIO and CISO experience, as well as my consulting advisory experience, that it is impossible to sell to the CIO and/or CISO without having a "champion" that will go to bat for you. They are often more accessible than the CIO or CISO, and most importantly, by building trust with the internal champion, you can inherit some of the goodwill they have built up with these roles.

The champion also helps the vendor to understand the strategic context of how a proposal for their solution will fit in with the overall plan and where the resistance to this proposal will likely come from.

> Note
>
> *In an average week, I would spend less hours on looking at innovation than I want, and that would be in smaller slices of time, not one block. Who do I trust to help me do that? It's an internal champion person that I know. That's who is going to help me.*
>
> **Scott Collary – Group CIO, Westpac Group**

As Scott notes, the C-suite doesn't always have the spare time to devote to looking at new technology to enable their strategy. Hence, these internal champions are also vital to the success of the CIO and CISO. Their career development and security are predicated on being able to deliver great results and without the champion, agitating for change only comes from the CIO and CISO, which is not ideal for many reasons. Most of all, the C-suite understand the strategy in terms of "what" is required, but they are not always the right leader to decide "how" this change should be delivered.

The champion comes in many shapes and forms, but they are often architects. Architects are well positioned to take on this role as they have responsibility for plotting strategic roadmaps and have a great understanding of the current gaps that need to be addressed. Plus, they tend to be trusted by the CIO and CISO, so they are ideal candidates to drive change.

> Note
>
> *In today's AI-driven world, architects bridge strategy and execution. They empower CIOs and CISOs to embrace bold change while ensuring every innovation strengthens resilience and security posture.*
>
> **Sunil Moolchandani – Chief Strategy Officer, Cohesity**

> Note
>
> *I am motivated by ideas that are strategically aligned, measurable in value, and strengthen the organization's security posture and operational maturity, particularly those that help the organization stay ahead of emerging and evolving threats.*
>
> *I believe organizations benefit most when CISOs foster business-aligned architectural foresight, informed by industry trends and vendor-agnostic discussions that enable balanced, outcome-driven security decisions. At the same time, I am cautious of ideas driven by market hype that add complexity without addressing a genuine business or security problem.*
>
> **Yaso Addanki – Head of Security Architecture, AGL**

This does not mean however that those in other roles cannot be champions. The most important attribute is that they have a willingness to champion new approaches.

I recall a project in my time as CIO at a bank where we wanted to develop an API layer for digital innovation. In this case, I was encouraging an architect to be the champion and take on a role in driving the API proof of concept; however, he was reluctant to be hands on and commit to the aggressive timescale needed to work with some vendors to pilot this idea. As the CIO I wanted an internal champion to help me drive the change, which the architect did after my encouragement and coaching. Ideally, of course the CIO and CISO want these champions to self-identify and volunteer to step up. Being personally inspired is much more of a driver than having a task that they are obliged to undertake.

> Note
>
> *Most CISOs these days like to empower their teams and direct reports to be part of influencing the direction on vendor selection. Most vendors just want to skip the team and go straight to the CISO or CIO. This is such an old-school "1-up" sales methodology that doesn't really work anymore. If someone sells to me, I then must sell it to my team. I'd rather the team sell it to me, then we're all aligned, and we waste less time.*
>
> **Nigel Hedges – Executive General Manager & CISO, Chemist Warehouse**

Champions ideally assist both sides in a sale – they partner with vendors, and they help to drive change internally with the encouragement and support of the CIO and CISO. In dealing with individual champions, you may have to adapt your approach to how committed the champion is acting.

> Note
>
> *Identifying internal champions at enterprise client sites is essential for driving meaningful progress and ensuring successful outcomes. These champions are individuals who not only possess deep knowledge of their organization's operations but also exhibit a genuine commitment to innovation and collaboration. Over the years, I've found that the most effective way to pinpoint these key players is by observing those who consistently step up during critical moments, whether it's leading a project, advocating for change, innovating or offering thoughtful solutions to complex challenges.*
>
> **Martin Dube – Head of Enterprise Application Solutions, Data & AI, NTT Data**

Essentially, the internal champion bridges the gap between the CIO and CISO and external vendors. Their advocacy and the delegated trust that they have been given from the C-suite provide the intel and context of the roadmap that you require. The following diagram provides an overview of this dynamic:

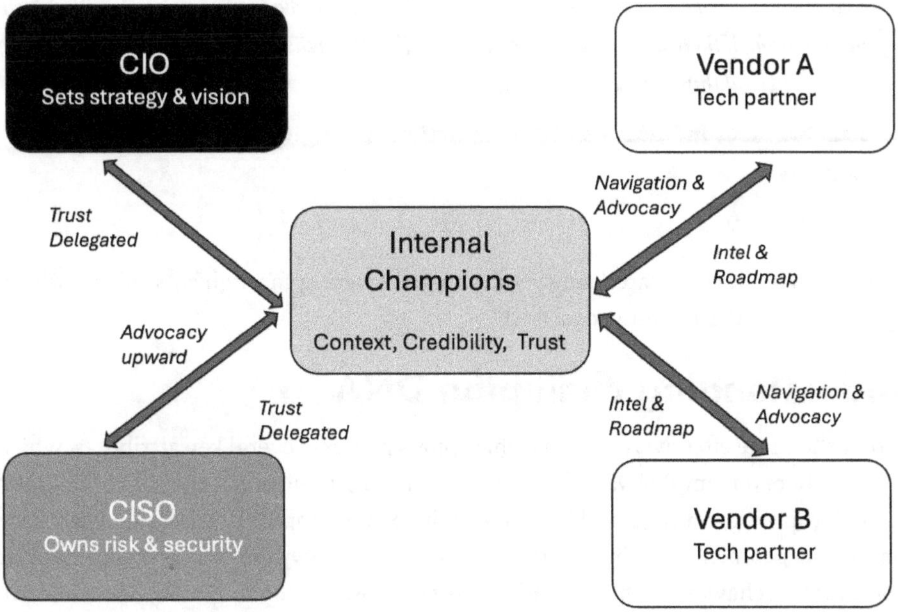

Champion inherits executive trust – vendors gain credibility that they could not reach by direct outreach

Figure 4.1 - How internal champion drives change

The internal champion's advocacy and the delegated trust that they have been given from the C-suite provide the intel and context of the roadmap and the personal advocacy that vendors require.

> **Note**
>
> *We need the CEO and the board to get much better at creating cultures of curiosity within the business, not even cultures of innovation, not even cultures of not being scared, that sort of thing. We need to enable our people and encourage our people to be curious. And as a result, you can then sort of create that internal champion around a particular point.*
>
> **Matt Boon – Senior Director, Strategic Research, Adapt**

> **Note**
>
> *Internal teams get more time, more context, and more direct coaching. They are living inside the same constraints I am. If the idea is not yet ready, I can say that plainly and help them make it stronger.*

> *External vendors get less time, more structured feedback, and a faster answer. I will not string a vendor along if there is no real path. A clean "no," with a reason where possible, is one of the more respectful things a buyer can give.*
>
> **Ram Kalyanasundaram – Chief Information and Digital Officer, Harris Farm Markets**

Note that in reality there are many vendors all advocating through champions, which creates "noise" that the C-suite must deal with.

Understanding champion DNA

To play their role effectively, internal champions possess several key attributes, which I refer to as "DNA" here for simplicity. It all starts with a strong mindset, at the core of this DNA—this is strategic thinking, courage, and learning agility. Skills support this mission with strong commercial acumen, combined with being politically savvy and a strong communicator. Then there are the behaviors of the champion; they take ownership and influence others through clear and effective business language. All these components make up the "champion" DNA. These include a specific mindset, skills, and behaviors:

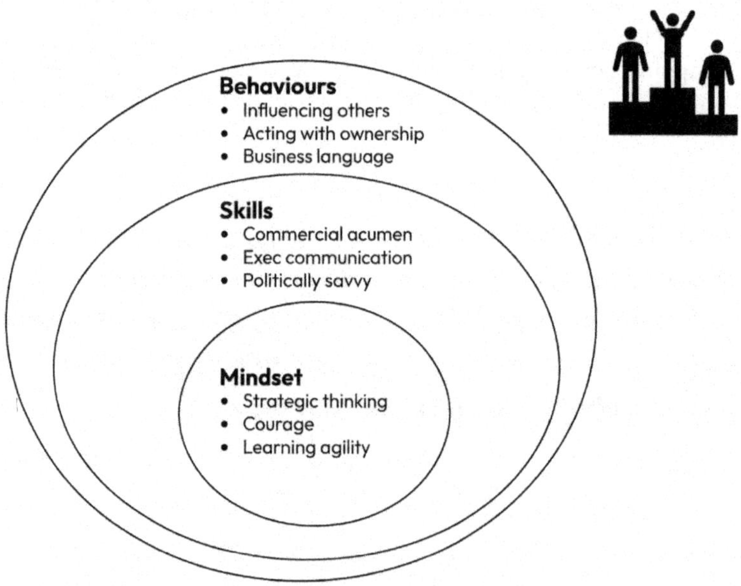

Figure 4.2 - Champion DNA

As you know, the term "champion" is not an official job title, and you cannot easily find them on an organization chart. They are in plain sight however, and you just need to follow these clues.

Just as human DNA is invisible to the naked eye and requires a scientific test, champion DNA operates beneath the surface of an organization, woven into how someone thinks, decides, and shows up under pressure. You can't always see this from their profile or CV.

> Note
>
> *Championing ideas has helped build my credibility when they succeeded. I also weigh timing carefully, because pushing new ideas while the organization is focused on audit findings or addressing red team results can create friction and slow my progress.*
>
> **Simon Blanchet – Security Architect and former HSBC Serai CISO**

In observing how these leaders show up you will begin to see some patterns of their attributes. The five attributes that I most commonly associate with and have used to identify these leaders are the following:

- **Acting with ownership:** The champion is often a leader that takes ownership of change. They are passionate about driving outcomes and will step forward to assume leadership.
- **Influencing others, without authority:** These leaders work to build coalitions across teams to influence without authority; they look for alignment of objectives with the synergy of different, disparate divisions.
- **Speaking business language:** They will be able to speak in business language about business growth and risks that are meaningful to the CIO and CISO.
- **Learning agility:** Champions are lifelong learners who reflect on their actions and are passionate about investigating any "dark corners" for missed opportunities.
- **Politically savvy:** They help guide vendors through politics and help both the enterprise and its partners to navigate these barriers. In taking on this role, they have "skin in the game," and this comes with some career risk to themselves.

Note

If you haven't been able to establish a relationship yet, remember there's 1st degree and 2nd degree separation. There are always champions around the CISO you can reach out to.

Gary Hayslip – CISO, Halcyon.ai, Board Director, and Investor

I've taken these five attributes and mapped them to the champion DNA to provide a synthesized picture:

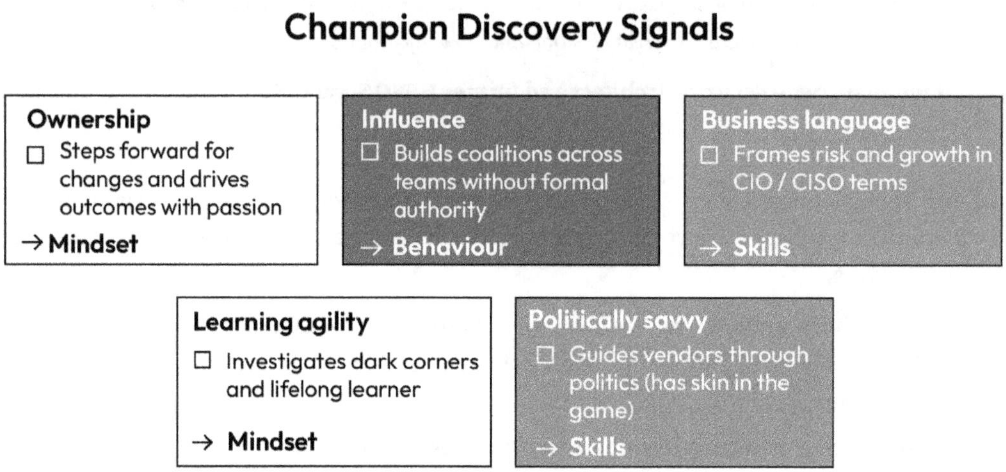

Figure 4.3 - Champion attributes and DNA

This can be used as a pattern framework to consider any potential champions. I'd argue that three of five of these attributes are going to be a basic foundation for your choice.

Using my baseball analogy, you are seeking raw talent to help you win the game. Each of these attributes is a signal to watch out for and ensure that you make good choices of where to invest your time to develop these champions.

While the champion is not the captain of the team, they are an individual that other team members will follow, not because of hierarchical authority, but due to their credibility. It is the champion that helps you win the game!

Note

An internal team member is much more likely to understand our environment, our strategy, our limitations, and our budget. They do not need to go through discovery because they already have that IP.

> *An external vendor (especially if they are new) is going to ask a whole bunch of questions to learn our environment, which does take up a lot of time. Time that we have less of, given resourcing constraints and never-ending additional risks to remediate.*
>
> *That is where a smart vendor will work with an internal team member, and the internal team member is more likely to bring things to attention that meet the brief or the focus of the current cyber program or needs.*
>
> **Nigel Hedges – Executive General Manager & CISO, Chemist Warehouse**

Champion DNA and their attributes explored, let's now consider more ways you can identify and nurture champions to be in your corner. These champions are busy leaders who have full-time day jobs, so they may be reluctant to commit to more; however, engaging with champions can be mutually beneficial (I explain this from the champion's side later in the chapter).

How to find internal champions

Champions are not always leaders who speak at conferences and are very visible with their views and opinions; however, the best champions have high internal visibility and influence. In this section I will share some further signals that I've used to identify internal champions.

> Note
>
> *I think vendors need to create cultures of humility...that drive a much greater level of empathy toward the customer as well. You must understand what the customer's going through.*
>
> **Matt Boon – Senior Director Strategic Research, Adapt**

The first and most obvious clue is, of course, leaders who are ***acting*** like champions. They are the ones who, when you meet them, ask strategic questions that challenge the current status quo. They are also tuned into the business priorities for growth and the risks to be mitigated. They appear proactive and perhaps a bit impatient for the next steps.

The second clue is an individual's **organizational position**. Champions are most likely in natural leadership roles that work across different silos; Digital Transformation Leaders, Enterprise Architects, and Heads of Technology (business-facing roles), for example.

> **Note**
>
> *I encourage and identify internal champions by focusing on the people closest to the business problem and who are most invested in the outcome.*
>
> *Rather than driving change from the top down alone, we work with prospects to build a network of cross-functional champions across Cyber, Data & AI and Infrastructure teams. These champions help drive adoption, accelerate decision making, and ensure that initiatives become sustainable organizational practices rather than one-time projects.*
>
> **Ryan Jones – Vice President, Cyera**

To build on the point on business language I made in the previous section, they use **distinct language** without too much tech jargon, which is understood by executives. They have the ability to frame their thoughts around what is keeping the C-suite awake, or what the board is worried about.

> **Note**
>
> *The strongest champions aren't just security advocates. They're business leaders who understand how transformation drives competitive advantage. They can clearly articulate why change matters in terms of reducing risk, lowering cost, and increasing productivity. We look for people with influence, not just the title, who can bridge technical depth with business context and move conversations forward across their peer group.*
>
> *These leaders are comfortable challenging the status quo. They're willing to say "no" or "yes, but" to refine the value proposition so it actually lands. When you find someone who can connect security decisions to business outcomes and communicate that effectively, they naturally become a catalyst for change.*
>
> **Bradon Rogers – Chief Customer Officer, Island**

Champions are very **career-oriented,** and you may see their contributions on industry forums, webinars, and LinkedIn posts. They are not shy to ask for career advice from mentors and will engage with their senior industry peers in a respectful manner.

> **Note**
>
> *When I'm working at large organizations, I would find at times the best person to learn about a department isn't the department leadership but an analyst or maybe an engineer who's been there for 20 years and has seen the stack change multiple times.*

> *They know some of the horror stories of previous technology integrations over the years and are the kind of people that you want to know because they usually have connections throughout all the other departments as well.*
>
> **Gary Hayslip – CISO, Halcyon.ai, Board Director, and Investor**

A final clue is that they are **connectors**. They seem to know everybody and are well trusted by colleagues and industry peers alike. They may, for example, serve on industry or organizational bodies, and their profile means that they keep getting invitations to further events.

> Note
>
> *Finding someone who falls in love with the problem, has a strong drive and a learning mindset, and isn't afraid to be wrong or make mistakes. A person with a growth mindset who listens first. Encouragement then comes through empowerment and communication.*
>
> **Jason Poley – Former Macquarie Group Global Head of Engineering**

I've summarized these key clues in the following figure:

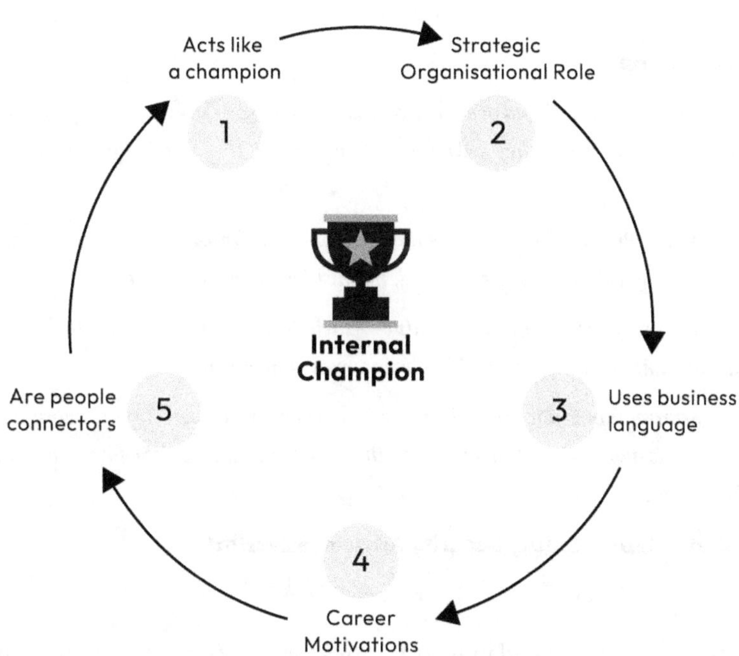

Figure 4.4 - How to find your champion

> **Tip**
>
> To help identify your champion ask your contacts at the enterprise who is the best person to talk with that has context of the strategy and the ear of the CIO and CISO.

Once you have identified a potential champion, you want to test their willingness to engage and see if there is synergy in terms of your offering and their personal interest in this topic.

> **Note**
>
> *Every successful security initiative is powered by an internal champion, someone who pushes the strategy into reality. These individuals are often more influential than formal leadership because they possess peer-level credibility.*
>
> *Interestingly, champions aren't always the most senior people. They are often the architects and engineers who live with the daily friction of existing gaps.*
>
> ***How to identify them:***
>
> *Look for "constructive skeptics," those who highlight risks before they become incidents, show a healthy frustration with current limitations, and influence their teams without formal authority.*
>
> ***How to enable them:***
>
> *Early authorship: Don't just "hand over" a tool. Bring them into the evaluation phase and let them shape the solution. When they feel a sense of authorship, they naturally become advocates.*
>
> *Equip the narrative: Provide them with the data to connect technical gaps to business risks. Help them explain why it matters to the board, not just how it works for the SOC.*
>
> *Engineer quick wins: Focus on immediate value— such as exposing a hidden attack path or cleaning up dormant accounts—to build their internal momentum.*
>
> *At its core, transformation is not driven by tools; it is driven by people who care enough to challenge the status quo. Recognition and visibility with leadership are the final "fuel" that sustains their impact.*
>
> **Abbas Kudrati – Chief Identity Security Advisor, Silverfort**

You can then start to share intel and industry stories that they can use to both help them make your case and look good to their boss and colleagues too. A great example is an insight I learned from a vendor that a recent ransomware attack was able to extract data within 25 minutes. This adds color and a sense of urgency that any CIO and CISO will notice. If they then start to respond to this approach, you are at the early stages of building your internal champion.

> Note
>
> *CIOs often need to build a coalition of the willing, especially for large investments which by their nature underpin the transformation agendas required to enter new markets or bring innovative new products and services to market.*
>
> *Building coalitions of the willing is more about enabling their success as opposed to motivating them to participate in the drive for change. Linking the agenda to the vision and purpose of the organization is an easy thing to do. Building enabling support is where the challenge lies. I encourage internal champions by giving them three things: clarity, ownership, and visible support.*
>
> *First, I make the purpose meaningful - linking the change directly to patient outcomes, safety, and staff experience, so they understand why it matters. Second, I give them real ownership - not just advocacy, but a role in shaping and improving the solution. That sense of agency is what turns supporters into champions. Third, I back them visibly - recognizing their effort, being honest about the challenges ahead, and reinforcing that change is ongoing, not a one-off event.*
>
> *When champions feel trusted, heard, and supported by leadership, they naturally bring others with them. Not because we ask them to—they do it because they believe in it and feel empowered to deliver it.*
>
> **John Sutherland – Chief Digital Information Officer, Calvary Health Care**

I've seen vendors take this further by sharing more information, including new unreleased product roadmaps for input.

Because champions often carry real career risk in advocating for change, they are putting their credibility on the line every time they step forward. Your role as a vendor or partner is to protect that investment by delivering on your promises and making them look good in front of their peers and leadership.

> Note
>
> *A key strategy for cultivating internal champions is to create opportunities for them to immerse themselves in the customer journey. This involves listening carefully to their insights, encouraging them to learn proactively, and supporting their development as strategic thinkers. By prioritizing empathy and stepping into the customers' shoes, they not only enhance their*

> *problem-solving abilities but also reinforce their commitment to organizational success. Ultimately, the goal is to ensure these champions remain focused, never lose sight of their objectives, and always strive to deliver value for their customers and their organization. Through this intentional process, we build a network of trusted advocates who can drive sustained positive impact across enterprise client sites.*
>
> **Martin Dube – Head of Enterprise Applications Solutions, Data & AI, NTT Data**

Once you have established a relationship with a champion the internal champion may find it insightful and useful to participate in advisory boards for your organization.

The advantages of advisory boards

For the champion, the advisory board is a source of competitive intelligence as to how peers and other industries are using your product. The benefit to you as a vendor is that inviting champions to participate in advisory boards can help to create some long-term advocacy and perhaps a little stickiness in terms of loyalty. Note that their presence at the advisory board is not for the purpose of selling to them, including product demos or talking commercials in the open meeting.

I should highlight that joining an advisory board is not likely to occur early in the relationship however, as this is usually reserved for existing customers.

> **Tip**
>
> I'd encourage internal champions to consider taking on this additional task. This will be rewarding in terms of broadening their personal network, and they can gain some advanced insights into how other companies are thinking. These associations can also provide unofficial sources of benchmarking across sectors.

In my career, I've served numerous technology and cyber advisory boards. As these are often non-paying, approval from the champion's manager and company is usually not an issue. The advisory boards that I have served on have been a great source of learning and have aided my ability to influence future product direction. There is a real sense of contribution in providing insights to a tech or cyber vendor that wants to gauge your perspectives on a new product feature or release.

Note that each advisory board is a little different in structure and format, but the intention is to gather a curated group of senior non-competing customers. The meeting sessions each quarter share product strategy and provide an opportunity to validate market directions.

> **Note**
>
> *The best interaction I've had with a vendor was with one who invited me to their APAC Customer Advisory Council. I will never forget that experience, as we had direct interaction with global product management and product platform owners. The council was held with other Asia Pacific customers, and we got to compare notes—what has worked, what has not, and align on similar challenges.*
>
> *We flew to an international location for 2 days and 2 nights. It was an opportunity to express pressures and limitations on both sides of the vendor/customer fence. They also combined interaction with a local charity, which made it personally meaningful and touching. It was rewarding to see us all as people, and the chance to influence the product roadmap. I thoroughly enjoyed that experience and will never forget it—or that vendor.*
>
> **Nigel Hedges – Executive General Manager & CISO, Chemist Warehouse**

Advisory boards I've attended are often in-person events and there is real value that the internal champion, (as well as CIO and CISO) gain from networking with other peers and colleagues from other industries. In my Eli Lilly USA CIO role, I was on Oracle CRM, Nokia, and HP advisory boards. Since then, I have served on many other advisory committees. My favorite advisory board ever was 3 days at MIT, where we were exposed to the innovation lab from the campus staff and students; the last day was HP-specific content on their product roadmap.

I'd argue that there is real value in having your chosen champion join these sessions with their peers, although this may mean that you don't invite the CIO or CISO to their equivalent session, as normally companies will not double up on participation.

The following table summarizes the mutual benefits for both the champion and the vendor with a well-designed advisory board program:

Category	Benefits to champion	Benefit to the vendor
Product strategy	Identify emerging customer needs Testing for blind spots Aligns roadmap to priorities	Identify and validate emerging customer needs Testing for blind spots Aligns roadmap to the CIO and CISO priorities

Category	**Benefits to champion**	**Benefit to the vendor**
Credibility	"Halo" effect of respected peers in the room	Brand trust is visible
Innovation	Opportunity to be a first mover Provides new insights to take back to the office	Gain and test new ideas
Go to market	Feedback on new pricing models	Focus group to test marketing messages on
Competitor insights	Opportunity to give feedback on what your competitors are doing differently	Opportunity to receive feedback on what your competitors are doing differently

Table 4.1 - Advisory board benefits to the champion, CIO and CISO, and to you as the vendor

In short, participation at the advisory board can benefit both sides and is a great mechanism to develop deeper relationships.

> Note
>
> Not every relationship becomes a partnership. For that reason, the CIO and CISO may want to keep a close eye on the vendor, and that might be their rationale for advisory board involvement. The "devil you know" is a saying that rings true when it comes to tech C-suite and vendors, from my experience in these roles.
>
> There can be a love-hate relationship between these parties at times, and there can be inertia to shift products unless there is a real trigger that makes the incumbent untenable.

For the champion, participating in an advisory board will provide strong industry recognition and have a positive impact on their own standing and reputation. This can accelerate their career both externally and within their own company. You can see from LinkedIn that leaders will often add their participation in these boards to their profiles.

I want to take the opportunity now to encourage more leaders to take the "golden" development opportunity of being an internal champion (for those of you in a position to do so). The personal growth that you will experience in this role, in being strategic, and thinking like a member of the C-suite, then learning how hard it is to drive change, is the best way to move your career forward in my opinion. As I love to say, you will grow by being uncomfortable, so take the plunge!

Becoming an internal champion yourself

Internal champions are vital to any enterprise. As a CIO and CISO, I was always looking to see which of my leadership team was going to have the courage and fortitude to accept this role. In this section I will explain the positive and negative sides that can come from taking on an internal champion role and look at what you do to get there.

I'll begin by highlighting some positive and negative factors, from a 10,000-foot view:

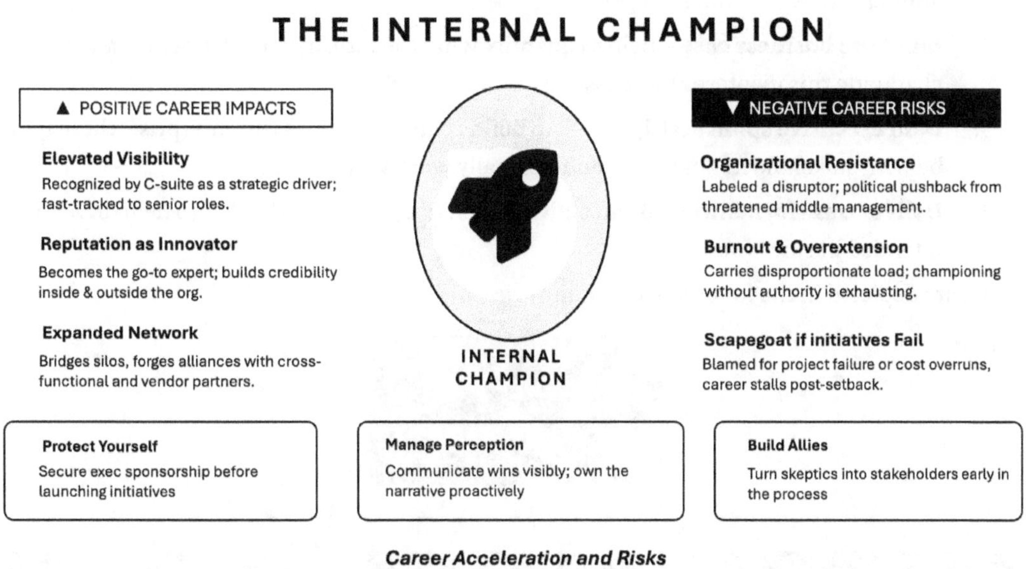

Figure 4.5 - Champion career impacts

As you can see, being an internal champion can both help and hurt your career. It is important to be under no illusion that there aren't downsides to taking on this challenge—I discuss this further later in this section.

It can be uncomfortable and is not an easy role to play, but from my own experience being a transformation leader, this is the most fun that you can have in the enterprise! I would repeat these experiences if given the opportunity.

Note

Ideas for improvement can come from many different areas of the organization. It is particularly important for leaders to spend time with front-line, customer-facing teams to understand the constraints that are inadvertently created by systems and processes.

Dan Chesterman – CIO, Teachers Mutual Bank

Being a champion, I have learned, is one of the fastest accelerators of an IT career, if you do it strategically. This can shift one's career curve much faster and much higher than is normally the case. I call this the "champion career accelerator".

But how do you become a successful internal champion? Here are some steps:

1. **Identify the strategic gap** – be the leader that spots the missed opportunity or the approach that can address a gap
2. **Build the business case** – help to quantify what the return on investment is and help champion this in internal discussions
3. **Gain executive sponsorship** – seek to build coalitions across the enterprise; these may be with stakeholders that you don't normally work with
4. **Deliver transformation** – Be an active leader, not just a cheerleader, to help drive the intended business outcomes

These are depicted in the following diagram:

Figure 4.6 - The Champion Career Accelerator

Note that while I've presented these steps in a logical sequence, it is not always possible or necessary for champions to achieve all these individually. Some may want to be seen as a leader of the first three, but perhaps not the actual "delivery," particularly when this is too far out of their comfort zone.

> **Note**
>
> *The key career question is: How can a CIO or CISO encourage me as an architect to champion change?*
>
> *A CIO or CISO encourages me to champion change by aligning on a shared long-term technical vision and showing they genuinely value my perspective. I respond best when they create psychological safety, provide visible support, and allocate resources for solid proposals.*
>
> **Simon Blanchet – Security Architect and former HSBC Serai CISO**

I personally chose to focus on transformation as a champion myself, as I felt passionate that this was going to be a challenging and great learning experience for me. I was also aware that this would be a great career acceleration factor, both if I stayed in the enterprise or if I decided to move on after the transformation was completed.

> **Note**
>
> *My "no" is rarely about the quality of the idea. It is usually about the queue.*
>
> *The technology roadmap is a queue, not a menu. Adding one initiative means delaying, changing or stopping another. That other initiative usually has its own sponsor, its own benefits, and its own risks. So, when someone asks me to champion their priority, they are also asking me to make a trade-off somewhere else.*
>
> *If I sponsor an initiative, I must be able to defend it when it is challenged and when it goes wrong. That means I need more than a slide and enthusiasm. I need to understand the assumptions, the evidence, the delivery capacity required, the risks, the failure modes, and what we are prepared to stop doing to make room for it.*
>
> *The quickest way to get my support is to show me that you have thought about the trade-off, not just the upside.*
>
> **Ram Kalyanasundaram – Chief Information and Digital Officer, Harris Farm Markets**

I've used being a champion to accelerate my own career and witnessed it with other peers. There is a caveat, however. I used the word "strategically" earlier as it is also true that change agents can attract negative press, as they are seen to be "rocking the boat." Allow me to provide some context for this; I'll then provide guidance to help avoid these pitfalls.

Some words of warning

While I am encouraging you to take on the mantle of being the champion to drive change, I want you to be fully aware of the downsides, which are less obvious than the potential for glory.

Before you commit to the champion role, you need to understand its full cost. You may see it as taking on an extra responsibility without having any specific accountability, but usually this is not broadcast, so some parties may be suspicious of your motives. When you are acting like a champion, there will be colleagues who will be pondering why you are taking the position.

There is a dark side to being a champion, and your efforts can backfire on you in terms of your career. I realized this as a champion myself when I could sense and feel that some peers and colleagues started to treat me differently. Your friendly suggestions may not be greeted with immediate warmth. There's the potential for your decisions to have a significant personal impact.

While there are many potential positive benefits of being a champion, I will outline several of the downsides that I have personally seen and witnessed:

Downsides	**Explanation**
Scapegoat 	Should the idea you have proposed or are supporting not succeed, then you are the obvious scapegoat that may be blamed for this failure. This is because champions are highly visible in their support.
Politics 	Any significant change moves the power dynamics and creates winners and losers. The champion is therefore seen as being ambitious and could be perceived as driving change for selfish, personal reasons.
Typecast 	There is a danger that you become seen as a "specialist" to fix all relevant problems, rather than, as you may wish, the leader to manage this once it is delivered and completed.

Downsides	Explanation
Workload 	Being a champion is an all-volunteer effort that is likely not formally recognized in your substantive role. Juggling these extra plates can lead to personal burnout and impact your other performance.
Brand 	When you are a champion and have decided on a path forward, then there may be a perception that you are biased toward the particular vendor you are supporting. This has the potential to negatively hurt your own brand.
Exec tokens 	The goodwill that you have built up with your CIO, CISO, etc., is not unlimited, and there is a risk that you will use up all the trust tokens you have with them.

Table 4.2 - Dark side of being a Champion

What can you do proactively to help protect your career? I've learned that there are a few approaches that can help you to be successful and at the same time not alienate other peers and colleagues in the workplace.

Risk mitigation strategies for the champion

Let's start with some advice from CISOs. I asked a question that internal champions rarely think to ask: *What do you wish your internal stakeholders understood about your role when they are seeking your approval?* Their answers will help you prepare to engage with these C-suite roles, and in doing so, help you avoid risks to your reputation.

> Note
>
> *They need to not just assume that because they are internal, I will naturally champion their initiatives. Often, they do not put in the required level of effort and diligence I would expect from an external vendor.*
>
> **Paul O'Rourke – former CISO, CRO and BCG Global Cyber Leader**

> Note
>
> *Approval does not transfer ownership. The role is to ensure alignment with strategy, risk posture, and enterprise architecture—not to carry the operational accountability for every tool or initiative. When stakeholders clearly articulate business value, risk reduction, measurable outcomes, and long-term sustainability, the conversation becomes collaborative rather than transactional.*
>
> **Sunil Varkey – CISO, Hexaware Technologies (Former HSBC CISO)**

While there is no such thing as full risk mitigation for the champion as you are supporting a new idea that may or may not work, I'll suggest some mitigations to help you navigate the personal risk.

Being generous and humble is the first principle that I've learned. A true transformation is indeed a team effort, and while there is pressure, it does not spread evenly to the top. Be sure to praise others for their roles and talk about the achievements of the "team" rather than what you personally did.

It is also wise to ensure that you document all key decisions in your own log, for the record. In the heat of the battle, when decisions are being made with much tension, it is easy to forget that a critical decision may be made with incorrect assumptions.

Your direct leader is likely your sponsor but be sure to develop other executive support structures by using this transformation opportunity to work closely with several other C-suite leaders that you would not normally get the chance to. One caveat of course is that executive churn can mean that your sponsor may depart prior to any change program that they were supporting.

Finally, while you build relationships and trust with vendors, always maintain your boundaries and sense of objectivity. Maintaining vendor distance while a transformation is in progress will encourage healthy challenge and debate and help avoid the risk of blame if it doesn't go to plan.

> Note
>
> *Internal teams have a contextual advantage—they understand our architecture, politics, constraints, and risk appetite. When they bring forward a proposal, it often comes with pre-validation and stakeholder alignment, which accelerates evaluation.*
>
> *However, internal advocacy can also create bias. Decisions still need objective evaluation against strategy, standards, and measurable outcomes. Familiarity should not replace due diligence.*
>
> **Sunil Varkey – CISO, Hexaware Technologies (Former HSBC CISO)**

> Note
>
> *The mistake internal champions make is forgetting that they are also selling. A good idea still needs a business case, an owner, a trade-off, and a path through delivery. The mistake external vendors make is forgetting that they are a guest in someone else's operating system. They need to understand the rhythm, constraints, and politics before they ask for commitment.*
>
> *Internally, I am willing to help shape the idea. Externally, I expect the idea to arrive already shaped for my context.*
>
> **Ram Kalyanasundaram – Chief Information and Digital Officer, Harris Farm Markets**

It's clear that there is a degree of self-sacrifice in taking the path of the internal champion. You may be asking yourself at this point whether taking this path is truly worth the risks it presents. Well, let me finish by adding a few of the factors that I considered to be important, from my own experience in this position.

Career acceleration

While I realized that becoming an internal champion would be very good for my CV and my future career, I wanted to really take on this challenge to help radically shape the technology direction of the organization I worked for at the time. The idea of operating in a greenfield manner with no constraints and no legacy to cater to was incredibly motivating to me.

I had seen earlier that different leaders did not try to impact the status quo, and I found that incredibly frustrating. Personally, I really wanted to be seen as a leader who got amazing results (I admit that there was a little ego involved, as I wished to be perceived as a strategic leader).

> Note
>
> *The key career question is: How can a CIO or CISO encourage me as an architect to champion change? A CIO or CISO encourages me to champion change by aligning on a shared long-term technical vision and showing they genuinely value my perspective. I respond best when they create psychological safety, provide visible support, and allocate resources for solid proposals.*
>
> **Simon Blanchet – Security Architect and former HSBC Serai CISO**

> Note
>
> *From my perspective, I feel most encouraged to bring new ideas forward when there is clear psychological safety combined with visible executive sponsorship.*
>
> *In the best environments I have worked in, leaders did a few things consistently well. First, they created structured pathways for innovation such as regular forums, or innovation sprints. So, ideas did not rely on informal escalation. Second, they were accessible and engaged; even brief, constructive feedback from senior leaders helped refine ideas and made the effort feel worthwhile.*
>
> **Bharat Bajaj – Technology Risk Partner, banking sector**

While the step up into this transformational leadership role brought many benefits, it also made me realize how very lonely you can be in these positions, and there are many moments of truth that you face alone. Often, it felt unfair that I was taking on this extra work and risk while everyone else was carrying on as normal with their roles and life not being impacted.

What I gained from these experiences was life-changing and addictive, however. I found I just wanted to keep doing this at different enterprises. I realized being a champion accelerated my own skills, knowledge, experience, and behavior in five specific domains:

- Stakeholder management and executive communication
- Business case and financial justification
- Vendor strategy, procurement, and negotiation

- Organizational navigation and influence skills
- Program leadership and transformation governance

What I did not expect was that the champion role and the development of these skills would shape every CIO and CISO role I held afterward.

> Note
>
> One extra benefit I gained, without realizing it at the time, was that my exposure to the C-suite became a regular occurrence, as the executives all cared about the potential of the transformation I was driving. I got exposure to how they thought and began to understand how I should present to them.

I learned that being a champion of change becomes part of your own brand. The success of transformation outcomes will lead you to further career opportunities and your reputation being elevated with the "halo" effect of having delivered *XYZ* global transformation.

> Note
>
> *Driving significant change at scale is hard. It takes several skills, including strong communication, influencing, strategic thinking, and strong execution. Leading change gives someone the chance to showcase their skills in a way not possible during day-to-day operations. It is also a great chance for the individual to be seen by other leaders in the organization. Clearly, there is also risk if it does not go well—but even then, there will be great learnings for the individual. No one ever learned to ride a bike without falling off.*
>
> **Gerard Florian – former ANZ Bank Group Executive & CIO**

Many transformations fail and this is the very reason why successful delivery carries such positive outcomes, accelerating your career within, and beyond, your current organization. I found this, for me, also led to consistent invitations to keynote conferences to speak about my learnings.

Deciding whether you want to be an internal champion

This section has been designed to help you think through the role of internal champion. If you are still undecided, asking the following questions to your CIO and/or CISO, and to a relevant vendor, might help you make up your mind.

	Question	**Rationale**
1	Is this problem on your priority list for next year?	Confirm there's genuine urgency before you invest your time and your credibility
2	What does success look like to you personally, and how will you measure it?	Understand what metric or outcome they need to be able to show
3	Who needs to be in the room to say yes to this, and who can kill it?	Map the real decision-making structure
4	What would make you say "no," regardless of how good the solution is?	For example, budget cycle timing, a competing initiative, or a prior bad experience
5	How much air cover will you give me if this gets resistance?	If an executive won't back the initiative when it gets challenged, you are exposed

Table 4.3 - Questions to ask your CIO and CISO before becoming a champion

Now let's turn to questions you as champion can ask the vendor you're engaging with or considering engaging with. As you will be vouching for them, it is critical that you are 100% confident in their capabilities. These will help you decide if they are a partner that you want your own reputation to be tied to:

	Question	**Rationale**
1	As champion, what will you need from me internally, and when?	Know exactly what the vendor is going to ask you before you commit to anything
2	How will you help me build the internal business case?	A good vendor provides reference calls, executive presentations, benchmark data, etc.
3	What obstacles did your champions at other enterprises discover?	Lessons you can learn in advance, before getting in the middle of this
4	If this goes sideways, what's your escalation path?	Know how the vendor responds under pressure before it matters

	Question	Rationale
5	What does your post-sale support model look like?	Who is my everyday routine support contact?

Table 4.4 - Questions to ask your vendor before becoming a champion

Summary

In this chapter I explored the critical role that the internal champion plays in driving a new change agenda. They can be the most powerful accelerant in any enterprise technology sale—they understand the environment, politics, and priorities in ways no vendor ever can. They also carry credibility that no external pitch replicates.

For internal champions themselves, championing change, although it presents various risks, is one of the fastest career accelerators available—providing C-suite exposure, transformation credentials, and cross-functional influence that normal roles rarely offer.

The relationship between vendor and champion is symbiotic. The vendor provides intelligence, peer insights, and roadmap access while the champion provides internal navigation, trust transfer, and advocacy.

The key learnings from this chapter are:

- **Champions are self-selecting, not often appointed** – they build from their own DNA (mindset + skills + behaviors) of ownership, coalition-building, business language fluency, and willingness to take career risks.
- **Five signals can help you identify a champion** – they ask strategic questions that challenge the status quo, they are in a cross-silo organizational leadership position, they speak in business-fluent language, they are career-oriented, and they are connectors.
- **Feed the champion with usable intelligence** – short, specific vignettes (e.g. "ransomware exfiltration now takes 25 minutes") that the champion can repeat upward. This will help them look smart in front of their own leadership.
- **Consider having champions serve on your advisory boards** – this offers mutual benefits– for the champion, they provide peer networking, product roadmap influence, first-mover pilot access, and career brand elevation. For vendors, they provide market feedback, competitive intelligence, and the opportunity to deepen your relationship.
- **The career acceleration the champion role offers is real but comes with risk** – for example, failure can make the champion a visible scapegoat.

5

Your Preparation

When you are cooking toast, the preparation for a poor chef like me is pretty easy. Preparation is more important for complex dishes where there are many components that are required to be integrated, and when certain food is very sensitive with cooking time. Good prep makes execution easier and less stressful. This chapter is my own "cookbook" for the preparation that you need to sell to the CIO and CISO.

I've seen the result of bad preparation when I, as a CIO or CISO, got approached by vendors or even internal champions who had not done their basic homework. I could (and still can) see, when I'm approached by someone for a discussion, if they are prepared or not and when confronted with an unprepared pitch, I'm immediately going to feel that this person is wasting my time. I'd argue that it is impossible to overprepare when you are planning to engage with a CIO or CISO.

In this chapter I explore some approaches that you can take to be better prepared—how to scout out information that is not easily available to gain context, and also, more importantly, getting into the head of the CIO and CISO, considering where they are in their career and how this will influence their thinking.

We will cover the following topics:

- Your research and preparation
- Knowing CIO and CISO pain points
- How does your product/service fit into their hierarchy of needs?
- Practice your elevator pitch
- Having a clear agenda

Your research and preparation

Research and preparation are essential to selling to the CIO and CISO. Products and services are very complex, and you want them to add yours to an existing smorgasbord, and it must blend in with these existing offerings and not cause any problems.

> Note
>
> *90% of vendors don't know anything about your company, what you're trying to do, whether the products are even relevant. They are just shooting in the dark. Usually, they believe in their product, but that's only part of the story. And then 10% probably have done some research and know what you are working on at a conceptual level. It's not great when it feels like they really don't care if it helps or not.*
>
> **Scott Collary – Group CIO, Westpac Group**

Preparation starts with detailed research and positioning. You must first understand the tech stack they are working with, which you can usually partially find out, although there will be some confidential components. How do you do this?

> Note
>
> All your research activities should comply with relevant privacy legislation and professional codes of conduct; the information you gather must be used solely for legitimate sales preparation purposes.

There are many public sources you can explore, including job postings where specific tools and platforms are mentioned as being required for different roles. Job postings are one of the most underutilized and most revealing sources of organizational intelligence available. When a company advertises for a role that specifies particular tools and platforms as mandatory requirements, they are publicly declaring their technology direction.

For instance, a posting that mandates experience with a specific SIEM platform signals where security operations investment is being directed, while another new role that requires Snowflake or Databricks experience but does not mention any legacy data warehouse suggests a cloud data migration is already in progress.

Conference coverage and early adoption stories in the press can also yield useful insights, as can LinkedIn. GitHub searches for public repos connected to the organization can also be an insightful approach, as can engineering blogs and technology review platforms, which can contain a level of architectural and operational intelligence about a target organization. Tools like **BuiltWith** (`https://builtwith.com/`) which can profile a public web stack, and Gartner® Peer Insights reviews (`https://www.gartner.com/peer-insights/home`) can also help.

Information you may be able to find from these sources can include:

- Network diagrams
- Details of architecture
- Authentication controls
- Third-party integrations
- Development practices

Through LinkedIn, you can further search for keywords to provide you with a sketch of a company's tech stack. This can include information about

- API
- OAuth, SSO, SAML
- Encryption keys
- XDR, EDR, SIEM
- Backup strategy
- Vendor names (Crowdstrike, CyberArk, etc.)
- Product names (Jenkins, GitLab, etc.)

> **Tip**
>
> Note that this research mirrors the reconnaissance phase of a cyber-attack. CISOs you may talk to will be acutely aware of this and may view vendors who demonstrate knowledge of sensitive infrastructure and application details with suspicion. Use this intelligence to sharpen your questions when talking to a CIO/CISO, not to display what you know about the details of the business/tech stack.

As you develop your relationship with champions, you can further test your understanding of their environment, blending this into the discussion. Note that at the beginning of the relationship, though, the champion may not be willing to share much detail with you, as you may not yet have earned their trust.

While access to the organization chart is often confidential, and job titles and levels can also be misleading and hard to understand from the outside, your preparation should also involve understanding the enterprise's hierarchy and who reports directly to the CIO and CISO. While this information may not be perfect, it will help you build a picture of the enterprise, what they are focused on from a strategy standpoint and who the key players are.

"High influence" leaders are often the acknowledged second in charge to the CIO and CISO. These leaders I would call "key node" – they deputise for the CIO and CISO in their absences. Their roles are often at the intersection of a few areas of the department, rather than having a narrow focus. They may have long tenure with the company or even have followed the CIO/CISO to this job from another enterprise.

They are often easy to identify in a room: when you do have the chance to have a meeting with the CIO or CISO and/or their team, watch who others defer to when the meeting starts and ends, then who their eyes look to when a difficult question is asked.

Your preparation is critical – your competitors will certainly have done theirs! Bear in mind, however, that the research you have done may change with new trends, issues, and incidents that have become key drivers since.

Note

Especially for the first meeting with any CIO, it is imperative for the Account Manager to prepare well and do prior research on the customer. For instance, read the customer's LinkedIn profiles, websites, research the organisational pain points and be aware of recent news and awards concerning the organisation. Do not go into a meeting with the CIO like an unprepared student and expect the CIO to spoon-feed all the answers to you. Instead, add value to the discussion through an in-depth understanding of the customer, the organisation, and pain-points.

Alvin Ong – Former Nanyang Technological University CIO

The secret is to build your depth of understanding of what they really care about—their pain points.

Knowing CIO and CISO pain points

This is the next level of research that is required. You need to understand the CIO and CISO's challenges. The masterful move is to really study their enterprise beyond the superficial level. For example, there is a $2B transformation underway, but it is not progressing well. In such a case, understanding the root causes and how this is impacting the CIO and CISO is great background to have going into your discussions with them.

I'd suggest starting with the CIO or CISO themselves: their background, where they have worked, what stage of career they are at, and who knows them well. Consider who could provide you with some information on how they operate and what their personal priorities are likely to be.

> **Note**
>
> *Show them their problem, prove your solution, and anchor everything in their risk reality. You're not selling to the person; you're selling to their problem statement. Consolidated visibility into risk, posture, and resolution is the only language that lands.*
>
> **Gautam Dev – CEO and Founder, Genix Cyber**

Understanding their career stage

The CIO's career will typically operate as an "S" curve—with an aggressive start, wanting to prove themselves, and they are also often fighting the normal imposter syndrome of being in a large role with more responsibilities than in past roles.

From my own experience, I've observed that the curve begins steeply. A new CIO arrives with something to prove to the board and executive that appointed them. However, deep inside, they may have imposter syndrome; this is more prevalent than most CIOs will publicly admit. Then the weight of a mandate that is larger than anything they have previously held, combined with the visibility that comes with a C-suite title, creates an internal pressure that manifests as urgency and a pronounced appetite for early wins. They want to move quickly, to make decisions and take on vendors and initiatives that their predecessor might have deferred.

This is the stage where vendors have the greatest opportunity. A new CIO in the aggressive early phase of their S-curve is more accessible, more open to new ideas, and more willing to challenge the incumbent vendor relationships they have inherited. But they are also more vulnerable as they are building their own internal levels of trust.

I've drawn up the typical career stages of a new CIO, from the early stages of aggressive hard work to moving quickly and getting results:

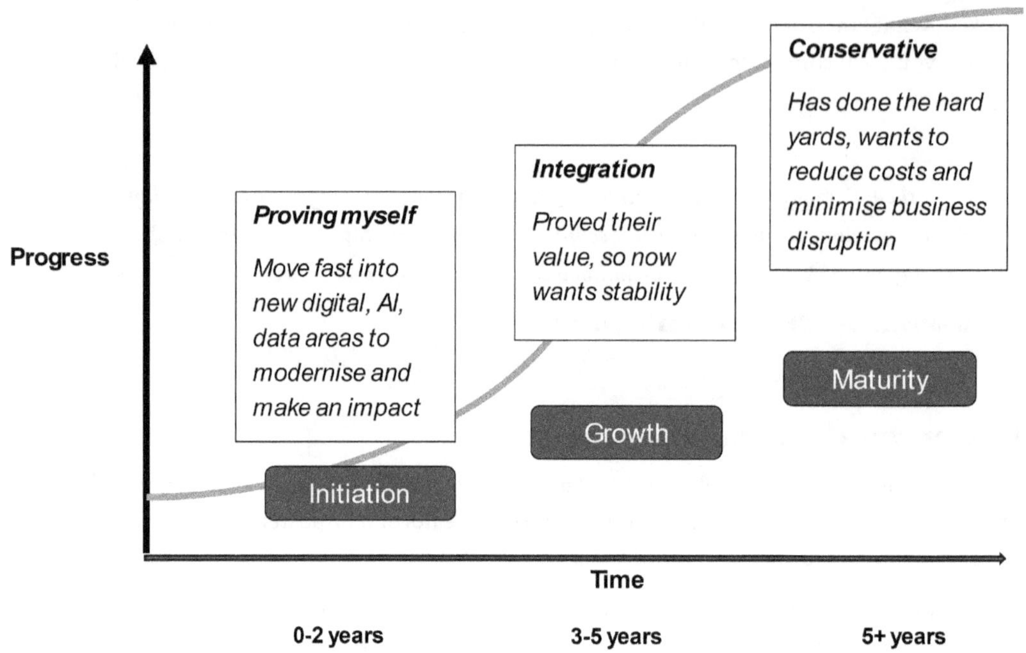

Figure 5.1 - Stages of CIO career

In the early stage the CIO will want to prove themselves by being able to deliver a valuable transformation change that will "mark" their career. The shiny object that the CIO delivers is their proof of doing a great job. Your product or service can be aligned to this objective, or if it isn't, it is not seen as relevant to them and therefore not prioritized. This can generate conflict as priorities may need to shift, and not every stakeholder will get what they have expected.

This is followed by a few years of consolidation following the transformation delivery (Integration), and the CIO wants to catch their breath and also address some of the "noise" created by the friction of the first stage.

Finally, the CIO in the last stage (Conservative) of their career wants to "keep the lights on" and not disrupt the business. They are going to be more careful.

Understanding the CIO's (or CISO's) career stage in this way can help you understand their pain points.

The CIO and the CISO often start at different times, so their career trajectories can create some opposing forces. Stakeholder conflicts can make your sell difficult, as aggressive and conservative stages may be in opposition.

Evaluate the next graphic, which shows the stages of the CISO career:

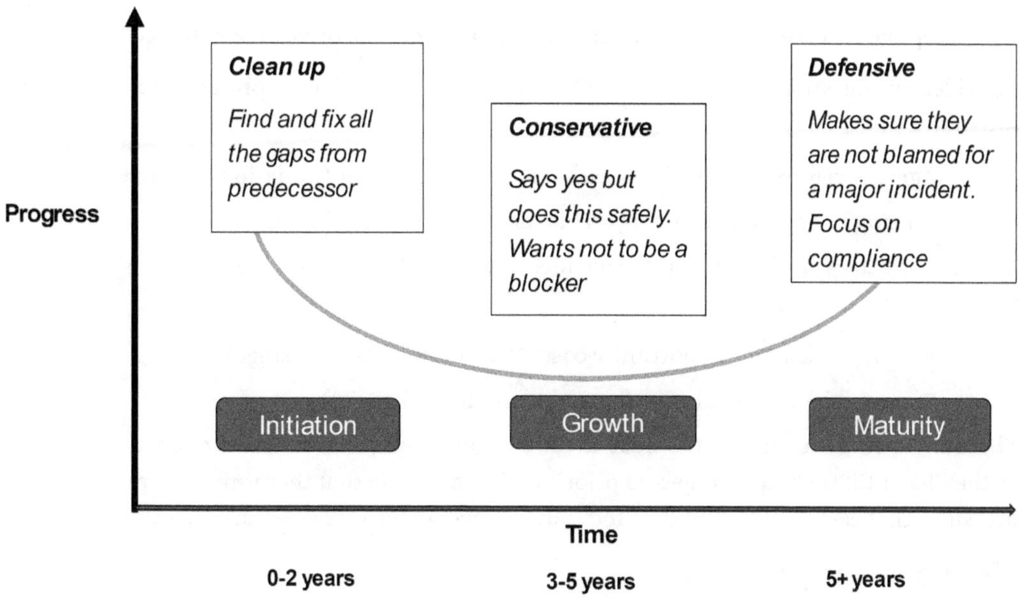

Figure 5.2 - Stages of the CISO career

There is a sweet spot in the mid-term when the CISO has finished their cleanup stage and the CIO has moved past the "prove myself" stage and they both seek stability. They are most aligned at this stage as a CIO and CISO team.

> **Tip**
>
> Your product or service will naturally be aligned to different career stages—innovative products versus those that are more about operational compliance.

In *Chapter 2*, I explored different CIO and CISO personas. Those different personas will combine with the CIO or CISO's career stage to amplify their preference – so for instance, a CIO who is Transformational will spend a longer time proving themselves and perhaps want to deliver several key initiatives before they feel that they are ready to move into stage 2. Similarly, a Risk CISO or Operational CISO will spend more time being conservative or fixing gaps.

Now that you understand the career dynamics, this is where you want to develop your hypothesis on how each CIO and CISO will operate and test this as you conduct your plans and preparation. Trying to work out where their personal "hidden agenda" is, is vital to maximizing your own efforts. Trying to sell a large transformation project to a colleague or staff member who is at a conservative stage is very frustrating for example.

Your emerging champion is a person that you can test your theories within terms of checking how receptive each executive is to change and their appetite to drive major change.

Consider this question: Is your CIO or CISO asking for more budget or protecting the budget? Are they:

- Aggressively making business cases for new investment (Initiation or growth stage)
- Cutting budgets and focusing on bottom-line efficiency (Maturity)

Another way to learn about this is to consider how the CIO or CISO is presenting risk to the board:

- Framing risk as an "opportunity cost" (Initiation or Growth stage)
- Framing risk as a regulatory fine to be avoided (Maturity)

These two questions can provide clues to the current temperature in the organization, as well as the CIO or CISO's career stage and priorities, but be aware that there are often macro-level pressures that cause reduced budget focus due to overall business revenue issues.

How are they feeling?

For CIOs and CISOs, their roles are full of challenges, and that is very much on their minds. When you have any discussion with them, be sure to watch their body language and how distracted they may appear.

Crises are commonplace for the CIO and CISO. During these periods of time, they are operating at a high cognitive load. Although this may not be obvious, these executives are experienced at hiding their feelings and may be fronting their real feelings. It's worth learning to read visual clues in their faces, however.

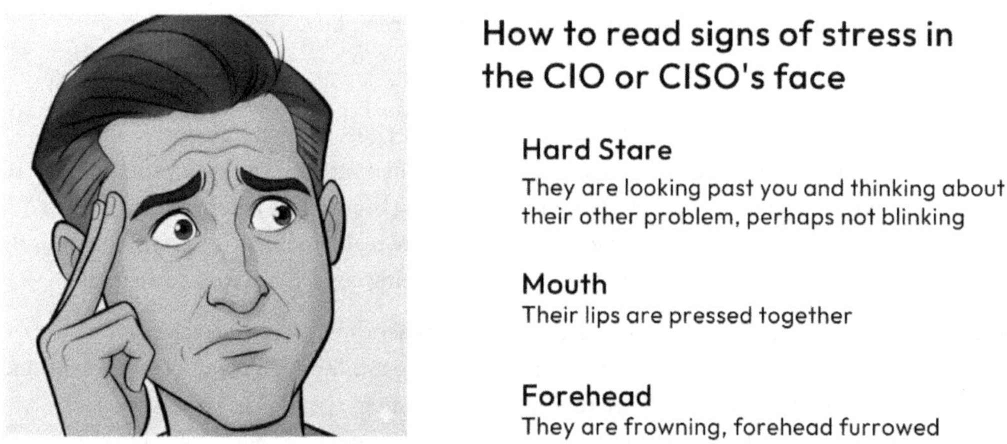

Figure 5.3 - How to read facial expressions

Of course, if the CIO or CISO is also incessantly checking their mobile device or looking toward the door, these could also be signs of stress. If you see these signs, I suggest this approach:

It looks like you need to be elsewhere. Is this a bad time? I'm happy to circle back when the dust settles.

The CIO and CISO will really appreciate your emotional intelligence. Trying to pitch to them when they are not mentally there won't achieve any of the outcomes that you want—unless, of course, their incident is related to your product and service.

The next question is to understand where the CIO or CISO's focus is in terms of strategic planning for the next cycle of planned projects, and how your product and service fit into that agenda.

Looking at the business agenda

CIOs and CISOs are high-powered executives, but do not operate in a vacuum; they are accountable to their direct supervisor and to the business strategy. To understand their business agenda and their broader world, you must read about the company in general.

Allow me to share a little vignette from Yigal Elstein on the importance of good preparation:

> Note
>
> *With the prep not being up to the mark and losing credibility with a very technical CISO that wanted to dive into very technical conversation and we did not prep for such eventuality, that was a missed opportunity to have a great meeting and have a top product person join and impress and allowed the competition to get advantage at a very senior level.*
>
> *We should have done more homework to study who the CISO was, tech vs. business mindset, and have a champion that prepared us better for the meeting – bottom line, always better to have a champion/change agent take you to the exec and build the agenda (that you then validate) with you to make the meeting a success.*
>
> **Yigal Elstein – Chief Revenue Officer, Checkmarx**

Business strategy and roadmap for listed companies are usually well documented and reported by the press. There will be many variations of this agenda with different labels and selected rhetoric, but you can boil down these clues into a sample set of 4-5 key strategic themes.

This could be, for example:

- Market expansion
- M&A growth
- Operational efficiency
- Regulatory compliance

These clues can come from public announcements on the financial quarterly earnings analysis, CEO and management interviews, new marketing material, and product roadmaps. When new roles are announced, there are also often cookie crumbs connecting these new positions to an approved strategy.

New enterprise strategic priorities have the effect of "crowding out" other initiatives due to financial and resource requirements. In truth, most enterprises struggle when trying to "stop" existing initiatives, and instead, these projects are not halted but just slow down with fewer resources invested.

These clues may provide some insight into the CIO and CISO's agenda that will be a direct input into their priorities. For the average executive, their list of priorities at 10,000 feet looks the same: cybersecurity, AI/machine learning (ML), legacy modernization, digital transformation, and compliance:

Emerging Business Agenda	**CIO and CISO focus**
Market expansion 	They are going to be tasked with accelerating digital transformation. This often means that there will be a higher risk appetite to allow short-term acceptance of legacy technology at end-of-life (EOL).

Emerging Business Agenda	**CIO and CISO focus**
M&A growth 	They are going to be tasked to help integrate a new acquisition into the corporate network. In the short term, cybersecurity will be the priority, and then there will be some data and applications impacted by this change.
Operational efficiency 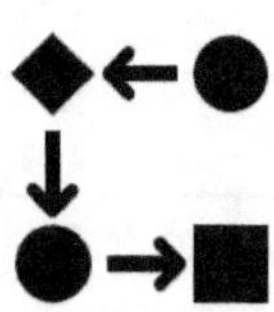	They are going to be tasked with helping reduce costs, with business departments being shut down or processes being re-engineered. They will be asked to automate and use AI to provide support. They may also be asked to contribute to cost reductions in the medium term.
Regulatory compliance 	They are going to be tasked with ensuring that all the required regulatory compliance homework is completed. There will be a strong focus on documentation and governance to enable these efforts. Some specific regulatory tech and cyber projects will be required.

Table 5.1 - Business agenda that the CIO and CISO care about

Remember, these are the priorities at 10,000 feet, and the actual priorities will vary depending on their status with regard to recent incidents, regulatory compliance, and progress in remediating their tech and cyber controls.

We must dive into the detail to understand more subtle aspects of this. If you interviewed the CIO or CISO, they would have a list of top 10 priorities. Across different enterprises and industries, this does vary somewhat in terms of actual order, but in general, the items tend to be similar, just with some ranking differences; for example:

	Top 10 priorities	
	CIO	**CISO**
1	Cybersecurity Risk Management	Threat Detection and Response
2	AI/Generative AI Implementation	Identity Management
3	Data and Analytics	AI Security and Governance
4	Digital Transformation agenda	Secure by Design Architecture
5	Legacy System Modernization	Cloud Security
6	Identity and Access Management (IAM)	Third Party and Supply Chain Security Risks
7	Business Continuity and Resilience	Data Protection and Privacy
8	Customer Experience and Engagement	Vulnerability Management
9	Talent and Staff Development	Cyber Culture and Awareness
10	Budget and Cost Management	Regulatory Compliance and Audits

Table 5.2 - Example top 10 CIO and CISO priorities

You will observe that there are some stark differences here. This does not mean that the CIO and CISO are not aligned as leadership but reflects the reality that their roles have very different focal points.

> **Note**
>
> There are different layers of strategic priorities that the CIO and CISO must manage. First, from the board and management, there are enterprise-wide initiatives, such as business growth, consolidation and reduction of cost. They will be responsible for supporting these as part of their role. But they will also have specific priorities that they will be personally held accountable for.

Their mental model of the stack of priorities is what shapes every conversation and therefore how you as a vendor are regarded by them. You are either in scope or not in scope. If you discuss a solution that falls into their list of priorities, then you will get attention. Otherwise, you are fighting an uphill battle to get this.

Every CIO and CISO will probably have a slightly different set of top priorities. The order may vary in terms of importance, but I'd argue that from my experience this list is more similar than different. However, the scale of operations in terms of complexity and geography will differ by organization.

What both roles tend to agree on is that cybersecurity is a top priority, although many CIOs will be happy to delegate this to the CISO and distance themselves from this domain.

In the following table I've reconciled the two lists around key priorities to show you where the CIO and CISO are naturally aligned:

Overall Priorities	Points of Alignment and Tension
Cybersecurity	CIO sees it as a strategic enabler CISO sees it as an operational imperative
AI Security	CIO wants to deploy AI CISO must secure it
Cloud Security	CIO drives migration CISO ensures security
Data Governance	CIO wants data quality CISO wants data protection
Compliance	CIO and CISO both share accountability to regulators and the board (this depends on jurisdiction, however)

Table 5.3 - Reconciling joint priorities

Remember that the CIO wants business value and the strategic outcomes related to the business agenda, while the CISO wants to keep the CIO happy but is focused on reducing threats and improving compliance. To make it more complicated, the CISO may be the project approver, but the CIO is the budget approver. Hence, you must make both stakeholders happy. This is the basis of deciding between needs (essential for survival) and wants (desirable things that make their lives easier). In the next section I explore how to operate when you are and are not a top 5 priority item.

How does your product/service fit into their hierarchy of needs?

Selling to the CIO and CISO can feel like you are playing an advanced game of "Bingo." The CIO and CISO want to tick off their card with as many of their business agenda priorities as possible. Indeed, the CIO will want, where possible, to tick off one platform that can solve a few of these priorities, even if these are not necessarily the best-in-class solutions, as the CIO is always afraid of architecture complexity (so is the CISO). The CISO is of course particularly focused on risk mitigation.

Getting the CIO and CISO to both agree that your product or service is a good fit is still a challenge. If your research suggests you address a top 5 priority, then the approach that you take will be different (from that you'd take if your solution fits outside this list).

A top 5 priority

If you align with a top five priority of theirs, this means that there is a real opportunity with allocated budget, and some current sense of urgency. The business case is less important and there is strong awareness among stakeholders of this being in the approved bucket.

Every time you speak to the CIO and/or CISO, you can refer to the top 5 priorities, and how your product and service are aligned with solving this problem. This is the time that your preparation requires you to research benchmarks and case studies that they would rate. A CIO who began their career in Australia, for example, will find more resonance in an example from a comparable Australian enterprise than in a Fortune 500 case study from the United States, not because the latter is less impressive, but because the former feels more directly applicable to the environment they are actually managing.

> **Note**
>
> *Understand my business, my role in the business, the likely challenges I might have. Second, provide some genuinely useful options for assistance and don't make it up as I will ask the tough questions and find out. Third, work more as a partner than simply a profit-making enterprise – think creatively about how we can develop a win-win relationship. Consider that unique value I might provide as a customer – especially given that most often my teams are outstanding contributors and thought leaders. Fourth, provide me with insights that I might not have already – after all, everyone needs ongoing education!. But do not start with the free giveaways as I will always turn away from any potential conflict of interest.*
>
> **Dr Maria Miloslavljevic – former ANZ Bank CISO**

From my own experience, I recall a vendor repeatedly referencing 3-5 different Indian enterprises that were his site references for a product. I had to keep asking him for a US-based one, which the company I worked at would take notice of.

The sense of urgency works in your favour, the CIO and CISO cannot afford to waste execution time. Consider how you can share best practices on expedited implementation, including a pilot that can provide confidence in the suitability of your product or service.

Not a top 5 priority

When the CIO and CISO are less interested in spending time to discuss your solution further, because it is not a top priority for them, you will struggle to gain traction. In these cases, you can theoretically try other stakeholders such as the CFO, CRO, or COO, but I'd advise against that approach as this will not be well received by the CIO or CISO.

My advice is to play the long game and see how your product or service is positioned beyond their Top 5.

If you can get an indication that this is on their radar, just not for this planning period, then your preparation becomes to share thought leadership and stay engaged with your stakeholders, but in a less active fashion. Your product and service are still relevant, it's just that the timing is off. This "Stay in Touch" approach is one that I've experienced many times. When someone says to a CIO or CISO, "I will check back with you in six months," then the CIO and CISO will usually say "yes."

I've seen this approach work well across many different countries:

Vendor: *I completely understand—priorities above 5 will not get funded this year.*

Let me get out of your way, but I'd like to set up two specific check-ins with your direct report or lead architect:

- *When your current vendor contract comes up for renewal* (Month-Year)
- *When does budget planning start for the next financial year* (Month-Year)*?*

Thanks, trust this makes sense?

Both of these check-ins are natural, and you are not asking them for any immediate action or special obligation. Your clear objective is to continue the dialogue and, where you feel this makes sense, with a staff member of the CIO or CISO's team.

> **Tip**
>
> A CIO and CISO will always understand passion; just be careful not to overdo it!

One thing to always be aware of is that timing can be everything. Timing can vary by industry and company - there are some companies that require a three-year strategy, and clearly, there is less confidence in the latter years. Companies taking this approach can form teams to look at programs that span multiple budget periods which often are labelled as transformation. These large-scale transformations I cover in more detail in *Chapter 14*.

There is a saying that "practice makes perfect". Even the best public speakers have to practice and ensure that their message is clear.

Practice your elevator pitch

Whenever I had a strategic presentation for the board, I would always practice beforehand. How I did this depended on my situation; in some cases, I would be speaking out loud only in my mind, and on a few other occasions, I'd enunciate the key points and test my own understanding, speaking without notes. I was also checking if the lexicon that I was going to use was impactful enough or needed to be changed.

Practicing this with others is even more dynamic and closer to the real thing. As a CIO and CISO, I've done trial presentations with my own team. I would ask them to specifically listen to how I present material and whether there are any style issues, or what questions would arise based on the current flow. Most importantly, I'd ask them to be skeptical rather than positive. This means that they should feel free to interrupt me mid-stream and ask questions, as that may point to a poor natural sequencing that then could be improved. I also wanted them to challenge and ask me the "so what" questions, so I must justify my assertions.

I'd advise you to practice your pitch in a similar way. When you present to any CIO and CISO, they are going to be straightforward with you and won't shy away from telling you that your message is not clear or that they simply don't understand your meaning.

Having this mock audience is better than just a video recording (which I know some people do to prepare), as that is very unlike any actual pitch that you must perform with executives or the board. Remember that "practice makes perfect." Your choice to use repetition builds your muscle memory and ensures that you really understand the essence of your message. It does not matter that your pitch is perfect to the letter in accordance with your draft. I've always felt that when you do this, your focus shifts to getting the words right instead of watching the CIO or CISO's reactions—and that means you miss the chance to adjust your message as needed.

So, who do you practice with? There are several options that you can consider, but of course, each of these is not equal:

- **CIO and CISO advisor**: Best of all is to use a CIO or CISO advisor – they will know how your message will land and can provide feedback on your approach and the language used.
- **Internal champion**: This depends on you having a strong and trusting relationship with the champion; then they are ideal to test run the pitch with. The champion can also provide specific advice on language that would work more effectively for their CIO and CISO.
- **AI:** I've not done this but practicing with your favourite AI engine is an option that you can take.
- **Your mother**: Honestly, I've never done this, but the adage of explaining to your mom applies. You must explain things 100% clearly and avoid making any assumptions.

The power of the pause is also worth considering; that is, learning to be comfortable with silence. A short pause after a strong point gives the executive space to absorb the message and respond. I've always felt that the moment of silence signals confidence and not anxiety.

If you do choose to record yourself as part of your preparation, watch it once with the sound off because your body language, your posture, and your eye contact will tell you more about how you are coming across than anything you say.

The 60-second pitch

Your preparation must be able to allow you to flex between different scenarios. The major difference is that in some cases, you will only have around 60 seconds to pitch, and in others you will be afforded more than 60 seconds and can speak according to what you understand to be the window that is available.

> **Note**
>
> I recall at Eli Lilly visiting hospitals with the sales representatives, who all travelled to different locations to wait for a few hours to try to catch the doctor as they made their rounds. The hallway was full of 3-7 different salespersons who were waiting for their 30 seconds to pitch to the Doctor.

How can you get a message across in this short time that will make sense and help the CIO and CISO with their needs? Allow me to expand on a couple of different scenarios:

Scenario	Scene
30 Seconds in the Hallway 	*Door opener* You are in the hallway, awaiting your moment to speak to the CIO or CISO as they make their way into a seminar session at a tech conference. You know that your solution aligns with one of their 5 priority areas, so your objective is to have them ask to hear more.
60 Seconds on the Phone 	*Build their interest* You reached the CIO or CISO on their personal phone, and they answered. Your objective is to get a meeting scheduled with them where you can show you support their strategic priority.
4–5 Minutes Pitch 	*Get commitment to the next step* The CIO or CISO has agreed to hear your elevator pitch. You have a little more time to establish your credibility, and your goal again is to ask for more time to explain in greater detail.

Table 5.4 - Your elevator pitches

Each of these scenarios is brief, and your preparation to be able to adapt to these windows is crucial. Ideally, you want to avoid the 30-second and 60-second paths, but they can be your entry points for a longer engagement.

Here are some example scripts for these scenarios:

Scenario	**Draft Script**
30 seconds in the hallway 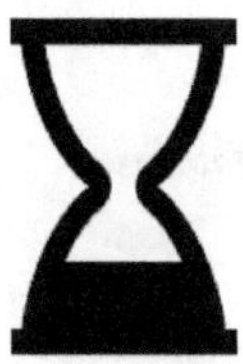	*Hi, I noticed your organization is moving toward* [specific priority]. *I've been working with 3 enterprises, and the early results have been very positive. Would love to share what we found if you have thirty minutes.*
60 seconds on the phone 	*Hi* [very quick small talk] *I appreciate you picking up, and I will be brief.* *We have been working with* [peer organization] *on* [specific challenge], *and I believe there is a direct parallel to what you are navigating right now.* *Could we find thirty minutes in the next two weeks so I can show you what we found?*
4–5 minutes pitch 	*From what I understand of your current focus on* [priority], *the challenge most organizations in your position face is* [specific problem]. *We worked with* [reference customer] *on exactly that—and the outcome was* [specific result]. *I would like thirty minutes to walk you through the approach in detail and show you how it maps specifically to your environment.* *Would* [specific date] *work?*

Table 5.5 - Your elevator pitch script

If you find that the CIO or CISO does not agree to a further meeting when you pitch to them, consider your approach:

- Did you forget to ask for the next step?
- Was your pitch not compelling or relevant?
- Did you not come across credibly?

It is also important to reconcile their body language with their responses. If the CIO or CISO was leaning in, nodding, and appeared positive, then you must move into discovery mode. Note that this same approach can be applied to other executives and potential champions to earn a chance to talk to the CIO or CISO too.

> Note
>
> *Be human and connect on a non-business topic/ice breaker (be informed ahead on what this might be, area of interest) but make sure it is genuine.*
>
> *Align on what is a good outcome for the meeting, revalidate the agenda in alignment to get to such outcomes.*
>
> **Yigal Elstein – Chief Revenue Officer, Checkmarx**

Listen, listen, listen, then be brief, be insightful

To progress the lead, it is imperative that you are tuned into the conversation and do not keep trying to sell the idea to the CIO or CISO. I know from my own experience when I've been in these circumstances, I start to think that I can't work with this person then, as they haven't listened.

As you have been observing the CIO or CISO, you can take the opportunity to take a small step into "discovery" by asking about their situation in more detail. Don't dive too deep, though; your intention is to learn more about their current plans, environment, and the existing problems. You are at the same time assessing how engaged they are in this project and if they really care, or if this is just a priority from management or the board.

> Tip
>
> Ideally, you want to understand more details about their pain points to be able to speak specifically to this topic rather than to features and functionality that are not relevant to that objective.

The truth is that most tech salespersons are not good listeners. I have been told by my own wife that I'm not a good listener, and that is probably mostly true. This is something I've had to consciously develop over time. To really listen takes discipline and focus.

There are different levels of listening:

Type of listening	**Description**	**How to develop**
Passive Listening 	• You are hearing not processing meaning • Present but not engaged • Interrupting to add your point • At the end you can't recall what was said	A simple test: if you cannot summarize what was just said in two sentences, you were not listening. Try to really tune into conversations so that you can effectively summarize them afterward
Active Listening 	• You are fully engaged and taking notes • You are asking questions to clarify • You focus on understanding • You repeat what the speaker said	Develop the habit of summarizing back to the speaker: "What I am hearing you say is...".
Strategic Listening 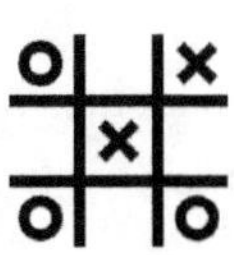	• You listen to understand the politics • You listen for what has not been stated • You relate to prior discussions • You try to connect the dots	During the conversation, listen for hesitation, repetition, and the topics that are avoided as much as the ones that are raised.

Table 5.6 - Different levels of listening

I've learned over time to be a better listener. I must be conscious about ensuring that I'm listening more than I talk. Taking notes is a great way to get yourself into this mode, and it signals to the other party that you value what he or she is saying. I've learned in my career that best practice is to be 70:30 - this means listening 70% of the time (and speaking 30%). This is based on the premise of allowing the CIO or CISO to take a journey of self-discovery, where diagnosis occurs before prescription.

As a CIO and CISO, when I've been in a conversation with a passive listener, this is when I've been likely to keep walking or hang up on a phone call. Then, of course, your access to them is going to be "blocked", as they have made up their mind that you are not interested in their problems but just want to sell them your product or service.

There is an element of ego involved here, as the CIO or CISO has an expectation of a conversation that may provide them some strategic insight that they were not aware of. They are focused on the future strategy as a priority, so this use of their time was granted to you with that notion in mind.

Just telling the CIO or CISO that there are more ransomware attacks is not something that they want to hear. They probably know this already, and in today's environment, the CIO and CISO want to hear what the hot topics are; these may not be immediate priorities, but are probably on their longer-term list of "To do's":

Hot topic	**Why are CIOs/CISOs interested**
Vendor consolidation 	How to reduce the number of vendors. They will want to understand that if they adopt your product, can they eliminate 2-3 others? Having some stories of reputable enterprises that have made this transition and the benefits is what they want to hear.
Operational Resilience 	Resilience of the business means bouncing back into shape from incidents. They want to learn how other CIOs and CISOs have made changes to improve their business continuity.

Hot topic	Why are CIOs/CISOs interested
Board Risk Quantification 	They are under pressure to justify their spending on technology and cybersecurity with new requirements to commence innovation investments. They want to learn how others are measuring these metrics and how this is used by the board.
AI Productivity Gains 	Every enterprise wants to execute and gain productivity improvements. The CIO and CISO want to understand how to avoid AI data leakage and incidents during this period of transition. They want to learn from other sites that have addressed these concerns.
Identity Security 	Identity management is becoming more complex with an increasing number of non-human identities, including AI agents. The CIO and CISO want to ensure that these new bots and access rights are carefully managed.

Table 5.7 - CIO and CISO hot topics

These "Hot Topics" will shift year to year but are very much on the CIOs' and CISOs' minds.

We must distinguish here between what are mandated board-approved priority projects that are funded, and what the CIO and/or CISO is concerned about that may not have approval. You are probably wondering why they have not yet sought approval to address these concerns. The truth is that there are natural conflicts that exist in the roles of the CIO and CISO which mean that operational trade-offs are always in play.

The CIO or CISO may be concerned about one or more of these topics, but they also probably recognize that their team is close to breaking point in terms of workload and stress from maintaining current progress.

> Note
>
> *Obviously, do your homework, and I know that that sells one-on-one. Do your homework. Understand who you're talking to.... quite often, vendors can't help themselves. A vendor walks in and they just, you know, for half an hour about talk about their product.*
>
> *Within the organisation in having that conversation, you can start to then identify what are some of the internal challenges that person is facing. Then how can you help them navigate those internal kind of roadblocks and challenges they're having while also recognizing who the other stakeholders are you need to be engaging with?*
>
> **Matt Boon – Senior Director, Strategic Research, Adapt**

> Note
>
> *In the first 10 minutes, strong vendors demonstrate that they've done their homework. They understand our industry, regulatory pressures, architectural landscape, and likely maturity gaps. They ask informed questions and frame their solution in the context of our operating model.*
>
> *Weak meetings start with generic slide decks and feature walkthroughs. Strong meetings start with context, relevance, and problem alignment. Technical solutioning should lead; marketing should support, not dominate.*
>
> **Sunil Varkey – CISO, Hexaware Technologies (Former HSBC CISO)**

There is also the reality that the CIO and CISO may not want to admit openly to the board and management their concerns about any of these hot topics. I know from my experience that raising these issues and not getting support can make you and the team feel "flat". The experienced CIO and CISO know when to pick their battles.

Now that you have prepared for your meeting with the CIO and CISO to understand what is on their mind and what they currently have in terms of technology stack, it is time to prepare your specific agenda for that meeting.

This is what I will cover in the next section.

Having a clear agenda

When you meet the CIO and/or CISO, you must have a clear agenda to avoid being labelled as a time-wasting vendor. Both the CIO and CISO have long workdays and are constantly being pitched to.

> Note
>
> *A waste of time is when vendors use the first ten minutes to prove how smart they are. They lean on slick slides, perfectly articulate their value propositions, and race toward the demo. That is the fastest way to lose a room. The only action that matters in those crucial early minutes is radical listening.*
>
> **Jayant Dave – CISO, Check Point Software**

Sharing a rough meeting agenda shows professionalism and respect for their time. Many CIOs and CISOs will not even accept a meeting unless an agenda is pre-shared and vetted by their Executive Assistant in advance.

Having a clear agenda also sets clear expectations for the meeting. This is particularly important as there will likely be attendees who are direct reports of the CIO and CISO who have been asked to join the meeting without any prior context. This can lead to confusion and unintended disruption in what may be only a 30-minute meeting.

> Tip
>
> Importantly, your agenda should address a specific business problem, rather than listing your product or service features.

I suggest sending this agenda via email 3 days before the meeting. This heralds the upcoming session and clarifies how you intend to use the limited time you have. Much earlier, it won't be read and the same applies to sending it later.

Having the agenda at the meeting regardless of whether it has been read or not, demonstrates the discipline that you want associated with your brand. This approach often reveals valuable context. Knowing this allows you to manage the upcoming discussion effectively, even if the participants arrive distracted.

Now with this preparation done, you are ready to walk into the office of the CIO and CISO, which is the focus of our next chapter.

Summary

In this chapter I explored how good preparation is the foundation of every successful CIO/CISO sale. My perspective is that most vendors skip prep and instead arrive with generic pitches that immediately signal they haven't done their homework.

Good preparation means you understand their tech stack and have mapped their strategic priorities and career stage. Your general reading of the broader business agenda for context and practicing your pitch until you can flex from 30 seconds to 30 minutes without notes will pay off.

Your goal is to walk in already knowing their pain points well enough that your questions sharpen their thinking rather than waste their time. With a CIO or CISO, you typically get one shot. They are extremely time-compressed, sceptical of vendors, and have seen every pitch. Walking in unprepared doesn't just cost you the meeting, it can cost you credibility that you may never get back.

The key learnings from this chapter are:

- **Research the tech stack before any meeting** – job postings, LinkedIn staff profiles, GitHub repos, and news articles reveal more than most vendors realize. You want to arrive with a solid hypothesis, not a blank slate.
- **Map the organization for influence** – a deputy (long tenured, cross-functional, trusted by the CIO/CISO) is valuable to identify (but may not be clear from an organizational chart).
- **Understand their career stage** – a new CIO, for example, in "proving" mode welcomes transformation pitches, while one is in "conservative" mode is likely focused on avoiding disruption. Selling the wrong thing to an executive at the wrong stage can be a dealbreaker.
- **Top 5 priority = real urgency and budget** – outside the top 5 = play the long game. If not in the approved cycle, offer a structured "stay in touch" with specific check-in dates tied to contract renewal and budget planning.
- **Know the CIO/CISO hot topics** – vendor consolidation, operational resilience, board risk metrics, AI productivity, and identity security, etc.
- **Abide by the 70:30 rule** – listening 70% of the time, speaking 30%. Strategic listening means hearing what hasn't been said and connecting dots across stakeholders.

6

Walking Into the Office of the CIO and CISO

You have done your preparation, established your contact with your target CIO/CISO and have finally secured a 30-minute meeting. This may be the culmination of many weeks and months of planning, as our CIO and CISO are busy executives, and it's likely difficult to get time scheduled with them. Even though you have prepared well at this point and even rehearsed with your CIO/CISO advisor and a few colleagues who have volunteered to give you a difficult time, there will likely be some doubt in your mind.

First, you get changed and wear an outfit that gives you confidence, is professional, comfortable, and appropriate to the culture you're walking into, with your preparation that we covered in *Chapter 5* all fresh in your mind. Then, as you are making your way to their office, you refresh yourself on the pitch that you have prepared, perhaps asking yourself whether there have been any other developments or other new market intelligence you can reference. Just before you walk into the lobby, you do a quick scan for any breaking news on their company. It's unlikely; however, it's always worth checking.

A quick reset and relaxation of the mind, to ready yourself for the meeting. You want to be early, so arrive at the meeting room 10 minutes in advance.

There you are, ready for your meeting. What do you do next? Well, read on, because that is the subject of this chapter. We're going to cover the following:

- The first 60 seconds matter
- Learning executive presence
- Building your confidence
- How to respond to CIO and CISO objections

- Bringing valuable insights
- Talking first base

The first 60 seconds matter

On entering the room, your first movement matters more than your first words. Make eye contact, the kind that signals you are present and confident. Walk tall. Then, when you sense this is appropriate, offer a handshake.

> **Note**
>
> Note that appropriate greetings differ across different cultures. In my experience working in Japan and across several Asian cultures, a bow is the appropriate greeting. Getting these right signals a level of cultural awareness that is noticed and respected.

Your goal as a vendor entering the office is to feel calm and grounded, even if the stakes feel significant. This is because the executive across the table will read your physical presence before they process anything you say.

> **Tip**
>
> The CIO and CISO you are meeting have likely sat across the table from hundreds of vendors. What you do before you speak tells them immediately whether you are someone worth listening to. So be sure to make those first thirty seconds count.

What you say first depends on your experience with the CIO and CISO and the relevant culture. In some countries, some degree of small talk is okay; it is often considered rude to jump straight into a pitch. (In a more traditional culture like Japan, it is quite normal to spend that first 60 seconds exchanging business cards (*meishi*) and then studying them.)

I'd always regard the first 30-60 seconds as a calibration exercise – you want to test the waters and understand how the executive is today, whether they are relaxed or stressed. These clues can be important to capture, and then you can adjust your approach for the meeting. If they walk in and reference that they're having a tough day, for example, then you might want to get straight to the point:

It looks like you are snowed under today. I'll get straight to the point so I can give you back some time.

These first few minutes really matter as you can lose the opportunity you have in an instant if you cannot gain their attention. They are always going to be thinking about what is next on their schedule and the rest of their day. Taking this approach requires some courage, but it pays off.

I'd add that there is an art in getting the right balance between small talk and getting straight into business. This is also massively dependent on the local culture and customs of doing business.

Small talk is not filler; it is the first part of the meeting, and the executive who mentions a regulatory review or a board agenda item is telling you exactly what matters to them right now.

The transition from small talk to the matter at hand works best when it is a bridge rather than a gear change, picking up something from the conversation and connecting it naturally. Let the executive lead the shift, read the signal when it comes, and follow it without hesitation.

I posed the question, *what does a vendor do in the first 10 minutes of a meeting that makes you think "this is going to be good" vs. "this is going to be a waste of time"* to a collection of executives. They shared some great insights that are worth reflecting on.

> Note
>
> *Some very basic things often set the meeting trajectory very early on, particularly for a first meeting, when salespeople have done their homework and they understand your background and experiences and take time to get to know you first. Conversely, when a vendor dives immediately into their content and why they are the best, with no context, I switch off.*
>
> **Paul O'Rourke – former CISO, CRO and BCG Global Cyber Leader**

> Note
>
> *The positive experience is when they get right into giving me insights. If I get 10-15 minutes of discovery questions or leading questions, it can be pretty frustrating. The most receptive first 10 minutes for me is when a vendor is describing (with data) what is happening out there, and any successful stories of customers like me having success establishing and then delivering on a project that supported their cybersecurity strategy and program.*
>
> **Nigel Hedges – Executive General Manager & CISO, Chemist Warehouse**

> Note
>
> *Follow through on commitments and respond constructively to inevitable challenges.*
>
> *When you meet a new vendor, how many minutes do you give them before you start to want to quit the meeting? It depends materially on how critical the capability is to my strategy and the quality, honesty and transparency of the participant.*
>
> *If both of those factors are low, it would take fewer than 5 minutes to finish a discussion.*
>
> **Dan Chesterman – CIO, Teachers Mutual Bank**

These guidelines equally apply to internal champions that are meeting the CIO and CISO. They may be a little more tolerant, since they already know them, but they will still be triggered into a negative posture if they don't start off strong. The key difference is that the internal champions will have a more natural understanding of the pain points and the potential benefits for these leaders in advance.

The CIO and CISO (most likely) do not intend to be rude or inconsiderate in their dealings with you. They must learn to be masters of both priority management and time management. In my last book *A Day in the Life of a CISO,* I explained this in more detail but allow me to summarise for you here. These executives learn that to succeed they need to focus on their priorities.

Priority management is strategic and ensures that the bigger picture is never lost. At the same time, they use time management as a secondary tool to ensure that they effectively manage their time and are ruthless with how they allocate it. In the context of their priorities, unfortunately your pitch is not going to be at the same high level that you yourself would place it.

> Note
>
> *Remember that your "critical meeting to present and discuss our solution(s) and advance our sales goals" is one part of your customer's incredibly busy day—dealing with staff issues, stakeholder engagement, security incidents and business escalations, improving operational resilience, and preparing for their next board presentation.*
>
> **Mark Trumble – Cyber Sales and Solutions leader**

Given this background, how you project yourself is as important as what you say. This is called "presence", and when you see this, it is instantly recognizable. Presence is hard to describe but we all know it when we see it.

For any technical or cybersecurity salesperson, developing executive presence will help you build relationships with the CIO and CISO. So, let's learn about it!

Learning executive presence

Presence is a personal quality that the most effective people bring into a room that is almost impossible to define but entirely impossible to miss. When you see it, you recognize it instantly, even if you could not explain exactly what you are responding to.

From my experience, presence is not loudness. It is a grounded quality of genuine engagement that makes the people around you feel that what is happening in this room, right now, is the only thing that matters. It is the ability to project self-confidence and maturity, an outward expression of your conviction, preparation, and clarity in approach and thinking.

Presence also has nothing to do with extroversion. Some of the most commanding people I have encountered in boardrooms and executive meetings are, by their own admission, naturally shy. I myself was labelled shy earlier in my career, but believe I have developed executive presence.

When a leader with presence speaks, people stop and listen. Then, when they listen, people feel heard. With their presence comes a sense that every word they contribute has been considered.

I was reminded of this during my time as CIO at Eli Lilly, when a senior stakeholder told me she had been waiting for me to speak—and that when I did, she expected to hear something different, something worth waiting for. That comment stayed with me because it captured something true about what presence actually is. It is not about filling the silence. It is about making what you contribute to the silence worth the wait.

My advice is that for every vendor working at the technical or cybersecurity level who wants to build meaningful relationships with CIOs and CISOs, developing executive presence is mandatory to be able to forge trusted relationships.

Your professional dressing and grooming provide some visual clues to this. Your body language plays an important part too, in that it reflects confidence, even without you speaking, and radiates positive energy. This means that you should work to minimize any distracting habits like fidgeting or restless legs that don't stop moving when you are seated.

Imagine you are meeting someone for the first time who looks like this, and in this setting:

Figure 6.1 - My executive presence

Would you stand up a little straighter? Not because they intimidated you, but perhaps because they made you feel the conversation would be worth your full attention.

> **Note**
>
> While crossed arms can often be misread as defensive, here they are relaxed, not closed. My posture in this photograph is grounded and my expression says, "I have heard everything you are about to say, and I am genuinely interested in what comes next."

As with most branding, executive presence cannot be faked, and you will always be judging or watching for these clues, whether you realize it or not. Once I meet a leader with executive presence, I expect that style to remain consistent. I would be incredibly surprised and shocked to see this CIO or CISO then lose confidence and composure. Of course, if they show signs of stress then I know that something else is happening behind the scenes.

> **Note**
>
> I learned the concept of resetting your perspective during my teenage years. Once, while playing in the basketball First team against our rivals who were all vying to win the competition, our coach Mr. Herb Barker, who played rugby for Australia and won a bronze medal at the Commonwealth Games in track and field, spoke to us. He could see

> that we all appeared a little tentative and aware of the importance of the occasion. Herb shared a simple story from his own experiences; he said:
>
> *When I played the All Black* (New Zealand Rugby) *team for the first time, I was also a bit scared to be honest, and then my coach told me:*
>
> *Don't forget – they also go to the bathroom like you do.*
>
> **Coach – Herb Barker (Wallaby #387)**

> **Tip**
>
> Whenever you feel the slightest sense of fear, remember CIOs and CISOs are human too and put on their shoes the same way that you do. Respect is important, but fear isn't necessary.

Humans all respond differently to different situations. To illustrate this, here is a spectrum of emotional responses you can experience when meeting an executive who is important to your career success:

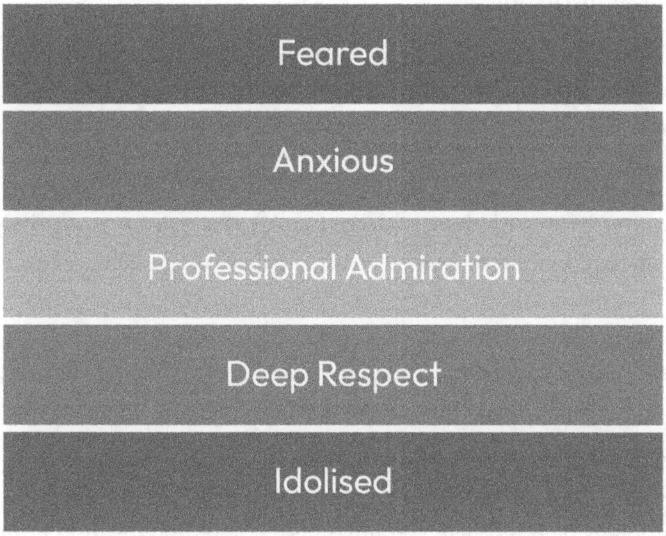

Figure 6.2 - Tech sales emotional ladder

Initially, when meeting the CIO and CISO you may experience the range of emotions depicted here. The sweet spot is to operate in the middle layer, by being respectful, and confident in having a conversation with them while maintaining your own degree of humbleness.

In my experience as a CIO and CISO it is often easy to spot which level the tech salesperson that you are engaging with is operating at. For example, when someone is anxious, there is hesitation in their voice and their body language reflects this.

Allow me to also touch briefly on the other end of the scale. When you "idolise" the CIO and CISO you may act a bit starstruck. You are aware of their distinguished career and may even mention this to them. In my view, while this is very respectful, it may impact the dynamic that you are wanting to build with them. Your goal is to develop a long-term partnership with them, where they gain a resource that can help them challenge their thinking and bring new ideas. However, if you are just agreeing to everything that they say, then your relationship will never reach that level. Successful CIOs and CISOs truly appreciate support but they also want to know the hard truths. Trust toward you may not develop for these executives if they feel you are just saying "yes" to everything they say.

True executive presence means that you are having a conversation with the CIO/CISO as a peer. They may not be an actual peer in terms of their experience, salary, etc., but none of these factors matter for this discussion.

You just want to be able to have a face-to-face discussion as an equal. Should you come into the discussion feeling that you cannot operate in this manner then you may not be able to be seen as a strategic partner.

> **Tip**
>
> Walk into a conversation with them with the framing that you are here to help them solve a problem that they are concerned about and discuss a possible way forward.

In my experience, I've seen some good and bad examples of tech and cyber sales. You want to avoid being seen as "cocky" and arrogant, rather than projecting presence.

There is a distinct difference between the confidence that comes with executive presence and that associated with arrogance. While you must be confident that your solution can honestly help with their problem, be humble in recognizing that you probably don't understand everything about the product and that there is a chance that this may not be a perfect fit for them.

Note

At times salespeople can be too eager or are so invested in the product that they are trying to sell, that they forget to understand the customer's needs. A sophisticated buyer will know why they are having a discussion – this can include having a problem to solve, education or due to relationships. Taking a step back and listening is key - The best vendors have been those who have thought broader and longer term without trying to hit a number.

John Taylor – Field CTO, Mimecast (former CIO & CISO)

I've met and engaged with a confident and humble vendor peer, and I learned something from the exchange. A salesperson understanding my problem and asking great questions is the sweet spot and over time this approach builds trust. The converse of course is vendors who engage poorly and then lose any right to meet with me again.

Note

My Red flags

People who talk much more than they listen

People who make their end of year your problem—rush deals, negotiate poorly, etc.

People who sell around you - no issues with vendors talking to other people in the org (just be transparent; it just creates more work later).

Gerard Florian – former ANZ Bank Group Executive & CIO

In my view when engaging with a CIO or CISO, the most effective approach is to adopt the following principles:

- Focus on listening actively more than delivering your pitch
- Go into the discussion with the goal of helping them instead of meeting your own targets
- If you don't know the answer, then be honest and say so

The time you spent to prepare for the discussion should give you a degree of confidence. Remember, your knowledge of the organization is a strong foundation that will support you.

Note

The good ones walk in and open with something like "Before I show you anything, can you tell me what's keeping you up at night right now?"

> *That tells me they've done their homework and they're here to solve my problem, not just hit a quota.*
>
> **Bharat Bajaj – Technology Risk Partner, banking sector**

> Note
>
> *Earn the meeting by showing understanding, not urgency. CIOs and CISOs want partners who make their complex world simpler. Speak to risk and business value, not technology alone. Approach each conversation as if their reputation is your own, because in enterprise security, credibility compounds or collapses fast.*
>
> **Michael Kazantzis – CEO, Cyborium**

Let's explore confidence further, as this is a foundation for success. Confidence is not the absence of doubt but the decision to act with clarity and purpose despite having some ambiguity.

Building your confidence

Many sales professionals are confident, outward-facing communicators, but effective salespeople come in a wide range of personality types and working styles. While some may be naturally extroverted, others succeed by building trust through careful listening and adapting to the situation. In fact, many CIOs and CISOs themselves often learn to adapt their natural communication style to suit different situations, audiences, and business needs.

> Note
>
> From my own experience, there is a high proportion of CIOs and CISOs who are introverted. These CIOs and CISOs did not reach the top of their profession by being the loudest person in the room. They got there by being the most prepared, the most rigorous, and the most trusted.
>
> The vendor who arrives believing they need to out-charm the executive across the table has fundamentally misread the room.

Adapting will turn your natural confidence into a distinct strength, ensuring that when you walk into a CIO's or CISO's office, you can absolutely nail the pitch.

Walking the tightrope between confidence and arrogance and at the same time, maintaining your humility is not easy. I'd like to share my tips on this:

- Practice makes perfect. After each session reflect on how you did and what you would do differently. Reflection is a powerful tool to help you look backward to help you going forward.
- Be comfortable in your own skin. Use the words and approach that are natural to you rather than following someone else's script. I've learned this from doing regular keynotes, podcasts, webinars and interview panels, and not looking at my notes and worrying about getting the words and pre-prepared sentences 100% correct. You want to come across as feeling real, while having a rough outline in your own head.
- Think positively. Always assume that the person you are speaking to respects what you are saying and this will end up in a positive outcome. Looking down when you are walking and counterbalancing can result in you falling from the tightrope.
- Identify your fears. Having a clear sense of what you fear will make you face up to that concern. Often the fear may be irrational or make little sense when you examine it.

You are now in front of the CIO, projecting your best executive presence. You take a seat opposite them and have your notebook open and ready to record some key actions. The detailed preparation that you have laboured over has earned you the right to take this meeting.

At the back of your mind, you may have your sales target and your different preparation scripts ready, but now is the time to relax and not allow these thoughts to dominate your mind. Your goal is to remain confident, maintain your executive presence and positively influence the outcome of this meeting. Try to depersonalise this discussion, as this will remove any sense of intimidation. This discussion is not about yourself or the CIO or CISO but the business problem that you want to assist them with.

Then comes your first test to project your confidence through your executive presence – when the CIO and CISO decide to challenge you and ask you a very specific and hard question. Let's cover this next.

How to respond to CIO and CISO objections

Most objections occur before first base. You have been listening more than speaking, but the question still came as a surprise to you. Perhaps you didn't expect this angle. Don't let this faze you; I'd say it is not unusual to have some potential objections expressed.

CIO and CISO questions are likely to be about the suitability of the solution; they are not questioning your competence. All these executives have a history with vendors overpromising and underdelivering.

Your role is to keep the conversation focused on outcomes, not resort to defensive justifications. Hence, allow them to express concerns and ensure that you understand them. Then ask yourself if the question is the real issue or whether there is another underlying concern.

You are at the assessment stage, and how you ask questions will be important; if you ask too many questions back, they might get annoyed. However, if you can, probe deeper where possible and add a new, valuable insight for them (see the next section on how to do this).

How they respond with their body language and dialogue is key. If they seem to be disengaging and trying to move on, then you are annoying them. If they are leaning forward and asking you questions back, they are still interested.

> **Note**
>
> Each objection made by the CIO and CISO must be addressed before you can close any deal. Your notes must capture this process, and you should ask for explicit confirmation that all issues have been adequately addressed.

In short, your approach is to focus on the quality of the discussion.

In closing off a discussion, given that your 30-minute meeting is soon ending, your likely goal is to schedule the next meeting and circle back to address any open issues and concerns.

I'd add from my own personal experience, when the CIO or CISO says they need more time or that the decision requires broader stakeholder input then you should resist the instinct to push them.

Instead treat it as an honest signal worth reflecting on. Ask yourself whether you clearly connected your solution to their priorities and whether the right people were in the room. Your concern should be earning the next conversation.

If there is no sales hook for a follow-up meeting, or discussion with subordinates or sponsor for the CIO, then there is cause for concern as there is not a strong enough reason for a follow-up session. The key to keeping sales moving is to always have a concrete reason to follow up and keep the sales pipeline moving. Now let's look at how you can add new, valuable insights when addressing questions.

Bringing valuable insights

You must bring valuable insights at the meeting when there are objections made. What you share should not be just the product features and a full rendition of functionality. The CIO and CISO want you to share broader global and industry thought leadership. They want to hear stories and insights that provide them with data points and sound bites, giving them talking points that they can use and reuse. At this point they are not yet committed to your product or solution, and they are trying to convince themselves that this is the most strategic use of their future capacity.

Some insights that the CIO would want include:

- What are our peers investing in right now?
- Are we overspending or underspending in specific areas?
- How does our risk position compare to similar industry peers?

For most cases, they will already have a view on these questions but want to validate their own theory and assumptions.

> Note
>
> *Good meetings start with focusing on my problem—not every cool feature in the product. Bad meetings start with PowerPoint slides and feature lists. If a vendor immediately aligns to business outcomes and value, I stay engaged. If it's clear they're running the same generic demo they gave 10 other CISOs that week, I mentally check out by minute three.*
>
> **Adam Palmer – CISO, First Hawaiian Bank**

> Note
>
> *First, understand my business, my role in the business, and the likely challenges I might have. Second, provide some genuinely useful options for assistance and don't make them up, as I will ask the tough questions and find out. Third, work more as a partner than simply a profit-making enterprise – think creatively about how we can develop a win-win relationship. Consider the unique value I might provide as a customer – especially given that most often my teams are outstanding contributors and thought leaders. Fourth, provide me with insights that I might not already have – after all, everyone needs ongoing education! But do not start with the free giveaways, as I will always turn away from any potential conflict of interest.*
>
> **Dr Maria Milosavljevic – former ANZ Bank CISO**

The CISO is also interested in these questions, but their questions will be specific to the context of the sale. If you are selling a **cyber threat intelligence (CTI)** service, then their questions may relate to new attack vectors and threat intelligence. If you are selling an **endpoint**

detection and response (EDR) solution, then the question will most likely be related to endpoint attacks such as phishing or malware protections.

Note that at this point in time the CIO and CISO are not that interested in reading business case studies that show the return on investment. This analysis is of interest later as progress is made with your product or service.

> **Tip**
>
> Also remember that the CIO and CISO want to speak to the best practices, so that they can repeat the same to the board and management. This is the path to being a trusted advisor. They may not tell you that they repeated your story to another stakeholder, but they will remember that you told them this valuable piece of information. I'd note that the very best tech salespersons are seen as industry experts first and foremost, that just happen to be representing a particular product now. They are renowned for consistently being able to provide valuable insights, becoming a true trusted advisor.

The insights you share with CIOs and CISOs help justify your positions with data points, and this can help remove emotion and reset challenging expectations to more acceptable levels.

One form of valuable information to share is benchmarking data.

Sharing benchmark data

The power of benchmarking data is that you help them make a better decision. This will help you build trust and the relationship that you seek with them. If you bring it into the conversation with them as an offer, rather than thrusting it upon them, then I'd say you have a better chance of acceptance.

In my career as a CIO and CISO I've valued receiving benchmarking information, but to be totally honest, when I first receive something like this, I look at it with a sceptical eye. My starting position is that this information is probably biased and of limited value.

> **Note**
>
> There are these common contradictory CIO/CISO fears to contend with: I fear being a leader who does not understand technology, but also I fear making decisions that only follow what others have done blindly.
>
> Both are career risks. They want to feel good about making decisions and being able to justify their rationale to their boss, fellow peers, and perhaps the board. There will also be moments when they've been challenged to adopt what *ABC* has done with their strategy.

I'd advise going to them and saying something like the following:

I have some new insightful industry data on the adoption of new AI LLM controls. If you are interested, I can try to access this benchmark information for you?

This approach works because:

- This may already be on their "hot list" of concerns
- Helps them be more educated on a gap that they suspect, but don't have sufficient info on
- Provides political cover for potential budget requests for next year
- Shares data on what their peers are doing

The data can provide an "apples to apples" comparison of best practices, spend, and outcomes. You may also choose to share a few select sound bites that provide an overview of the benchmark.

Note that most of these credible benchmarks are paid services rather than being vendor-based. Of course, I'd not recommend providing benchmark data that is not credible or is an edge case. This will only serve to hurt the trust that you want to build.

> **Tip**
>
> Benchmark data is a tool; only use it as required in the circumstances. I'd say that, given that CIOs and CISOs can be sceptical of such information, use this sparingly—perhaps in cases that make direct sense and at the right time.

The CIO and CISO are very interested in justifying their technology and cyber investments. Despite what you may think, this is not an easy task, as most enterprises have basic or few **cyber risk quantification (CRQ)** processes that are embedded.

Return on investment

A return on investment is what the CIO and CISO both want as the outcome. The technology solution is merely a means to the end. Thus, as you walk in their office, this is what is on the back of their minds. (Note that this topic will be explored in further detail in *Chapter 18, Business Case Approval.*)

This is where the internal champion's assistance is most valued by the CIO and CISO. Return on investment is a contentious topic and there is always competition from different business groups for funding. Hence both the CIO and CISO face a lot of internal conflicts due to the growing size of their combined budget. This spend is likely justified without much understanding of the return on investment.

When this technology investment is aligned with a digital transformation initiative then it is usually easier to gain approval, as this has direct alignment with generation of new revenue and driving market share. These programs and projects are strategically associated with the board and CEO-approved plans. An example is where there is a $5m digital customer channel transformation and included in this is $1m cybersecurity uplift for something like a "passwordless" interface. I've seen many examples of such projects being wrapped into a broader program of work as a project dependency.

Gaining approval for any digital or AI project is easier as the business is playing "offense" and not "defence". There are some very distinct differences between the psychology of this investment, compared with cybersecurity investment. The following table summarizes the 3Bs of Digital AI vs Cyber projects:

3 B's	**Digital AI Project**	**Cybersecurity**
Business Motivation	Return on Investment	Risk Mitigation
Board Driver	Fear of Missing Out (FOMO)	Fear, Uncertainty and Doubt (FUD)
Budget	Capital (Strategic growth)	Opex (Expense)

Table 6.1 - 3B's comparison of Digital AI vs. Cyber projects

The three 3 Bs (Business Motivation, Board Driver, and Budget) in the table contextualize how investments are viewed by the business departments compared to the board and compared to the **Chief Financial Officer (CFO)**. While this is the same project, each stakeholder has a slightly different lens.

Note

A passwordless program is a strong example of this in practice. When evaluated through a cyber risk quantification framework, eliminating password-based authentication can represent a measurable reduction in breach probability, quantified at $1 million or more in risk reduction. Framed that way, it is no longer a security project competing for budget on technical merit alone; it becomes a portfolio investment with a demonstrable return, sitting alongside other capital and operating expenditure decisions and winning on its own terms.

It is important to remember these subtle variations as this can impact the effectiveness of your communications. In contrast to an AI project, gaining approval for a standalone cybersecurity program is a more complex experience. The board and management often do not fully understand what this investment is and how this helps them to avoid loss. The argument is that the investment provides a risk buydown to reduce the likelihood and impact of a new cyber incident. CRQ is the approach used to provide a probability-based analysis of different risk scenarios being successful. Enterprises that have invested in this capability are able to understand how the probability of a certain past attack has been reduced from 15% to, say, 10% using Monte Carlo simulation analysis.

Note

This methodology measures cybersecurity risks in financial terms, allowing enterprises to understand their potential cyber losses in dollars (rather than just qualitative ratings like "high", "medium", or "low").

CRQ calculates metrics like **Annual Loss Expectancy (ALE)**, and this can help the CIO and CISO provide a common language that can help bridge the communication gap between security teams and executives/board members.

This approach can assist the board to prioritise security investments based on which risks pose the greatest financial threat and to determine how much to spend on different security controls. Then the business can make investment decisions based on risk appetite.

Taking first base

You have started your dialogue with the CIO and CISO; it is not yet a win and while you feel that progress has been made, this is not the time to celebrate. Your hope is that the CIO and CISO have marked that meeting as "useful," and if that is the case, then you have achieved first base.

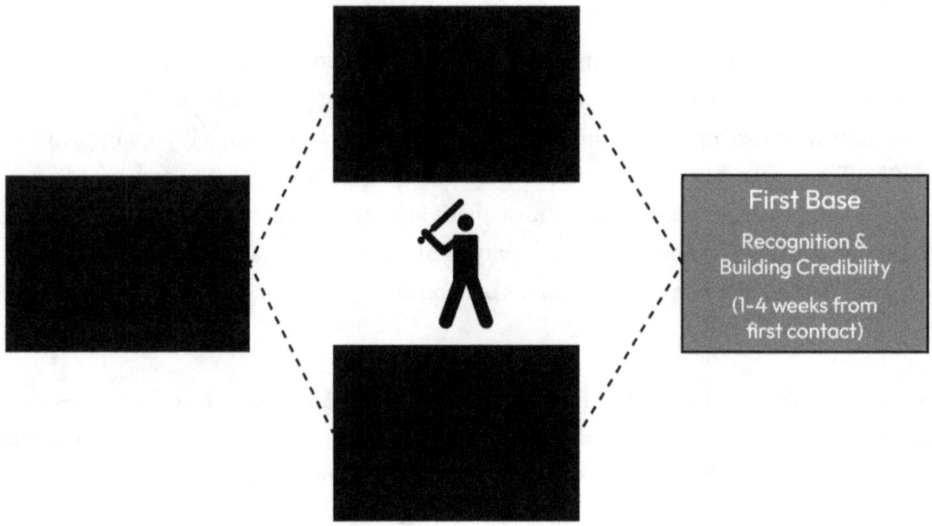

Figure 6.3 - Taking first base

Note

A good vendor interaction feels like this:

- Here's what we're seeing in the field.

- Here's where we win, and here's where we lose.

- Here's the maturity level we fit best.

- Here are the metrics customers achieved and what it took operationally.

Sam Ghebranious – Director, Axcelerate/Senior Advisor, Frost & Sullivan

Getting to first base has taken some effort. Allow me to summarise what this required:

- Planning your agenda ahead of the meeting
- An effective first 60 seconds to build executive presence
- Building your confidence
- Being ready for objections
- Providing the insights the CIO and CISO really care about

This whole process will feel like an accomplishment as you have been trying to gain recognition and build your own credibility. You are now motivated to look ahead and consider how you get to "second base" and what is required to achieve this.

In the meantime, another batter has come to make a hit with the CIO and CISO. There is real competition in this game, and competitors are also as motivated as you are and want to achieve the same end goal. Now how do you proceed to second base?

> **Note**
>
> While I'm not a massive baseball fan, I've seen the Kobe Hanshin Tigers and New York Yankees respectively play at their home stadiums – both are awesome teams. I learned that baseball is a game of strategy and tactics; a team sport but also based on individual performance. A good vendor interaction feels like this.

First base brings a humbling realization that you know far less about how the CIO and CISO truly think than you assumed. The closer you get, the more clearly you see that their world is more complex, more pressured, and more nuanced than you considered. In the next chapter, we deep dive into their perspective, the foundation everything else is built on to help you move your relationship with them forward.

Summary

In this chapter, we explored how once you have gotten into the room with a CIO or CISO, that is the start and not an end to celebrate. The access to them is hard-won—and the first 60 seconds can either validate all that preparation or undo it instantly. Your meeting with them is won or lost on soft skills: executive presence, active listening, and your ability to demonstrate you already understand their problem before they have explained it.

Remember, the goal of a first meeting isn't to close anything; it's to be marked "useful" and earn the right to a second conversation. This is still first base.

The key learnings from this chapter are:

- **Read the room in the first 60 seconds** – should the CIO/CISO signal they are under pressure, skip small talk and get straight to the point (emotional intelligence here builds more goodwill than any polished opening).
- **Learn to project executive presence and confidence** – be careful not to be seen as cocky or arrogant, however.
- **Handle objections by probing deeper, not defending** – ask "are you ok if I ask a few more questions on this?"
- **Share valuable data with them, such as benchmark data** – offer it as resource, use it sparingly and only when it directly addresses a known priority gap.

Part 2 (Second Base)

Problem Validation and Trust

In this second part of the book, you will move beyond getting in the room and into the harder, more consequential work of validating the problem and earning genuine trust. I will explore how to see the world through the eyes of the CIO and CISO: their dual mandates, competing metrics, and the external events that can reprioritise everything overnight, before stepping into the shoes of the architect, whose influence on your deal is often invisible until it isn't. You'll learn how to conduct a gap analysis before the client does theirs, how to navigate the organisational politics that derail more deals than poor products ever will, and how to use analysts, peer validation, and benchmark data to build the credibility that carries you through a proof of concept (POC) or proof of value (POV).

I will also confront the harder strategic questions: when to recommend best of breed solutions, when a package makes more sense, and how AI is disrupting both simultaneously. I have included two detailed case studies to close this part; one on major transformation sells where three buyers speak three different languages, and one on the costly ambiguity that surfaces when ownership is unclear. By the end of this part, you'll have the frameworks and the judgment to validate problems with precision and start to build trust that holds under pressure.

This part of the book includes the following chapters:

- *Chapter 7, Deep Dive Into the CIO and CISO Perspective*
- *Chapter 8, Stepping Into the Shoes of the Architect*
- *Chapter 9, Gap Analysis*
- *Chapter 10, Navigating the Maze of Politics*
- *Chapter 11, The Value of Research Analysts and Advisors*
- *Chapter 12, Proof Positive*
- *Chapter 13, Packages vs. Best of Breed Solutions (vs. AI)*
- *Chapter 14, Selling Into a Major Transformation*
- *Chapter 15, When Ownership is Unclear*

7

Deep Dive Into the CIO and CISO Perspective

The CIO and CISO are always busy and not just calendar busy. Their minds are constantly processing competing demands, strategic pressures, and organizational noise. When you arrive to sell, you enter that world without a map. You do not know what is truly on their mind or which of their many priorities is the one that matters most right now. That gap between what you assume and what they are thinking is where most deals are lost before they even begin. In today's enterprises there are two major business priorities, that are strategically driving digital and AI technology to enable transformation, while maintaining operations and ensuring cybersecurity and resilience.

These two objectives of going fast and being safe are in inherent conflict, like you are trying to put both your feet on the accelerator and brakes at the same time. Executives face extreme commercial pressure to operate within this paradox, managing what amounts to a dual mandate.

New technologies must be adopted without extensive proof points or while risk frameworks are still being built. While your resources are already stretched with existing approved priorities, there is incredible pressure on internal teams to keep up with these new demands and requirements too.

CIOs and CISOs are expected to lead at a speed that is taking their own breath away and is beyond their personal risk tolerance. As a senior employee with short-term incentives at risk, this becomes challenging. The culture of enterprises is such that if they resist, they risk being seen as the department of "No". This can limit career opportunities in the short and medium term of the CIO, CISO and even the internal champion.

However, I've seen firsthand that the board and management offer little support to the CIO or CISO who fails to align with organizational priorities and even less sympathy when the reason is resource constraints or pace of change. The CIO and CISO are expected to deliver regardless, which is precisely why the vendor who helps them close that gap, rather than adding to it, is worth more than any feature set can convey.

In *Chapter 5* we explored the preparation needed before walking into the office of a CIO or CISO. Any prep you complete is useful but ultimately incomplete, because you will never fully understand how they think until you get inside their head. That is exactly what this chapter does. We step into the mind of a CIO and CISO and explore the many voices echoing around in there.

In this chapter we cover the topics that will turn you from a fortune teller into a mind reader. Rather than guessing what a CIO or CISO requires, you will learn to analyse how they think and where your solution genuinely fits. I explore understanding CIO and CISO strategy, reading the mind of both executives, their career concerns, why current industry trends shape their priorities, how budget cycles and approval processes influence decisions, and the polylemma that sits at the heart of every CIO and CISO role. By the end you will have a good chance of knowing what they need.

The topics we will cover in this chapter are:

- Understanding the CIO and CISO strategy
- Reading the CIO's and CISO's mind
- CIO and CISO career concerns
- Why current industry trends matter
- Budget cycles and approval processes
- The polylemma of the CIO and CISO

Understanding the CIO and CISO strategies

As a vendor (or as an internal champion) your objective is to understand the CIO and CISO's strategy. Once aligned, you are best positioned to assist these leaders in shaping the future direction.

Of course, the challenge is that the CIOs and CISOs are often guarded and may not be willing to share their personal ideas, as these may not be approved and budgeted. In this scenario your goal is to understand where they are in their strategic refresh cycle and when that plan can be shared. Note of course that this strategy process varies from company to company in terms of timing and intensity of effort.

While this might seem simple, it is often difficult to gain that understanding. Most strategies are shared on a need-to-know basis and only once they are fully approved. In truth, most strategies are high-level and are agile due to the dynamic nature of the IT and threat landscape. Some organizations also treat strategies as a living document and will have it updated regularly and as required. For many CIOs and CISOs, the planning horizon requirement is mandated by the CFO and their planning team.

> Note
>
> *I can do the three-year strategy, but in a dynamic environment with a lot of change it's like wishing, even 18 months is sketchy. This is why my teams are focused on the first six months, but they can see where we're going.*
>
> *They like it because they have a better enterprise view of where they sit in all the projects and running services around them. It helps them understand what they are working on and where the company and its business units are going.*
>
> *Doing a three-year strategy to me doesn't make sense. It's good from a financial standpoint to see what resources and funding you believe you will need, but then realistically, it's hard to be confident about what's happening 3 years out. I usually do 18 months, and my team and I work in 6-month sprints, because you go ahead and you do an assessment, whether you're doing NIST or whatever you're using to baseline yourself so that the board's satisfied you are providing them a report which shows the current baseline of the company's identified risks and how the business measures against competitors or peers. "Here are the areas where we are immature," and it's here I break those areas down into projects. "These are the things that we're going to be working on over the next 6 months."*
>
> *So, I use that data to provide an 18-month timeline, and I make sure that the board understands this is flexible. We're doing it in 6-month sprints, and we may need to adjust this depending on the business.*
>
> **Gary Hayslip – CISO Halcyon.ai, Board Director, and Investor**

Note that in evaluating a new solution, as part of their overall strategy, CIOs and CISOs need to be able to see how this fits within their big picture, from a 10,000-foot level, while also evaluating the solution more closely. This movement from strategic intent, to addressing a business gap, to then adopting a new solution can feel like a significant leap of faith.

> Note
>
> *I look for what is working somewhere on the planet. Chances are I am not the first person with this problem—maybe in another country or another industry but looking for what good looks like is key. This helps inform the strategy and will then influence the shortlist. You are rarely evaluating a solution on tech spec alone—factors such as the vendor track record, including informal references and commercials, are key.*
>
> **Gerard Florian – former Group Executive & CIO, ANZ Bank**

While the stakeholders and peers of the CIO and CISO recognize these pressures, they are unlikely to support any deceleration of progress. Let's return to the "Carrots and Sticks" analogy I referred to in *Chapter 2*—what motivates the CIO and CISO is progress and metrics that measure their achievements.

What metrics tell you about the CIO and CISO

Metrics are the clearest indicators of what is on a CIO and CISO's mind. Therefore, they are worth paying attention to—what they are being measured on—so that you can address these with your solution. For example, does your solution improve the trajectory, or worsen it as attention is diverted from other priorities?

Metrics can be confidential and sensitive, so it is not easy to gain access to these artifacts, but I can outline the most common types in broad terms by reflecting on my experience as a CIO and CISO in the banking sector. Let's explore what metrics look like in a typical enterprise. The CIO and CISO will often have these metrics imposed upon them by the board, management, and the risk committee.

The following diagram shows the natural hierarchy of KRIs, KCIs, KPIs, and OKRs that exist within enterprises:

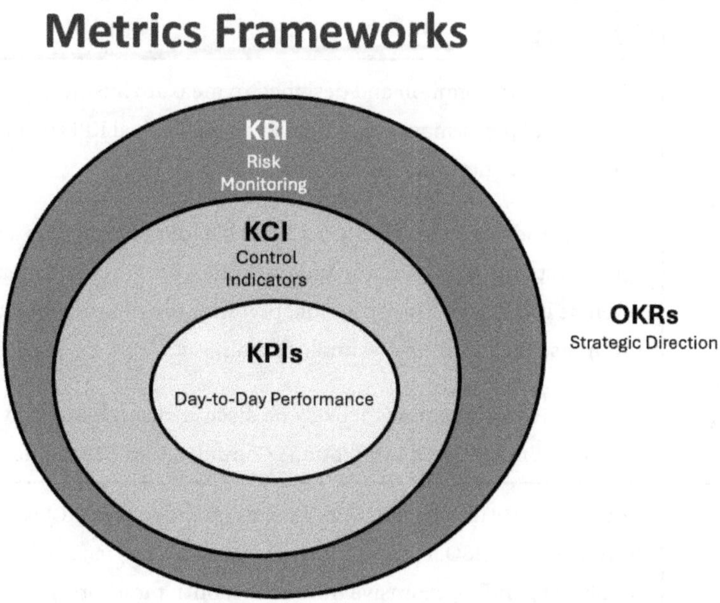

Figure 7.1 - What metrics matter to the CIO and CISO

This hierarchy mirrors how decisions flow through an organization. KPIs measure what is happening today, KCIs confirm that the controls enabling that performance are functioning correctly, and KRIs provide the forward-looking risk context that the board and audit committee speak in.

OKRs sit deliberately outside the operational circles entirely because they do not measure how well the organization is running; they define where it is trying to go.

In the enterprise, the CIO and CISO have a series of key measures that they are accountable to deliver. Usually, the metrics are tied to their performance objectives; therefore, there is likely a direct correlation to the bonus that they receive.

Allow me to explain how this help you understand exactly how much skin is in the game for the CIO and CISO:

Metric	Description
KPIs (Key Performance Indicators)	These are very common and designed to measure business health and operational performance on a regular basis. Typical KPIs include employee turnover or digital channel conversion rate. The CIO and CISO are directly accountable for these metrics and therefore are expected to both monitor and track their progress. KPI measures will often be included in their personal performance plans; hence, these are often cascaded to all the technology team. For the CIO, KPI reports will likely be discussed at the monthly governance meetings, including the Operations Committee and Technology Committee.
KCIs (Key Control Indicators)	These indicate if a control is working as intended. The KCI is the "bread and butter" of the CISO. I know this from my own experience in the role, which involved spending extensive time each month monitoring cyber and technology controls and the progress of remediation, then attending 2-3 Key Control Effectiveness meetings to ensure that these plans were being adhered to as expected. The CISO will be closely monitoring KCIs on Vulnerability Patch Management, MFA Adoption rates and Security Awareness Training. These metrics are all included in the board and management reporting and usually on an exception basis, which means a KCI is reported if it is not effective. CIOs, on the other hand, will pay attention to KCI metrics that measure operational stability, including outages and incident response. The CIO radar has a strong bias to avoid business disruption and that motivates these executives' behaviour.

Metric	Description
KRIs (Key Risk Indicators) 	These are the metrics used by the board to measure risk appetite; hence, their purpose is to provide a metric that demonstrates that the enterprise is operating within or outside of the stated risk tolerance objective. These metrics can be highly political, as they are used by the board and are accordingly very sensitive even within the enterprise.
OKRs (Objectives and Key Results) 	These have been around since the 1970s, with Intel and Google using this framework extensively. In current practice, there will likely be 3-5 OKR measures, cascaded from top down. These are enterprise-wide ambitious goals emanating from the CEO and board. OKRs are designed to "stretch" the enterprise and the executives to strive for market growth or net promoter scores or leading customer experience. OKRs are often discussed in press briefings by the CEO and board members as their strategic ambitions that are measuring their new strategy. As such, these measures are usually widely known, not at all confidential. They are designed to drive alignment in the enterprise, however, are usually decoupled from personal performance reviews hence may not be a major focus for the CISO.

Table 7.1 - KPI v KCI v KRI vs OKRs

There are many metrics that the CIO and CISO will need to produce; however, only some of the measures are vital from their own points of view. And not surprisingly, what they prioritize is very different. In the following graph, I have plotted these four categories of metrics and their relative importance to each executive:

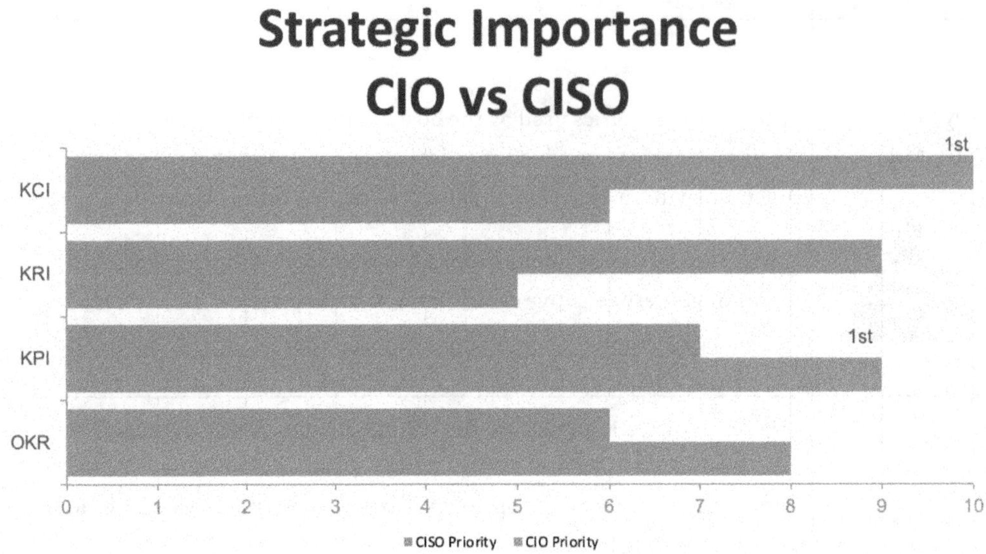

Figure 7.2 - How the CIO and CISO prioritize metrics

Understanding the strategic importance of these different metrics is essential, as it allows you to identify exactly which data points are most relevant to your key stakeholders.

First, the average CIO and CISO will be usually inundated with different metrics that are required for various governance forums. The trick is to learn which they really care about and want to move the dial on.

Also in reality, as a vendor your access will be limited to a small subset of this information, essentially only what the executives are willing to share. These could perhaps include service level agreement (SLA)-specific KPIs, service performance metrics, and relevant operational data for their own service. Specific OKR, KRI, KCI metrics and any internal performance dashboards are usually off limits as they expose weaknesses that competitors or threat actors could take advantage of.

Given the sensitive nature of this information, if you can gain some insights into any of this content, this is a win and it can provide some valuable insights into where the management is paying attention. You can therefore figure out how your proposed solution aligns or doesn't align with this direction.

Note

In practice, most organizations use KPIs as their foundation, add OKRs for strategic initiatives, and embed KCIs/KRIs depending on their industry's operational and regulatory complexity.

Financial services and healthcare (where I have worked in my professional career) typically need robust KRI frameworks, while tech startups might focus more heavily on KPIs and OKRs.

Internal champions may have near full access to these metrics. However, they will still require a conversation with the CIO and CISO to understand what is dominating their attention span. As we will discuss, there are often competing pressures and usually too many metrics that can splinter their focus. The CIO and CISO will often pay most attention to their personal preferences, but when there are polylemma (multiple) pressures, you may spot this in the metrics with the degree of divergent measures that the CIO and CISO are being held accountable to. For example:

Metric	How it's measured	Value Proposition
Metric 1	90% of projects delivered on time	Speed
Metric 2	Regulatory Compliance %	Compliance
Metric 3	Emergency Patching (unplanned work)	Security

Table 7.2 - Polylemma pressures example

Identifying the metrics they care about is your assignment. This knowledge is vital for your pitch because the CIO and CISO are under constant pressure to show progress in a domain that their peers often struggle to understand. This goes back to being curious when having that conversation about which dials they want to move. This is where a CIO and CISO can start to disclose they are worried about a specific metric. For example, a metric for "change failure" rate, which will measure how fast the team recovers from a change-induced outage. This metric should be kept below 15%, and if your technology can provide automation to address this gap, then this is a potential opportunity.

To help you uncover these priorities when you are meeting with the CIO and CISO, here are a few questions that can help you gain these clues:

- Is development security (DevSecOps) a priority now?
- How are you tracking the Change Failure Rate as a joint KPI to ensure that security checks aren't becoming a bottleneck for your digital growth?
- How are you balancing the "Run vs. Change" ratio?
- Are you prioritising the retirement of legacy core systems, or are you more focused on digital channels?
- Given new regulatory requirements, has this changed the priority of resilience over prevention focus?

To provide some context, there are many CIOs (in banking particularly) that focus on speed and stability. For a typical enterprise, you may be able to discover the following KPI, KCI, KRI and OKR metrics for the CIO.

Metric	**How is it measured?**	**Target**
Running the organization vs Change Ratio (KPI)	Percentage of IT budget allocated to run-the-business activities versus change-the-business initiatives, tracked through budget categorization and project portfolio reporting	< 60% Run
Backup and Recovery Testing (KCI)	Frequency and success rate of tested recovery procedures	100%
Unplanned Outage Frequency (KRI)	Number of unplanned outages breaching agreed tolerance thresholds per quarter	Zero critical incidents
AI Transformation Progress (OKR)	Percentage of defined AI initiatives delivered against board-approved roadmap	Set by board

Table 7.3 – CIO Metrics for Speed and Stability

The CIO must achieve these metrics while working with extensive legacy technology, making the challenge formidable. This makes the budget spend hard to free up from operational spend and be reallocated to project investment. Even a 99.999% uptime still converts into 5 minutes of outage per year, which is tough.

The CISO, on the other hand, will typically have KPI, KRI, KCI and OKR metrics that cover key measures that demonstrate stability and security. Here is an example:

Metric	How is it Measured?	Target
Mean time to recovery (MTTR) (KPI)	Average time measured from incident detection to full service restoration, tracked through incident management and reported as a rolling average across all priority (P)1 and P2 incidents	< 2 Hours
Third-Party Risk Score (KRI)	Percentage of third-party vendors assessed against the organization's vendor risk framework within the defined review cycle	100% 3rd party reviewed
Multifactor authentication (MFA) Identity Health (KCI)	Percentage of user accounts with MFA enforced and actively verified as operational across all identity providers, measured through identity governance	95–100%
Cyber Resilience (OKR)	Validated through quarterly red team exercises, penetration testing results, and incident management reporting	<4 Hours MTTR

Table 7.4 - CISO Metrics for Stability and Security

The key is that you understand what kinds of metrics CIOs and CISOs are judged on and how your solution helps to improve these data points.

Both the CIO and CISO will be asked to frame their concerns with existing frameworks used by the business. Let me explain these approaches, so that you can better understand how you could support their efforts.

Value stream mapping

This approach is popular with enterprises that are undergoing large-scale process transformation. With this approach, the existing processes are mapped end to end, then the value extracted is visualized. This can include new cybersecurity and resilience requirements added into the new process map.

> **Note**
>
> Value stream mapping is a lean methodology that can be traced back to the Toyota Production System.
>
> To learn more, see `https://www.lean.org/lexicon-terms/value-stream-mapping/`.

Impact vs. risk framework

Most enterprises operate an existing risk framework (see *Figure 7.3*) where there is an assessment of impact and likelihood. All the major programs and projects are plotted onto this portfolio with other non-tech initiatives. The ideal is to seek the business impact with the lowest risk exposure.

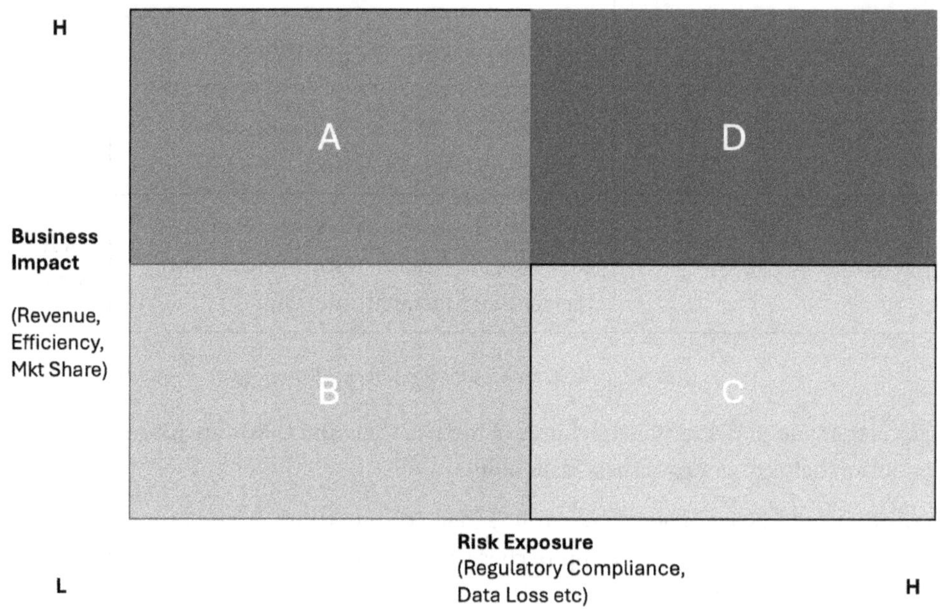

Figure 7.3 - Impact vs. Risk Framework

In this framework, projects that have business benefits and low risk are the most desired. The CIO will gravitate to the "Green" zone (A and B quadrants) where they can make the greatest impact on the business. On the other hand, the CISO will naturally want to reduce the largest risks, which can gravitate them to the D and C quadrants.

> **Note**
>
> *I'm not buying software — I'm buying a measurable improvement to my risk posture. Show me where I sit today, where your solution moves the needle, and how that maps to the frameworks I'm accountable to. Everything else is noise.*
>
> **Samir Sherif – Global Field CISO, Fastly; Investor and Board Director**

The CIO and CISO may not favor a particular approach and will probably prefer to get things done with the minimum governance, which is commonly seen by them, in my experience, as a "hand brake". The key lesson here is understanding the content that the CIO and CISO want to use in their business case.

It is unlikely that they will directly request this material, especially given the governance complexity of gaining approval. They need content in business language that is risk-framed and provides competitive context.

Supporting their business case

Any program and project that is approved must have a business case. This is a barrier required by governance processes, and there are some parts to this process that you can assist the CIO and CISO with.

The typical business case that the CIO and CISO must complete for approval includes a lot of details, but a template will look something like this:

Business Case	**Explanation**
Executive Summary	Short summary of the business case
Business Problem	Outlines the gap with the current situation
Strategic Alignment	Alignment with the approved business objectives
Proposed Approach	A non-technical explanation of the proposed solution detailing how this addresses the current gap
Financial Analysis	ROI, NPV, Payback assumptions according to enterprise standard approaches
Success Metrics	What outcomes are expected and how are these measured in the short and medium term

Business Case	Explanation
Alternatives	This summarizes the other options that were considered
Board Action	Review and approve as per governance framework

Table 7.5 - Business case template

Let's take two examples from the CIO and CISO world that add some colour to this stage of the process. There is a growing concern about business resilience and cyber resilience to help ensure operational sales and growth expectations can be achieved.

Many enterprises have assumed that their backups are safe from cyber-attacks, and there is a growing investment into establishing tertiary data backups that are segregated from production systems.

> **Note**
>
> When I was at HSBC, we implemented one of the very first "air gapped" (isolated) tertiary backups that covered their crown jewels (most critical assets) and we had full backups of these production systems. As this investment was significant you can imagine that the business case was highly scrutinized.

The following table highlights some of the key components where the tech and cyber sales vendor ("Vendor A") can assist with providing more historical incident context in relation to these concerns, taking the threat of ransomware as an example:

Ransomware Resilience - Business Case
Executive Summary *Uplift the business operational resilience by implementation of new systems and processes that fundamentally* transform *the Restore and Recovery processes with a* tertiary backup *that meets new SLA requirements.*
Business Problem *In our industry, the incidence of ransomware attacks is accelerating, with 2x over the last 12 months. These events have disrupted operations for many of our own competitors. The current backup solutions are unable to guarantee the recovery time objective that Regulators and our Stakeholders are expecting.*

Ransomware Resilience - Business Case
Strategic Alignment *Business Objective - Safely grow business and* maintain *stable operations*
Proposed Approach *Implement a new* immutable backup infrastructure, EDR solution and enhanced incident response capabilities from Vendor A.
→**Financial Analysis** *Infrastructure $20m operating expense* *Payback: 1.4 years*
→**Success Metrics** *Expected loss without: $80m ransom cost + recovery cost +* lost *business opportunity* *Risk reduction value: $12M*
Alternatives *Do nothing, Vendor B, and Vendor C*

Table 7.6 – Ransomware business case example

I've marked with two arrows where Vendor A can provide external insights that could make the most difference.

The benchmarking data on ransomware incidents and average recovery times from these events is useful – if you do your homework, you should be able to provide them with this. Similarly, success and financial metrics that have been achieved can provide a degree of confidence for the business case team.

This next example is one that the CIO would be more familiar with and therefore most likely to sponsor. Many enterprises suffer from a gap in their customer data foundations, often maintaining four or five separate, non-integrated databases.

In the era of AI, there are new opportunities to create new markets and explore micro segmentation. However, the lack of a single view of the customer will be a barrier to this opportunity. The following example business case will be very common given the new focus on AI by the board and management:

Customer Data Foundation for AI - Business Case
Executive Summary *A Customer Data Foundation is required to grow our business and take advantage of existing clients that have current business with our enterprise. There is also an opportunity to grow new markets from AI analysis of these customer segments.*
Business Problem *Our business operations have fragmented data analysis capabilities, and the single view of the customer is lacking. As a result, AI-enabled marketing to seek further new business opportunities is constrained. In addition, new privacy laws require a single view of the customer to provide as an "on demand" request.*
Strategic Alignment *Business Objective - Make strategic business decisions based on data.*
Proposed Approach *Implement a program for unified customer data with help from Vendor A.*
→Financial Analysis *Infrastructure $8m operating expense* *Payback: 3.5 years*
→Success Metrics *Share of customer wallet - increases from X to Z*
Alternatives *Do nothing, Vendor B, and Vendor C*

Table 7.7 – Customer data foundation business case example

Again, Vendor A can add considerable value by sharing examples of financial benefits and success metrics from other client sites.

Many enterprises recognize that their Customer Data Foundation is lacking, yet they remain reluctant to invest due to the longer-term return that is expected. This program of work is understood to be universal but is unattractive due to the degree of technology debt and the organizational friction that this will require. Now the new AI focus has reinforced the need to address this gap and allow offensive data strategies to be enabled.

In both business case examples, you will see that there are references to "Business impact" and to "Risk exposure". The mind of the CIO and CISO will likely be split between these, as well as other concerns, driving what they are focusing on at any one point in time.

Reading the CIO's mind

CIOs are not thinking about your product or service. Instead, their time is consumed by a few "north stars," strategic priorities that remain at the front of their minds. In a lot of cases, the CIO will have been asked by their manager and the board to drive enterprise change and enable competitive advantage.

> Note
>
> *If you're selling to CIOs, you should know how CIOs think.*
>
> **Matt Boon – Senior Director, Strategic Research, Adapt**

There is a common theme of **revenue and business velocity,** that the CIO is under extraordinary pressure to deliver. In recent years, CIOs have been asked to drive the business platform transformation, with a specific focus on simplifying the tech stack. This translates into reducing the number of moving parts in play and buying integrated products.

Most recently however, the focus has shifted to now asking the CIO to make AI successful. This means using AI technology to both increase revenue and reduce costs.

Here's an example of some "north stars" driving the CIO:

Cost savings	Delivery
Enable New AI Revenue	Deliver Business Transformation
Cost savings from integration	Retirement of Legacy Technology

Cost savings	Delivery
AI Productivity Savings	Data Integration Foundations

Table 7.8 - Example CIO north stars

These are the result of pressure from each of the CIO's stakeholders as well as factors such as what career stage they are in and perhaps also how their executive remuneration has been structured. (There may be a direct connection between a CIO north star and what their reward package has defined as success.)

Let's look at who influences CIOs the most:

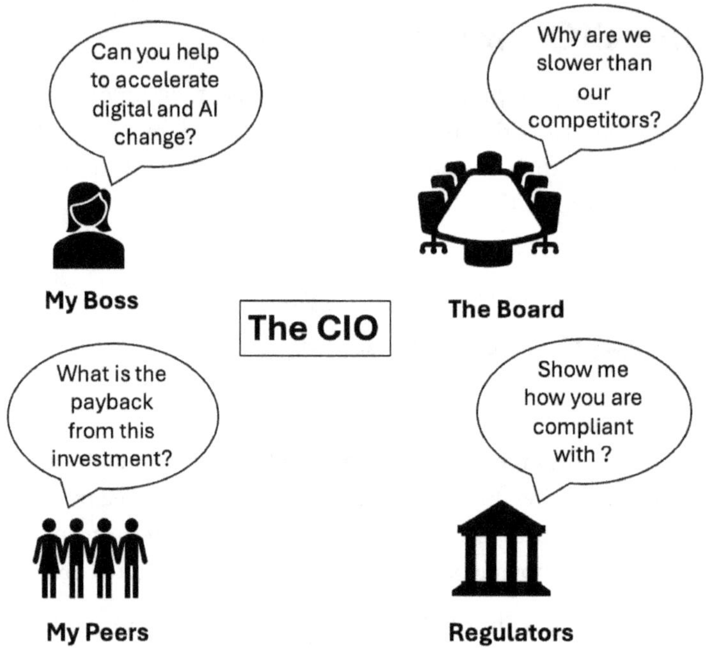

Figure 7.4 - Who influences the CIO the most

Each of their questions may have some degree of overlap but also, each of them has a particular perspective that matters to them.

I'm sure that these are not a surprise, but what is subtly different are the primary questions that they will be asking the CIO to address. In addition, the CIO will have a few of their own personal influencers that will drive their view on how they think and act.

The CIO is constantly switching between competing priorities, emerging incidents, and the kind of urgent organisational noise that can consume their mental bandwidth before the working day has properly begun. A regulatory deadline lands on the same morning as a critical system outage, for example, or an urgent board request arrives in the middle of a vendor negotiation.

This is the CIO's real work. This means that the vendor who shows up with a fixed pitch and an expectation that the conversation will follow the structure they prepared for will most likely be surprised.

> Note
>
> *For the vendors who invested time and were there during the quiet times as well as the "spend cycles" - I would always say the following. I don't like playing battleships - the kids' game where you try and guess the coordinates of hidden battleships (where I hide my strategy and vendors have to try and guess where the deals are).*
>
> *I would rather turn things around and show partners where the "battleships" or opportunities are. I will also say—I want you to think about some opportunities, but for others, I already have a good partner; don't waste your time and mine there.*
>
> **Gerard Florian – former ANZ Bank Group Executive & CIO**

Reading the CISO's mind

The CISO, as you would now expect, has a very different perspective and their own set of "north stars". In theory, the CISO's north stars are aligned with the CIO's, however I'd argue that there are many circumstances where this may not be the case.

> Note
>
> *Internally, successful pitches are based on alignment to priorities and strategy. If someone pitches a new security tool but can't connect it to our strategy and show how it is reducing risk or improving a key business function, it's a hard sell. I look for value to our business and risk reduction goals, not "Here's a cool new tool."*
>
> *The biggest mistake internally? Assuming I can wave a wand to fund or approve things without lots of other approvers. The CISO doesn't bypass the process; it's often just the first major step. I'm a gatekeeper to the larger approval process that has many people involved before any large investment is approved.*
>
> **Adam Palmer – CISO, First Hawaiian Bank**

CISOs generally realize that their job is nearly impossible and the question is when they will be breached, not if. For them, what's top of mind is the difficulty of their job and legislation that holds them with personal accountability for a major incident. Hence, it is not surprising that the CISO has an ongoing focus on how they can limit the blast radius (a metaphor taken from explosives in military terms, about containing the potential impact of any rogue bomb).

CISOs don't like to think about Cybersecurity Insurance and Directors and Officers Insurance (D&O), which are only invoked after a major cyber incident. Such a case may lead to their own role being eliminated too. Instead, the CISO will think about how any incident, even a minor one, can impact their own career opportunity in the longer term. In the event of a major incident, if they keep their jobs, their bonus and incentive plans will be negatively impacted in the short term at least.

The CISO cares about both Operational Resilience and their own Resilience. You must consider how your solution or service can help them achieve both objectives. Clearly their own Resilience is never going to be a topic that you as a Tech and Cyber sales vendor can raise directly; however, being aware of this means that your messaging can also infer how your solution will allow them to sleep well at night.

> Note
>
> *As a CISO, you have legal obligations and these are paramount. Many people do not understand how a CISO often needs to walk a fine line because accountability in decision-making matters—a lot. There must be a good reason to invest time and money into something—it must matter and it must solve a problem that is a priority.*
>
> *There are countless problems to solve but they are not all priorities! If it's an important risk that is being addressed by the initiative but it is being addressed sufficiently already without that initiative, and will continue to be well-addressed for a reasonable time into the future, then I should be investing in areas where important risks are not fully under control or where there is a likelihood they will increase beyond tolerance levels in a short time period.*
>
> *Further to the above, many people do not understand that security risks are constantly changing. So CISOs MUST continually scan the external and internal environment to assess how these risks are changing or may change based on many different indicators.*
>
> *This means that what was the top priority last week might not be this week. And CISOs also need to continually judge how much is enough – we can't afford to overinvest in one area while underinvesting in other equally important areas. It's a constant juggle.*
>
> **Dr Maria Milosavljevic – former ANZ Bank CISO**

Here's an example of some north stars driving the CISO:

Risk reduction	Strategy
Address Largest Risks	Deliver Cyber Transformation
Cyber Control Remediation	Retirement of Legacy Technology
Design New AI Controls	Focus on Secure by Design

Table 7.8 - Example CISO north stars

You can see that in both CIO and CISO north stars, "Retirement of Legacy Technology" is commonly desired by both parties. While their reasons for wanting to support this may be different, the result is that it is a plus to their business case if you are able to enable this benefit.

> Note
>
> *If you believe in your product's value to the CISO and the organization(s) he defends, be patient and professional, listen more and speak when it's impactful. Have a plan—test it with colleagues and your customer(s) to validate the path to the outcomes expected. CISOs will need time to source budget, align your solution to their strategy and gain support from their stakeholders for the value increase and risk reduction goals that will be achieved.*
>
> **Mark Trumble – Cyber Sales and Solutions leader**

The CISO answers to many. Despite often having a reporting line to the CIO, the strategic and sensitive nature of cybersecurity means direct questions come from every corner of the organization and beyond. From my own experience, the heat on the CISO is considerably more intense than anything directed at the CIO. Many CIOs quietly acknowledge that cybersecurity is all downside and will, often instinctively, seek to limit their own exposure. They are managing their blast radius. Knowing this gives you a sharper, more empathetic lens when engaging with both leaders.

Let's look at who most influences CISOs:

Figure 7.5 - Who influences the CISO the most

This graphic looks similar to the CIO example, but I'd argue that these voices are all louder, stronger, and more emotional. I've never seen these stakeholders relax the pressure on the CISO.

Theoretically, each of these parties is a potential engagement that you can consider in influencing the CISO; however, this approach won't be welcomed by the CISO.

CIO and CISO career concerns

The CIO and CISO north stars I've raised are also impacted by private thoughts around their own **remuneration** and the **career stage** that they are in. Frankly, this is even more opaque and therefore harder to detect.

Remember we are all human and subject to our own fears and desires. This may be latent but comes into what is at the back of the CIO and CISO's mind. Therefore, this can have a significant impact on their actions and decisions.

Note

There is a joke that circulates quietly among technology leaders that captures the precariousness of these roles better than any statistic could:

CIO = Career Is Over.

CISO = Career Is Soon Over.

Behind the humour is a truth that every CIO and CISO carries into every significant decision they make. These are roles where the downside is disproportionate to the upside. They are very conscious that their success is largely invisible, but failure is very public. The vendor who understands the weight of that joke is operating at a different level than the one who has never stopped to consider what it actually feels like to sit in that chair.

The direct accountability these roles face can be ruthless and very direct. I would highlight also that the CIO and CISO must deal with the emotional and mental strain of working hard and under much stress.

In terms of remuneration for the CIO and CISO, being a Senior Executive usually means that their package includes fixed and variable salary with bonus and stock options. I myself have regarded these as being akin to "golden cufflinks". What I mean by that is yes, I will pay attention and care for this as an incentive, but I have also been cognizant that my career is not necessarily long term with the enterprise.

Note

You start getting through that plateau area and it's like, I've got a mortgage, I've got kids, I've got private school. I don't want to rock the boat, that kind of thing... I think that tends to lead to stagnation from an innovation point of view in a lot of organisations as that bench gets full of that.

Matt Boon – Senior Director, Strategic Research, Adapt

In pure math terms, the variable part of the package is usually in the range of 40-100% of the total package. There is a recognition that some of this may be lost if you change roles or that this is negotiated with the next employer.

The bonus component can be impacted by negative clawback if there are major issues after the departure of an executive. Hence, there is often a percentage of every bonus that is retained and vests over a few years.

Each CIO and CISO will be thinking about their potential exit in x number of years and how they want to tie their performance to a particular stage. For instance, a CIO will want to deliver innovative digital and AI change that positively uplifts the stock price (the north stars I mentioned earlier). Thus, there is a bias toward programs and projects that have a shorter-term payback.

The CISO, on the other hand, will want to ensure that during their tenure they avoid any major incident. This can lead to them having a bias toward higher cost short-term fixes, although these may not be meeting other goals of integration and reducing complexity. I've seen myself and worked with peers who at times made strange decisions that did not appear aligned to the objectives that had been agreed.

The following graphic presents how different career stages are aligned with the CIO and CISO's own thinking about remuneration. As you progress through different stages, motivations can change, and what is valued also shifts.

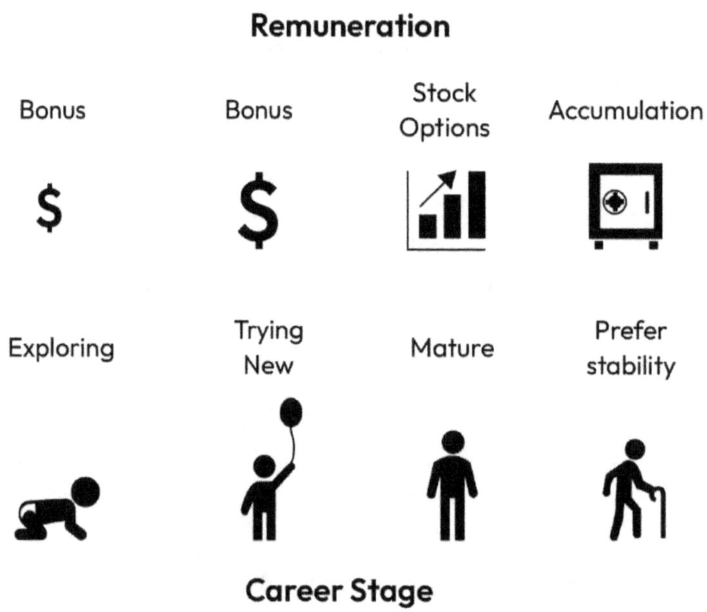

Figure 7.6 - The influence of remuneration and career stage

Not every CIO and CISO thinks the same way, and career stage is one of the biggest reasons why. Their motivations around remuneration and personal values shift as they move through different stages of their careers, as we discussed previously.

Early on, they are building; in the middle, they are establishing. Later, they are protecting. As a vendor, if you walk in with the same pitch regardless of where your executive sits in their journey, you are leaving opportunity on the table. The smartest vendors read career stage as carefully as they read company strategy. It tells you what your CIO or CISO values most right now, and that is exactly where your conversation should begin.

Taking a cynical view, the average CIO and CISO are sometimes not building toward a long-term vision but instead have a bias toward delivering results that provide immediate outcomes and are aligned to their own investing or perhaps the exit date they plan. This may help or impede your own progress depending on your solution.

Why current industry trends matter

Every CIO and CISO cares about industry trends and broader pressures as these are leading and lagging indicators for their own strategic plans. These trends and pressure points change dynamically every year; however, the top priority items do not tend to change that much year on year.

At the time of writing, these are the top priority areas – I also include here how you can address them to aid your pitch:

1. **Cyber resilience** – Resilience rather than Cybersecurity. Help here by sharing how their peers have used this focus to minimize the impact of attacks that are successful.
2. **AI delivery of value** – Show "quick wins" of actual delivered AI outcomes with productivity realized
3. **Cost avoidance and reduction** – Share how your solution is future-proofed and further functionality can be deployed without adding new cost
4. **Talent and resource gaps** – You can note how your product solution is an attractive feature to new starters
5. **Platform consolidation** – Show why your best-of-breed solution is worthy of an exemption from this approach based on peer benchmarks

The CIO and CISO will appreciate it if you share stories from other clients and industries. They want vignettes of what has worked for their peers. These 5 priority areas may already be on the CIO/CISO's roadmap, hence are not necessarily new items and are likely to be a combination of "Known Knowns" and "Known Unknowns".

This has been named the **Rumsfeld Matrix** (popularized by Donald Rumsfeld). The Rumsfeld Matrix is a 2x2 decision-making and risk management framework that categorizes information into four quadrants based on levels of certainty: Known Knowns, Known Unknowns, Unknown Knowns, and Unknown Unknowns.

Using this framework, we can see that the value of the industry trends is correlated to the scarcity of the intel:

	Definition	Value of Intel
Known Knowns	Facts and things we know.	Zero
Known Unknowns	Gaps in our current knowledge	☆☆
Unknown Knowns	We know that we have not learned this yet	☆☆☆
Unknown Unknowns	A "Black Swan" vulnerability that we have never expected or anticipated	☆☆☆☆

Table 7.8 - Value of Intel

> **Note**
>
> When you are sharing intelligence that is already understood then that is of limited value, and indeed the CIO and CISO will not value this. The sweet spots here are the "Known Unknowns" and "Unknown Knowns". Note that "Unknown Unknowns", are the most valuable. But frankly these will not be available.

An example of "Known Unknowns" is the ROI that other peers have been able to achieve from Agentic AI projects for Fraud Reduction. Another example could also be the CIO and CISO's suspicion that their fourth-party suppliers have cyber weaknesses in terms of unpatched legacy systems, but they do not have a rough estimate to understand this gap. This is a typical question asked by the board, and the CIO/CISO do feel very exposed when they are unable to provide any answer.

Speaking of "Known Unknowns", as a Tech and Cyber Vendor you are always strongly interested in budgets. So, let's explore this topic.

Budget cycles and approval processes

Let's start by saying that traditionally the CIO and CISO are not the natural allies of the **Chief Financial Officer (CFO)**. The CFO is used to dealing with business cases that have strong **net present value (NPV)** and paybacks that they can compare A vs B vs C. This may be harder for the kind of solutions we are focusing on here.

They also do not like the fact that technology budgets always seem to increase, and there is a perception that these budgets are "fat" and that there is poor planning inbuilt into this process. Often the CIO and CISO are the budget holders; however, given large spends, they are likely not authorized to purchase without formal approval from multiple parties.

All expenditure relates to a budget year. It does get tricky when planned projects are delayed and run into the next financial year. Typically, most CIOs and CISOs are not that focused on financial management as a discipline and must learn this the hard way when their CFO challenges their planned or existing spend.

The financial planning cycle can be prolonged, and I've seen teams that are full-time and run this all year long rather than being just a short planning session before budgets are fixed.

Note

Most suppliers I've worked with underestimate how structured business buying cycles are. There are times of the year when it's much easier for a CISO to commit to OpEx spend; understanding that cycle makes a real difference.

Lee Barney – CISO, Ventia

As a Tech and Cyber Vendor, you may be asked early in the cycle for estimates of costs. These are for planning assumptions for the next financial year. While this is a good sign, it does not imply a commitment or a guaranteed sale.

The question that you may be asking is "should I provide a high-ball estimate or a low-ball estimate?" I've seen this backfire, so here is my advice: It's best to give a range, with plus and minus 25%. As you probably don't know enough, this is the safest approach.

A high-ball estimate makes you look expensive, and there is a chance that the project can die at this stage. On the other hand, a low-ball estimate can look too good to be true. Yes, this can get you to the next step, but then you can lose all the trust that you have been working on building. Just saying that you had *different assumptions* will make you look unprofessional.

Now, let's talk about the budget approval.

Gatekeeper heaven

Gatekeepers are usually parties that you have not dealt with but can impede your progress. Regardless of if you are internal or external, the first gatekeeper is the CIO and CISO Executive Assistant (EA). I have seen that EAs are often impossible to navigate and protect their boss's diary as if they are guarding treasure.

Once you have negotiated your way past the EA then there are more formidable gatekeepers ahead.

There are three key gatekeepers as shown in the following table – the CFO, Legal and the board. The CIO is also an internal gatekeeper (for CISOs), but we normally assume that this is where the CISO has started lobbying first and the CIO is aligned that this goes forward for formal approval. The CIO therefore has already reconciled that any budget or resource constraints with their own priority projects can be accommodated. (Remember that they are on the same team but often have very different priorities.)

Gatekeeper	Their challenges to the CIO and CISO
 CFO	If I approve this solution, how many resources can we reduce? What is the impact to the business if we delay to next year? How does the return compare to other proposals?
 Legal	Where is the data stored for this new service? Why should we accept the vendor's terms for ABC? How is data sovereignty managed?
 Board	Is this strategically aligned with the current strategy? How is this proposal going to align with the long-term vision? How do I get comfortable with this product being new and not used by our peers?

Table 7.9 - Budget approval gatekeepers

If all goes well, the request is approved and these items are added to the approved annual budget. In some enterprises these funds are transferred into the technology budget and in other cases there is a separate programs and projects budget established.

Over time, budget is allocated to these accounts. There are often "triggers", that have been pre-defined by the CFO to ensure cash flow during the year, and that certain revenue or cost targets are first met before funds are released.

For the CIO and CISO, as they are usually owners of many new initiatives, IT and Cyber Strategy approval governance presentations provide context for this budget. There is significant preparation by the CIO and CISO for these presentations. And there are usually a few run-throughs first with the CEO and CFO, the Management Committee, then with the board. Depending on the contention for resources and funds, they can iterate again with management members.

During these weeks and months, you should expect the CIO and CISO to be totally unavailable, unless they call you for some urgent data (known unknowns) to support their case or because there have been some questions from the strategy process.

Once their case is approved, the CIO and CISO will still often not communicate with you. There is now a bucket that can be applied, and they must make further investigations before it can proceed.

In any opportunity there is usually an incumbent. Thus, it is insightful to understand contract expiry and how to navigate this.

Contract expiry

Time is running out; the CIO/CISO's existing vendor may have their contract up for renewal. There is usually some degree of likes and dislikes with that product and service. As you are building your relationship with the CIO and CISO (or more likely with their team), it may be mentioned that this is coming up for renewal later this year. For you, this is the opportunity that you have been waiting for and means that now is the time to position your product and service.

The CIO and CISO will already have an opinion about the quality of what they have received from the incumbent and what they see as gaps that they would like to address. At the same time there is inertia, the desire to not spend too much effort on a new solution unless it is seen as having strategic value. My advice is don't wait until the last 3-4 months and start talking to your stakeholders at least 6 months before expiry. There is always the danger that by default the internal team runs out of time to review options and then this decision is delayed. Then you will be fighting for the *next* renewal cycle.

Earlier I talked about different career stages of CIO and CISOs. It's worth noting that there may be personal sensitivity by these parties if they had been the leader who had brought in the current solution:

Exploring 	They have just arrived; it is too early to tell if they should switch, as their plan is not yet developed
Trying New 	They like to kill legacy contracts to free up budget for innovation
Mature 	They want to go for consolidation, merging a few expiring contracts into one platform.
Prefer stability 	Prefer the status quo, although they may renew just to avoid the "Unknown Unknowns"

Table 7.10 – Career stages and contract renewals

Some of these career stages are not favorable to a new entrant. Either way, what you don't want is to try to compete. If there is a lack of internal focus on the current contract, it implies this is a zombie contract, has simply expired, and is just running month to month. Additionally, if the volume of contracts is high, it means that some of these arrangements are auto-renewed if the notice period has been missed. If this occurs, it is usually a sign that the CIO and CISO do not prioritize this activity and it probably means that you should focus elsewhere.

But I want to note that my own pessimistic view is counter to what I heard at an interview with Matt Boon:

> Note
>
> *As you start getting up toward the end of your career, I don't think that you're doing rash, risky things. I think you're bringing a level of knowledge and ability to make the big calls that you couldn't make before.*
>
> **Matt Boon – Senior Director, Strategic Research, Adapt**

As I have discussed, the mind of the CIO and CISO is busy and often cluttered with many details. This is combined with the fact that often many of these priorities end up being "number 1", and here lies the dilemma: how do the CIO and CISO make trade-offs when this happens? Unfortunately, this can be quite a regular issue to resolve.

At times the CIO and CISO must make this trade-off across three or more options, which describes a polylemma, which is what I explore with you next.

The polylemma of the CIO and CISO

Most of us have probably come across the Project Manager Triple Constraint – on time, on budget, and high quality is what is desired, but when delivering, you find yourself choosing which will be given less priority. No one likes to make this trade-off, but this is just a reality of modern enterprises. Allow me to introduce you to a polylemma, which describes a situation when you have multiple complex options to address. The CIO's and CISO's role often encounter polylemmas.

Take a CIO in a bank today; they are trying to achieve something that sounds straightforward and is anything but: speed with stability. Every bank wants to move at the pace of a digital startup, with modern payment systems, AI-driven customer interfaces, and the kind of seamless experience that fintechs deliver. At the same time, the engine powering all that ambition is frequently a core banking system built on COBOL (an older language that predates the internet and the advent of the personal computer).

This is like a CIO trying to achieve the performance of a formula 1 with an original combustion engine under the hood. The car looks modern from the outside, but the engine is ancient.

The vendor who understands this paradox does not arrive promising formula 1 performance. They arrive having already thought about the engine what it can sustain, what it cannot, and how to extract more speed without taking a corner too fast.

The CIO wants to use metrics reflecting this internal battle of speed with stability. In today's digital world, the CIO usually must work on maintaining systems resilience (stability) while supporting legacy technology that is end of life (EOL) and facing pressure to have hourly/daily (speed) systems releases. These are just two of the main factors; the reality is that the CIO must address two other key factors—compliance (extensive regulations) and cybersecurity (brakes)—that make their role extremely challenging.

Allow me to illustrate this with the following graphic:

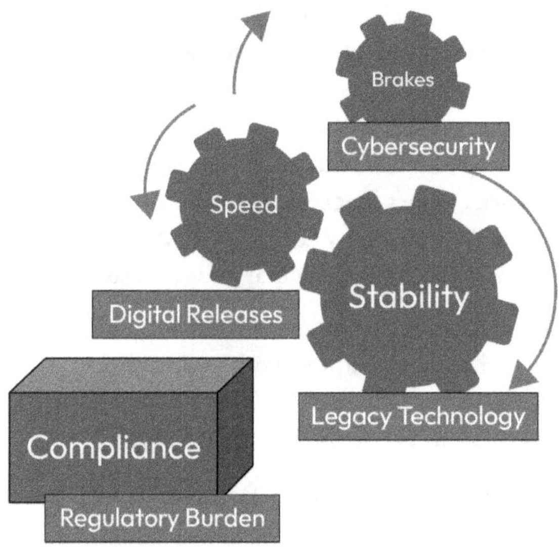

Figure 7.7 – CIO's polylemma to juggle

I've talked about the legacy struts; most CIOs and CISOs are reluctant to take any risk with their core systems, as any serious incident means that the business stops. The expectation is that these critical systems are 100%, or as good as available. At the same time, there is business pressure to operate at top F1 speed with customer experience and daily release cycles. They also need to find time to patch systems to ensure they are safe and add more security such as **multi-factor authentication (MFA)**, which can create friction to slow the vehicle down. And watching over all these elements is the regulator, who expects these competing compliance objectives to be 100% met.

In reality, the CIO and CISO are asked by their boss and senior stakeholders to meet Speed + Stability + Security, such that often Compliance becomes a trade-off item and is escalated to be a priority only after a major incident has occurred.

The CIO and CISO must try to balance all these objectives. When I'm working with different CIOs and CISOs, it's clear they all operate with various levels of detail. Some work at a high strategic level and others at a more granular level.

In *Chapter 2*, I talked about the respective CIO and CISO personas which highlight the natural preference for each of these leaders. However, these leaders will have to adjust when there are economic and business headwinds that dictate new tactics to meet the current market requirements. These events, such as new regulations, major incidents in the industry, mergers, and acquisitions, or new market entrants are not within their control.

The following table illustrates the impact of such factors on how the CIO and CISO will adjust their thinking and response. This highlights how personal preference is required to morph, given the polylemma challenge:

External Event	**Priority Shift ->**
 New regulatory requirement	Compliance
 Major Incident in industry sector	Cybersecurity

External Event	Priority Shift ->
 Competitor M&A or new entrant	Digital Transformation

Table 7.11 - CIO and CISO priority shifts from external event

Every CIO and CISO will have their list of top strategic priorities, that they will prefer to be their north stars to guide their execution. However, they will have to always make trade-offs regarding managing the broader agenda. This is a permanent dynamic and has significant consequence.

As the vendor who wants to help CIO and CISO, it is important that you are aware of how they navigate competing priorities. They must operate with incomplete information, resource constraints, and personal risk exposure. Accordingly, it is critical that you position your solution to support this.

> **Tip**
>
> Here are my tips on this:
>
> - Acknowledge the complexity based on this reality
> - Show how you can reduce cognitive load and not add to this.
> - Address how you will help them sleep at night
> - Respect and support their resource constraint

Other second base blockers

In our game of baseball, we are looking over to our next objective: second base.

While the CIO or CISO is the "Manager" who signs off on the vision, the champion is often the "Shortstop" guarding second base. However, they aren't the only players on the field you need to worry about, and getting to second base requires navigating a few other fielders:

Fielder	Their Goal	Second Base Blockers
Procurement	Governance	Need to ensure that the vendor risk profile is acceptable.
End Users	Stability	Not wanting to accept the process change and disruption to the business.
Executives	Judgment	Can raise objections in terms of competing priorities or resistance to change.
CFO	Budget	Can deny or ask for trade-offs or that the cost be absorbed in existing budgets.

Table 7.12 - Fielders who can block second base

From my own experience as a CIO and CISO, you do expect that there will be some degree of resistance and anticipate that some socialization with other stakeholders (fielders) will be required. In some cases, this is just general "noise" that must be expected, including some further input into and reconciliation of expectations from these other stakeholders involved. But in other cases, there can be a hard "no"; then it may become impossible for the CIO and CISO to get their ask across the line.

Only some of this dialogue will be visible to you, and there will be limited transparency as to what is going on with some of these parties.

Reaching second base requires a full understanding of the customer's problem and significant progress in validating that the proposed solution is technically viable with key stakeholders.

To gain the respect of a CIO or CISO, you must first align with the Architect, who is focused on how a solution fits and works effectively within their enterprise, but there are these other roles to bear in mind too. The Architect is a key leader that we need to get onside and that is what I will cover in the next chapter.

Summary

In this chapter we took a deep dive into the CIO and CISO perspective – what is on their mind, metrics that they care about, how they write business cases, and how they manage budgets, gatekeepers, and contract expiry.

I've noted that CIO and CISO are caught in a complex polylemma, where they must balance the drive for "F1" speed digital innovation with the limitations of fragile legacy core systems. While the CIO strives to shift budget from "keeping the lights on" to adding new features, they are often hindered by technical debt that consumes capacity needed to achieve 99.999% availability. At the same time, the CISO must maintain security standards, such as a specific MTTR, despite aging infrastructure that lacks monitoring.

Overall, their decisions are shaped by a hierarchy of metrics (OKRs, KPIs, KCIs, KRIs), career stage self-interest, stakeholder politics, and budgeting gatekeepers who don't speak technology.

Understanding this complexity and helping CIOs/CISOs build the business case rather than just pitching a product helps you be successful in your sales attempts.

The key learnings from this chapter are:

- **Dual mandate creates permanent tension** – CIOs are pushing the accelerator (AI, transformation, revenue), CISOs are steering the corners (risk reduction, compliance). Your solution must address both or you create internal friction between both executives.
- **Metrics reveal what they're accountable for** – CIOs care most about KPIs (speed and stability),CISOs care most about KCIs (control effectiveness) KRIs (board metrics) are politically sensitive and rarely shared with vendors, and OKRs are enterprise-wide measures.
- **Career stage drives decision bias** – a new CIO in "proving" mode chases transformation wins, one in "conservative" mode avoids risk. While a CISO near tenure end will often over-invest in short-term fixes to protect their record (therefore read the stage, not just the personas).
- **Three gatekeepers to prepare for** – CFO (ROI and cash flow), Procurement and legal (data sovereignty and contract terms), board (peer validation and management consensus); the CIO/CISO need ammunition for all three.
- **External events override persona** – new regulation, a peer-sector breach, or a competitor M&A will instantly reprioritize the agenda, stay close enough to pivot your relevance when these occur.

8

Stepping Into the Shoes of the Architect

When your goal is to sell to the CIO and CISO, you must first gain the respect of the head architect. They may be the first internal stakeholder you engage; they are a natural choice for an internal champion. To successfully drive change, you will need the support of this leader; otherwise, your mission may fail.

All architects are not the same, but they are certainly wired differently from other leaders. The CIO and CISO are focused on "what" and "when", with the CIO caring about the outcome and the delivery of the business strategy, while the CISO wants to do the same but with minimal risk. In contrast, the architect cares deeply about "how;" they want to understand how your solution will fit into their environment and work effectively. It makes little sense to get the CIO and CISO happy if the architect is not aligned.

In this chapter we will look at this role and explore how you can build a relationship with them to aid your sales strategy and get you to second base. We will cover the following topics:

- Understanding architects
- Speaking the language of the architect
- Evaluating the architect's influence
- When the architect is not on your side

Understanding architects

I've worked with many architects, and they are an interesting group of leaders who are looking forward to which direction the enterprise needs to move toward. The reality is that architects are the brains in the team that are charged with thinking about the future.

A great architect is extremely hard to find, as they must be adept at strategic thinking while remaining grounded in understanding the details of the existing tech stack and able to map a safe migration from the current state to the future state (often carrying that entire picture in their head).

The key thing to remember is that they are often the left hand of the CIO and CISO (from my view, the right hand is the operational leaders who keep them in their job). The architects have the forward-looking perspective that many in the C-suite find exciting. In short, they are a trusted internal advisor.

Note

Maybe you are not talking to the CISO, but you're talking to the lead architect and some of the network engineers—they can give you a lot of the intel you need so you understand what stage the environment and security stack is in right now. This is what I'm doing currently to provide security services to the company; these are some of the projects they're working on.

Gary Hayslip – CISO, Halcyon.ai, Board director and investor

Architects are interested in:

- Reducing complexity
- Future proofing
- Fixing technology

Note that these three goals are all important; however, if forced to choose, then the architect would probably rank them in this way:

	Architect's Priority Ranking	Rationale
1	Reducing complexity	Architects recognize that they have too many systems and applications, which makes maintenance less efficient and increases the attack surface.
2	Future-proofing	Architects prefer to avoid tactical solutions and instead recommend new scalable options that align with their roadmap.

	Architect's Priority Ranking	Rationale
3	Fixing	Architects accept end-of-life and legacy only when they have no other choice.

Table 8.1 - Architect priority ranking

While architects aim to achieve all these goals, they may, if necessary, defer addressing technical debt and push it to the next year or planning cycle.

Architects can veto a decision or recommendation as they have an internal gatekeeper role to provide approval for new technology. Strictly speaking they may not have formal approval decision rights, but in any enterprise proceeding without their blessing can be difficult.

Their perspective is mid-term and long-term. Their short-term decisions are therefore shaped by a long-term perspective. Therefore, leading with product features is not the way to engage the architect.

> **Note**
>
> *Cold outreach rarely works for me. If I need a vendor urgently, then I usually know how to find them. Instead, vendors should spend time with the people who actually make buying choices, such as architects. They're the ones who hold the keys, they are the ones who recommend your product over your competition; sell to them, and they will be your biggest partner inside your target customer.*
>
> **Lee Barney – CISO, Ventia**

> **Note**
>
> *A productive meeting with a salesperson often happens when they are accompanied by an engineer/architect type. A great meeting is when the salesperson directs the meeting, doesn't say much, and the interaction is between the technical people to understand if there is alignment between the business outcome and the proposed solution. When it then comes down to next steps, commercials, and relationship, the salesperson takes the lead and adds value in those areas.*
>
> **John Taylor – Field CTO, Mimecast (former CIO & CISO)**

The architect is always evaluating several market solutions as part of the overall roadmap of transformation. They are the key enterprise stakeholder that you will need to convince to gain second base. It is not impossible to move ahead without their endorsement, and I've seen this occur. However, you will want the architect to be fully supportive of your solution and formally endorse this approach.

> Note
>
> *I'm willing to champion ideas I strongly believe in, especially when I can see a real improvement in security risk reduction or operations efficiency. I pull back when I don't have enough data to support it, when the timing is wrong or when I feel it might create more problems than it solves.*
>
> **Simon Blanchet – Security Architect and former HSBC Serai CISO**

Given the architect's priorities, how you, as a vendor, can succeed is to learn to speak their language. In the next section, I will cover how you can specifically address their goals to reduce complexity and map the future architecture roadmap.

Speaking the language of the architect

The architect thinks in terms of blueprints, in light of the direction that is planned and how what you are talking about is relevant to this journey. The architect's "blueprint" maps current gaps in architecture and is therefore restricted to a need-to-know basis. If, during a meeting with the architect, their dialogue suddenly stops, it may be because the discussion has touched on a confidential topic. Knowing their key goals, which we covered in the previous section, will guide you, however.

> Tip
>
> At this stage of exploratory discussions, it is too early to suggest a **non-disclosure agreement (NDA)**. As you expect, signing an NDA takes a bit of effort, so while the architect will feel more comfortable speaking openly, introducing one too early can slow down your progress.
>
> I've seen that there will be moments when, in the discussion, the architect can start to ask questions that are sensitive to your own organization. That may be the ideal time to suggest exploring a mutual NDA, as this will protect confidential information from both sides.

> **Note**
>
> *A good architect is worth their weight in gold; they will be the primary gatekeeper for new technology for the busy exec. I put a lot of trust in the recommendations that architects bring to me. They know the landscape and how new technology fits in.*
>
> **Lee Barney – CISO, Ventia**

While focusing on discovery to learn about the current pain points, you want to learn some basics from them, for instance, key areas to explore around the legacy vs new cloud technology infrastructure and any brittle components that have caused recent incidents. Or, for example, whether there are concerns about the flat network and the lack of segmentation that stops lateral movement by a threat actor.

> **Note**
>
> *Championing well-informed and strategically aligned ideas helps build credibility as a forward-thinking security leader who can influence outcomes and drive meaningful transformation. I consider it a privilege to be in such a position, though it is both rewarding and challenging, as successful initiatives strengthen trust, while failures, regardless of cause, carry personal accountability and impact leadership confidence. This is why it is important to focus on championing ideas aligned to business values and the organisation's risk appetite.*
>
> **Yaso Addanki – Head of Security Architecture, AGL**

Your overarching objective is to gain some understanding of the current architectural patterns. The architects want to ensure that any new technology is consistent across the enterprise. They don't want to allow the creation of more tech debt and need to ensure that the new components are interoperable.

These patterns are in effect the reusable blueprints that the architecture team has established for how new systems must be designed. They can cover several different domains including:

- Event driven architecture
- Microkernel architecture
- Microservices architecture
- Layered architecture

What matters is that when the architect mentions one of them, you recognize it as a signal about how they expect new technology to be integrated and you ask how your solution aligns with that pattern.

In your conversations with the CIO and CISO, you would have focused on specific messages around speed of delivery, ROI expected, compliance achieved, and digital experiences transformed. In contrast, when talking to the architect, you must provide more specific data that explains the "how". For instance, you might say, "This solution has integration patterns and APIs for your existing stack and access management systems."

To tick the architect's box on "complexity," you must provide a blueprint on how your solution integrates with what you know of their existing tech stack. This should outline how industry-standard third-party solutions have already been proven in live environments in combination with your product. Similarly, the architect wants to ensure that there is ample shelf life for new solutions – they want "future proofing."

Addressing their key goals also puts you in good stead with architects. Here are some examples of what you can say regarding the integration of your solution in alignment with these goals:

Solution integration	**Reduce Complexity**	**Future Proofing**
Identity	Standard Azure AD, etc., is supported	Automated user lifecycle for scaling from 100 to 100,000 users
Data Interface	Single source of truth with data managed by APIs	API allows your enterprise to change vendors later without breaking your integration
Network	Operates within the existing "Zero Trust" perimeter	Track record of evolving with changing global data regulations
Data Analytics	The existing data warehouse can be utilized	Data portability with no proprietary structures

Table 8.2 - Solution integrations mapped against key architect goals

If the CIO, CISO, and architect are all in the same session, you will of course need to consider all perspectives and ensure that you are able to bridge them. The CIO will be wanting to achieve business outcomes, and this will be their focus. At the same time while the architect also wants this, they will be desiring more specific technology advancement that is aligned to their architecture roadmap and the patterns that have been agreed. Here are some examples:

CIO	Architect
The ROI is achieved in 12 months	Kubernetes with auto scaling execution
15-month rollout to achieve business outcomes	Quantum computing readiness has already been tested and validated
API gateway reduces incidents by 90%	Agentless AI integration with *ABC* using CASB Technology
Endpoint protection was rolled out in 90 days, including testing	Encryption key management integrated with Machine Learning to provide tamper-proof detection

Table 8.3 - CIO vs Architect focus

The architect operates at a more detailed level compared to the CIO and their focus is different, as expected. What they want from vendors is to understand your reference architecture, which includes:

- Data flow patterns
- How components interact
- Security model
- Capacity planning
- API integration
- Authentication and authorization

The architect also wants to understand how this migration will be staged, the technical, and operational requirements, including the detailed operating system requirements, plus the known performance bottlenecks. All this means that when dealing with the architect, there may be a level of detail that you find impossible to cover without some more detailed tech support from your team.

I would like to share what I consider mandatory items you must provide to the architect to satisfy their concerns:

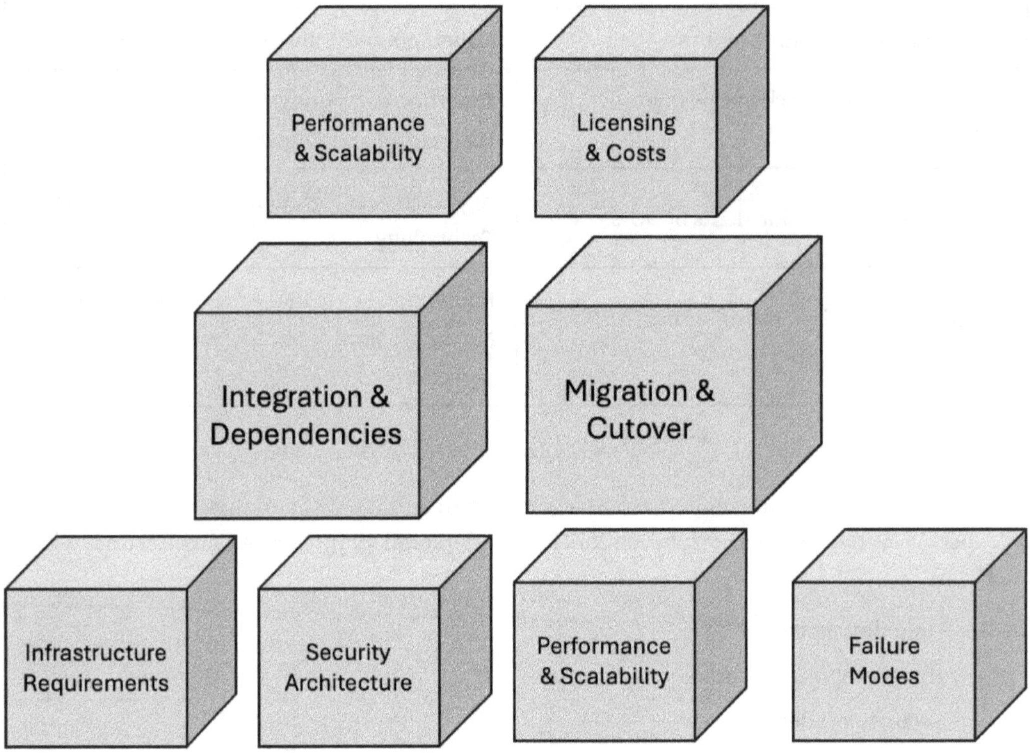

Figure 8.1 – Mandatory architect concerns to be addressed

As you can see from the preceding image, there are eight mandatory items that you must address to progress. If you cannot address these, the architect could block your progress. Note that the larger boxes in the middle row correlate with their importance to the architect.

If you can provide these items early, then this is an accelerator for your sales cycle. Let's look at these further.

Addressing the architect's concerns

In essence, the architect will want to learn from your meeting whether your solution can work at their enterprise, and whether they need to add other technology colleagues to this discussion. These colleagues might be other direct reports of the CIO and CISO, not necessarily them directly. The CIO and CISO will be kept informed but won't be the ones to discuss this level of detail normally.

Allow me to add a few notes on each of the eight mandatory items I've mentioned, with the two most important (denoted by the larger boxes in the middle in *Figure 8.1*) being the most critical and the remaining of roughly equal importance:

- *Integration and dependencies* - they want to understand how this new system will work with existing technology. This will be at a detailed technical level of data formats, protocols and network connectivity.
- *Migration and cutover* - they want to see a plan to transition from the current to future state. This includes migration approach, data migration, rollback plans, etc.
- *Performance and scalability* – they want to ensure that this technology can operate at the scale and loads that this enterprise requires including expected growth. Details will include bandwidth, memory consumption, latency etc.
- *Data flow* – they want to know how data moves, where it resides and data residency. The details required include data sovereignty, data backup and recovery, data synchronisation etc.
- *Security architecture* – they want to only deploy new solutions that meet the existing security policy and patterns. This includes network security, audit logging, vulnerability management and authentication approach.
- *Infrastructure requirements* – they want to ensure that the existing technology stack can support this new component. This includes detail on compute, storage, network, middleware etc.
- *Licencing model* – they want to know about the Total Cost of Ownership (TCO) to address business case requirements. This includes cost per user, per instance, add-ons and support tiering etc.
- *Failure Mode* – they want to know if this technology component stops working correctly, how gracefully does it fail?

The architect will welcome written content that covers these items, including reference architecture whitepapers that include the details that are expected. Some access to Reference Sites (other sites) that have peer architects willing to speak is also valued.

Because the architect prefers facts and details, you should avoid vague answers or flowery marketing jargon. Bear in mind also that the architect cares to look good in front of the CIO and CISO, so helping them with ammunition for the business case will be appreciated.

Note

Approaching the members of my team who are at the coalface of things is often best because they are the ones who are mostly feeling the pain of issues day-to-day. If my trusted team member has worked with a vendor to solve a problem, and they can collectively demonstrate the value under scrutiny, then that's often the best way forward.

Dr Maria Milosavljevic – former ANZ Bank CISO

Preparing business case materials

In the previous chapter, we talked about financial analysis and success metrics being potential content to share for the CIO or CISO's business case; in addition, stories from industry peers always resonate strongly. Ideally, the discussion you have with the architect should also provide them with new perspectives that can add more colour to their business case blueprint (which is a "living" document).

Let me add a few examples of how this could work:

Sharing with the architect	**Echo to the CIO**	**Echo to the CISO**
Reference Peer	*ABC* has achieved 100% digital migration in *x* days	*ABC* upgraded to strong MFA as they migrated to the new platform
Benchmarking Data	We would reduce complexity and process 3× faster	This closes our 3-year-old audit issue

Table 8.4 - Storytelling echoes to CIO and CISO from the architect

The overall impact is that the architect shifts from a type of gatekeeper into being an internal champion for your product, moving you forward from first base. In short, to get yourself to second base, you must prove to the architect that you pass their two tests:

- Does this solution *fit* the environment (and is it within the risk appetite)
- Does this solution *align* with the enterprise technology roadmap?

While the architect does not have approval authority as a gatekeeper, they do have influence. When they say they are not supportive for any reason, then it is going to be hard for you to succeed.

> Note
>
> *Champions often sit within enterprise security architecture or operations. They value influence and credibility internally. Engage them early, support their success story, and make them look good. My goal during any cycle is to ensure everyone has a voice and alignment feels natural rather than forced.*
>
> **Michael Kazantzis – CEO, Cyborium**

In essence, the architect's role is to ensure strategic alignment of the architecture and technical validation. If you can meet this threshold, then they can be a valuable internal advocate to help accelerate the sales process. In my experience as a CIO or CISO, I could act independently of the architect, but I rarely moved forward without their support.

Evaluating the architect's influence

I know from my own experience as a CIO and CISO that executives can get very frustrated with the architect but must also respect their expertise and strategic perspective. Your degree of care is directly correlated to the architect's degree of influence. This is a factor that you will be able to assess as you engage with them.

The "acid test" is how they operate when the CIO and CISO are in the room. Observe if the executive leaders really listen to the architect's advice and recommendations. From my own CIO and CISO experience, I found enterprises to be mostly poor at architecture, and architecture practices are not strongly followed. The architect's degree of influence may not just be caused by their personal drive, but also the culture of the enterprise. So, I recommend mapping the degree of influence of the architect as being "high" or "low", in the context of the enterprise level of maturity. You can then design your pitch in alignment with this combination.

Here are a few little clues:

High Influence	Low Influence
The architect talks about the roadmap "To-Be" state, and you see the CIO and CISO refer to this artifact.	The architect talks about the "As is" state and focuses on tech requirements with little reference to this artifact.
Architects often refer to the Architecture Review Board (ARB) and how they intend to get approval in this forum.	The architect is not leading this approval process and acts like a spectator.
The architect talks about their recent engagement with the CIO and CISO.	The architect is reluctant to join or engage in a meeting with the CIO and CISO.

Table 8.6 - Architect Clues on their degree of influence

A "low"-influence architect in a "weak" practice enterprise will require more assistance and documentation. They may also be less engaged and therefore a weaker champion that you can rely on. Thus, you will have to extend your reach to a broader group of stakeholders.

> **Note**
>
> I've heard a recent story of a tech vendor that conducted more than 1000 interviews with business and lower-level stakeholders to prepare properly for their pitch to the CIO and CISO. When I heard this story, I first applauded their strength of preparation but then thought about the actual cost for both the enterprise stakeholders and vendor to go for this level of engagement. I'm not sure that this effort is sustainable and necessarily a good return on investment.

High influence often correlates with strong architecture maturity. I classify architecture maturity as follows (note that these estimates are from my own experience):

Architecture maturity	**Estimated population**	**Symptoms to look for**
Measured 	15%	Architecture practices are embedded into the business culture and there are no backdoor alternatives.
Defined 	35%	The architecture processes are defined and starting to be enforced.
Under Development 	35%	Architecture is reactive and there is approval, but processes are immature and can be bypassed.
Unrecognised 	15%	Architecture as a formal discipline does not yet exist in any meaningful sense.

Table 8.7 - Architecture maturity breakdown

Architecture as a discipline across different industries and countries does vary to a large degree in terms of maturity. My estimate is that only 50% of all sites have a measured and defined practice. This means a large part of the market is navigating technology decisions without these mature processes.

The organizations that lack architectural maturity will need more than a product; they also need a partner who can help them think clearly about where the solution fits and why.

> **Note**
>
> Low architectural maturity means the internal champion will carry more personal risk, making choosing the right vendor to support not just a technical decision but a career one.

You can leverage your relationship with the architect to help build and develop your engagement with the CIO and CISO. Having this leader vouch for you will act as a trust multiplier and is key to proceeding.

But what do you do when you are facing a hostile architect who is not open to engaging with you?

When the architect is not on your side

Unfortunately, not every architect you encounter will be a potential champion; some may be actively hostile and obstructive. You never want to work with one that appears supportive in the room but undermines the process the moment you leave.

Before reacting, try to diagnose the reason for their hostility. I've found it is most commonly rooted in feeling bypassed, but there may also be a genuine technical concern that has not been addressed that you can then respond to. At times there may be a loyalty to a competing vendor that is historical and will be hard to overcome.

> **Tip**
>
> The most important rule is to engage early and directly. The architect who is brought into the design early becomes invested in the outcome. Ideally you want them to feel that ownership and see this as aligned to their own roadmap.

In the next chapter, we will discuss the gap analysis that you will want to start with the architect and have them start to involve other stakeholders in the sessions, which will be a real validation exercise for the potential solution.

Summary

In this chapter, we explored why the architect is so critical to your success and why bypassing them is a risk you cannot afford to take.

Unlike executives who care about "what" and "when," architects care about "how": whether your solution reduces complexity, fits the existing stack, and will not create new technical debt.

Converting the architect from gatekeeper to champion is a powerful outcome, and you do this by giving them the ammunition to advocate internally to the CIO and CISO.

The key points from this chapter are:

- **Architects are key to reaching second base** – bypassing the architect creates internal friction that can surface later and damage your credibility with the very executives you're trying to close with.
- **Architect priorities rank in this order** – (1) reduce complexity, (2) future-proof the architecture, (3) fix tech debt.
- **Speak their language** – architects want reference architecture, API patterns, data flows, and security models.
- **Assess their influence before investing heavily** – high-influence architects reference the "to-be" roadmap, lead ARB processes, and engage directly with the CIO/CISO; low-influence architects focus on "as-is" and act as spectators.
- **Help the architect look good** – provide peer reference stories and benchmarking data they can echo upward to the CIO and CISO (this is how a gatekeeper becomes a champion).

Summary

9

Gap Analysis

You've established your product and service as a contender now that you have met with the architect, CIO, and CISO. There may have been several meetings and reviews of slide decks to establish that your solution appears to fit an existing problem that is important to the executives.

From my own experience, CIOs and CISOs expect many of these promising new initiatives to fail. The architect may have agreed to give your product and service some further consideration, but this does not mean that they are sold on your product or service; rather, they want to discuss it further, ask detailed questions, and take a peek at how it works.

This is where a gap analysis comes in, the focus of this chapter. A gap analysis compares features of the new solution with the actual business requirements. I'd add that the gap analysis itself is also as much a test of your professionalism as it is of your product.

This chapter explores the gap analysis stage and explains how you can prepare for it, why it is so important for this to be an honest assessment, and what to do if your proposal doesn't make it through this stage.

Essentially, we'll cover the following topics:

- Moving forward with trust
- Gap analysis preparation
- Undertaking gap analysis discussions
- Head-to-head gap assessment
- Keeping your gap assessment honest
- What to do if the outcome isn't positive

Moving forward with trust

From my 25+ years in the C-Suite I've seen that most enterprises operate with the very invisible but critical attribute that is "trust". I've seen internal and external peers succeed and fail, based on their own ability to be seen as trustworthy.

Trust acts as an invisible filter at every stage. Vendors, partners, and internal teams who are perceived as trustworthy get the benefit of the doubt when things get difficult. Without this attribute, small missteps become disqualifying. No amount of technical capability or commercial attractiveness fully compensates for a trust deficit at the C-Suite level.

At this point in your sales journey, you are still trying to secure "second base," and this is where real trust can be established. In these meetings, you are starting to understand the business and technology drivers of these leaders, plus a flavor of the political dynamics. Your meetings with the architect and perhaps a few other team members are a great start, but now the real work must commence.

> **Tip**
>
> Remember what you are selling to the CIO and CISO is not their prime focus.

> **Note**
>
> *I don't buy tools; I buy measurable reductions in risk, complexity, and cost.*
>
> **Mathias Bücherl – Group CISO, Heidelberg Materials**

In my experience, this is where the best vendors step up; they have met with different stakeholders and handled the questions of the architect. You don't yet understand all the politics in the enterprise (we will cover this in the next chapter), but these conversations have started to gradually shift and are a little warmed up with prior discussions and initial questions being addressed. Thus, there is an increased weight to the quality of the dialogue as the CIO and CISO team will begin to open and disclose more detail to you. They will be more willing to share artifacts with you and may invite other colleagues to your meetings. The cadence of the meetings starts to become more frequent. This will lead to harder questions being asked, as you have moved beyond the product pitch stage and the CIO/CISO and team are thinking more positively about how your solution could operate in their enterprise. Trust underlies all of this.

As a former CIO and CISO, I know that trust varies by individual, but trust toward vendors usually starts at a lower level. No offense here, but most leaders I know have been burnt by past bad behavior of a vendor or two, at some point.

> **Note**
>
> *Too many vendors treat the CISO as a buyer of technology. I am a buyer of outcomes. Technology selection happens at the end of the journey—not at the beginning.*
>
> **Franco Marconcini – Group CISO, Electrolux Professional**

I've always judged who I work with in my own manner; I give and expect respect. Personally, I value honesty, smarts, and diligence. When someone works with me in this manner, it builds greater trust. It is during the gap analysis when this foundation of trust can be developed further, so let's examine what has worked and what has not, in my experience in regards to building trust.

Building trust

Trust is developed through honesty and valued engagement. In your mind, perhaps unconsciously, there is an equation being calculated in real time about who you do and don't trust. This is akin to a bank account with deposits and withdrawals made, which either build trust, or erode it.

Your trust deposits are made through consistent delivery and showing up with insight. Trust withdrawals happen the moment you overpromise and do not deliver.

The balance of this trust account determines whether you are tolerated or genuinely valued and it is being calculated in real time by the CIO and CISO whether you are aware of it or not. This development of trust cannot be accelerated by spending money or trying to build the relationship at an unrealistic pace.

Note that building trust is not a short-term outcome; this takes performance over time. For this reason, I have a chapter on building a partnership of trust later in this book (*Chapter 21*). This is your longer-term objective, and your consistent behavior will enable this outcome.

> Note
>
> *We recently evaluated several vendors for a cloud-based platform. Most of them talked about detection rates, AI, or the latest analyst report rankings. They assumed that's what drove our decision. It wasn't. What influenced the decision were operational and trust factors.*
>
> *I asked, "How fast can my team deploy this?" The vendor who showed up with a pre-deployment plan, a strategy, and engineers ready to work alongside my staff — that's who won.*
>
> *Another differentiator was transparency. One vendor proactively admitted they'd hit problems in another bank deployment and explained how they fixed them. That honesty told me they were an honest partner, not just a seller.*
>
> *Their CEO joined multiple calls, not to sell, but to ask, "What would make this successful for you?" That helped the trust factor.*
>
> *The technical differences between finalists were marginal — 90% of features were the same. But the vendor who made it easiest for my team to succeed operationally, and who demonstrated value, readiness, cultural alignment, and transparency, won.*
>
> **Adam Palmer – CISO, First Hawaiian Bank**

In Chapter 2, Table 2.10, I explained different levels of vendor trust; now let's build on this with the process of moving from being a "Stranger" to being a "Trusted Partner". It is important that you don't assume that your product or personal charisma can allow you to bypass levels and jump straight to "Partner," the desired target.

> Note
>
> I've seen sales staff act a little too familiar after just a few meetings, and this can feel inappropriate. There is also the risk that your internal champion will not be happy if you act in this manner in front of their CIO and CISO. In short, your behavior must match the level of trust that you have built.

The hard question to ask yourself is where you are right now with your relationship with the CIO/CISO. There is little point in overestimating the degree of trust that they have developed. Trust takes time and sustained effort to achieve, and this may also be a function of the product and service that you represent being on their radar.

We, as leaders, can only build upon strong foundations. You cannot "steal" second base; it must be earned. Gap analysis is a step toward building this relationship; ultimately, the CIO and CISO care about solving their business problem, rather than a partnership at this stage.

The following table provides you with insights into how trust matures over time with CIOs and CISOs (this is based on my own observations):

Level	Vendor Persona	Trust Level	CIO & CISO Behaviors
0	Noise	Stranger	*Short and guarded responses*
1	Known Quantity	Acquaintance	*Comparing you to other solutions*
2	Credible Vendor	Industry Colleague	*More candid with you*
3	Preferred Vendor	Advisor	*Happy to meet regularly and share information*
4	Strategic Vendor	Partner	*Happy to introduce you to C-Suite*
5	Trusted Advisor	Trusted Partner	*Actively refers you to their peers*

Table 9.1 - Trust Maturity Model

As your trust builds over time, you earn the right to gain more respect. This means that the behavior of the CIO and CISO will start to change from "short and guarded responses" to improved levels of trust.

How can you accelerate this process of building trust then, so that you know what the CIO and CISO want? Well, you can:

- Have a genuine interest in understanding their business
- Help them look good using insights and intel
- Make an introduction to someone that they value
- Solve a problem that they care about

The architect relationship that we discussed in the previous chapter is a proxy approach; you want to build trust with them to bridge the trust that the CIO and CISO have with them.

I would like to share the personal model I've applied over the years to determine who I trust and the basis for that judgment. In my opinion, trust is a conclusion that you reach based on some behaviors that you have observed. The three C's rule is the intersection of my own beliefs, and I trust those who demonstrate these three C's:

Trust = Competence + Character + Consistency

Of these three C's, "Competence" is the easiest to try to detect for the CIO and CISO, as they have seen many thousands of pitches. Bluffing through technical questions is difficult to sustain, and your credibility suffers each time you must defer to another team member. On the other hand, "Character" is revealed when there is an issue and depends on how you react to it. Finally, "Consistency" will only show up over time with your ability to coordinate and show up for the CIO and CISO.

I need all three to trust someone. Just being strongly competent and with character, but not consistent, will reduce my trust in that person.

The following image presents the three Cs and the factors that demonstrate them:

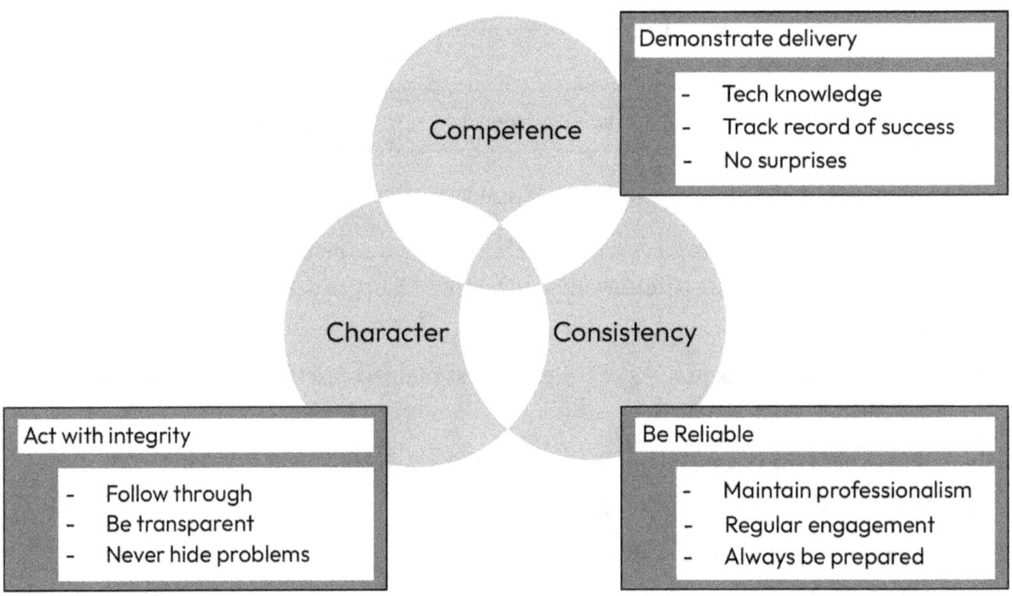

Figure 9.1 - How I build trust

Now, if you are a tech or cyber sales leader and your team has told you that a CIO or CISO sees you as a "Preferred Vendor", how can you verify this? "Trust but verify" is an essential approach to adopt.

There will likely be a bias toward overestimating your maturity level. Table 9.2 uses the Trust Maturity Model to pose some questions to consider. You can use this to test the trust level your team believes has been achieved:

Level	Trust Level	Questions to consider
0	Stranger	*Do you have to remind them who you are and where you work?*
1	Acquaintance	*Do they remember your name?* *Do they recall the context of your discussion with them?*
2	Credible Vendor	*Do they see you as an industry colleague?* *Are they open and candid with you?*
3	Preferred Vendor	*How often do you meet?* *How long are these sessions?*
4	Partner	*Do they contact you via text messages?* *What other advice did the CIO and CISO ask for?*
5	Trusted Partner (MVP)	*Have other peer CIOs and CISOs been introduced?* *What board presentations have you made?* *Are you invited to strategic planning workshops?*

Table 9.2 - Example questions to test trust maturity

Now that we have explored how to build trust, let's move to the gap analysis process. This will be a series of meetings to explore the solution and how well it addresses the business problem at hand.

In this meeting there will be a huddle of several stakeholders. This includes the architect, technology and business subject matter experts (SMEs), vendor sales engineers, and so on. Your preparation before the session really matters and will contribute to the success of the discussion. Let's explore that.

Gap analysis preparation

Your prep sessions with the architect and team would have established some basics around what problem they are trying to resolve and what technology stack is already in place, including where they want to avoid any further workloads being added due to legacy frailty.

Your preparation for the gap analysis discussions is to anticipate within your own team what the hypotheses are in terms of the problem and what requirements are addressed and not addressed. In short, you are doing your own mental gap analysis.

Then, what do you do when you are aware of the gaps in your own solution? In my experience, the worst-case scenario at this stage would be to allow this to proceed while hiding the gaps. It is best to consider whether there is a way for you to control this narrative before the client team discovers this themselves.

I recommend disclosing gaps proactively and early. In my experience as a CIO and CISO, honest disclosure of a weakness paired with a credible workaround and a roadmap builds more trust than a flawless pitch that unravels under questioning. Hiding these facts will destroy all trust, while admitting them and working through the approach to addressing them in the future allows you to remain in the game. In your preparatory internal hypotheses exercise, known gaps should be categorized as:

- Deal Breakers
- Significant
- Nice to Have

It is hard to address a "Deal Breaker" unless there are no other solutions that can meet the CIO/CISO's requirements. For each of these gaps, I recommend preparing a gap analysis document. This might look like the following:

Component	**Explanation**
Gap	Description of what is missing
Workaround proposed	Tactical alternative
Product roadmap	Release schedule to address aspects of the gap

Component	Explanation
Industry context	What other competitors have done to address the gap, or similar gaps

Table 9.3 - An example of gap analysis

I'd note that the CIO and CISO are typically only concerned about the biggest gaps—hence they will focus attention immediately on the "Deal Breakers" and usually will not care as much about "Significant" and "Nice to Have's".

Your sharing of this analysis with the CIO, CISO and champion will provide broader context and will enable you to see if there is any flexibility on the identified gaps.

Note that the CIO is more likely to accept a non-perfect solution than the CISO. For many categories, the CIO is happy with "good" and doesn't need "great". With the CIO, there is a bias for getting results and getting them quickly.

> Note
>
> *A minimum viable product (MVP) for a CIO is a non-customized/black box solution that doesn't require significant costs and time in customizing for a company's environment. It is quickly deployed and provides market-relevant data on CRQ that has been obtained and matured across multiple organizations.*
>
> **Paul O'Rourke – former CISO, CRO and BCG Global Cyber Leader**

Disclosing gaps during gap analysis will help you build credibility, particularly as you acknowledge a weakness but in doing so, also share how others have addressed this in the short term.

Undertaking gap analysis discussions

During gap analysis, you are likely painfully aware you probably have at least one other competitor and perhaps also an existing incumbent. What can you say about them that will be received well?

Directly criticizing the competition is not a good option. Having seen it as a CIO and CISO, this approach has not landed well with me. Instead, I'd advise you to respectfully address the product differences.

I've seen a vendor say, "Actually, *ABC* is a great product and stronger than we are at *XYZ*, but where we are better is in addressing *123*." This style of honest differentiation does land well. It is one that the CIO and CISO will listen to and may provide you with further context as to what is more important to them.

Your product competitor will likely have their own script, and your champion will be reconciling both statements to work out what they see as the truth. If this message resonates with them, it will probably be repeated when you are not in the conversation.

When possible, this is the ideal time to suggest that the evaluation team speak with another customer of yours for a reference. This can address their concerns about any gaps and provide credibility to the gap analysis preparation that you have shared.

Note

A lot of evaluation goes into risk around a new product. We look at the company: is it going to survive in the long run? What are their financials like, do they have a good go-to-market (GTM) approach, who runs the company, and what is their track record? All the new and emerging third-party risk and compliance obligations, which are designed to make things safer, better, and more transparent, put a huge burden on new companies selling to banks and the banks themselves to attest to them. Having said that, I have had some excellent results with some new and emerging companies and technology and some not-so-great ones too, but I'm a firm believer that you have to know the risks and implications of your decision, and that comes with due diligence and experience.

Scott Collary – Group CIO, Westpac Group

Another aspect to consider is product or feature workarounds. As a CIO and CISO, I never liked to buy a product with a workaround. This always carried additional costs later to integrate the workaround back into the solution, and some upfront expense to enable this approach. Additionally, whenever I was promised this feature would be in an upcoming release, I treated it with a degree of skepticism. In normal situations, it is hard for a vendor to guarantee a new feature or functionality due to the broader product requirements to address a large customer base.

However, I've also been in the situation where a feature did not exist, and the vendor asked me to develop a custom API Layer. I recall convincing the vendor that I'd prefer to partner with them on co-developing the capability. This was in the spirit of partnership, rather than the traditional approach of contracting for a waterfall development. The example was for a core banking system and in this example, the project work was integrated into the overall product.

There are many types of gaps, and I'd like to explore these in order to have a common language that we can use going forward. It is interesting that what emerges as a gap on the CIO and CISO's end may not be what you have considered significant.

Types of gaps

We can put gaps neatly into one of three buckets. These relate to capabilities that the architect and the evaluation team have established as functionality required to address their existing problem statement:

Functional **(Technical Gap)**	**Business** **(Process Gap)**	**Workload** **(Resource Gap)**
Our backup restore process does not support Yubico authentication	*Our API gateways require a manual approval step*	*4-5 Agentic AI specialists are required for training the models*

Table 9.4 - Types of gaps and examples

Any gaps in these areas will be assigned a risk rating from "Very High" to "Very Low". In some instances, for example when these relate to compliance matters, these will be mandatory items, and a "Very High" and "High"risk rating is likely to rule your product out of contention. However, workarounds may be acceptable for medium and low risk impact gaps. All products will have some gaps. Summarizing the overall situation with the team could be expressed verbally like this:

Gaps 1 and 2 are both being delivered in next month's release.

Gaps 3, 4, and 5 workarounds are available that ABC *company has also installed.*

Gap 6 is unfortunately not available.

Alternatively, this can be written up in a formal report; when this data is plotted on a Priority-Alignment Matrix, this can provide a clear understanding of context:

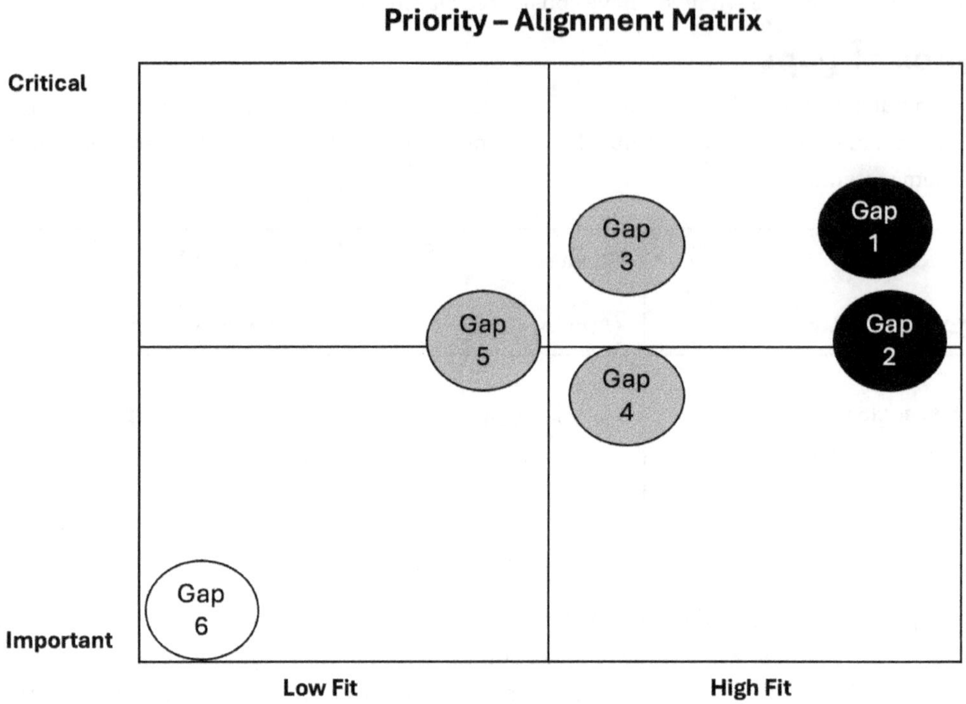

Figure 9.2 - Priority-Alignment analysis

What matters more are "critical" attributes that also have a high fit for your requirements. In this example Gaps 1 and 2 are more critical and doable and therefore are a positive fit in the gap analysis. Gap 6 is lowest risk and a low fit, so is not concerning.

It is likely that the CIO and CISO do not attend the evaluation and only hear anecdotal comments from their own internal team. Remember that your product will be compared against both competitors and incumbents, so, you need to make your case as clearly as possible.

> Note
>
> *I select vendors based on a comprehensive evaluation of various factors, but when scores are nearly identical, I often take our existing relationship into account. This helps deepen our current relationship and indirectly contributes to improving the quality and performance of the services that the vendor provides to my company, beyond just the services being procured.*
>
> **Group CISO – Large Japanese Bank**

If the CIO or CISO is not present during the evaluation, you may want to find a way to ensure your narrative reaches them directly so you don't need to rely solely on the internal team's retelling. Request a brief executive briefing, provide a concise leave-behind document tailored to their level, or leverage any existing relationship contact to give them your key messages firsthand. In relationship-driven markets like Japan, this direct touchpoint can carry more weight than any scorecard.

The gap review process may not always go as planned. Insights into why it goes poorly can often provide valuable lessons.

> Note
>
> *Challenges arise when vendors or clients are overly theoretical (PowerPoint consulting), lack transparency, or rely on junior teams without deep expertise. For instance, a client engagement faltered due to poor communication, inflexible processes, and misaligned KPIs. The organization could have improved the outcome by engaging in joint planning, simplifying intake processes, and prioritizing business impact over bureaucracy.*
>
> **Linus Lai – Group Vice President, IDC**

So far, I have discussed a gap assessment that measures a single solution against a defined standard or requirement, answering how far it falls short of where it needs to be. In the next section I outline a head-to-head gap assessment which does the same but across competing options simultaneously. Therefore, gaps are measured relative to each other as much as against the standard, making it a more powerful decision-making tool but one that requires rigor to avoid bias toward a predetermined outcome.

Head-to-head gap analysis

The gap analysis can be approached as the new solution vs. existing application or can be two to three new products being compared directly. An evaluation of multiple vendors helps the enterprise to identify the best solution, but this does create a larger workload on the CIO and CISO's team.

In my opinion, when the CIO or CISO is evaluating multiple vendors, the question becomes, "what separates the winner from everyone else?" Is it price, relationship, features, or something else?

Note

Above the RFP threshold, vendors succeed by understanding our business context and delivering credible outcomes. The decision is driven by fit, execution capability, and trust. Price matters, but it is never the sole—or decisive—factor.

Franco Marconcini – Group CISO, Electrolux Professional

The CIO and CISO will be expected by Procurement to have a degree of competitive pricing tension, and that is covered in more detail in *Chapter 19*. However, at this stage, what really counts is to separate the winner from the other solutions.

Note

If the solution is more commodity, then cost will be the main factor. If it is strategic, then the solution itself will be the main driver. What matters are:

- *Solution – present something that delivers business value and addresses the minimal requirements.*
- *Strategic thinking and potential – ability to go beyond the current solution. This represents long-term value and the ability to grow with the business.*
- *Price/Value – the commercials will be kept separate from the solution information, and until the technical assessment is completed, the procurement person and I will be the only viewers. This will ensure that points 1 and 2 (in this list) are the focus.*
- *Total cost of ownership – including cost to serve and cost to grow to understand how much the solution will cost to run post implementation.*
- *Relationship – this will often represent a tie breaker if the assessment process is close.*

John Taylor – Field CTO, Mimecast (former CIO & CISO)

Separating commercials from the technical assessment, the evaluation ensures decisions are made on merit first, preventing cost from distorting the scoring of solution quality. Together, the criteria John Taylor has shared create a balanced view of both immediate fit and long-term partnership potential, rewarding vendors who think beyond the brief rather than those who simply meet it.

Keeping your gap assessment honest

An honest gap assessment is one that is clear-eyed and lacks bias. There is little point in overstating strengths and sugar-coating weaknesses. The CIO and CISO will be exposed if this assessment is in any manner fabricated.

A fabricated (flattering) gap assessment does not stay in the room where it was presented. Unfortunately, it gets shared with the board, referenced in audit responses and used to make investment decisions that affect the entire organization.

When the gap between what the assessment claimed and what the environment contains becomes visible, the consequences land on the CIO and CISO who signed off on it, the champion who commissioned it, and the vendor who produced it.

An honest assessment is the only one that is acceptable. From my experience, a best practice gap analysis process must have these attributes:

- Collaborative (this is done *with* the client, not *to* them)
- Prioritized (focus on mandatory requirements)
- Contextualized (rough understanding of risk, costs, etc.)
- Trustworthy (honest assessment of fit)

> **Note**
>
> Since the CIO and CISO are likely not likely to be present at the final summary session, do you send this gap analysis result to them directly? My advice is that doing this is a high-risk but potentially high-reward approach.
>
> I'd recommend that if you believe you are a "Preferred Vendor" and the degree of gap is not extensive, then this is a viable solution. If your trust level is not high and the gap is considerable, then you will look a bit desperate, and this is not a path you will want to take.

In the scenario where there are many gaps, and you do not look like the right fit for the CIO/CISO's organization, then how do you bow out gracefully?

What to do if the outcome isn't positive

The truth is that many great proposals don't succeed. The first thing you should understand in these circumstances is that an unfavorable outcome from a gap analysis is not necessarily a lost relationship.

How you respond in the moment of losing will tell the CIO and CISO and their teams more about your character than anything you did during the initial pursuit.

> **Tip**
>
> Your being totally professional will be remembered long after the decision itself is forgotten.

If you are playing the long game, then you will want to wish the team well and perhaps also consider recommending an alternative approach. In my mind, providing a short verbal recommendation carries some kudos for your own character and respect for your integrity. Here is what you could say:

I've genuinely appreciated the access you gave us and the candor of your team throughout this process. We learned a great deal about your environment, and I have a lot of respect for what you are trying to build. I hope the path forward goes well.

Remember the CIO and CISO community is small and very interconnected. While you may have to bow out here, the leader that you are talking to is likely to show up in another account within a couple of years. Vendors that display strong integrity will build trust for another day.

It's important to stay engaged and stay curious. I'd recommend maintaining the relationships you have developed without an agenda.

> **Tip**
>
> The vendor who learns from a loss and returns better prepared next time is the one who eventually wins.

> **Note**
>
> *If you lose the bid, think about maintaining the relationship for the next time. If you have come second, it usually means that you've done most things right.*
>
> *Don't just walk away... the level of engagement may be light touch or less frequent, but you are demonstrating that you are interested in the relationship going forward.*
>
> **John Taylor – Field CTO, Mimecast (former CIO & CISO)**

In the next chapter, I cover how to navigate the maze of political dynamics that may arise at this juncture. While you do not want to play politics, this does happen and is frequently seen when we approach making a new strategic choice.

Summary

In this chapter I explored the gap analysis phase. This is where real trust is built or permanently lost. It is the moment vendors either demonstrate competence, character, and consistency, or they expose themselves as sellers with no substance.

The best vendors arrive having already done their own honest (internal) gap assessment. They also disclose weaknesses proactively and frame gaps in terms of workarounds, roadmap timelines, and peer context rather than hiding them.

Your goal here is to move from "Credible Vendor" to "Advisor" on the trust maturity scale while confirming technical fit with the architect and evaluation team.

The key learnings from this chapter are:

- **Trust = Competence + Character + Consistency** – competence is tested through technical questions. Character is revealed most when problems arise. Consistency only shows over time. All three must be present to advance.
- **Do your own gap analysis before they do theirs** – categorize known gaps as "Deal Breakers", "Significant", or "Nice-to-Haves"; prepare a gap analysis document with workaround, roadmap timeline, and industry context for each.
- **Honesty about gaps is a competitive advantage** – proactive transparency (including admitting problems at other deployments) is a decisive trust signal.
- **Never criticize competitors directly** – respectful product differentiation is the only acceptable approach.
- **Operational gaps often matter more than feature gaps** – the key underlying principle is that you're not buying software, you're entering a relationship with an operational dependency.
- **Know when to bow out gracefully** – if gaps are extensive and trust is low, recommending an alternative builds long-term character credit.

10

Navigating the Maze of Politics

In the previous chapter, you navigated gap analysis and moved your solution from contender to preferred option. Now a different challenge emerges, one that no amount of technical preparation can fully protect you from: internal politics.

As your gap analysis has progressed, your solution is getting broader attention. The champion has been quietly helping you to navigate the inherent politics that exist within the enterprise. Some of these politics are overt and surfaced, but the majority are covert and you have little awareness that this is playing out.

Your solution is starting to look like a contender, but not all internal parties may be aligned yet. This is akin to seeing the whole baseball field but not noting that there are divots on the surface that can trip you over as you make your way around the bases. Politics are hard to see but have a real impact on progress. The other stakeholders may be concerned about resource or budget conflicts, or that accountability in this domain is shared and impinges on their silo.

How do you now navigate the maze of politics to ensure that you can progress and your efforts up to this point are not lost?

Navigating organizational politics is a critical, learnable skill for CIOs, CISOs, champions, and vendors alike; those who master it treat it as the operating system of the organization rather than something to avoid. Each role must earn influence differently: CIOs by aligning technology to business outcomes, CISOs by reframing security in financial and risk terms, champions by building trust across both sides of the table, and vendors by making their internal advocates look good without overreaching. The CIO and CISO are very conscious that they need to try to control the narrative, so that the right messages are being received. In highly political scenarios the vendors are the first to be blamed if things don't go as expected. The internal champions also have some degree of exposure that they have to manage as they have been endorsing these new directions.

Across all these roles, political capital is built through proactive relationship management, coalition building, and transparency. This can be destroyed by surprises or hidden agendas. We'll dive into these political dynamics in this chapter to help you to navigate the maze of politics at play.

I will cover the following topics:

- Understanding politics through the eyes of CIOs and CISOs
- Navigating the maze
- Preparing CIO and CISO for the board
- Insurance for the champion

Understanding politics through the eyes of CIOs and CISOs

Politics in the business context refers to organizational tensions where leaders and their staff take actions to influence others or to gain power for themselves. Self-interest is key here—it plays out above the surface and, unfortunately, also below the surface. For yourself as a third party, these are mostly, if not completely, invisible, and you may not even be aware of the tension. However, CIOs and CISOs often will see and observe politics, and this may change how they operate and can manifest in how they show up in meetings.

I've learned that politics can involve tactics applied to form alliances and perhaps even to control information sources. I can say from my own experience, this can lead to a very negative and toxic environment.

Given this, the very thought of politics can be immobilizing. Most people do not like to play politics or engage in the game. Some career-minded leaders may find this distasteful but, nevertheless, accept it as a necessary evil to achieve their own goals, including career advancement. Also, remember that power is not equally distributed. The CIO and CISO may appear powerful with large teams, significant budgets, and substantial remuneration packages, yet they are rarely experts in politics. However, in today's era both the CIO and CISO must learn how to navigate in what is becoming a politicized position.

> **Note**
>
> *Stay above internal politics. If you find yourself being dragged into it, then walk away. You no doubt have other leads and other customers who need your help. Remain impartial and protect your future relationship with whoever comes out on top of the internal bun fight.*
>
> **Lee Barney – CISO, Ventia**

I'd note that from my experience, power, in the end, is not what you are given by a title or a budget. It is what others are willing to extend to you because they trust you, value your judgment, and believe that your success is connected to theirs. For CIOs and CISOs, building that kind of power requires acknowledging honestly that their expertise, however deep, does not automatically confer it. The champion will have some sense of the power that each executive holds, but they can also confuse hierarchical position with true influence.

> **Tip**
>
> Treat trust with the utmost respect. Every decision, communication, and alliance should be measured against whether it builds or erodes it.

The CIO's natural role is to seek alignment and to try to make everyone happy with the balance of strategic plans on new digital investments, resilience, and regulatory compliance. As a result, the CIO often must learn to be a strong diplomat and an authoritative voice on the executive management committee. The CIO and CISO are constantly trading off their own agenda to reduce risks for what others are asking of them and the team. They are asked to go faster, then they risk their peer executives being upset that change is occurring too quickly.

Having established how the CIO and CISO operate politically, what does this mean for those who work with them? The vendors and champions who understand the diplomatic constraints of the CIO and the agenda trade-offs of the CISO will engage with them far more effectively than those who treat them as unconstrained decision-makers.

Concerns around politics and the associated friction they can cause can drive the behavior of these leaders. For many CIOs and CISOs, it is not the technical complexity of a decision that shapes their behavior, it is the political consequence. They need to be aware where friction will come from, who will resist, and what it will cost them personally to push through it. This narrows the range of what they are willing to propose or defend themselves.

The following diagram maps the stakeholders whose disapproval CIOs and CISOs tend to most fear, and whose concerns will be amplified whenever political noise reaches them:

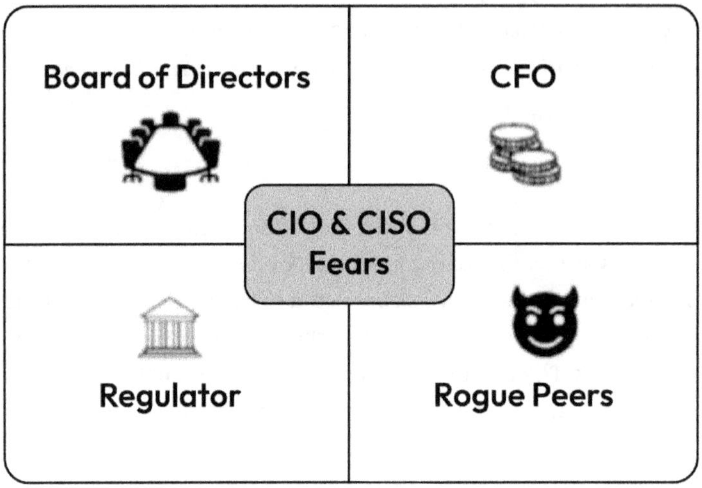

Figure 10.1 – Who the CIO and CISO fear disapproval from

This is a careful balancing act for CIOs and CISOs. They do not want to get on the bad side of the board, the CFO, or regulators in particular.

> **Tip**
>
> The CFO rarely opposes technology investment directly; instead, they apply traditional financial measures to non-linear transformation programs by demanding ROI timelines and payback periods that bear no relationship to how technology value is delivered.
>
> The CIO and CISO who cannot speak the CFO's language fluently enough to push back will find their most important change programs consistently underfunded or deferred. The vendor who helps them navigate both relationships with board-ready narrative and a CFO-proof financial case earns a position that no competitor can easily displace.

Then there is the rogue peer, who sits closer to home than the board or the CFO. Rogue peers are often business unit leaders, marketing executives, and operational managers who procure and deploy technology or AI solutions outside of the approved governance process. Unfortunately, these peers are a persistent and growing reality, accelerated by the ease with which software as a service (SaaS) platforms and AI tools can be activated.

The CIO and CISO are rarely consulted before these decisions are made. But they are almost always consulted after, specifically when something goes wrong. The rogue peer who deployed the solution is rarely the one who answers for it, and they don't usually attend the risk committee after an incident has occurred to explain an issue.

Should any political "noise" be heard by any of these parties, CIOs and CISOs may fear that this would then be amplified and even that their own job may be placed on the line.

When attempting to introduce new ideas, tools, and strategy, CIOs and CISOs can come up against additional tension as peers realize that if the CIO or CISO gets this new investment approved, then there is less money in the overall budget to be spent on their own projects. They can then take pre-emptive strikes to weaken their business case.

Also posing a risk to the CIO or CISO's attempt to advocate for your solution is what is known as "not invented here" syndrome. This is politically dressed resistance to external ideas, and it is often a symptom of an organization that has not created enough psychological safety around change. This can lead to new ideas being dismissed as lacking credibility and often occurs to protect egos at stake.

It is against this backdrop that the CIO and CISO will be mindful of power struggles when different colleagues are competing for their own power and influence. These so-called turf wars rarely surface openly, yet significant positioning made by politically minded colleagues occurs in the background to take territory, akin to the Chinese game of *Go*.

How you assist the CIO and CISO to navigate the political maze they face can be the difference between success and failure.

Navigating the maze

Politics is an unspoken dynamic; you can see it, sometimes feel it, but it often remains unacknowledged, operating just below the surface of every meeting and approval process in the form of power, territory, and fear that nobody puts on the agenda but everybody brings into the room.

The following diagram summarizes the key factors that can potentially be root causes for politics:

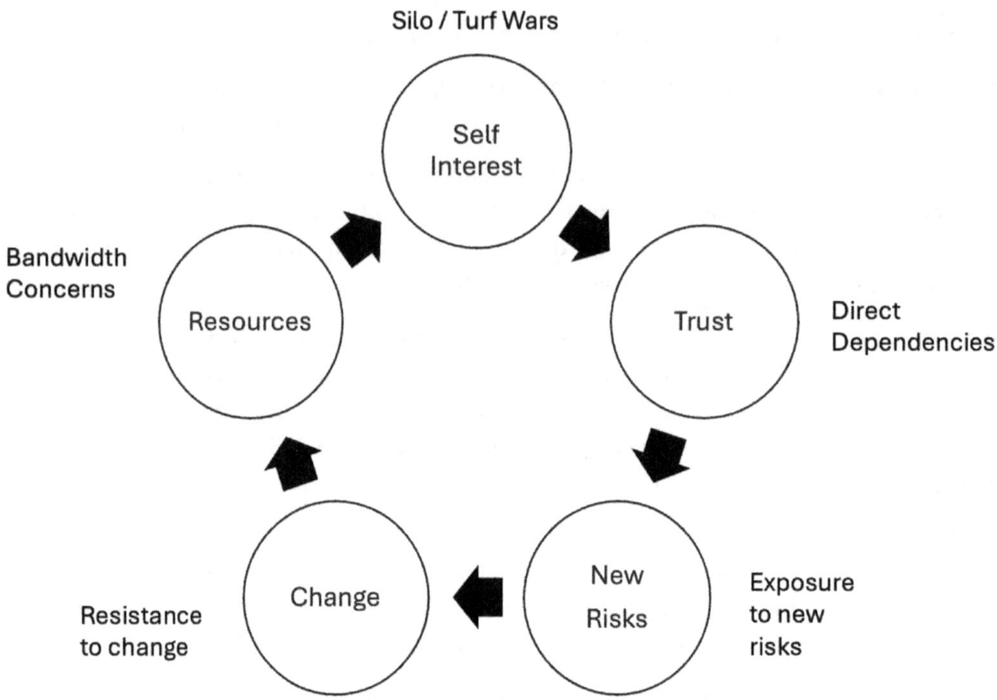

Figure 10.2 – Root causes of politics

Your internal champion is your guide and must be your starting point in navigating the politics around the sale of your solution, because this is a trust exercise. Having been in similar situations myself, it at times feels like being blindfolded in a maze, having to move carefully, rely on instinct and touch rather than sight. I've learnt that the most practical thing you can do is find others who have walked this maze before to walk it with you.

Helping your champion to prepare answers to these questions will aid navigation:

	Top 10 questions to answer	**Relevance**
1	How does this address our problem?	*Walk me through exactly which pain points on our roadmap this solves*
2	How does this connect to our existing stack?	*What gets deprecated, what new dependencies do we assume?*

	Top 10 questions to answer	Relevance
3	Where does this sit in our transformation journey?	*Does this accelerate this journey or create a detour?*
4	What is your security position?	*SOC 2, penetration test results, software development lifecycle (SDLC), etc*
5	Where will our data live and who can touch it?	*Data residency, data handling, encryption at rest, and in transit, etc*
6	What happens in the event you are breached?	*Your notification timeline, liability, etc*
7	What is the real total cost of ownership?	*Licensing, integration, internal resource load, etc*
8	What resources will be required for this to work?	*Timeline and the internal headcount required*
9	Give me three reference customers who are similar to us	*Similar industry, scale, and similar complexity*
10	Will you still be here in five years?	*Financials, roadmap, and your acquisition risk*

Table 10.1 – Questions to answer

The quality of your answers to these ten questions will tell the champion almost everything they need to know not just about the solution, but about you as a potential long-term partner.

Going back to *Figure 10.2*, these are the areas that you, as a vendor, can particularly assist with:

- **New risks.** You can share case studies of how other organizations have managed similar new risks.
- **Change concerns.** Again here, sharing examples of how other peer organizations have managed this change is useful.
- **Resource concerns.** The actual (or at least likely) headcount and expertise required.

Since extended stakeholders will likely review the gap analysis, you'll need to ensure you can carefully meet these challenges if possible.

> **Tip**
>
> Ask your champion a simple question: what friction can we expect and what can I do to help prepare for this?

Helping CIOs and CISOs reduce political noise

The CIO and CISO will hear about friction; most likely, they'd have heard this before you were informed. They will always back their team, but they'll also be cognizant of the politics and want to reduce "noise" levels. This "noise" rarely stays contained; other peers not involved may overhear it. The CIO is particularly sensitive to managing these relationships.

While they may not personally be across all the details, the gaps identified, and the sources of friction, as executive leaders, CIOs and CISOs must drive change with as little noise as possible.

A useful practical approach you can take to help CIOs and CISOs reduce this political noise is to offer customer references, allowing these executives to speak on a peer-to-peer basis. Both the CIO and CISO can gain great perspective and insights from talking to organizations that are "live" with your product or service, and which serve as proof points for the solution.

> **Note**
>
> Long-term customer references are valuable because a peer can explain what it is like to work with you, perhaps in comparison to another vendor, and how the product you are selling has evolved over time. This gives them a sense of what a long-term partnership with your company will actually feel like.

Political concerns tend to be the number one career risk that the CIO and CISO care about. This can be their career killer if they cannot drive a change to deliver an expected business outcome due to political resistance (this is very real for the CIO in particular, and their longer-term career survival depends on navigating this successfully.) This is why, to build consensus, the CIO and CISO will likely be willing to slow down progress and have direct conversations with known resistors.

Let's now explore the CFO and board of directors through their lens, as being the most feared stakeholders by the CIO and CISO and look at how you can assist the CIO and CISO with this engagement.

Calling the CFO an adversary is not entirely unfair, but many CIOs and CISOs would recognize the characterization immediately, even if they would never say it out loud. I've met several CFO executives who seemed to take delight in challenging the IT spend of the CIO and CISO. The reason for this is simple: IT spend is a large part of discretionary investment, and it is often hard to articulate why this is required.

Defending against CFO attacks

Once you gain a level of trust with your champion, they may tell you that the CFO is challenging the project. In today's business environment, there is a constant cycle of budget cuts that occur whenever economic headwinds are experienced. The CFO will always heavily scrutinize IT and cyber spending as they tend to see this as pure expense with hard-to-measure returns. (Some of the new investments in AI, however, come with a promise to increase productivity and, for that reason, may have slightly less scrutiny.)

To appease the CFO, the CIO and CISO will need to have bulletproof ROI and payback justifications, which you should provide them with. The CFO will care about cost avoidance and will also prefer either OPEX (operating expense) or CAPEX (capital expense). Their preference varies by company: some CFOs want OPEX for flexibility, others want CAPEX to avoid hitting quarterly earnings. You will want to frame the investment to match their bias. They typically also care about total cost of ownership (TCO), and unfortunately, they will include any write-off costs in this equation.

> Note
>
> *When you are a businessperson, you want to go faster because you're not constrained by the resources or constrained by the other projects. We have an annual budget process and on January 1st everyone runs off and starts 800 projects, but we do not have 800 architects or project managers or SMEs.*
>
> **Scott Collary – Group CIO, Westpac Group**

Most CFOs will accept a three-year ROI, and in some cases, I've seen them deduct operating expenses from forecast budgets of the CIO in anticipation of future savings. Two factors are in play here—first, the CIO may not be here in 3 years' time, so is willing to commit to this, and second, I've seen CFOs sometimes forget these forward commitments.

When you are providing data to the CIO and CISO for these justifications, be aware of the distinction between Type 1 and Type 2 savings:

Type 1 "Hard" Savings $	These are direct $ reductions in budgets.
Type 2 "Soft" Savings 	These are time saving or cost avoidance savings.

Table 10.2 – Hard vs. soft savings

CFOs only really care about hard savings. For example, we have made an investment of $1 million, and the hard savings of $1 million over 3 years are cash that can be re-allocated into the CFO's pool for new investment.

The CFO also likes to hear about headcount reduction from automation. For example, removing three full-time equivalent roles from your Sydney team's established staff budget. They also like to hear about application simplification and how the new solution will, for example, allow two other legacy products to be retired.

To be totally honest, CIOs and CISOs would probably prefer to have some budget buffers rather than commit to hard savings. CIOs and CISOs like to negotiate and speak to the CFO about achieving Type 2, or soft savings. This means that there would be some efficiency gains or cost avoidance. For instance, the investment will improve data loss prevention controls and avoid a privacy fine of $3 million, or that our software engineers can use GitHub Copilot, and they can then increase code output by 30%. As the disapproval of the CFO is generally feared, CIOs and CISOs will likely focus on hard savings to appease them, however.

> **Note**
>
> I've seen commercial deals where outcomes can be tied to the delivery milestones. This usually is driven by the CFO and Procurement, but I'm not going to recommend or not recommend this approach. Suffice it to say that delivery is hard enough without this added pressure.

The CFO is often going to argue for "doing nothing" and deferring this expense to the following year to prioritize revenue generation over new added expenses. New risks that the CIO or CISO have been escalating as concerns are frankly not high on their radar.

As a vendor, one way you can potentially help the CIO and CISO with addressing the CFO's concerns is by offering to put the CFO in touch with another reference site CFO.

I've said *potentially* here given that financial positions and budgets are heterogeneous, meaning this may be of limited value. The same net present value (NPV) calculation, the same payback period, and the same financial business case can land entirely differently in another organization.

In either case where the CFO is winning the argument and no new budget is available to fund your project, your position may appear bleak. Before giving up, try to establish whether this is an advanced negotiation tactic being played out. For example, the messaging from the architect, CIO and CISO are all positive, but they all confirm that there is no room in the budget. However, if there are other large projects commencing and new demands to cut your price, then this may be a negotiation tactic.

When friction is met, another option is pursuing a small pilot or proof of concept (POC). The CFO is often happy to fund this with the goal of getting started and getting some data to prove the potential benefits. I've also seen vendors offering to fully fund a POC. I will discuss POCs further in *Chapter 12*.

You can explore the appetite to start with a small department or location with a limited user base. With this approach, the CIO and CISO will feel that they are making progress, rather than coming to a halt. Plus, there will be learnings to prove the actual value your solution provides. This will also serve to reduce risks around a larger implementation.

> **Tip**
>
> Explore a pilot to keep progress moving ahead; this is most likely to get alignment of CFO, CIO and CISO.

We will discuss packages (integrated platforms) vs. best of breed solutions in *Chapter 13*, but it is a potential approach to consider raising in this broader scenario to consolidate some tools, if you are selling a package.

> **Note**
>
> Note that best of breed, as you expect, would give you the "best" tool for every job but with the burden of making them work together, while a package gives you a coherent environment but at the constraint of a single vendor's roadmap and their pace of innovation.

The CFO with procurement team counsel will always favor packages with the promise of overall lower investment cost. Raising this is very opportunistic but I'd caution that it can complicate matters and add in a broader requirement that was not previously considered.

> **Tip**
>
> You could also consider some innovative pricing model where your product or service is discounted at the beginning.

Finally, if none of these approaches is gaining traction, your best option may be just to postpone the engagement, while ensuring that you continue to assist the CIO and CISO with any further preparation for a later business case in terms of other queries that have not yet been addressed.

Of all the conversations the CIO and CISO will have in their career none carries more weight or more personal consequence than the one that happens in the boardroom.

Preparing CIO and CISO for the board

A large investment that requires meaningful trade-offs does not stay within the technology function. It earns its way onto the board agenda precisely because it is significant enough to slow down other strategic priorities or change the shape of what the organization can and cannot do in the short term. You can make a real difference here to support the CIO and CISO.

The CIO and CISO will have to provide a clear, non-technical explanation of why the proposed solution makes sense, considering it likely cannot be achieved without sacrificing some other projects' spending first.

You can help with anticipated board questions by referring to those you know that have come up at other organizations. This will often be around risks to operations by this solution not working, and the degree of disruption of this change, as the board has a high focus on operational continuity and what risk mitigations have been considered.

To address these questions, you can provide some board presentation materials that have been successful at other (de-identified) enterprises. It's worth including content that provides insights into risk mitigation, financial justification, and implementation timelines.

The board, the CEO or the Chief Operating Officer (COO), will likely also express some curiosity about the company behind the solution being proposed. They understand that a great selection of business partners is vital for long-term success. In this case, then the CEO may benefit from meeting your own CEO and having a briefing to better understand your company as a partner.

The agenda for such a briefing may cover:

- Overall company strategy and growth
- Overview of peer companies that have been successful with this solution
- How are risks mitigated

The board engagement is one of the highest arenas of fear for the CIO and CISO. This can be a strong case to use external advisors to help navigate politics. This can be an independent advisor or one of the more strategic ones such as Bain, BCG and McKinsey. There are also specialized vendor advisory groups like Gartner®, Forrester®, and some boutique firms—this I will cover in *Chapter 11*.

Insurance for the champion

I've noted that the role of the champion is tricky and that they will be involved in helping the CIO and CISO to navigate politics. For this reason, I wanted to ensure that I provided some guidance for them.

Previously I noted ten questions you can provide champions to help navigate the political maze and to ensure that they have 100% confidence in you and your solution. There are however a different set of questions that champions need to consider when thinking about internal politics and navigating their career while driving this change:

	Top 10 reflection questions	**Notes for champions**
1	Who owns this problem?	*Align to the person accountable for the problem, not just affected by it. Ownership drives urgency and urgency drives decisions.*

	Top 10 reflection questions	Notes for champions
2	Who benefits and who loses if this solution succeeds?	*Every technology decision creates winners and losers; map them before you start advocating or you will be surprised by the resistance you encounter.*
3	Have I built my coalition before I need it?	*The relationships that protect you when the politics get difficult are the ones built before the politics arrived.*
4	Where does this sit on the CIO and CISO's actual priority list?	*What executives say they care about and what they are measured on are not always the same thing.*
5	Which stakeholders need to be briefed before the meeting?	*Surprises in executive meetings are rarely welcome, regardless of how sound the idea is. Pre-brief the key players.*
6	Who are the quiet blockers?	*Identify who has the most to lose and engage them privately before they engage publicly against you.*
7	Can I articulate why now?	*Is this a critical priority, regulatory deadline, a strategic inflection point or addressing a major risk?*
8	Have I translated the technical case into a business consequence?	*What the solution does, but what the organization avoids, gains, etc.*
9	Is the minimum viable version to be approved first viable?	*Knowing when to scale down your ambition in order to get it moving is one of the most important skills in organizational change.*
10	If this goes wrong, what is my exposure?	*Understand what you are putting on the line; ensure the vendor understands it too.*

Table 10.3 – Reflection questions for champions

Summary

In this chapter, we explored the reality of navigating the politics the CIO and CISO will be facing behind the scenes. Unfortunately, political friction is the hidden killer of deals that are technically sound and commercially justified. And as a vendor, you are largely blind to it.

The winning approach is to stay neutral. Support your champion with information, evidence, and peer references rather than trying to own the politics yourself. Arm them with this and let peer credibility do the heavy lifting.

The key learnings from this chapter are:

- **Politics is a black box** – work only through your champion. Your role is to ensure that you equip them with your expertise, peer references, and gap analysis context that neutralizes resistance without appearing to take sides.
- **There are three friction points where you can genuinely help** – these are resource concerns, where you can provide headcount and implementation data from comparable sites, new risk fears, which you can address with case studies, and change management resistance, where you can share peer adoption stories.
- **CFO defense demands hard savings** – they care about hard savings: headcount reduction, application retirement, cash that flows back into their pool. Soft savings such as efficiency gains are useful context but rarely move the needle alone. When budget is genuinely frozen, a small, contained pilot can maintain momentum and preserve the relationship without requiring full commitment.
- **Board preparation is an underutilized vendor opportunity** – you will not be in the boardroom, but you can shape what happens there. Provide board presentation materials based on anticipated questions from other engagements.

11

The Value of Research Analysts and Advisors

In the previous chapter, I explored how to navigate the maze of politics. This chapter covers how research analysts can be used to assist with that. Referencing an independent research source can take the heat out of the equation. While the CIO and CISO still own the decision, these resources provide trusted validation from a third party. Sometimes external advisors are given more time and attention than internal executives.

Many specialized research analyst firms such as Gartner®, Forrester®, IDC® and some boutique firms like IT-Harvest® or Frost & Sullivan® are particularly valued by the CIO and CISO for their advice.

Then there are strategy consultants as well, such as McKinsey, Bain, and BCG (commonly referred to as MBB), or Deloitte, KPMG, EY, and PwC (commonly referred to as the Big 4). These trusted advisors' research can lend credibility to CIO and CISO recommendations.

All these analysts also serve you, as vendors, by providing an independent source of intelligence that you can share with your clients.

I'd argue that there are very few enterprise technology purchase decisions that occur without some degree of reference to analyst research. Technology solution integration is a complex challenge, and the CIO and CISO are only human. They want to ensure that the strategic change they are planning will not cost them their job or negatively impact their company.

In this chapter I explain the role analysts and advisors play in the tech and cyber sales journey, with insights into these major players, including how you can use their insights to help your case.

The key topics we will cover in this chapter are:

- Understanding how analysts work
- Understanding boutique advisors
- Big 4 vs. MBB

> Note
>
> *If you walk into a boardroom meeting as a CISO tomorrow and say, "Look, I've been doing my research on ChatGPT and here are the products we need to buy," you have very limited aircover.*
>
> *Walk in and say "According to Gartner these are the products we should consider," heads will nod and say "well, that must be okay then."*
>
> *The risk of course is that tried and true often stymies innovation. Take a blended approach and use ChatGPT to identify options and an analyst firm to qualify their capabilities.*
>
> **Matt Boon – Senior Director, Strategic Research, Adapt**

Understanding how analysts work

When there is doubt, analysts can provide a clearer view of the situation. By providing independent third-party validation, their research tends to be trusted as expert opinion on different technology domains.

> Note
>
> *We use available research and expertise to help inform us on what's coming and what's good. This helps us narrow down what we should be looking at.*
>
> **Scott Collary – Group CIO, Westpac Group**

Personally, as a CIO and CISO, I've used Gartner, Forrester, IDC and other boutique firms. These services have different levels of subscription, and each provides a different level of support and service. I've summarized the three major market leaders in the following diagram, with some context on where they focus and how they are different:

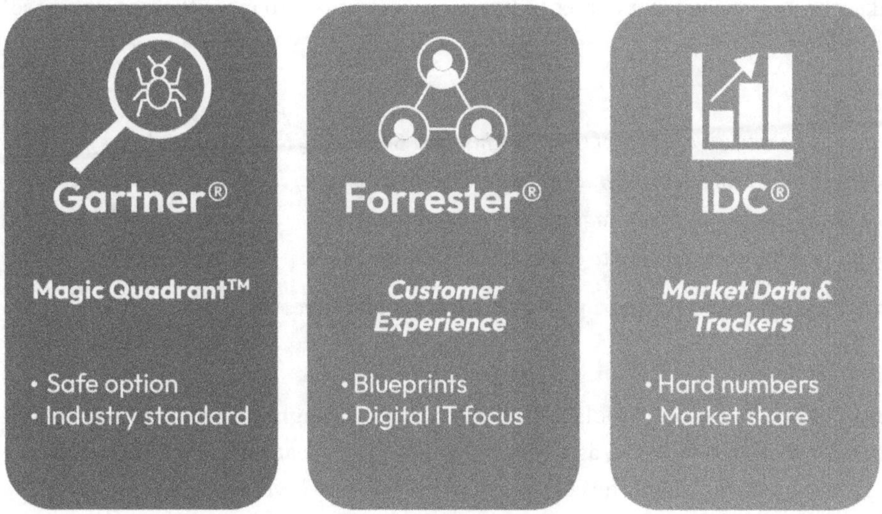

Figure 11.1 - Gartner vs Forrester vs IDC

As you can see, there are some distinct differences across the three major providers in terms of their approach and focus areas.

When CIOs and CISOs receive a challenge on why they have chosen any particular product, they typically respond with reference to third-party research. For example:

Gartner	*Gartner put them in the Leaders category of the Magic Quadrant™*
Forrester	*They are rated highly by Forrester*
IDC	*IDC shows them as being a market leader*

Table 11.1 - Analyst justification

> Note
>
> *The difference with an analyst is that we won't tell you what you want to hear. We'll tell you what you should hear.*
>
> **Matt Boon – Senior Director, Strategic Research, Adapt**

The CIO and CISO will be aware that no analyst is perfect. They will use them to guide and validate their decision, not to make the decision for them. Using multiple analysts is well accepted by large enterprises. For medium-sized and small enterprises, however, cost will most likely be an issue when it comes to having subscriptions to more than one of these research bodies.

> Note
>
> *Typically, I like to use a couple of them, not just one. Every place I've been has always used Gartner for one thing or another, but they're expensive. Forrester is getting to be expensive and they're also not as wide in coverage. So, there are times when they may not be covering a specific niche, so then you have to go out to IDC or another firm.*
>
> **Gary Hayslip – CISO Halycon.ai, Board Director and Investor**

CIOs and CISOs will use these tools to help them think through the problem they are trying to address. On the other hand, you, as a vendor, will probably read these reports with a competitive eye, seeing where the competition is placed vis-à-vis your own products.

In the following sections, I offer brief primers on each of the market-leading firms, drawn from my own experience as a subscriber and user of their research services.

A primer on Gartner's research services

Gartner is generally renowned as a safe sounding board that has good coverage across the technology stack, including many niche areas. They are particularly known for the Gartner Magic Quadrant™, which is a standard for market ownership. The dominance of Gartner is such that most enterprise vendors have an existing contract with them.

There are many levels of Gartner membership. I've personally been a member of the Gartner Executive Program (ExP), which is their highest tier for senior technology executives. This program provides regular 1:1 meetings and they assign an Executive Partner (EP) who can act as a coach.

I have also been a member of the Gartner® Research Board, an elite service for the largest enterprises only. This comes with a premium price tag and the service serves as a network of peers that you can brainstorm with, ask questions, and learn from.

> Note
>
> I understand that there is also a Gartner® Enterprise IT Leaders (EITL) service for senior IT Directors and those who are direct reports of the C-Suite, and a membership group, Gartner® Technical Professionals (GTP), for "hands on" technologists.

Most CIOs and CISOs will use the Gartner Magic Quadrant™, usually on an annual basis, to help them become more educated on the market and, where possible, to gain some intel on respective vendors and how they compare to each other.

The quadrant provides a 2x2 matrix with four boxes: Challengers, Leaders, Visionaries, and Niche Players:

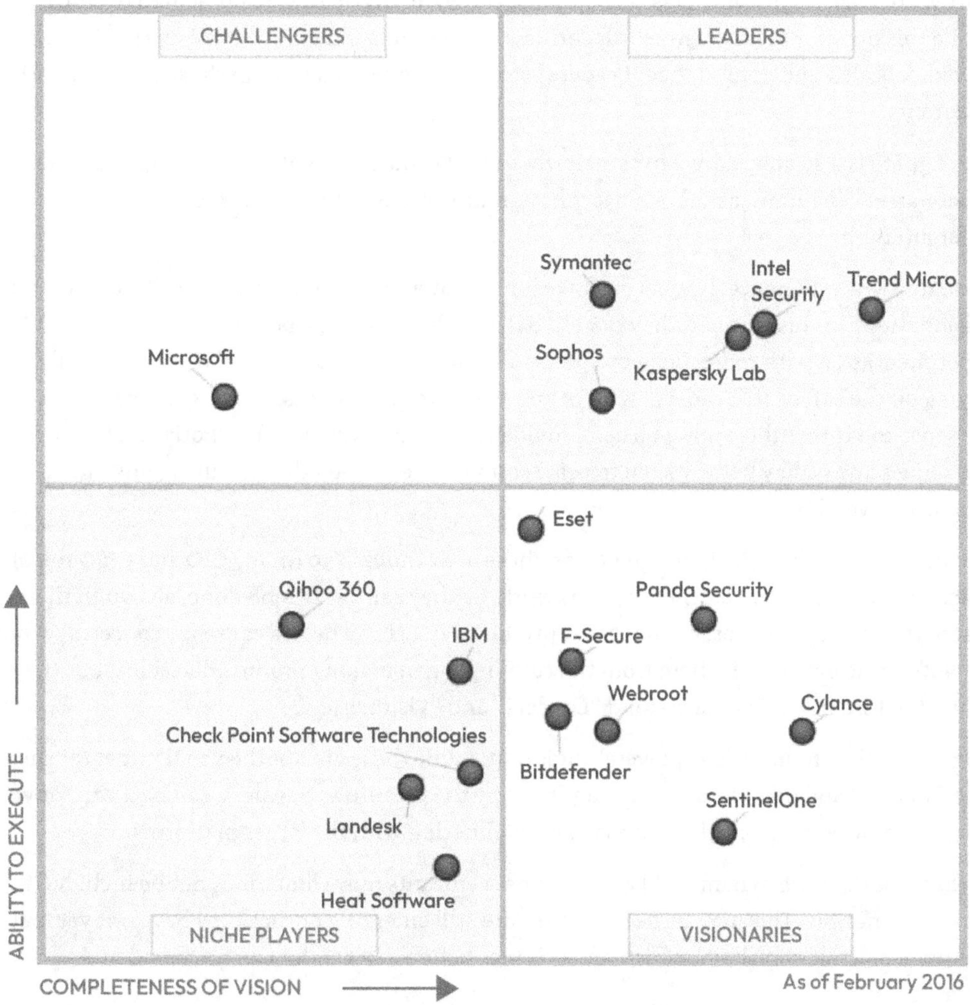

Figure 11.2 - Example Gartner Magic Quadrant™ (2016) (licensed for use under CC BY-SA 4.0: https://creativecommons.org/licenses/by-sa/4.0/deed.en, via Wikimedia (https://commons.wikimedia.org/w/index.php?curid=47558996))

The "Leaders" box in the top right-hand corner highlights the solutions that Gartner considers as having completeness of vision and ability to execute. This is the sweet spot that every CIO and CISO will want to examine and that every vendor wants to inhabit.

This quadrant helps CIOs and CISOs to build their shortlist of contenders and it also assists with risk management around the decision, since it is the natural and lowest risk option to start with. Clearly, personal bias will influence how much risk they are prepared to consider. While this quadrant will get much attention, this does depend on the problem that is being solved. It is also understood that "Leaders" can be more expensive than those players in other quadrants.

When there is a strategic drive to transform, the CIO and CISO will more strongly consider the "Visionaries" quadrant, as these players have more potential for future-proofing differentiation.

From my own experience, leaders can take joint strategic positions with both "Leaders" and "Visionaries". In this manner, they plan to balance their strategic portfolio with experimentation with more niche products in some non-mission-critical use cases, while relying on the safety of "Leaders" with prime-time proven systems, such as systems of record. My sense too is that this approach can provide the CIO and CISO with negotiation leverage as emerging players may be very keen to price competitively when they are up against an established vendor.

Moving on to the "Challengers" quadrant, these are vendors I've (in my CIO and CISO roles) considered as being safe partners to work with, as they can get the job done, although their roadmap at the time the assessment was produced may have been a cause for concern. I would not automatically exclude them from the running when making product decisions, but they would be third in line for me, behind "Leaders" and "Visionaries".

Being classified in the "Niche players" quadrant, while these are not the usual target for the CIO and CISO and don't tend to be sought out by the C-Suite as partners, can be a win for you if you are a new best-of-breed solution that is competing with the larger platforms.

As these markets are dynamic, I'd note that new entrants may sometimes not be included in the latest analysis. This may be because they are still emerging or that they have not yet met Gartner's revenue threshold, which must be met before any vendor can be considered.

Note

Analysts themselves typically will engage with vendors that they find interesting and will be guided by what they're hearing from end users as well. I'm not being a Gartner cheerleader, but it is a very independent objective. Basically, it's very, very strict.

Matt Boon – Senior Director, Strategic Research, Adapt

The CIO and CISO will always pay attention to what Gartner says but will also be questioning whether the problem they are trying to solve aligns with their analysis. There can be subtle differences in how these markets are defined in terms of their micro segments, and the CIO and CISO are often learning this and the associated jargon as they explore. They do usually, therefore, want to look at the details in these analyses, not just the headlines.

Note

Every purchase decision stems directly from the business-aligned cyber risk appetite. Vendors often think their placement in a Gartner Magic Quadrant™ (just an example) matters most. For large enterprises, it rarely dictates the final call.

I have seen vendors positioned at the absolute top of an industry quadrant become operational disasters in a live production environment. What actually wins the deal is customization, flexibility, and the ability to adapt to exact use cases.

Jayant Dave – CISO, Check Point Software

Technology hype cycle

Gartner also produces the Gartner Hype Cycle™ which maps the maturity trajectory of emerging technologies against the cycle of expectations that typically accompanies them.

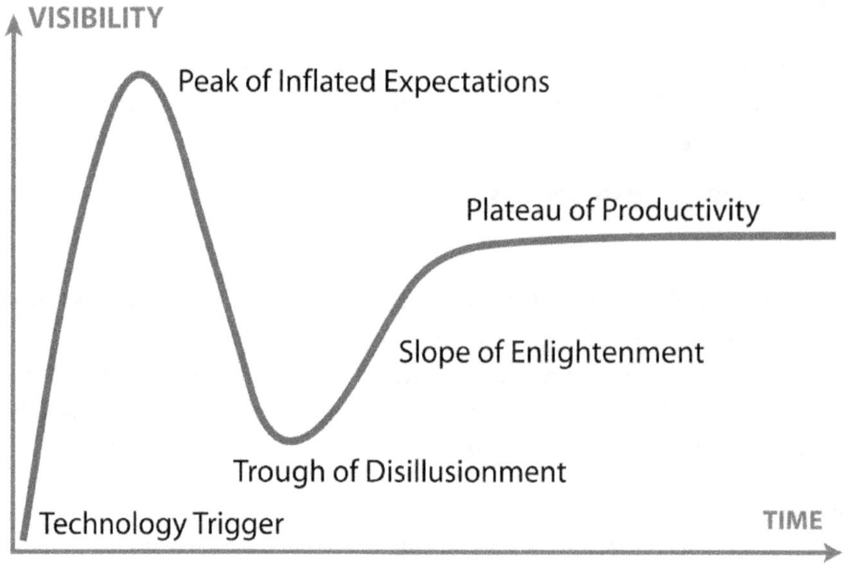

Figure 11.3 - Graph based on the Gartner Hype Cycle™

(Image by Jeremy Kemp at English Wikipedia, used under license CC BY-SA 3.0, https://creativecommons.org/licenses/by-sa/3.0/deed.en)

In this framework, any new technology will progress through this "roller coaster ride":

- Innovation (or "Technology", as above) Trigger
- Peak of inflated expectations
- Trough of Disillusionment
- Slope of Enlightenment
- Plateau of Productivity

This is the natural cycle that new technology travels through, albeit at different speeds. There will be early recognition of the new tech, followed by hype that inflates expectations, before people become disillusioned with the actual reality of the solution. This then leads to the final stages of adoption, where what this technology actually can provide is accepted.

Note that this framework is about the overall category of technology, rather than specific brands and products. This provides a great perspective for the CIO and CISO who are window shopping new technology to understand the relative maturity of product categories. Some CIOs and CISOs will use this analysis to inform their thinking about the relative timing of when to consider evaluating new or alternative technologies. For instance, if this hype cycle shows Agentic AI at the "Peak of inflated expectations", the CIO or CISO will exercise some caution, not expecting a new solution in this area to be perfect but to have some areas requiring improvement.

When Gartner says you are past the "Trough", then that is when your product will be more seriously considered. The average CIO and CISO will often wait for the last two stages of the Gartner Hype Cycle™ to signal when they want to engage in considering a category of technology. The rationale for this is that at stages 4–5 of this cycle then:

- There is real ROI evidence
- Best practices have matured
- Vendor market has stabilized
- Compliance frameworks are available

The CIO and CISO's job is to minimize operational risk, not to win innovation awards. When a technology has reached stages 4 and 5 this is when the technology may finally fit the risk tolerance of a regulated budget-constrained enterprise.

Having said that, I should note that different CIO and CISO personas may work to a different set of assumptions. It may be the case that how your efforts in pitching new technologies and sharing industry intel land will be correlated to the comfort zone of each of the personas. For example, in the following table I have mapped how the different personas I identified earlier in this book may operate at different stages of the curve:

Persona	**Comfort Zone**
Transformation CIO 	Being a more natural risk taker, the Transformation CIO is more likely to want to be a "first mover", and hence may act quickly to evaluate new technology when they are at the "Innovation (or Technology) Trigger" stage.

Persona	Comfort Zone
Operational CIO 	A very conservative leader, operational CIOs worry about business continuity, so may ignore technology that is not at the "Plateau of Productivity". These leaders tend to hate hype and want certainty over the unique and funky.
Risk CIO 	This leader thinks in the eyes of the risk committee. They therefore operate aligned with the risk appetite. Hence, they work through the whole curve and can accelerate or adopt innovation early or late, depending on this appetite.
Business CIO 	This CIO cares about positive business outcomes, such as driving new revenue and customer experience (CX) improvement. They see IT innovation as the driver of this improvement and, as such, they act as a "fast follower" and might act at the "Trough of Disillusionment" stage.

Table 11.2 - CIO personas and Gartner Hype Cycle™

How the different CISO personas may react is much the same in the first two of the four types. However, they diverge in the remaining two personas. This divergence is not about risk appetite in the generic sense; it is about what each persona is actually waiting to learn. When that trigger point has been reached, then they are ready to act (note that this does not mean that they are ready to buy):

Persona	Comfort Zone
Transformation CISO 	The Transformation CISO likes to act quickly and has a higher risk tolerance; hence, they are more comfortable operating at the "Innovation (or Technology) Trigger" stage. (Note that this persona is not very common.)
Operational CISO 	This CISO is very binary and prioritizes safety. Hence, this leader is patient enough to wait until technology has matured and reached the "Plateau of Productivity" stage.
Risk CISO 	The Risk CISO is pragmatic. They can act fast to take advantage of a crisis when there has been a recent breach event to learn from that facilitates risk mitigation and remediation. Their natural preference may be to wait until the "Trough of Disillusionment" stage, as at this stage there is further clarity.
Business CISO 	These CISOs are extremely business sensitive and exercise caution to not take any action that can upset their business colleagues. Their natural bias is to be a "fast follower," so they generally wait for the "Peak of Inflated Expectations".

Table 11.3 - CISO personas and Gartner Hype Cycle™

Note there are pressures on CISOs to be more business-focused now, rather than just worrying about isolated technology outcomes (such as tool deployment, patch cycles, or system uptime). Instead, they must leverage security to enable business value strategic objectives, like accelerated digital transformation, regulatory compliance, and market trust. Managing the cybersecurity risk appetite is a top priority for all enterprises.

I'm certain that every technology leader has seen the dynamics of the Gartner Hype Cycle™ play out. The real question is about timing, as predictions are often wrong in terms of when each curve will start to shift in a new direction. CIOs and CISOs can only read the clues which act as signals.

> **Note**
>
> I recall a cab driver talking to me about the various cryptocurrencies that he held with the rationale that there was a killing in the market to be made. Clearly, this was a signal for the "Peak of Inflated Expectations", but like picking equity stocks, while you can observe the trends it's harder to accurately predict the peaks and troughs.

A primer on Forrester's research services

Like Gartner's Magic Quadrant™, the Forrester Wave™ also plots industry leaders and ranks them in terms of the strength of their offering and their strategy.

While the Gartner Magic Quadrant™ is generally considered prevalent, in my view, Forrester may feel like a better option when the selection is highly contentious. This is because they provide more quantitative data and there is more transparency of their weighting, along with documented strengths, weaknesses, and differentiators for each vendor. I personally feel more confident in their findings in this specific scenario. This also means that tech teams can apply their logic to their own comparisons and specific home-grown weighting more easily.

The Forrester Wave™ plots vendors across the two dimensions of "Strength of Offering" and "Strength of Strategy". These vendors are segmented into "Leaders", "Strong Performers" and "Contenders".

From my own experience in reading these reports, a CIO and CISO will be glancing into the top right-hand corner ("Leaders") to see which solutions have been plotted there.

> **Note**
>
> *Both enterprise leaders (e.g., CIOs, CISOs, CDOs, etc.) and tech vendors read Forrester reports as a trusted, third-party frame for understanding markets, clarifying fast-moving technology shifts, and aligning their thinking with how the market is evolving rather than relying on internal opinion or vendor marketing alone.*
>
> *What's different is the intent and lens. Enterprise leaders read primarily to decide and defend. They try to seek clear recommendations, trade-offs, risks, and operating guidance they can use to prioritize investments, reduce uncertainty, and justify choices to boards and peers.*
>
> *On the other hand, vendors read to interpret and influence. They look for insight into buyer behavior, evaluation criteria, narrative signals, and gaps in their own positioning, products, or go-to-market strategy.*
>
> **Charlie Dai – Vice President and Principal Analyst, Forrester**

Forrester analysts have a strong following in their cybersecurity offering; given that CISOs are often more technical, the detailed approach they provide has particularly strong appeal for them. Forrester has a slightly different focus to Gartner, with a strategic digital and customer experience (CX) focus. This service can be valuable help for the CIO and CISO to better understand their own sales and marketing colleagues and peers.

When the CIO and CISO have access to both Gartner and Forrester reports, then they will read and review them both in tandem. I'd add that from my own experience they probably aren't required to reference more than one of these analyst reports, but they will value both and keep a mental note of relevant factoids, just in case they need to reference them later when asked by management or their executive peers.

The CIO and CISO will correlate Forrester and Gartner "leadership" categorizations as being a positive sign of affirmation that they are on the right track with considering a new solution. They will not be too distressed if this doesn't match on both as they will recognize that these technologies are changing and assessment is ongoing.

A primer on IDC's research services

A third option is IDC, who are well known for being the publisher of many of the most established technology publications. IDC is a great source of technology market share data and trends that are occurring across this field.

IDC also owns International Data Group (IDG), which was rebranded a few years ago as Foundry. In full disclosure, I've written freelance for both IDG and Foundry for their *CIO*, *Computerworld* and *CSO* publications for over 12 years. I have also been a regular speaker at their conferences.

A key difference from Gartner and Forrester services is that IDC access is less widely available for the CIO and CISO, but very commonplace for tech vendors in their Go-to-Market (GTM) strategy planning. IDC's foundational business strategy and revenue model are inherently vendor-centric, while Gartner and Forrester have targeted end-user buyers such as the CIO and CISO.

However, the CIO and CISO will trust data that is shared with them by IDC as an independent source that is reputable. When I've been presented with this data, as a CIO or CISO, at the early stages of trying to scan the market, this has helped me to scope out my first longlist and, in some cases, my draft shortlist.

> Note
>
> *CIOs and CISOs prioritize strategic alignment, measurable outcomes, service quality, and assurance. Product leaders focus on innovation and technical differentiation. Marketing teams value thought leadership and market visibility.*
>
> *Missteps occur when organizations use a one-size-fits-all approach or fail to tailor messaging to audience priorities.*
>
> **Linus Lai – Group Vice President, IDC**

The IDC MarketScape™ offering provides an assessment of vendors with a focus on market leadership and size. This is designed to serve as a data benchmark for these vendors. This product operates at 10,000 feet, so it lacks detailed product evaluation, focusing purely on competitive positioning:

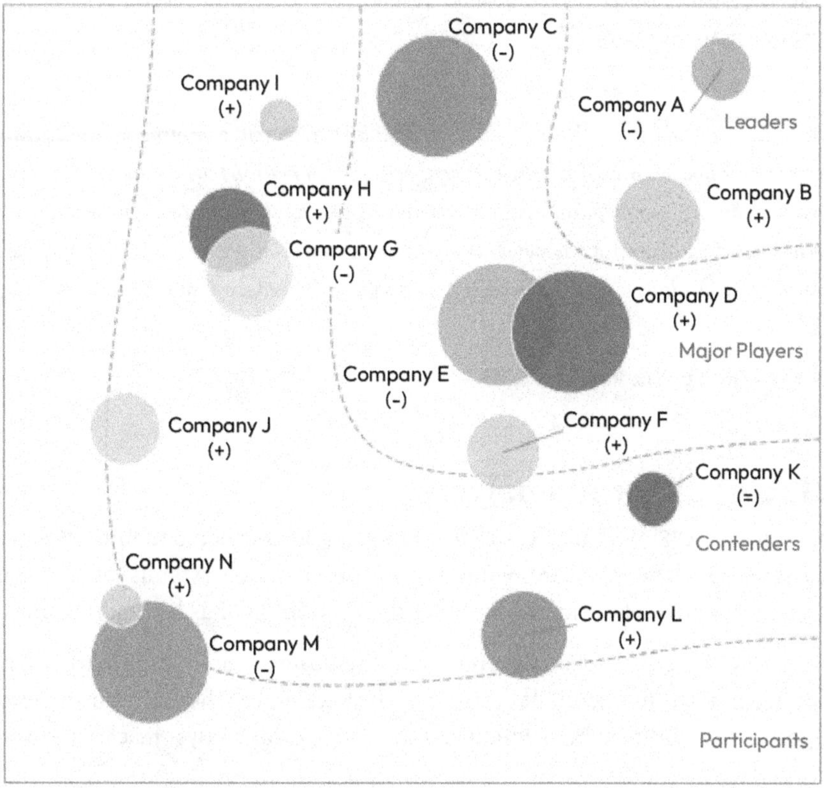

Figure 11.4 - Example IDC MarketScape™ report (used with IDC permission: https://www.IDC.com/promo/IDCmarketscape/)

I spoke to Linus Lai, IDC Vice President, about how analysts work across the sales process. The first question I posed was to ask his advice on how best to engage analysts.

> Note
>
> *IDC analysts prefer structured briefings for product updates, inquiry-driven discussions for deep dives, and executive-level conversations for strategic alignment. Ongoing dialogue and access to senior experts post-project are highly valued.*
>
> *The most productive engagements are those that combine formal briefings with informal, collaborative exchanges, allowing for real-time feedback and co-creation from a variety of stakeholders, depending on the nature of the engagement.*
>
> **Linus Lai – Group Vice President, IDC**

A second question that I posed to Linus was "What do vendors most commonly misunderstand about how analyst firms operate?"

> **Note**
>
> *Vendors often misunderstand the independence of analyst research, assuming influence can be bought or that rankings are solely based on vendor input. In reality, IDC's methodologies are rigorous, combining market data, customer references, and analyst expertise. Inclusion in research is based on relevance and evidence, not commercial relationships. Advisory services are considered consultative and independent, subject to a defined scope of research and qualifications.*
>
> **Linus Lai – Group Vice President, IDC**

The value of all three analysts

The average CIO and CISO will use research analysts but also speak to their trusted network. Of course, this is feasible when they are evaluating a "Leader" that is established, but this can be more challenging when looking at a new emerging solution that has less market presence.

For CIOs and CISOs, the value of analyst research is typically greater at the start when they are trying to learn about the market and then also at the back end as they move into more formal pricing negotiations. This results in what I call the U-Curve for analyst research value:

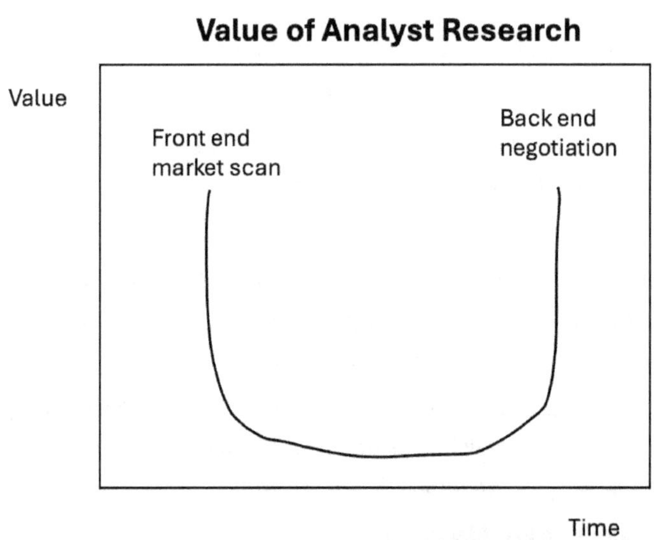

Figure 11.5 - U-Curve of value of research

In *Figure 11.5*, in the center of the U-Curve, we can see that there is a major dip in value, and that is likely when the proof of concept (POC) process and evaluation are underway. This is because the reports are generic and do not provide any insights into how this will work in the CIO and CISO's own environment. That's why, at this stage, reference site checking is much more valuable. Then, finally, at the back end, as we progress through contract and procurement processes, the value of these advisories increases as some benchmark data on price negotiation can help to sharpen the agreed price.

CIO and CISO time is short, so any shortcuts to accelerate the vendor evaluation process and shortlisting will be adopted. This market scan is of the highest strategic value to the CIO and CISO (despite a common industry belief that vendors pay these advisors for assistance, leading to them being included in upcoming reports, etc.). At any one point in time, there are thousands of options available. The CIO and CISO already have an extensive inventory of applications and systems, always too complicated and numerous.

> Note
>
> *We use Gartner in market scanning and have also leveraged industry analysts at times. It is one potential source of market intelligence but not the defining factor in many cases, as more specific, tailored information is more useful.*
>
> **Dan Chesterman – CIO, Teachers Mutual Bank**

Analyst research is also particularly valuable during gap analysis (which we explored in *Chapter 9*), where it can provide supplemental insights on scope differences between different solutions.

Given that using these analysts is de-facto best practice for the CIO and CISO, the reality is that there is a bias toward established players. Smaller entrants lack the same level of financial resources, so this becomes a barrier to entry. Tech and cyber vendors that are positioned in research analysts' reports bring instant credibility, making it much easier to get meetings with stakeholders. If you aren't included, gaining brand awareness and acceptance is trickier. Remember, while you are running for the next base, the CIO and CISO are only interested in the home run.

There are players beyond Gartner, Forrester and IDC, who I refer to as "boutique advisors". They operate with the CIO and CISO to provide a more personalized advisory service, albeit on a smaller scale.

Understanding boutique advisors

There are boutique advisors that provide specific market information on technology solutions – IT-Harvest, Frost & Sullivan, Adapt, Emertel and so on. They act as specialists in that they operate at a more granular level with the provision of quantifiable "hard" data and advise CIOs and CISOs on, for example, how to negotiate with vendor *ABC*, who has 35% market share, and "here is the approach to achieve a 15% discount."

While it could be the case that the CEO and board care less about the opinion of the advisor and instead want to know why the CIO themselves is comfortable with a recommendation, coverage and support from a friendly advisor provide the CIO and CISO with a degree of cover and safety.

> Note
>
> *The fastest way to lose me is to treat me like a channel:*
>
> - *Turning a briefing into a deal pitch*
> - *Withholding limitations (I will find them anyway)*
> - *We do everything positioning—no maturity fit, no wedge*
> - *Not knowing competitors (signals don't understand the category)*
>
> *I believe that advisors amplify vendors who bring market truth, not marketing.*
>
> **Sam Ghebranious – Director, Axcelerate / Senior Advisor, Frost & Sullivan**

In this section I examine IT-Harvest and Frost & Sullivan, as examples of what these services can offer. Unlike analyst firms that primarily guide enterprise procurement decisions, IT-Harvest and Frost & Sullivan strategically focus on mapping ecosystem growth.

They therefore serve technology vendors, venture capitalists, and the enterprise C-suite simultaneously. While IT-Harvest delivers data-driven tracking of cybersecurity vendor metrics like headcount and investment rounds, Frost & Sullivan provides macroeconomic growth forecasting and strategic advisory to fuel corporate mergers and acquisitions (M&A) and vendor go-to-market pipelines.

A primer on IT-Harvest

IT-Harvest is a cybersecurity specialty firm that was founded by Richard Stiennon (a former Gartner Analyst). At IT-Harvest Richard has built a strong reputation for providing depth of data at a real-time "live" level.

At the time of writing, IT-Harvest tracks more than 4,500 cyber firms and some 12,000 products. They monitor the landscape in terms of the health of the vendor, for instance, their headcount growth, funding, etc. This can provide clues around future-proofing that is vital for the CIO and CISO. Vendor products are also mapped to standard industry frameworks such as MITRE and NIST.

Figure 11.6 - IT-Harvest dashboard (image courtesy of Richard Stiennon)

The IT-Harvest business model is mostly vendor funded. The value of IT-Harvest for you as vendors is that this data is input for your Go to Market (GTM) plans to identify new opportunities. In evaluating your market segmentation, for example, you can focus on who is in the market and who is not, and hence where there is a delta that can be explored. This data can also provide you insights into how your competitors are faring in the market and even who might be considered in your M&A planning.

A primer on Frost & Sullivan

Frost & Sullivan functions as a global growth strategy and market research firm that focuses on helping clients identify, evaluate, and execute powerful business opportunities.

Frost&Sullivanspecializeinlookingahead.Theyoperateonboththebuyerandsellersides they are a bit more balanced than IT-Harvest. They are well known for the Frost Radar™, which is a benchmarking tool that evaluates tech companies' ability to build market share. This radar plots an "Innovation index" and "Growth index," which provide clues to the momentum of different firms:

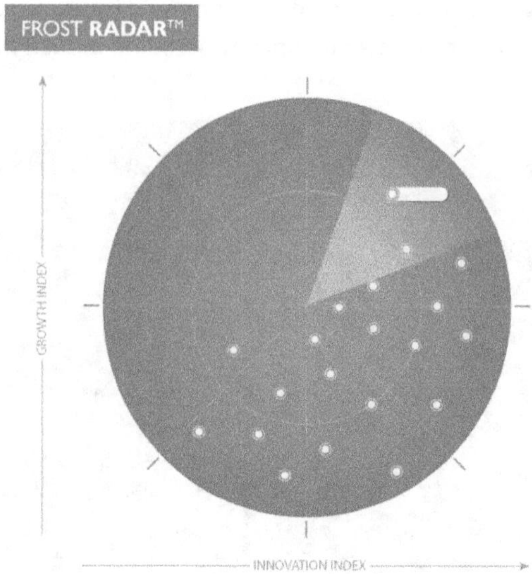

Figure 11.7 - Frost Radar (https://www.frost.com/transformational-growth-journey/frost-radar/)

The view that they want to provide is a longer multi-year horizon. Their service is aimed at assisting CIOs and CISOs in their forward planning, looking at the next wave of change. They also have specialist depth in specific sectors such as Healthcare, Energy, IT, and Industrial.

They also offer "Growth Pipeline as a Service," which combines customized market intelligence, strategic consulting, and corporate training to guide executives and investors through long-term industrial and digital transformations.

In terms of peer support, they brand themselves as providing growth coaching. This activity assists the C-suite with their forward roadmaps. I've attended Frost & Sullivan events myself, and they were considered and mature sessions.

In terms of helping the CIO and CISO to navigate politics, IT-Harvest and Frost & Sullivan are valuable, as these advisors have a strong reputation with their advice being more specific than Gartner or Forrester.

Ultimately, the use of analysts is very dependent on the organization and their own culture. Gary Hayslip explains this dynamic very well.

Note

If, as a CISO in government, we were going to look at any kind of new technology, we would be required to pull the Gartner report on that technology. We would be required to show the quadrant, who the leaders were, and we were expected to pick one of the top 3 leaders—that was just the way that they did things in government.

In private industry, it's more of - we trust you as the technology leader and security leader for the company so you can go ahead and make choices and many times, it may not be the top of the quadrant.

Gary Hayslip – CISO, Halcyon.ai, Board Director and Investor

I'll now look more broadly at a wider set of advisors.

Big 4 vs. MBB

Advisors can assist you with your thinking by providing a rich depth of experience and critical thinking to challenge your own assumptions and they come in many shapes and forms. Comparing these different entities is like comparing an Apple Watch to a Rolex and then to a Patek Philippe timepiece.

Gartner and Forrester are equivalent to the Apple Watch. They get the job done and are a safe choice. The Big 4 (Deloitte, KPMG, EY, and PwC) are the consulting arm of accounting and audit firms, the equivalent of a Rolex watch. There are also large system integrators, including Accenture, Capgemini, etc.

Note

Be clear on the strengths and weaknesses of each other. Strategy consultants typically operate at the highest levels of the organization, have trusted relationships with business decision makers and can help the client make decisions objectively.

Sometimes the right decision might go against the tech and cyber vendor, but this means the client's needs are being prioritized. Help the consultants understand your solution – invest in enablement and knowledge sharing, including what it takes to successfully implement your platform (and what often goes wrong).

Joseph Edwin – Senior Partner, Bain & Company

Then there is MBB, which is the acronym for McKinsey, Bain, and BCG (the Philippe Patek in my analogy) which represent the high end of strategic advisory consulting. They are the most prestigious strategy consulting firms that have a strong global reputation.

Joseph Edwin, Senior Partner at Bain & Company, provided some thoughts on the value of this independent advice.

> Note
>
> *The reality is that some firms will use multiple advisors during an engagement. For instance, advisors should play an objective role in shaping and defining the transformation in business outcome terms, rather than as a technology replacement program.*
>
> *They should help the client make tough trade-off decisions (e.g., cutting non-performing products from the portfolio), set up effective program governance and a value delivery approach.*
>
> *They should not have a vested interest in the choice of platform and instead help the client select a platform that fulfills the business outcome best, in the most efficient manner, and has the potential to support future needs.*
>
> **Joseph Edwin – Senior Partner, Bain & Company**

Both MBB and the Big 4 advisors are well respected for their expertise. Thus, they will be operating close to several of the peers of the CIO, including the CEO, Chief Financial Officer (CFO), Chief Operating Officer (COO), Chief Risk Officer (CRO), etc.

Some firms may use all three types of advisors during an engagement, for instance:

- Gartner or Forrester for product selection
- MBB for strategy
- Boutique firms for custom assistance
- Big 4 for execution and project delivery
- System Integrators for complex program delivery

> Note
>
> *Global System Integrators (GSI) firms play a very unique role versus analysts and vendors (OEMs). We have extensive experience in dealing with many clients across all industry sectors. Based on these, we have built strong local capabilities in individual countries as well. With millions of hours of delivery with our clients, we have gained unique insights into our clients' problems and have built robust methods which have stood the test of time. We can bring*

> *unique industry perspectives and learnings from our previous implementations to help our clients better understand the transformation journey.*
>
> *Based on this experience, I feel we differentiate ourselves in the following areas:*
>
> - *Vendor agnostic perspective right from the battlefield. Based on our experience on what has worked and what has not, we can share experiences and provide a "trusted advisor" role which is vendor neutral. This can help clients understand what is in the best interest rather than a specific tooling.*
> - *Zoom-in approach: we have the ability to go deep technical into the aspects of implementation and transformation. This is where we can provide deeper, granular details depending upon the stakeholder engaged.*
> - *Zoom-out: Ability to see things at strategic and macro levels and how the transformation program in cyber security can help with achieving business objectives. We can connect the platforms to business outcomes.*
>
> *In a true sense, GSI's role should be to act as the orchestrator of decisions into outcomes—connecting analyst perspective (market truth) and vendor perspective (product truth) to the client's context (operating truth)!*
>
> **Gautam Kapoor – Cybersecurity Lead, Accenture**

In terms of navigating politics, a combination of different advisors can assist the CIO and CISO with the maze that transformation programs can become. Large-scale transformation for core banking or insurance systems particularly is complex and has claimed many CIO careers. These are therefore prime candidates for MBB advisory given the typical reasons for failure of these programs (poor case for change, inadequate sponsorship, dysfunctional governance, etc.). Granted, this will cost more, but the price is often well worth the costs avoided, which include on the CIO and CISO's own career.

Summary

In this chapter, I explored how the CIO and CISO engage these different research analysts to provide an independent perspective on the marketplace and trends. Research analysts serve as credibility infrastructure for CIOs and CISOs—independent validators that help defend their high-stakes technology choices upward to boards and CFOs. I've argued that the value of these services to CIOs and CISOs follows a U-curve—highest at the shortlisting stage and then again at contract negotiation, with a significant dip in the middle where generic reports can't account for their specific environment.

For vendors, research analyst recognition is the golden ticket to market credibility and enterprise pricing power.

The key learnings from this chapter are:

- **Know which tool fits which job** – Gartner dominates for market scanning and shortlisting, Forrester is more transparent in its methodology and stronger for technical and cybersecurity audiences, IDC is primarily a vendor GTM tool. Big 4 executes, MBB provides board-level strategic credibility, and boutiques like IT-Harvest and Frost & Sullivan provide specific market information and also serve vendors.
- **Analyst positioning is a double-edged sword** – being in a "leaders" category opens doors, anything else creates a credibility headwind that is genuinely difficult to overcome. Smaller vendors face a structural barrier (Gartner has revenue thresholds, annual cycles leave out new entrants, and the CIO and CISO bear personal career risk adding unlisted vendors to a shortlist).
- **CIO and CISO personas determine where in the Gartner Hype Cycle™ they might engage** – for example, a Transformation CIO may act at "Technology Trigger" stage; an Operational CIO waits for "Plateau of Productivity". Selling without understanding where your buyer sits on that curve and which persona they are may be tricky.
- **Analyst reports help mitigate risks for CIO and CISO decisions** – citing Gartner or Forrester, for example, is career risk mitigation. It provides the CIO and CISO political insulation when a decision is later challenged. Understanding this dynamic means your job is not just to win the evaluation, but to make it easy for the CIO and CISO to defend their choice with credible third-party support already baked in.

Endnotes

1. Gartner® and Magic Quadrant™ are trademarks of Gartner, Inc. and/or its affiliates and are used herein with permission. All rights reserved.
   The Forrester Wave™ is a trademark of Forrester Research, Inc

   IDC and IDC MarketScape™ are trademarks of International Data Group, Inc.

   Frost & Sullivan® and Frost Radar™ are trademarks of Frost & Sullivan and are used herein with permission. All rights reserved.

12

Proof Positive

You have now made it to the point of having proof of concept (POC) and/or proof of value (POV). This is a milestone that shows progress and a level of commitment to potentially proceeding with your solution.

Although this stage brings you significantly closer to finalizing a deal, note it does not signify a full agreement or that the budget is secured, however. An evaluation of your offering likely means that your solution is in running against the incumbent and perhaps 1–2 other products. The team that is involved in the evaluation is usually a cross-section of internal stakeholders including business analysts, architects, and operational technology staff.

The CIO and/or CISO are keen to see this be successful. There is a saying that "you need to kiss many frogs to find your prince or princess". The POC and POV are akin to this, designed exactly to help them make the decision of whether to keep talking to you or not. The POC/POV can be beneficial for you too—often vendors invest significantly in pre-sales and the POC/POV provides validation on whether this investment is likely to be converted into a sale. This is a significant step in the overall sales process.

This chapter covers the full evaluation journey from what makes a good POC and POV, through the process of running them well, to avoiding POC and POV creep and dealing with an impasse that can derail promising opportunities.

In this chapter we will cover the following topics:

- Understanding POC and POV
- The POC
- The POV
- The POC and POV process

- Avoiding POC and POV creep
- Anticipating an impasse

Note

I start with my own research, including previous experience working with known vendors or their competitors and gathering feedback from my network of strong cyber-SMEs (subject matter experts).

I treat the Gartner Magic Quadrant™ as helpful context when available, but never as the main driver, and I push for interactive demos followed by proof of concepts to validate how the technology performs in our environment.

Simon Blanchet – Security Architect and former HSBC Serai CISO

Understanding POC and POV

The terms proof of concept (POC) and proof of value (POV) represent different things even though they are often used interchangeably. Most CIOs and CISOs are probably not that fussed about these definitions, to be honest; evaluation teams are usually much more concerned about the scopes of these items being properly differentiated.

Allow me to use an analogy to explain this difference: A POC builds the campfire to prove it can be done; a POV decides whether fire is even the right way to stay warm.

I've expanded on this in the following table:

Dimension	Proof of Concept (POC)	Proof of Value (POV)
Aims to check	Technology feasibility *(Can we build this?)*	Business feasibility *(Should we build this?)*
Measures	Performance *(in the sandbox)*	Business impact *(real data workloads)*
Integration needed	Minimal integration *(Does it work?)*	Some integration *(To validate assumptions)*

Dimension	Proof of Concept (POC)	Proof of Value (POV)
Scenario scope	Edge case scenarios *(Will this break?)*	Actual use cases *(Will I get real value?)*

Table 12.1 – POC vs. POV comparison

Since the POC process operates at a greater level of detail than the POV, it takes longer to complete, usually 3–8 weeks (but this can be shorter). In contrast, the POV process is faster and all about getting to a "go"/"no-go" decision, so it generally only requires 2–4 weeks. But note these times will vary with different companies and also take into account what other normal business as usual (BAU) work is being undertaken.

Note

The whole POC process is frustrating for both sides. It takes too long to get vendors in the door, get vendors onboarded and for NDAs to be processed.

At Halcyon, we do a POV, a proof of value. This is what we're installing, and this is what we're going to prove. This is what we're going to test, and then at the end of it, were we successful?

The POV is our pilot. Then you say: let's negotiate.

Gary Hayslip – CISO, Halcyon.ai, Board Director and Investor

At the time of writing, there is growing consensus that POV, which proves a business payoff, may be a better approach than the POC focus on technology. In essence, the POC proves the solution can work, but it is the POV that proves it is worth buying, and those are two entirely different conversations. The champion who presents a successful POV arrives with the answer "here is what it costs, what it delivers, what it means for our risk position, and why the timing is right." That is a considerably stronger and safer position to advocate from.

Some enterprises may want to do both a POV and a POC for new solutions. However, most CIOs and CISOs would consider this, like most vendors, to be undesirable because doing both takes time, money, and discipline.

Note

Also note that some enterprises like to also use a "pilot" process as a longer evaluation that can follow the POC and/or POV exercise. The pilot will test the solution with production data and actual users, often in a smaller location. These pilot exercises can measure the outcomes of running the solution in a more realistic use case.

Doing a POC and POV can be valuable, but you need to understand why you are going through this process so that you can discern real opportunities from those that are likely not to go anywhere. Could this, for instance, be an intellectual exercise primarily for an architect's curiosity? Or might a leader want to do this for political reasons, or to be able to dismiss any questions in the future by stakeholders? These motivations can be a waste of time for all parties.

Note

A POC in a sanitized development environment tells me almost nothing. You simply cannot replicate the sheer chaos of a high-volume, low-latency peak trading floor in a lab. To prove a tool works, I insist on two things.

- *First, production stress tests – test critical use cases on a small, controlled user group in the live production environment. If it breaks there, it does not get bought.*
- *Second, geographic reality. Never assume regional parity. A control that deploys flawlessly in North America might fail spectacularly under the infrastructure or regulatory constraints of Asia.*

Jayant Dave – CISO, Check Point Software

POC and POV are important processes as they can provide insights into the degree of fit of the product and highlight some potential issues. So, CIOs and CISOs will likely ensure that the procurement team is aware of the exercise being performed (in *Chapter 19* we will cover procurement in detail); however, they may not be interested in being invited to be a part of the evaluation team at this stage.

Note

The CIO and Chief Procurement Officer (CPO) should work very closely together. The technology strategy and future state architecture and delivery of these rely on a

> commercial strategy. However, in my experience, the average CIO and CISO may not be meeting that regularly with the CPO.

When a POC or POV moves from an "interesting idea" to "approved and budgeted," it usually comes down to three things:

- The solution clearly solved a measurable business problem that stakeholders had already agreed was a priority
- The total cost of ownership and ROI were tangible enough to survive a Chief Financial Officer (CFO) conversation
- At least one internal champion had both the conviction and the organizational capital to push it across the finish line

Without all three, even a technically superior product can stall in committee.

Let's look at the POC in more detail.

The POC

What constitutes a good POC? What separates a high-quality proof of concept from a box-ticking exercise? Who needs to be involved, what does success look like, and how long should it realistically run?

In my opinion, a good POC is one that is laser-focused on validating the 1–2 most critical risks that would kill the deal if left unanswered. This is not a demo of all features, but has a clear, pre-agreed success criteria signed off by all key stakeholders *before* it starts, and the right mix of technical, operational, and business voices involved. (Then later, no one can say "but we never tested *our* use case.") It should run long enough to be credible but short enough to maintain urgency (perhaps 4 weeks).

At the end of the process the CIO and CISO should have documented evidence that the solution solves their specific problem on their scale, and the people who have to live with it daily are confident enough to stake their reputation on it.

For further insights, I consulted a couple of executives about their perspectives on POCs from their extensive experience with these: John Taylor and Tony White.

> **Note**
>
> *POCs often fail due to lack of clarity of what success looks like. Success can be a set of functionality or alternatively it can also be an exercise to see what the solution can do i.e.: formulate requirements (not ideal, but an approach when you know there is a fit to a problem*

but can't articulate it properly – a good example is a solution that identifies shadow product usage or similar).

My key checklist revolves around:

- *Agreed success criteria – only 3 or 4 items, not a long list. Pulling together a long list will add to overheads and will likely cause the POC to fail regardless.*
- *Dedicated internal staff to work with the supplier – this is a common mistake, and I've made it, where the POC is not given the right amount of attention which comes down to BAU activities or other project activities getting in the way.*
- *Exit criteria – how is the POC going to end? Often a POC will become a production dependent system without the service wrappers etc. put in place to be production ready. This then causes a lot of friction and a perceived failure of the POC when in fact that was never the intent.*

John Taylor – Field CTO, Mimecast (former CIO & CISO)

Note

A rigorous, well-designed POC is essential for evaluating strategically important applications and services. Vendor selection should begin with an assessment of how well each proposal addresses the business problem or opportunity you have defined.

That said, avoid overly prescriptive functional specifications as these can limit innovation and prevent you from discovering superior approaches. Instead, articulate the problem clearly and allow vendors to demonstrate how their expertise and technology can help you achieve success; they are often the true specialists in their domain. A simplistic example—specifying that a vehicle must have a 2-litre petrol engine eliminates the possibility of a potentially superior solution, such as an electric vehicle.

POC design and execution is a well-documented process with excellent frameworks available; however, my significant "must-haves" for success are:

- *Clarity concerning the problem to be solved and business need, its priority within the business overall and that top level management's reward structures are clearly linked to solving this business problem.*

- *Rigorously measurable success measures/acceptance criteria - vague measures allow scope "wander", up-selling and more revenue for vendors.*
- *From the very beginning involve all relevant stakeholders: IT, security, procurement, compliance, business owners, and internal and external end-users with clear responsibility and availability commitments.*
- *Use real world data and representative use cases, including low frequency but recurring scenarios. e.g. take three months of actual transactions and as well as including routine use, go looking for the rare cases to ensure they are all included in the testing.*
- *Document POC findings, challenges, and remediation steps thoroughly. Not all the rare cases may be accommodated by the system and in the testing be clear how these will be handled in the future – evaluate the service and cost impacts if "workarounds" are needed.*
- *Conduct pilot rollouts in real world environments before full deployment.*
- *Ensure that the pilot location has a proactive, open and communicative culture. A wider roll-out will be difficult if the pilot is "rubber stamped" in a location where the boss said yes and staff must suffer the consequences.*
- *For global organizations, consider cultural and operational differences across regions, as this may result in multiple pilots in different regions. What works in one country may fail in another due to differing norms.*

Tony White – Former Qantas Chief Procurement Officer

Procurement has deep expertise in the POC process; this is why Tony White's reflections on what really matters, from his extensive experience, are so valuable here.

There are five key steps required to complete a successful POC:

1. Define exactly what technical question the POC needs to answer.
2. Agree on success criteria before any work begins.
3. Build the simplest version that can prove the concept.
4. Test it against real infrastructure, not a lab setup.
5. Present findings as a clear go or no-go decision.

What I've seen is that step 4 is where most POCs cannot meet the objective to the right level. Unfortunately, everything works perfectly in a controlled environment, then breaks when it hits the organization's actual systems, legacy integrations, security policies, and real data volumes. This is the step most teams shortcut, and the one that causes the most expensive surprises later for the CIO and CISO.

> Note
>
> *A well-structured POC validates not only technical capability but also team collaboration and cultural alignment. It should measure value realization speed, not just feature testing. Always run it with business-impact metrics agreed upon upfront.*
>
> **Michael Kazantzis – CEO, Cyborium**

A good POC for a CIO or CISO proves the technology works within their actual environment, their real infrastructure, constraints, and security boundaries. It delivers a clear answer on integration complexity and performance under test load before a dollar for full deployment is committed. Now that we know broadly what makes a good POC, let's dive into POC scope in more depth.

The scope of the POC

The POC process must be able to address high-risk factors so that there is some degree of comfort that your solution works as expected. As a principle, POC need to be designed to be time-bound (I earlier outlined the range of 3–8 weeks). It is improbable to expect the process to be able to examine all possible high (technology) risks in a restricted time frame, and so POC should aim to test no more than three critical assumptions.

In essence, the scope is a negotiation between all the stakeholders (including you as vendor) to ensure that there are minimum requirements to validate if the solution is suitable from a technology standpoint. Hence it is not realistic to expect the POC to address all possible business scenarios and every variation of business process. The scenarios chosen should test the boundaries of how the system works, for example when there are extreme loads or there is corrupted data.

> Note
>
> *A successful POC is hypothesis-driven, time-boxed, and tests technical feasibility under real-world conditions. Essential characteristics include clear success criteria with explicit metrics and timeline constraints, realistic test scenarios with actual customer data, defined scope that proves value without full scale, stakeholder alignment secured before launch, and thorough integration tests with existing systems. Organizations should match their validation approach to their maturity and risk tolerance levels.*
>
> **Charlie Dai – Vice President and Principal Analyst, Forrester**

The goal is that the POC proves the business value of your solution, but its scope should be narrow enough to be accelerated if needed.

> Note
>
> Typically, the resource requirement of this exercise is derived from extra effort by staff on top of their day jobs, and as a result, CIOs and CISOs tend to be wary of the time taken by this process.

Best practice is that the POC only begins when the success metrics are clearly defined. These metrics must be signed off by the POC evaluation team and be quantitatively measured (rather than being subject to a leader's subjective judgment). You and your champion have a key role to play in helping to identify these measures.

> Note
>
> *POC criteria should be fully defined and signed off by both parties upfront, including mandatory criteria and weightings, so there is no ambiguity about whether the evaluation was successful or not.*
>
> **Paul O' Rourke – former CISO, CRO and BCG Global Cyber Leader**

A sound POC process gets the balance right between technology risk and business uncertainty. For example, technical risk can be "high" and business uncertainty "low" if there are multiple systems to be integrated to address data quality issues and legacy technology platforms. In this way, the POC acts as a mini stress test of how complex this exercise will be.

In *Figure 12.1*, I've tried to illustrate getting this balance right. The reality is that there are four different scenarios that can result from these two independent variables:

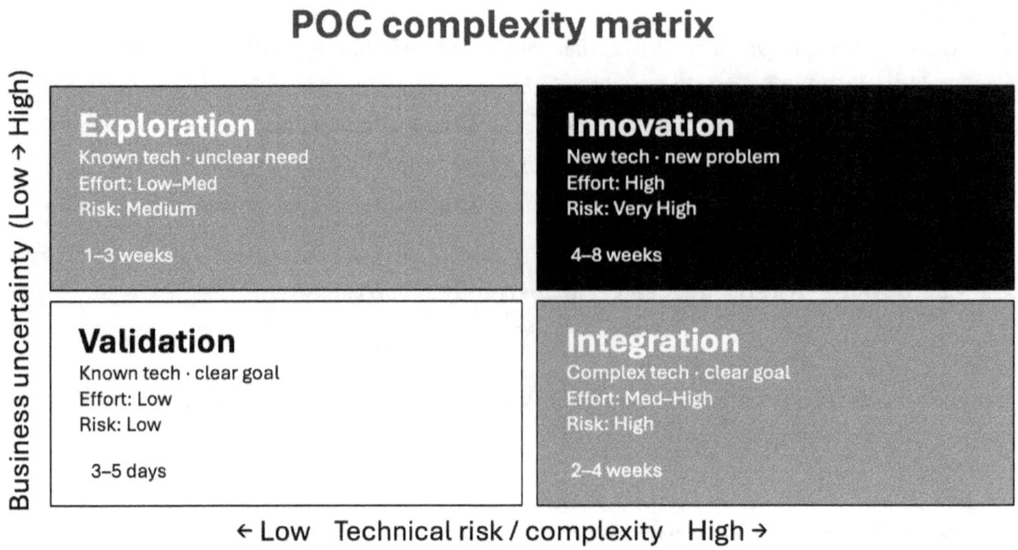

Figure 12.1 – Business uncertainty and technical risk

Of these four scenarios, the "Innovation" quadrant, when both technology risk and business uncertainty are "high", is likely a worry both to the C-Suite and to you. There's a recognition that the risk of failure is high and the POC will take longer as there is less clarity on what good looks like.

CIO and CISO will both probably be most concerned about the "Integration" quadrant, as it means that success falls mostly in their realm of responsibility, since the business has strong clarity on what they want and therefore has a clear expectation of what good looks like.

The area which you as vendor will likely find most concerning is the "Exploration" quadrant, as the business requirements are uncertain. Ideally, you will want the POC to be in the "Validation" quadrant, where there is well-understood tech and clear goals. This makes the probability of success much higher.

The POV

I've always used the words POC and POV interchangeably; as a CIO and CISO I was looking for the positive outcome and saw these as a means to an end. As I explained earlier, however, there is a difference between a POC and POV.

> Note
>
> *A successful POV is not just a technical validation; it is a business-focused exercise that demonstrates measurable value, validates outcomes, and builds confidence for long-term success. The best POVs are outcome-driven, collaborative, and focused on solving real business problems. Success is measured not by how many features are tested, but by how effectively real business value can be delivered.*
>
> **Ryan Jones – Vice President, Cyera**

> Note
>
> *A good POV answers practical questions. Can the solution handle the customer's data reality? Can it integrate with existing systems? Can business users or operations teams adopt it? Does it reduce effort in a measurable way? Does it produce evidence that an executive sponsor can take to an investment committee? If the proof does not help the customer make a decision, it is just a demo with extra steps.*
>
> **Sundar Iyer – Managing Director, Emertel**

To my mind, a good POV includes the following steps:

1. Identify the business problem and the expected outcomes.
2. Define the metrics that will measure success.
3. Map the real use cases and user workflows to be tested.
4. Validate assumptions with actual stakeholders, not just sponsors.
5. Measure business impact against the agreed metrics.
6. Present a clear "invest" or "walk away" recommendation.

Of these six steps, where this process can stall is usually at step 4. The real test is getting honest input from the people who will use it day to day, who have no political stake in the outcome and will tell you what isn't working. These SMEs are harder to access, harder to align, but their feedback is the only validation that actually means something.

> Note
>
> *When I was at my previous employer as a CISO (SoftBank)...if we were looking at a new technology or service, we would have an architecture review meeting. So, every time that we were going to do a project, we were going to bring in a new technology and make a change to*

> *the stack, and if it involved a POV, you had to bring it through the architecture meeting, which was basically IT and cybersecurity.*
>
> *You would present a business case package as to what problem you are trying to solve and the basic architecture of what you're doing, what changes you were making. And then the test that you were going to run and the expected results, and at the end, if there were any deliverables.*
>
> *After the testing was complete, we would be expected to come back and brief again on the results. Our boss (CTO) wouldn't let us go ahead and submit to procurement to buy until we had done that to make sure when he and I were before the CFO and the board, we could answer, yes, we did test, and it met or exceeded our requirements.*
>
> *In doing a POV, I always wanted to do at least 40 endpoints, with those 40 endpoints being in technology, including at least 10 in finance and 10 in other departments. I wanted to make sure that when doing a POV, we tested in different business departments to ensure it not only worked with our stack but didn't adversely impact any applications or services being used by these other departments.*
>
> **Gary Hayslip – CISO Halcyon.ai, Board Director and Investor**

The scope of the POV

A good POV defines the specific business outcomes being validated, such as cost savings, risk reduction, productivity gains, or revenue impact. That is tied to metrics the organization already tracks. It tests against real use cases and actual user workflows, so stakeholders can make a confident invest-or-walk-away decision.

> Note
>
> *The deals that progress are not always the ones with the most exciting technology. They are the ones where the vendor can make the buyer confident. Confident that the problem is real. Confident that the approach fits the enterprise. Confident that the value is measurable. Confident that the vendor can deliver in a complex environment.*
>
> *Proof of value is critical. Enterprise buyers rarely want a science project, but they do want evidence. A POV should be designed around the decision the customer needs to make. It should not just demonstrate features. It should test the business case, integration path, operating model, security assumptions, adoption approach, and success metrics.*
>
> **Sundar Iyer – Managing Director, Emertel**

When I was a CIO and CISO, the POC was more a focus of mine than a POV. This was because my accountability was operational, not commercial. As CIO I was held responsible for systems staying up and technology scaling without chaos, and as a CISO, I was responsible for nothing getting breached, compliance being maintained, and risks staying within acceptable boundaries. I gravitated toward proving *can we safely run this?* over *is this worth it?* I would get to that in the business case later, so why focus on this now was my thinking.

The POC and POV processes

There are subtle differences between the POC and POV processes. The weighting criteria against actual end usage is fundamentally a POV discipline because it is asking not whether the solution can work technically, but whether it will deliver the outcomes the organization needs when real users interact with it in a real environment. On the other hand, in a POC the weighting reflects technical complexity and integration risk.

> **Note**
>
> *When I was at Gartner® years ago, it showed me that POCs were actually more successful when they were not done face to face. And I'll tell you why: because you can bring along subject matter experts to that POC that you couldn't otherwise do.*
>
> **Matt Boon – Senior Director, Strategic Research, Adapt**

In these processes, in most cases, the evaluation team will have further questions for you to ensure that their scoring is appropriate. How you respond to these queries is critical.

> **Tip**
>
> Aim to respond promptly and informatively, but concisely. It is best to answer a question simply and only supplement it with more information if you are concerned the evaluation may have missed a key feature of the solution's functionality. There is little point in arguing, however.

While responding to these queries in writing, try to copy all members of the evaluation team, rather than just your champion or contact. The client wants to learn how good it is to work with you and your team. If you are responsive and honest, then this "brand" will be associated with your company's solution, in their minds.

The POC is like a dress rehearsal for being seen as the client's partner. As such, the evaluation team doesn't always focus specifically on the product; they also keep an eye on the team that supports this effort. The personality that you bring to the table provides them with a glimpse into what it will be like to work with you as a vendor. Even though this might not be a primary criterion in the evaluation, it always factors into the decision.

How you match up to the client's internal vendor evaluation rubric will now again be in the hands of the evaluation team. This process is about elimination of poor choices as much as it is about getting to the final two alternatives. (There are instances where more than two options are considered, but honestly most enterprises lack the capacity to investigate every option in depth.)

The CIO and CISO understand the POC is seen as critical for you, and they will always ensure that the POC and POV dates you have selected are met. Vendors usually assign their "A" team to this task and CIOs and CISOs expect them to highlight what they think these leaders want to hear about their strengths.

> **Note**
>
> CIOs and CISOs have the ultimate authority to stop the exercise at any time. I've only seen this exercised when the POC has been an absolute failure and there is very little to learn from it.

The typical CIO and CISO will not be that transparent with the POC unless perhaps there is much political jostling that is underway with your peers. As the POC itself is an exercise in risk management, the CIO or CISO has little incentive to share progress reports with their boss or stakeholders until they see this as being for their own benefit. This may be a source of frustration for you, but that is the reality.

Should the POC exercise be successful then there will be calls for the CIO and CISO to check on the experience of their industry peers. Once the POC has proved feasibility, the natural question that is asked is "Has anyone else done this at scale?".

> **Note**
>
> *Enterprise buyers value references, but only when they are relevant. A logo slide is useful, but it is not enough. Buyers want to know what was implemented, how long it took, what changed, what value was realized, what challenges came up, and what the customer would do differently. A credible reference story is balanced. It does not pretend everything was perfect. It shows maturity, delivery experience, and honesty.*
>
> **Sundar Iyer – Managing Director, Emertel**

The CIO and CISO's peers in the same industry carry more weight than standard vendor case studies because they share the same regulatory environment, similar infrastructure complexity, and comparable risk appetite. Therefore, their experience is directly transferable.

The role of peer feedback

Vendor evaluation is often preceded by informal, as well as some more formal, reference discussions with peers. These are vitally important. The CIO and CISO always take peer feedback seriously as it provides valuable insight into how you have collaborated with similar enterprises in terms of size, complexity, and reputation.

> Note
>
> *Features come first. I ask many questions such as: Does this solve the problem in situ? Does it work well in our environment, and scale in the way it needs to? What are the support arrangements for when things (inevitably) go wrong? Do they operate like a genuine partner or are they just looking to make a profit?*
>
> *Second comes price and lock-in risk. And some further questions: What do their longer-term customers say about them and their prices after the honeymoon period? Do they fit into an architecture that allows them to be replaced?*
>
> *Another thing I always consider is the likelihood of them being bought out—especially when working with smaller players (which is often something I like to do, especially if they are sovereign). This could present further risks to the above. For example, if a competitor buys them, then the product might be replaced and features might change. Architecture likewise—too many vendors purposely design for lock-in. And if they are small and bought out by a big player, the pricing will probably change. And so can the question of sovereignty.*
>
> **Dr Maria Milosavljevic – former ANZ Bank CISO**

> Note
>
> *Price is important, especially when working in an organization that prioritizes cost efficiencies. However, a solid roadmap and investment in improving the product are important. Part of this is making sure that future features are not "added modules" where I need to pay for more.*
>
> *A commitment to improving a product to include more capabilities enriches the partnership as it makes my life easier. I want to spend the least amount of time on commercial negotiations and discussions, and more time on protecting my organization. Relationship is key. Vendors who play the long game and are willing to say they can't meet my requirements are more likely*

> *to be engaged later when something I'm seeking can be achieved using their offering. It's a good way to get trust. Sales folks who are transactional and short term never stay in my contact list.*
>
> **Nigel Hedges – Executive General Manager & CISO, Chemist Warehouse**

I'll note, from my own perspective, that your reputation among the enterprise's peer group is a significant factor and usually accounts for 20% of the overall evaluation. There are a few reasons why this is important:

- **Risk mitigation**. Knowing that the solution works effectively serves as proof for the CIO and CISO. Conversely, when there is "noise" about the solution then the average CIO and CISO will not bother to take the discussion further.
- **Industry standing**. When a reputable enterprise client also uses your solution, this creates a "halo" effect.
- **Validation**. This feedback can provide comfort that your solution works in practice and not only in theory.

> Note
>
> *POCs and POVs are time-consuming, resource-intensive, and rarely prove anything other than what the vendor has chosen to demonstrate. I often place more weight on credible customer and peer references. A structured RFP process will validate the rest.*
>
> **Lee Barney – CISO, Ventia**

In addition to peer group feedback, there are also reports from reputable industry analysts, such as Gartner®, Forrester®, etc., which may play a role in the evaluation process, as I explained in the previous chapter. The feedback reports from these parties are usually trusted and may be referenced at the start of the sales process to assist with understanding of the major players in a category. Their solution recommendations will help you to get to the CIO and CISO's shortlist; however, they will not be the final decision point.

The final decision is always signed off by the budget holder. This is usually the CIO, CISO or relevant business stakeholder, but some enterprises may have some pooled investment that is allocated for spend. I cover this further when discussing business cases in *Chapter 18*.

Even when the CIO or CISO is more passive in the process, they will lean on their staff to recommend the best option to proceed with.

Note

The most trusted proof is peer validation combined with credible customer outcomes. Technical depth matters, but when backed by independent assessments or shared lessons from similar organizations, financial strength is secondary to evidence of consistent delivery. A simple "how we maintained this customer's uptime during X challenge" is far more effective than a dozen product awards.

Michael Kazantzis – CEO, Cyborium

In my role as a CIO and CISO, I was usually supportive of the POC as my focus was on the problem that needed solving. I personally entered this process with an open mind, without talking to too many of my peers, but never discounting their feedback or the consideration that I would need to go down that path later.

Note

When CISOs ask you for vendor shortlists or market direction, what criteria consistently matter most? CISOs shortlist vendors who reduce risk without creating new fragility:

- *Outcome fit (will this reduce incident impact or improve evidence?)*
- *Operational fit (can we run this with our current team?)*
- *Integration fit (does it work with what we already use?)*
- *Proof (peer references in similar environments + metrics)*
- *Trust (how they behave when challenged)*

What vendors think matters (often doesn't): feature count, platform claims, and AI branding without workflow change.

Sam Ghebranious – Director, Axcelerate/ Senior Advisor, Frost & Sullivan

While the POC and/or POV are a key step on this journey, there is always a concern that this can be too protracted. What I call "POC creep", is where the initial scope is simply extended.

Avoiding POC and POV creep

With both POC and POV you must have clear scope and governance. Unfortunately, POC and POV creep can and does occur—this is a free trial that keeps being extended as the team is too busy and gets distracted from their review of the solution.

Scope creep is one of the most common reasons POCs and POVs never convert into real projects. It usually starts innocently with a stakeholder asking to test one more scenario; another team wants their use case included, and suddenly a short exercise becomes a 6-month project with no clear finish line. The exercise loses its original purpose, budget and patience run out, and by the time results are presented the business context has already moved on.

I've seen examples where POC/POV creep is an excuse for the exercise effectively being deprioritized as "I've been too busy" or that there has been a major incident or issue to deal with. The root cause of this creep, however, is often that the review was started without a clear decision framework—who owns the decision to say "yes" or "no." This is where you and the champion have to both do yourselves a strong favor by being very disciplined.

Treating this like a project requires progress to be reported, and there are explicit entry and exit criteria. These targets will enable the team and yourself to avoid POC/POV creep, where invariably nobody is happy with the outcome.

> Note
>
> *I'm very iffy on the generic offer of POCs. I want highly defined criteria before we start one—what constitutes a yes for success and failure. And I don't like paying for a POC that then tells me I should pay for the product. If a newer vendor wants to invest in a POC and we think it has value, we will provide the success criteria and help with it.*
>
> *Established partners, if they want to test something out that they know is aligned with what we want to do, I would be more amenable to.*
>
> **Scott Collary – Group CIO, Westpac Group**

The fix for creep is rather simple and requires discipline: lock the scope and timeline and treat any expansion request as a separate conversation.

Being open to stopping the POC or POV that has not succeeded is key here; this will help avoid everyone wasting further time. Stopping a failing POC/POV is, culturally, harder than it sounds, unfortunately. At this point, the relationship between you and your target organization has deepened, you have internal advocates, and stopping can feel like personal failure. Instead, I'd argue that a POC/POV that eventually concludes "not right for us at this time" is still a success, as this has stopped you perhaps from taking on a lose-lose outcome, and stopped the enterprise from a poor fitting long-term commitment.

I've seen numerous articles from McKinsey and Gartner suggesting that POCs and POVs fail around 50–70% of the time (for example: `https://www.gartner.com/en/articles/genai-project-failure`). (I should note that recent research has tended to be on AI projects, so this is perhaps a biased sample.) Given these experiences, it is often the case that a POC or POV ends in a stalemate and does not proceed. I refer to this as an "impasse", a non-decision on moving ahead.

> **Note**
>
> I'd note that an impasse is more likely after a POC than a POV. This is because a POC produces a technical conclusion that still requires a separate commercial decision, while the POV produces a business case that the key decision maker helped build and therefore already owns.

Anticipating an impasse

An impasse is a source of frustration for both the client and you as the vendor. It is therefore important to anticipate why this happens.

Usually, this exercise provides insights into a client's previously unexplored requirements. This is often the case for new domains since their needs are not well understood, particularly how different systems will work when integrated.

A POC or POV ends up in this state if it becomes unclear that the risk management that was the root cause of the exercise has not been addressed in its entirety. In this scenario, some parts are likely well catered for while others are partial gaps; this is when it falls into this "no decision" state. The problem still exists, but the POC/POV team is not convinced that your solution is the right one.

Let's boil this exercise down to further understand why you may reach an impasse. The POC and POV are seen by the CIO and CISO as a means to an end. What they really care about is achieving their own goals.

The CIO is only focused on the POC and POV if they meet what the CIO sees as the tangible outcomes that they desire—improved customer experience, increased sales, reduced costs, etc.

Figure 12.3 – Key CIO question about POC / POV

CIOs are usually less fussed about how elegant the solution has been engineered but instead want a workable solution that helps reduce the current risks. They also want to work with vendors that will stay in business.

The CISO, on the other hand, cares about risk and security. The POC/POV is for a potential new product that will either increase or reduce their attack surface, so this is something that they care deeply about understanding.

Figure 12.4 – Key CISO question about POC/POV

When a POC or POV reaches a dead end, you have one last move: an honest postmortem conversation that acknowledges the issues, owns them without deflection, and presents a credible path to resolution through workarounds or future releases.

I'd note that the probability of a reprieve is low, but the vendor who handles a dead end with integrity leaves an impression that no pitch ever could. To reflect on the trust maturity model that I shared earlier in the book, how you act in a scenario like this can determine if you move into the "Credible" level or slip back into "Noise".

A better outcome, of course, is the evaluation that went only okay but keeps you in the race. This is often less about the solution itself and more about the CIO or CISO's strategic preference for an integrated package solution over a best-of-breed tool, a factor that can override even a strong POV result. That strategic tension between the best individual solution and the right fit for the overall architecture is where the next chapter begins.

> Note
>
> *The most valuable engagements are those where the vendor and end-user organizations are transparent about their goals, bring senior stakeholders to the table, and actively collaborate with analysts. For example, a recent digital business strategy project succeeded because the client defined clear business objectives, involved executive sponsors (CIO/CISO), and encouraged open dialogue.*
>
> *IDC was able to bridge strategy and execution, mobilize quickly, and provide tailored, actionable advice. The organization's willingness to share data, challenge assumptions, and co-create solutions enabled a strong outcome.*
>
> **Linus Lai – Vice President, IDC**

Summary

In this chapter, we covered the POC and POV stage, the most structured and high-stakes phase of the sales cycle. Let me remind you that this is a dress rehearsal for your partnership and not just a technical test.

The winner isn't always the best option objectively because the criteria, determined purely by the client, are subject to their requirements and conditions, among other things.

From my experience, winning a POC or POV is not only about product performance but also about how your team behaves under pressure, how quickly and honestly you respond to queries, and whether your references and peer validation hold up to scrutiny.

The key learnings from this chapter are:

- **POC and POV are similar but distinct** – POC tests technical fit and POV tests business impact. Avoid being pushed through both sequentially and letting it drift into a pilot without a clear decision point in-between.

- **Define success criteria before the POC/POV starts** – quantitative metrics signed off by both parties upfront; subjective evaluation leads directly to impasse and wasted cycles.
- **Your team's behavior is part of the evaluation process** – how you respond to queries, handle gaps, and show up under pressure is a preview of your partnership.
- **Peer validation from comparable enterprises carries ~20% of the final decision** – industry reports play a role in this too.
- **POC/POV creep and reaching an impasse share the same root cause** – no named decision owner and no exit criteria. Treat it as a project, not a favor, and be willing to stop a failing POC/POV early if needed.

13

Package vs. Best of Breed Solutions (vs. AI)

There have been a series of major mega shifts that I've seen over the last 30 years of my career, with enterprise technology transitioning several times, and the landscape radically changing with each wave.

Over this period each CIO has gone forward to present their IT strategy to their board and propose a strategic direction based on the assumptions of how the lay of the land is appearing.

The CIO and CISO must make a purposeful tradeoff between adopting a "best of breed" solution or using an integrated package. By "best of breed" I mean selecting the best specialized tool for each specific function, even if they are from different vendors. While by "package" I mean choosing one vendor's integrated ecosystem that covers many functions together, even if no single module is the absolute best in its category.

For the CIO and CISO this is a fundamental strategic decision on where to invest. There is a danger if they put "all their eggs in one basket" that they are taking a risk. Of course, there is the counter argument that having an integrated package means that there are no gaps in their technology. CIOs and CISOs may decide that they want to get the optimum mix of both of these types of tools. That is, they might want to select best of breed when it comes to the most strategic processes where innovation can provide the greatest advantage, however, they may also want to select a package to efficiently and effectively have an end-to-end solution that is easy to operate.

These are the considerations going through the minds of the CIO and CISO as they are processing their proof of concepts (POCs) and proof of values (POVs). In truth there is no wrong answer, just that a poor selection either way may lead to instabilities in production systems, hence the stakes are high.

The strategic choice between a best of breed tool vs. a package is fundamental to your relationship with the CIO and CISO. If you are a package vendor and they would prefer to go for a best of breed solution, you are selling them a migration of their current perspective and that is a much harder deal to close.

The internal champion will be intimately engaged in this activity, and I'd argue plays a key role in the direction of whether to adopt a best of breed or a package solution.

In this chapter, I will explore the thinking around this decision to help you navigate this process with the assistance of your internal champion. We will cover the following key topics:

- Waves of change
- The difference between best of breed and package solutions
- Now, enter the AI era
- The CIO and CISO perspective
- AI considerations

Waves of change

In my own working career, there have been endless patterns of change. I started on an IBM 8086 PC. This was a floppy disk computer with an external hard drive that took 8-9 minutes to boot up. That was state of the art in the 1980s, and I've seen enterprises move from standalone PCs to networked PCs, to diskless PCs, to virtual PCs and now containerized enterprise browsers.

The pace of change is now accelerating, with each wave arriving faster than the last and with less time between disruption and adoption.

Along with these changes there is a graveyard of once successful companies that have in the past dominated this market. But the market has far less tolerance now for organizations that choose to wait and see. The vendor and champion who understand this are not just selling a solution for today's environment they are helping the CIO and CISO build architecture that is designed for the next wave of change.

Looking back, there have been a few major application eras for enterprise technology:

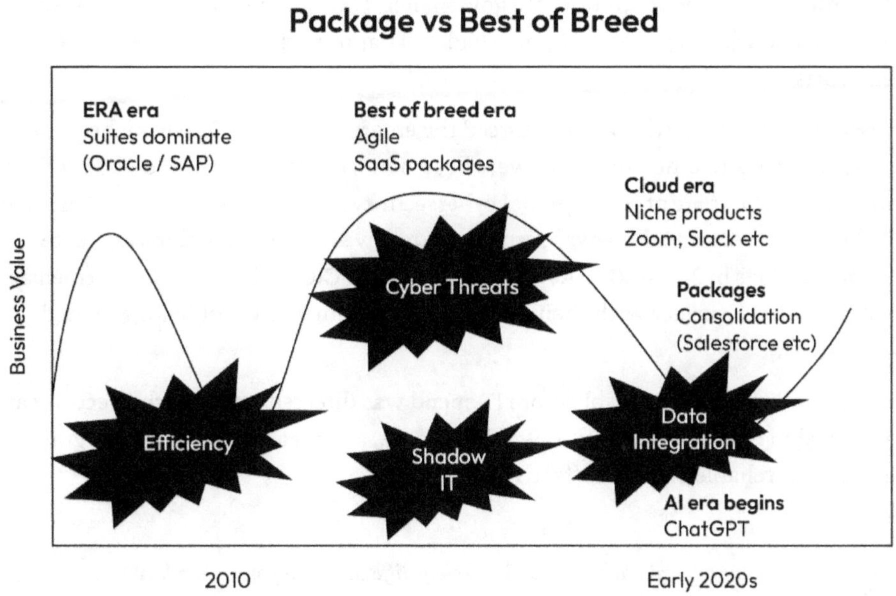

Figure 13.1 – Enterprise tech waves of change

As you can see from the preceding graph, the first is the adoption of enterprise resource planning (ERP) systems by different enterprise divisions. These disparate systems were later consolidated into enterprise-wide ERP systems programs. The scope initially was accounting, ordering and inventory systems, then this also started to include customer relationship management (CRM) systems too.

I've personally driven such transformations to consolidate over 40 different systems into one process, one server and one set of source code. The efficiency gains of these global and regional efforts are very evident in terms of ongoing total cost of ownership.

The scale of these ERP programs served to crowd out resources for other digital efforts and this led to the emergence of "shadow IT"(unapproved business technology) with the adoption of software-as-a-service (SaaS) applications at the speed of a credit card payment, bypassing technology and procurement processes. Without this being a stated IT strategy objective, there was widespread focus on best of breed products as the default to success.

Most CIOs were struggling to maintain their operations with a heavy ERP requirement and at the same time, satisfy the hunger of the digital natives who wanted to adopt new technologies and ignore large package upgrades.

The emergence of major cyber threats was now apparent with many new systems that had been onboarded, and without appropriate governance. CIOs and newly hired CISOs worked to reduce the risk and where feasible, migrate shadow IT apps to those supported and governed by the enterprise.

The following Cloud Computing era reinforced the emergence of previously niche products such as Zoom, Slack and other apps that were best of breed (alongside new cloud products and services). Following a spate of major global cybersecurity incidents around 2017-2018 and concern about data security, there was resulting extensive regulatory actions to create remediation backlogs in 2020-2021. At the same time, the CIO and CISO were alarmed at the growth of their attack surface with their legacy systems vulnerable, not being patched or able to be patched.

The end result was that considerably more IT spend was directed toward cybersecurity and this only served to reinforce the drive toward packages, as a means to have an integrated solution that was reliable and cost effective.

> Note
>
> *There is a movement toward packages. It's extremely difficult when you're in a large organization and you have 50, 60, 70,000 endpoints, and your team is having to go through dozens of different technologies when you're threat hunting. That is one of the drives for CISOs to look at packages where you can consolidate. If nothing's proprietary, you can consolidate and then integrate so you have data to make decisions in real time. To me it makes sense you're going to move toward packages because it's just more economical.*
>
> **Gary Hayslip – CISO, Halcyon.ai, Board Director and Investor**

> Note
>
> *Execs want to move away from in-house system integration since it is not core to security, they want to rely more on package vendors that can consolidate point solutions successfully—very much the case in the application security space.*
>
> *Security teams need to evolve and be better partners to development teams, understand the development process and work in an environment aligned to it. The same goes for sellers of security technology.*
>
> **Yigal Elstein – Chief Revenue Officer, Checkmarx**

Striking the right balance will continue to be a significant challenge for the CIO and CISO to address. There will always be pressure to consolidate the technology stack and a desire to use the best available tools for the most critical requirements.

The difference between best of breed and package solutions

This debate is the first philosophical fork in the road of any enterprise technology decision. Best of breed says, "buy the best individual solution for each problem and integrate them," while packages say, "buy a suite from one vendor that does everything well enough and trade some capability for simplicity, unified support, and lower integration overhead."

A CIO or CISO's answer to this question telegraphs their entire technology strategy. A best of breed buyer values precision and is willing to manage complexity, while a package buyer values coherence and is willing to accept some functional compromise.

I asked Geoff Stalley, a Non-Executive Director who sits on several boards, a former CFO and Big 4 Partner, his views on consolidating vendors versus buying best-of-breed point solutions.

> Note
>
> *The biggest gap I have found in taking on a consolidated vendor program versus best of breed implementations is the sheer scale of such a project. Often these are managed by a systems integrator of a lead vendor who have experience in implementing technology. What they don't usually have is specific experience in technology in our organization and thus the ability to judge whether the organization can adopt and adapt to the new technology.*
>
> *I have been an advisor to a major airline, a major hospitality company and a major city utility business where the board was advised to halt a large, consolidated technology implementation purely because the organization couldn't cope with the magnitude of the change. On the other hand, I have also advised a major global tech company to adopt a common package and to effectively force it into the organization to drive change across the businesses.*
>
> **Geoff Stalley – Non-Executive Director and former CFO**

From my experience, any CIO tends to look at best of breed solutions seeing both opportunity and operational burden simultaneously. The inherent promise of best-in-class capability in each domain is attractive, but they are afraid of the hidden cost of integrating and managing a sprawling portfolio of vendors, contracts, and APIs.

Also from a CIO's lens, best of breed solutions only really make good sense when the functional superiority of the individual solution is so significant that it justifies the integration tax and the CIO is also convinced that the internal IT team has bandwidth to own that complexity long-term.

For CISOs, this view is even more skeptical. Every additional vendor in the stack is another attack surface—another set of credentials, another compliance conversation, and another third-party risk assessment to run. Therefore, best of breed products are not favored and the CISO will most likely run a strong security review before these can pass their veto decision rights.

Note

CIOs and CISOs often misunderstand how global systems integrators (GSIs) think about vendors and platforms. The common assumption is that GSIs are simply "implementation partners" who push whichever vendor they have the deepest commercial relationship with. In reality, GSIs evaluate platforms through the lens of operability, scalability, integration, and future support talent availability into the client's ecosystem.

The bias, if any, is usually toward execution safety, not just margin or commission. We recommend what we feel will work best for the client. Having the right talent in the market for a particular product is also one of the evaluation criteria. Sometimes local talent is just not available in the local country, which makes it difficult to implement the solution. The same happens if the CISO picks a "Cool Niche Startup" for which there is little or no talent/skills available in the open market. Recommending this startup is a massive delivery risk for the client.

Gautam Kapoor – Cybersecurity Lead, Accenture

That said, a seasoned CISO also knows that a package solution with mediocre security capabilities can be far more dangerous than a best of breed solution that does one thing exceptionally well, particularly in high-stakes domains like identity, endpoint, or threat detection where "good enough" is not acceptable.

Note

"Best of breed" became a euphemism for tool sprawl. Our research found organizations now run an average of 50 application security tools, and 67% of security leaders say managing them is the bigger problem than any individual capability gap. It's no surprise, then, that nearly every organization we surveyed (97%) says they have plans to consolidate their application security tools in the next 12 months. The right balance isn't a ratio, it's a question: does the package actually correlate signals across the agentic development life cycle (ADLC), or is it just point tools rebadged under one logo? Pick packages where the data model is unified

> *and the context compounds; stay best of breed only where the function is truly differentiated and the integration cost is one you're willing to own.*
>
> **Amir Kazemi – Senior Director, Product Marketing, Cycode**

Ultimately both the CIO and CISO will privately admit that the best of breed vs. package decision is rarely purely technical. It is as much about the organization's integration capability, internal talent and risk appetite.

The CIO and CISO must source the best solution for the outcome that they are seeking. However, this can sometimes mean that the very best option is not the product they will choose.

Figure 13.2 captures the fundamental tension at the heart of every architecture decision the CIO and CISO face; on the left, a best of breed approach that offers specialized capability across multiple vendors but carries the weight of integration complexity, resource burden, and a total cost of ownership that is only visible once in operation mode. On the right, a package approach that trades some of that specialized capability for a unified stack, shared data, and operational simplicity that reduces total cost of ownership (TCO) (this approach is also aligned with the CIO's budget priorities and the CISO's security and risk obligations):

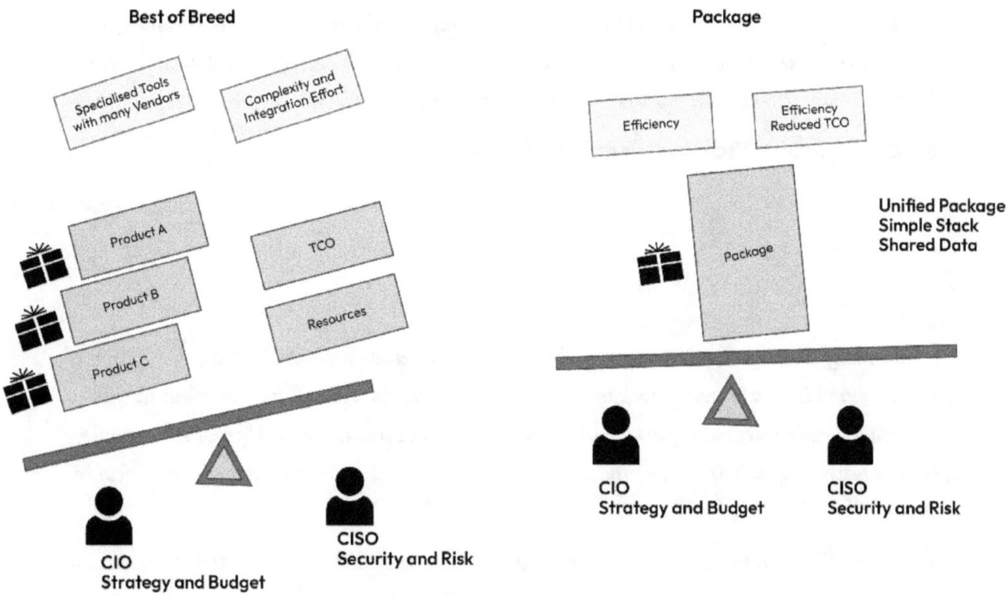

Figure 13.2 – Best of breed solutions vs. packages, as seen by the CIO and CISO

There is also pressure from different stakeholders on establishing a balance between best of breed and package solutions. While there is no one right or wrong answer this is the fundamental question that the CIO and CISO will constantly be trying to discuss and ensure that there is a clear approach that makes both business and technical sense.

I'd argue that the Chief Financial Officer (CFO) will want cost efficiency and simplified vendor management. The business units want the best tool for their specific need. The architecture team wants coherence and governability. The CISO wants security controls that work across the entire environment without gaps at the integration points. And the board wants a technology strategy it can understand and defend.

> Note
>
> *The truth is that there is no universal formula, the right balance depends on organizational maturity, integration complexity, and risk appetite. That said, a practical framework is the 70/30 rule: anchor your architecture on 2–3 core packages that handle the majority of your needs (70%), and selectively layer in best of breed point solutions (30%) where there are genuine capability gaps that your package vendor cannot close within a reasonable roadmap window.*
>
> *For CISOs specifically, package consolidation often wins on visibility and control—fewer integration points mean a smaller attack surface and simpler audit trails. For CIOs, the calculation is more nuanced: packages reduce operational overhead but can create vendor lock-in and slow innovation cycles. The key question to ask is: Does this best of breed solution solve a problem that will still exist in 3 years, or is my package vendor likely to absorb this capability?*
>
> **George Lee – Senior Vice President, Proofpoint**

> Note
>
> *This isn't really a technology debate. It's a business performance decision. The key distinction is between commoditized "buying packages" that bundle features without improving outcomes and architecturally integrated packages that actually reduce friction and improve how people work. The latter tend to win when productivity, speed, and operational efficiency are critical to the business.*
>
> *Best of breed still has a place, especially when specialized capabilities create real differentiation or meet strict regulatory needs. But the real test is simple: does your approach help people work faster, improve customer outcomes, or create competitive advantage?*

If it doesn't deliver on at least two of those, it's adding complexity, not value.

Bradon Rogers – Chief Customer Officer, Island

Note

My default position is package first, with best of breed by exception. That is not ideology. It is operating discipline.

Every additional product creates a tax: integration, data, identity, security, procurement, contract management, training, support and upgrade paths. In a large organization, that tax can sometimes be absorbed. In a leaner environment, it compounds quickly and shows up as complexity, duplicated cost and slower delivery.

That said, best of breed absolutely has a place. I will defend it where the capability gap is material, where the risk is too important to accept an average answer, where the package is clearly behind the market, or where the capability creates genuine differentiation. The point is not to avoid specialist tools. The point is to make them earn their place.

The test I like is simple: if the specialist tool disappeared tomorrow, would the package alternative do 80 percent of what we need without unacceptable risk? If yes, the specialist needs a very strong case. If no, defend the exception and document why it exists. Best of breed has to buy its way in every year.

Ram Kalyanasundaram – Chief Information and Digital Officer, Harris Farm Markets

Note

There are many considerations, including:

- *Criticality of the capability for the business strategy and whether it creates distinctive value for the customer*
- *Level of integration with other systems and capabilities within the organization*
- *Whether there is the potential to leverage the package solution into other parts of the organization*

> *Essentially the key is to ensure that the decision is driven by the business strategy. Investing in a strategic capability (whether best of breed or package) in my view is only valuable if it is followed up by leverage of that capability.*
>
> **Dan Chesterman – CIO, Teachers Mutual Bank**

Indeed, the challenge is going to be how to balance the depth of a best of breed solution vs. a package which has integration simplicity and cost efficiency. This is a question that I posed to Tony White, an old colleague of mine who was a business transformation leader that pivoted in his career into Chief Procurement Officer at Qantas.

> Note
>
> *Reliance is increasing on third-party packages and point solutions and while this gives companies benefits in speed, innovation, and operational agility, this approach can also bring greater exposure to risk, costs and governance challenges. Procurement vendor managers must navigate:*
>
> - *Selecting between specialized best of breed tools and integrated packages*
> - *Running disciplined, evidence-based POCs*
> - *Assessing vendor resilience and long-term viability*
> - *Securing favorable and sustainable commercial terms, and*
> - *Coordinating governance across diverse internal stakeholders and numerous vendors*
>
> **Tony White – Former Qantas Chief Procurement Officer**

Getting this balance right is the job that the CIO and CISO will have to grapple with. This is not an exercise in just selecting the "best" product, instead this is about managing this in the context of a portfolio view. I asked industry expert Abbas Kudrati about this, who has seen this equation from both sides.

> Note
>
> *The idea that a CISO must "choose a side" between a package and a best of breed solution is a false dichotomy. In practice, the most effective security leaders don't optimize for tools—they optimize for outcomes. The balance isn't ideological; it's contextual.*
>
> *Large packages bring undeniable advantages: simplified architecture, reduced integration overhead, and the ability to move faster with lean teams. For foundational controls—identity*

> *providers (IdP), endpoint security, and cloud posture—packages often provide the necessary "connective tissue" to establish consistency.*
>
> *But "enough" is where the tension lies.*
>
> *In mature environments, the greatest risks rarely sit within the 80% of coverage that packages handle well. They reside in the remaining 20%—the specialized gaps that attackers actively target. This is where best of breed solutions earn their place.*
>
> **Abbas Kudrati – Chief Identity Security Advisor, Silverfort**

There is a choice that leaders will need to make on what is the right ratio to adopt. Going for everything best of breed is not economically feasible and going for only packages means that you may be missing out on capability for a critical control.

> Note
>
> *"Size matters not. Judge me by my size, do you?"*
>
> *Moving from the classics to popular culture and Jedi Master Yoda, there is wisdom to be found in this challenge to the Padawan, Luke Skywalker.*
>
> *Yoda's point is that capability and impact are not necessarily correlated with physical size. The mentality of nobody getting fired for buying IBM is rightly relegated to the dustbin of history. Sellers should focus on impact. Impact can be seen in terms of faster innovation, better customer service, greater flexibility and superior outcomes. In my experience it's better to be a big fish in a small pond, that is, to deal with smaller, more hungrier partners.*
>
> **John Sutherland – Chief Digital Information Officer, Calvary Health Care**

My own view is that when we boil this down, the decision is sometimes made not by strategy at all, but by whoever has the strongest relationship in the room.

> Note
>
> *This is a constant tug of war for any security leader. Go all in on a single package, and you inherit massive concentration risk. Stack a dozen best of breed tools, and you drown your security operations center in integration debt and operational overhead.*
>
> *My evaluation comes down to a strict balancing act governed by three criteria:*
>
> - *First, risk alignment. Does it fit our specific risk appetite?*

> - *Second, speed. Does it reduce our mean time to respond and recover?*
> - *Third, operational drag. Can we deploy and manage it without adding headcount*
>
> **Jayant Dave – CISO, Check Point Software**

This is the backdrop to any discussion about best of breed solutions vs. packages. Most CIOs and CISOs have seen at least part of this transition over the last 25-30 years. The delicate balance between these types of technology has now been interrupted by the AI era.

Now, enter the AI era

How will the massively disruptive force that is AI affect the status quo, particularly when it comes to the balance between best of breed products and packages? I firmly believe that this is one of the most consequential questions in enterprise technology right now, and the answer is uncertain.

I've observed that traditional package vendors, such as Salesforce, SAP, etc. have had their market valuations impacted somewhat in recent years as a result of emerging AI tools. How they respond to this will be their challenge to maintain relevance in the marketplace.

As such, package players are making necessary strategic and defensive moves to embed AI capability directly into the packages themselves—for example, Copilot in Microsoft 365 and Einstein in Salesforce.

Similarly, every CIO and CISO has strong board pressure to make significant AI progress, and they are acutely aware that this comes with risk. In the short term these packages will probably continue to win as they mitigate their own personal risk.

In effect, new AI products (at the time of writing at least) are a best of breed variant, however there is some significant difference between these and more traditional best of breed products, as these were built around the assumption that workflow and data live inside their boundaries. What I mean by that is that new AI agents can operate autonomously, to orchestrate across systems without the user ever opening the native application.

> Note
>
> *There's been swings back and forth about whether to focus on deploying packages or purchasing best of breed and my view is that we want to have packages as much as possible, but then best of breed where it's new and innovative.*
>
> **Gary Hayslip – CISO Halcyon.ai, Board Director and Investor**

The traditional argument for packages was coherence: one vendor, one data model, one governance framework, one contract. The traditional argument against best of breed was fragmentation: too many vendors, too many integrations, too much operational complexity.

Potentially an AI agent architecture removes the fragmentation argument almost entirely. If the agent handles the orchestration, then we no longer require a specialized vendor for integration.

I'd note that this does not mean package strategies are wrong today. It means they need to be evaluated with one additional question that most organizations are not yet asking: how does this decision look in a world where an AI agent handles orchestration?

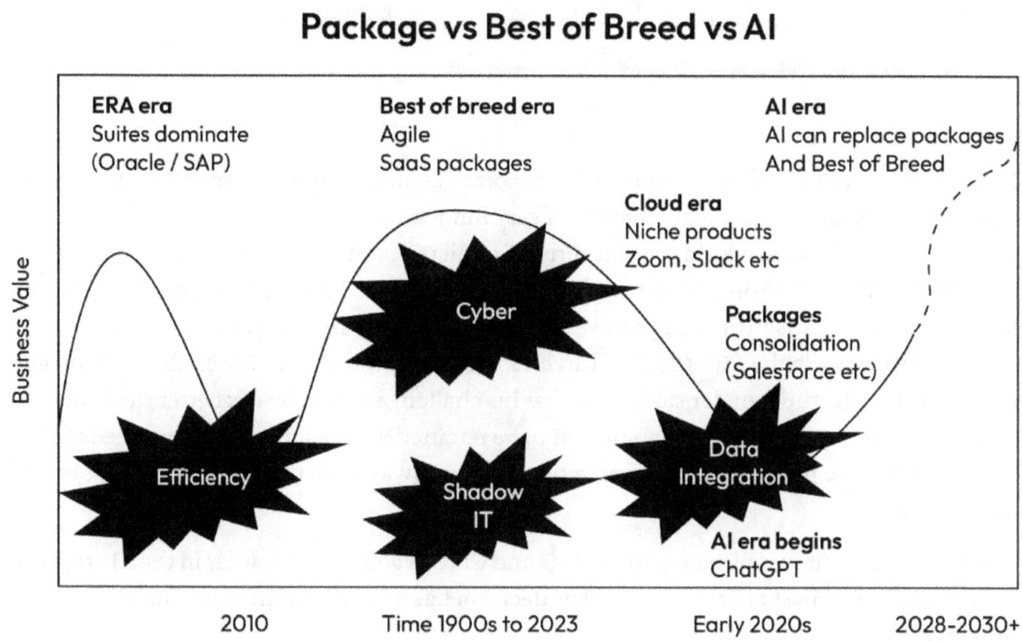

Figure 13.3 – Waves of change in the AI era

Either way, this will mark a difficult period where there are no safe answers in the long term. Both packages and best of breed products will struggle to compete when there is an earthquake occurring on the baseball pitch.

The new best of breed players must integrate into the stack, and CIOs and CISOs must evaluate their AI capability, which is so rapidly moving that it can make one dizzy with the speed of change.

The problem, though, is that for the CIO and CISO, the risks are magnified and where previously they innovated on the edge but had packages for core systems that were robust and safe, there is now pressure to fully embed AI best of breed everywhere.

In addition, third- and fourth-party suppliers have AI embedded in their products too, making it much more complicated to have an accurate inventory.

> Note
>
> *The right balance isn't a formula but a conversation around risk and your vision. Packages reduce integration debt and operational complexity, which matters enormously when your security team is already stretched thin. Best-in-class solutions make more sense when differentiation is mission-critical or provides a significant business advantage.*
>
> **Dan Wheatley – Vice President of Sales, Gravwell**

Comparing AI product "A" vs. AI product "B" becomes an interesting challenge. Recently I was speaking to an Israeli Tech startup that had a very innovative AI detection approach, able to gain visibility of AI usage within the enterprise. I recall reflecting and saying that to test this properly in a fair head-to-head comparison, it would require a POC to be run concurrently so there can be a comparison of false positive AI leaks when comparing product A to B. This would in effect enable the CIO, CISO and architect to see if product A or B was able to manage this better. The startup founder said to me that his challenge was to be 10x better than the established solutions, just "good enough" AI to be retained. I fully agree that there needs to be a sufficient delta to provide enough motivation to move away from the known and trusted existing vendor.

I'd anticipate that the act of selling to the CIO and CISO is going to be harder in the AI era, now that the traditional best of breed vs. package decision has mutant variants that include varieties of AI.

With all this in mind, this is a fitting starting point to examine the difficult set of decisions around selling these products to the CIO and CISO.

The CIO and CISO perspective

So far in this chapter, we have explored that when you sell to a CIO and CISO, you are caught between two competing philosophies: best of breed solutions vs. packages. We have seen that the market has shifted toward packages as the preference (although the emerging AI era may change that). However, if you asked the CIO privately, they would probably say they prefer best of breed solutions. Why is that?

From my perspective, the CIO has likely seen interesting monopolistic behavior by many of the ERP era vendors in the past and perhaps even from more recent ones. The battle scars of working with vendors when in a "lock-in" state have been quite deep and hard to easily forget. CIOs now also face AI packages while also making strategic choices about these new packages. They also need to consider where to host the data/application that the AI system utilizes. From my experience, I would say that CIOs ideally want the best of both worlds.

> Note
>
> *At the end of the day, it comes down to value. I will default to the architectural principle of "buy before build, re-use before buy" which will always lean toward systems that integrate and are part of a package, these will be better than point solutions.*
>
> *The best assessment criteria is a true net present value/total cost of ownership analysis as intuitively, package solutions will represent a lower cost to serve/grow within the business as usual (BAU) environment. Often, packages will represent a consolidation opportunity over best of breed (but not always) and from a unit cost perspective, be cheaper as you can often do more with a package.*
>
> *I also push for a basic 80/20 rule approach i.e.: is it good enough? Coming back to the architectural principle, can an existing solution be modified to address an emerging business requirement before going to market to identify a new solution?*
>
> **John Taylor – Field CTO, Mimecast (former CIO & CISO)**

There is a fundamental tension that exists between technical depth and operational efficiency. A hybrid approach to adopting both makes common sense, regardless if you are buying a package or best of breed solution.

What about CISOs? I would argue that a CISO wants a security baseline that is unified to ensure that reporting is embedded and that there are no gaps from integration of disparate systems. When your career is on the line, you want this baseline to work efficiently and be reliable. Thus, packages may be favored.

Having said that, there is however a risk that CISOs (as well as CIOs) will be aware of: if you put all your eggs in the same basket, you end up with concentration risks that make your enterprise resilience a concern. As a CIO and CISO you will enjoy potential cost savings, but a single point of failure is not a principle that you will want to embrace. Once an attacker has gained access, then theoretically they will have all the keys to the kingdom, and they now own your environment.

> Note
>
> *Often concentration risk is captured in an organization's enterprise risk register as a key risk—this then facilitates a discussion about associated risk appetite and any mitigating actions/controls required.*
>
> **Tanya Graham – Group Executive, iCare (former CIO)**

> Note
>
> *It just makes sense that a lot of the packages integrate with each other now, so they actually give you a better picture, and it's actually easier for your team. Of course, if you flip the whole discussion around from an attacker's point of view, it could also be easier as well because if you were able to break into that package, you would now have access to quite a lot of information and tools.*
>
> **Gary Hayslip – CISO Halcyon.ai, Board Director and Investor**

The CISO will also be aware of critical controls that are dynamic in the enterprise, and for these they may favor specialized tools as a "shield". This is where best of breed will have an advantage.

> Note
>
> *A package may provide multifactor authentication (MFA) and basic access management, yet it often lacks deep visibility into service accounts, non-human identities, and lateral movement paths across hybrid environments. A specialized identity security solution addresses these high-impact gaps that a generalist package might overlook.*

> *For a strategic balance:*
>
> - *Package for consistency: Use packages to reduce operational drag and create a "security baseline."*
> - *Best of breed for risk concentration: Introduce specialized tools where the risk is too high to accept "standard" coverage.*
>
> *The mental model for a CISO should be: Are we consolidating for convenience, or are we reducing actual risk? Those two outcomes are rarely the same.*
>
> **Abbas Kudrati – Chief Identity Advisor, Silverfort**

Taking Abbas Kudrati's perspective into account alongside my own views, this graphic shows how packages and best of breed solutions work best when used side by side to provide a comprehensive defense:

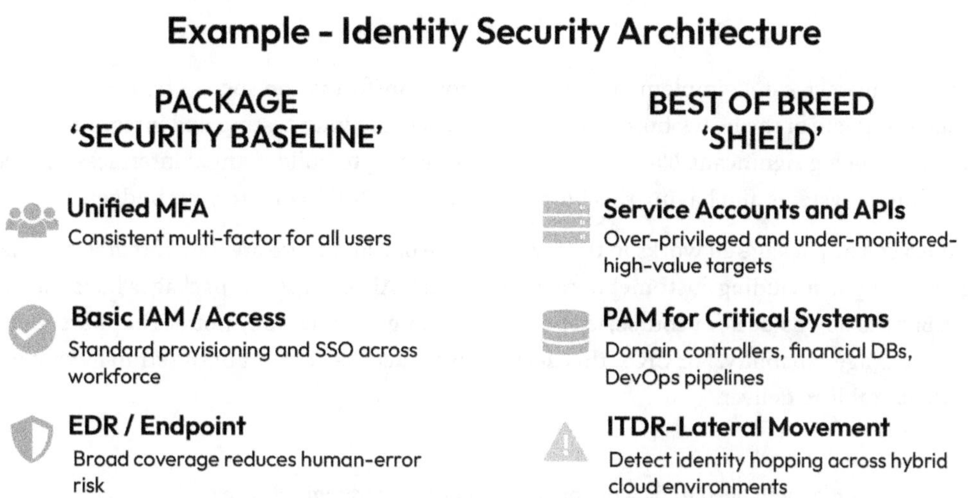

Figure 13.4 – Packages and Best of breed

These are the decisions that the CIO and CISO must make across their entire portfolio with their key concerns in mind, while also being mindful of the costs involved.

> **Note**
>
> Any vendor will naturally fall into one side of this equation. New innovative products are naturally best of breed, and these can, over time, be developed into a package. However, it is also feasible that packages will acquire new innovative components and

> develop into best of breed options. Take the example of Google acquiring WIZ or Microsoft acquiring GitHub for instance.
>
> The "package" effect is often not always transparent and at times, companies do not rebrand newly acquired solutions. I've also seen that innovative startups may lose their edge when absorbed into a larger enterprise body which moves more slowly and with more governance.

> **Note**
>
> *The other factor in looking at best of breed is just a point of time variable. Provided the vendor can demonstrate a clear roadmap and commitment behind the product, this needs to be factored into the decision on the vendor selection.*
>
> **Paul O'Rourke – former CISO, CRO and BCG Global Cyber Leader**

Having in my own career implemented core systems transformation such as banking, I'm personally aware of the heavy burden of changing packages with testing and integration investment being significant. The CIO will also fear having to build manual interfaces between best of breed systems and having this burden continue as BAU load into your budget.

In contrast, the package all works in theory out of the box and there are data integrations that are built for you including customer data management. Also, in theory, packages have a lower TCO. But the downside is, of course, that you are settling for what may not be the "best" but just an average capability. For CIOs, this decision is in fact the key part of the strategy that you are accountable to deliver.

> **Note**
>
> The champion will need to be a major supporter of the strategic choice and argue for a specific approach that is aligned with the thinking of the CIO and CISO.

Making the right choices and considering a combination of strengths and weaknesses through this strategic selection is strongly correlated to the scale and complexity of the enterprise. A CIO in a small startup will likely never choose a package, as this is too large a tool with a cost that is not bearable. A CIO in a large enterprise, however, has the freedom to choose between a package and a best of breed solution.

Note

The optimal balance depends on organizational maturity, risk tolerance, and capability requirements. Effective approaches usually use packages for core controls and augment with best of breed tools for specialized needs where package components fall short. Organizations should choose packages when operational efficiency and vendor consolidation are priorities but opt for best of breed when specific capabilities require specialized depth or regulatory requirements demand purpose-built solutions. Most successful organizations adopt a hybrid approach with packages as the foundation and strategic specialists for capability gaps, with interoperability through open APIs essential to prevent vendor lock-in.

Charlie Dai – Vice President and Principal Analyst, Forrester

Matt Boon, a former Gartner® analyst, reinforced that analysts look for how these packages and best of breed solutions work together well, and explained that these linkages really matter to the buyer.

Note

Within all the analyst firms, you'll get analysts who are focused on those bigger players... the package players. They're looking for much greater collaboration... there's a real sort of focus on how we can identify some of those interdependencies and potential sort of linkages between some of these vendors.

Matt Boon – Senior Director, Strategic Research, Adapt

The CIO and CISO essentially focus on capabilities and make choices of which capability to implement when they may have invested in duplicate functionality.

Tip

Not every process is equally important, so best of breed solutions are naturally more attractive for strategic capabilities that differentiate your enterprise from the competitor.

Strategic, core, or essential capabilities

In my career as a CIO at Eli Lilly across Australia, China, Asia Pacific, Japan and the USA we used Boston Consulting Group (BCG) for new market entry analysis, so over my 15 years there we were heavily exposed to their approach. Eli Lilly then published an internal paper that was written with BCG to help us all use their strategy development approach, then called the "4 column framework".

As my career progressed I kept using the BCG Eli Lilly strategic approach and this facilated my own thinking through future directions.

One of the favorite approaches within this framework was around strategic capability assessment. This approach segmented all capabilities into current ability to deliver a specific outcome at an enterprise level. Thus leaders, when undertaking an IT strategy exercise, are making conscious choices as to which capabilities to invest in, which vendors to partner with, and what to de-invest.

All capabilities fall into one of three categories:

- **Strategic:** Gives competitive advantage
- **Core:** Systems of record
- **Essential:** Services used by the business

CIOs and CISOs today will be thinking about capabilities in this manner.

Evaluating this at a portolio level we would classify strategic capabilities like AI, digital innovation and some parts of data analytics and perhaps a small part of cyber as "Strategic". These capabilities differentiate us from our rivals and we want to be "Above Parity" with these to compete effectively in the market.

ERP and CRM systems were probably considered to be "Strategic" when they were first deployed and now these have reverted to being "Core" systems that are important to run the business but no longer a strategic edge. For any "Core" systems we just want to be as good as our competitors; being "Above Parity" is overinvesting.

"Essential" capabilities are services that we use every day such as the help desk or payroll. These are usually outsourced or if performed internally, we may invest only the bare minimum to provide a baseline service. We want to run these essential services efficiently, and for many CIO and CISOs, these may be candidates to outsource or potentially offshore to lower cost centers, if they haven't already been.

This analysis is depicted in the following graph:

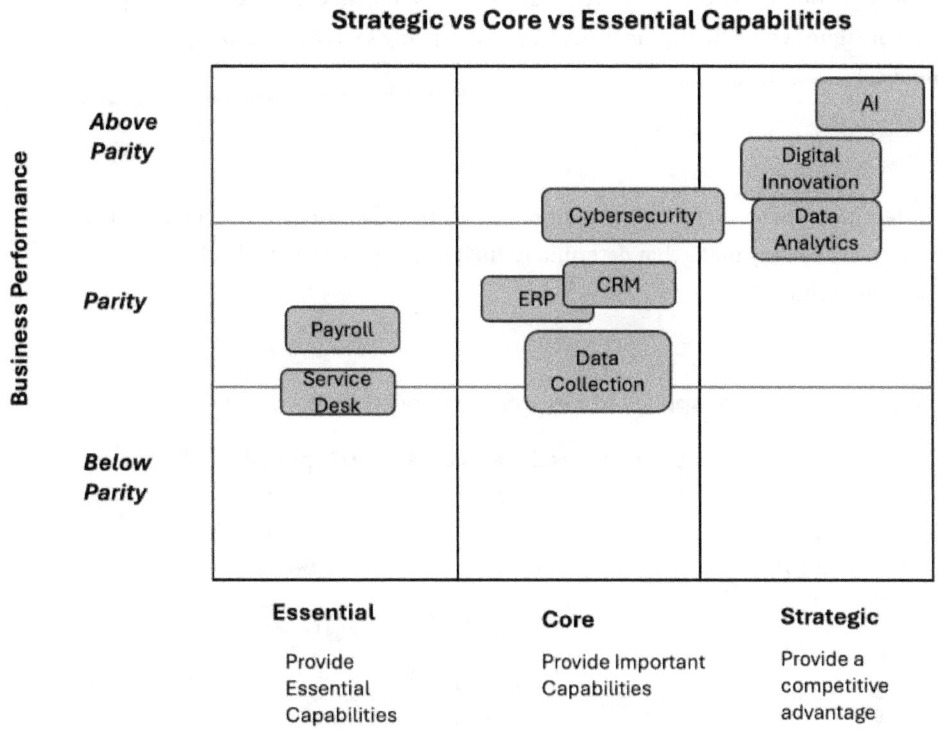

Figure 13.5 – IT Capabilities ranked by importance

You can see that some products are entirely positioned in "Strategic", "Core" and "Essential" segments, and there are some products crossing two different categories.

Using this framework, I have, as a CIO, then made strategic decisions to invest in best of breed solutions for that "Strategic" category and over time, as those shifted left, to consider moving this investment to a package.

> **Note**
>
> The CIO, while they network, tend to have a sense of competition with their peer CIOs. This is not necessarily a personal thing, but more that they are rewarded for helping their business compete and be differentiated in the marketplace. This will mean that their "Strategic" capabilities are then extremely confidential and they will not desire to talk about this too openly or to share too many details. There may however be exceptions to this, for example when asked to provide benchmark insights to non-competitors in other industries or different geographic regions.

I'd add that the CISO is similarly secretive about revealing too many details of their security portfolio, however they often have a select group of CISO peers that they compare notes with and they may gain a sense of being secure by adopting similar products.

Tip

While you may want to try to dress up your product and service as "Strategic", in truth the CIO has already made that determination. It is tricky to try to make that conversion, but it can be done.

This same approach can be applied to a cybersecurity portfolio by CISOs:

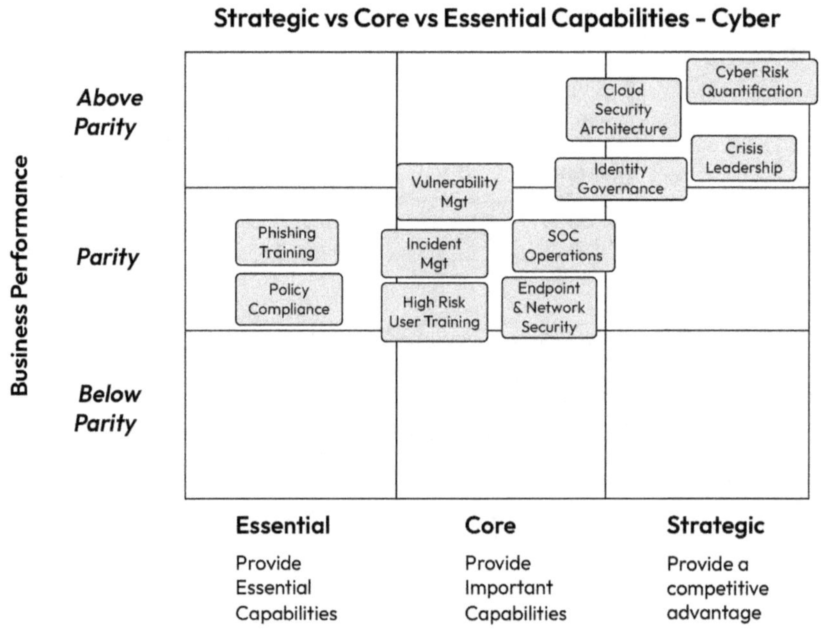

Figure 13.6 – Cyber Capabilities ranked by importance

Note

The average CIO and CISO prefers multi-cloud architecture where workloads can be logically split across different providers. This can reduce concentration risk—putting "all eggs in one basket"—and allows future usage pivoting, depending on how these major players are innovating with their latest cloud or AI offerings.

Allow me to highlight "Crisis Leadership" as an example. This is "Strategic", as leading and communicating exceptionally well in a crisis assists enterprises in being able to reduce market impact in terms of customer churn, share price reduction and industry reputation. The associated capability of "Incident Management" is a "Core" capability as following a process of escalation and communication when there are system issues being experienced is important but doesn't need to be cutting edge.

The CISO may use such analysis in trying to convince the CIO that additional investment funding is required for "Strategic" and "Core" capabilities when there is a gap in the required maturity.

> Note
>
> *During school time, if possible, every top student wants to be no.1 student in the class, not no.2. A similar ambition happens in the product or solution fields sometimes as well. So, we have seen more packetization players are coming.*
>
> *There is no absolutely right or wrong in being packetization players, but the fact is, due to legacy technical architecture and business history, not every customer would completely switch all the existing solutions into one package solution overnight. So, a deep understanding of the pain points and focusing on integration, not just complete replacement, sometimes would be more tangible.*
>
> **Frankie Shuai – Vice President of Information Security, Bitdeer**

From my own experience there will likely be pressure by the CIO to ensure that capabilities in the "Strategic" and "Essential" categories use packages rather than best of breed solutions. There will be exceptions of course, but the CIO will be under pressure to reduce IT spend and packages can provide this opportunity, plus they may have the advantage of already being an incumbent.

Of course, this analysis can be dynamic and for instance, new agentic AI modules within security operations products, to automate log management for example, can then elevate part of the capability into the "Strategic" segment. This is where great vendor sales team can help the CIO and CISO rethink how they have mentally positioned different capabilities.

Note

Traditionally, log management has been classified as an essential capability, albeit unglamorous. It sits in the operational budget, is evaluated on cost and compliance coverage, and attracts almost no executive attention. But when an agentic AI module is embedded into that log management capability, autonomously correlating events across the entire environment and identifying threat patterns that no human analyst could detect, that capability changes from "Essential" to "Strategic".

Understanding whether your solution is classified as "Strategic", "Core", or "Essential" by the CIO and CISO determines everything that follows. This determines who owns the decision, which budget it draws from, how the business case should be framed, and what level of executive sponsorship is realistic to expect.

The classification is equally consequential for the internal champion, as a solution positioned in the wrong bucket will attract the wrong decision makers, the wrong funding conversation, and the wrong success criteria.

Given the tectonic shift toward packages, from best of breed solutions, what happens when the small innovative vendor that the CIO or CISO has identified as best of breed is acquired by a much larger mega vendor? I've touched on this briefly already, but let's consider this in a little more depth.

Concerns about acquisition risks

We'll start with the CIO. The CIO sees that there can be potential disruption to their technology roadmap and operational continuity should the best of breed solution that they have standardized on be at risk of being acquired by another vendor.

From my own experience, you then start to worry about product discontinuation and whether the new acquiring vendor will "sunset" this solution in favor of their own competing product.

CIOs are also very concerned about whether support quality will deteriorate during the transition. They have chosen these new innovative solutions and often enjoy great support as are seen as strategic clients by the vendor, versus being just another customer in a larger list.

Note

My approach to package/software selection vs. best of breed, needs to account for additional variables. The previous mantra in cyber was "Defense in Depth", which resulted in multiple bespoke solutions. The complexity this introduces is that the company is then forced to pay for bespoke integration costs, ongoing, every time the vendor updates versions. This also introduces additional licensing costs and complexity in managing multiple vendors.

> *My preference in selecting new hardware or solutions is to look to leverage existing vendors and have them accountable for the integration costs and reduced licensing costs. An obvious example is Microsoft E5 and leveraging their security suite across multiple areas. Microsoft Defender is not necessarily best of breed, but I have selected and integrated it due to the above reasons.*
>
> **Paul O'Rourke – former CISO, CRO and BCG Global Cyber Leader**

On the other hand, the CISO sees security and compliance exposure with vendor acquisitions. In my time as a CISO, I would worry about potential changes to data handling practices, data residency, and whether security commitments would be maintained post-acquisition in these scenarios. Most of all, CISOs will be concerned about the new acquiring company's security posture, whether it's weaker, and whether that might increase breach risk.

> Tip
>
> If you are ever in this scenario and there are discussions about acquisition of your company that start to leak out, then I'd advise being transparent with your clients and those you're hoping to bring on as clients, as much as possible about the situation and any timeline that may exist.
>
> How a vendor communicates significant change such as mergers and acquisitions (M&A) activity, I'd argue is one of the most defining trust moments in the entire relationship. The CIO and CISO are expecting to be treated as partners who deserve to hear difficult news directly and before everyone else.

AI considerations

The CIO and CISO will often have both a natural preference and some friction against core systems of record being migrated to the latest and greatest new technology. (We just have to look at the speed at which banks have made a shift to become digital banks.) They want innovation and operational stability at the same time. Of course, as some legacy packages have design flaws, the constant tension between these two factors will remain a key part of the CIO and CISO's strategy.

Two concepts are reshaping the platform vs. best of breed decision in the AI era. **Data density**, which refers to the volume of data within a unified package, and **governance surface area,** which refers to how broadly that data is distributed across systems, third parties, and AI models that may not be fully understood or auditable.

I'd note that packages have traditionally been data dense by design, and that concentration is what makes AI genuinely powerful, but the simultaneous pressure to embed AI everywhere is expanding the governance surface area to create the worst possible scenario for the CIO and CISO.

I'd argue that the safe bet though is in-between these two factors. Rather than going in fully on either strategy, the best approach will be isolating where AI-assisted development can operate without touching core data integrity boundaries, then treating those boundaries as non-negotiable until observability and explainability tooling matures. This will allow the enterprise to capture necessary velocity gains without betting governance stability on tooling that is still evolving rapidly.

Many CIOs and CISOs are dealing everyday with fragile legacy products. They know that security patching will not be always possible and have accepted this risk as part of their strategy. Similarly, with the new AI tools that are emerging, they are aware of the risks around model drift, hallucinations and that auditability will be only feasible using another AI to keep up with the volume. For their own career's sake, CIOs and CISOs need to consider how they contain the risk while also accepting a degree of new AI risk.

There will be bets made on new AI technology and how this works with existing packages and best of breed solutions, striking a balance between the existing fragile technology debt and then carefully using AI for some isolated steps in the process such as coding, automation, documentation or testing.

This way, CIOs and CISOs can feel more comfortable that the systems that run core systems and business are in effect isolated (air gapped) from the new and potentially unstable new AI systems.

This balance of the old and the new is depicted in the following figure:

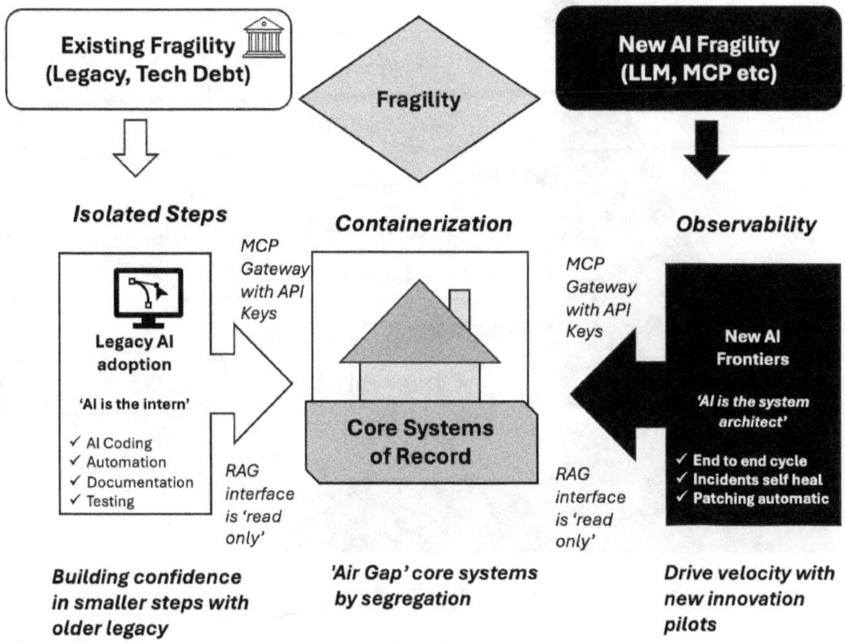

Figure 13.7 – The CIO and CISO balancing new and old

This approach brings velocity and what will be real time systems that rebuild and self-heal whenever there is an issue or incident. This is nirvana for the Innovation CIO persona, but a complete nightmare for most of their CIO peers.

Even with AI capabilities effectively isolated from key systems and with a human in the loop, when you fully commit to AI and work at AI speed, then your only control against negative effects may be observability.

For the CIO and CISO, the oversight required in the AI era shifts into a more complex model that requires a combination of layers of control. The reality is that the role of the CIO and CISO moves from being the "pilot" to being the "air traffic controller". There still must be humans in the loop that review exceptions that are out of tolerance. Then there are policies that must be enforced, ensuring that changes to access or data operate only through specified guardrails. A layer of AI for observability will also be added to track all the actions that both humans and AI are performing:

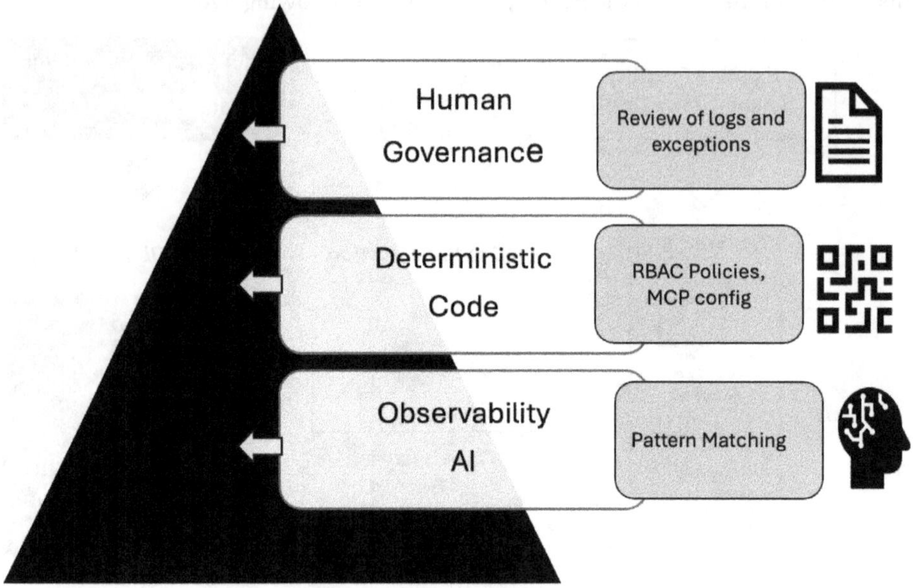

Figure 13.8 – AI Era Oversight

This is a new era, and many will be fearful of this change. I suspect this will be a key discussion point when the CIO and/or CISO you are trying to sell to is trying to drive new change.

There are discussions of removing humans from the loop entirely to enable true AI era speed. The logic is that 1:1000 level of human to agent supervision will only serve to slow down AI, so we must begin to accept this process may become human-less. That is a huge leap of faith that I for one do not yet support.

Future charging models

A final item worth considering from the CIO and CISO perspective is that with the rise of AI and agentic AI, we have seen package vendors start to charge differently; from cost "per seat" (user) basis to a "per interaction" (transaction) model.

We have seen major players adding AI to their existing package, this includes ServiceNow (Now Assist), Microsoft (Copilot) and Salesforce (Einstein). These new features are charged add-ons with a best of breed flavor.

While this is a clear upsell strategy, CIOs do want to extract value from their existing core capabilities, and this is a hybrid approach that will enable them to move faster than trying to build this new capability themselves.

Up and coming best of breed vendors face less high pressure here as they are usually sold at a premium per seat, for strategic capability. And then they are likely to already have a direct competitor that has operations already established in their go-to market.

It is my prediction that in the future we will see some morphing of the current models with packages continuing to grow through mergers and acquisitions, continuing to charge their base seat fees as well as interaction fees for AI capabilities. As a result, this will force smaller best of breed solutions to offer seat-based costing for traditional use and similarly, some interaction-based costing for AI features.

The key difference will be the extent of the pricing, and how each decides to take (perhaps aggressive) positions in the market. The CIO and CISO will usually let the procurement team manage these details, with the knowledge that there is often little negotiation that is possible on the terms and conditions. However, with one eye to the future and the next big change, they are always wary of how the budget can be a constraint for their IT strategy.

Summary

In this chapter I explored the complex topic of packages vs. best of breed solutions. The package vs. best of breed debate has never been fully resolved, and the AI era is now making it significantly more complex.

CIOs tend to privately prefer best of breed solutions for strategic capabilities but are often pushed toward packages by integration burden, TCO pressure, and board risk aversion. While the CISO would think similarly when it comes to selecting cybersecurity products for their own portfolio, they would be more likely to favor other business stakeholders selecting packages as these are more tried and tested.

The key learnings from this chapter are:

- **Best of breed solutions for strategic investment** – strategic capabilities (competitive differentiators like AI and advanced cybersecurity) warrant best of breed investment, while core capabilities (such as ERP, CRM) better suit packages. Essential capabilities such as helpdesk or payroll can be outsourced.
- **AI is disrupting both sides simultaneously** – package vendors are adding AI as upsell modules, while agentic AI bypasses traditional user interfaces entirely, eroding vendor lock-in (neither packages nor best of breed solutions have a guaranteed safe position).
- **Pricing models are shifting** – the move from per-seat to per-interaction charging for AI features will force CIOs to renegotiate their cost models (best of breed vendors will face margin pressure competing against package economies of scale).

- **Acquisition risk is a real CIO/CISO concern** – when a best of breed vendor is acquired, CIOs fear product discontinuation and support degradation while CISOs fear weakened security posture and data residency changes. Transparency from you about any M&A timeline helps to preserve their trust.
- **The winning AI strategy is not full commitment to AI nor resistance to it** – it is deliberate isolation, using AI where it accelerates without touching core systems, governing through observability rather than direct control.

14

Case Study – Selling Into a Major Transformation

Despite all the reports by Gartner®, Forrester® and IDC® about increased IT spend across all industries, the truth is that most enterprises have limited capacity for IT transformation spend. In my experience, I've observed that typically 70-80% of the IT budget is for business as usual (BAU) requirements, leaving just 20-30% for strategic programs of work which are often referred to as "discretionary" spend. Surprisingly, there is often less for this than you may think. The fund of money for major investments tends to be a closely managed pot of dollars with high political visibility.

Only when the market gets wind that there is a major transformation on the horizon and there are heightened expectations of a massive payday can this transformation then become the key strategic driver for the enterprise and, as a result, take the lion's share of the budget and resources. I've seen many examples of large transformation programs crowding out other projects.

Selling a solution in a major transformation can be a blessing, but it can also be negative for you. When there is a broader transformation, the competitive dynamics are higher, with every competitor trying to bid for the real estate. Similarly, on the inside, there is competition between insiders, all trying to influence the future decision to go in their preferred direction.

A transformation signals that there will be funding for the proposed change. But at the same time, this can also have implications for how this is funded and approved. In general, the process will slow down due to the strategic implications and the additional governance that will be required.

Selling to the CIO and CISO when there is a major transformation changes the equation, I explain how in this chapter. There is now a Chief Transformation Officer (CTO) that is a key stakeholder, and I will provide perspectives on how to sell to this role.

By definition, a CTO is the executive accountable for driving and delivering large-scale organizational change, owning the mandate, the budget, and the program governance required to move the enterprise from its current state to its desired future state and at pace. Note that while in some organizations the job title may be different, what matters here is that this executive has a mandate to drive large-scale change. We will cover the following topics in this chapter:

- The dynamics of enterprise transformation
- How to sell to the Chief Transformation Officer
- How to reconcile the C-Suite

The dynamics of enterprise transformation

CIOs and CISOs are often the center of attention when it comes to transformations. They are under board-level pressure to deliver outcomes and, at the same time, they may be inundated with attention from you and other vendors wanting to be included.

> Note
>
> *Some vendors will read about our Transformation program and jump to the conclusion that this means we want to modernize or simplify some platform or product, without taking the time to understand if this is what our strategy is trying to achieve. I get that without time with us, they won't get that information, but I don't and my team doesn't, have time to educate potential new partners on what and how to sell to us.*
>
> **Scott Collary – Group CIO, Westpac Group**

This is good news and bad news at the same time. You are not wasting your time with pitching new ideas, but you often have to start again with building relationships and understanding the stakeholders.

As a vendor (or even internal champion), I'd argue that your immediate response upon learning of an impending transformation may not be positive. To start with, you may be concerned that you will get lost in the details, and/or any progress you have already made will slow down. Champions may fear that their own credit will be watered down by a large transformation effort.

In my own experience, I've seen many instances of a fairly simple "widget" sale get later caught up and incorporated into a broader, more strategic transformation business case.

> **Note**
>
> *I assess vendors through a strategic architecture and risk-based lens, prioritizing alignment to the organization's security strategy and the suitability of product capabilities to internal requirements. Selection is based on demonstrated fit in our environment—security maturity, integration, operational supportability, scalability, compliance alignment, vendor roadmap credibility, reference calls, and total cost of ownership—with strong emphasis on proof-of-value in real operating conditions.*
>
> *Importantly, I am conscious of decisions that create long-term lock-in or rigid dependency; I prefer solutions that maintain architectural flexibility and minimize future switching and integration constraints.*
>
> **Yaso Addanki – Head of Security Architecture, AGL**

There are several mega-trend factors that are driving the forces of transformation, and often this is outside of the direct control of the CIO and CISO. As a CIO that has led many transformations personally, I can say that considering and understanding the market broadly and strategically is essential for them in the early days of these efforts (however it is very likely that the transformation requirements are outside of their current horizon and therefore they may have some "blind spots" in enablement of this vision).

> **Note**
>
> *When talking about transformation, you are looking for a fundamental change and improvement to the way you work. You should take those critical changes and have the vendor demonstrate them as part of any POV. This enables you to carve out the first steps in a transformation program and provides the vendor with an opportunity to demonstrate they can get you moving in the right direction while forming a proving ground for whether you can work together.*
>
> **Dan Wheatley – Vice President of Sales, Gravwell**

Given the expected impact of transformation work, there is often the involvement of strategic consulting advisories such as McKinsey, Bain, and/or Boston Consulting Group (BCG). (We covered the value and roles of these advisors in *Chapter 11*.) An advisor will be engaged at the C-Suite level to provide strategic thinking capability. This position requires the advisor to be a sparring partner and not a "Yes" person. They provide slightly provocative hypotheses of a problem statement and act to help their clients see their full potential when constraints and assumptions have been removed. Joseph Edwin provides great framing for how strategic advisors work in this scenario.

> **Note**
>
> *When I look back at some of my engagements, the best ones are those where the client is strongly bi-lingual – i.e. well versed in both technology and the business it supports and speaks the language both groups understand. They expect the advisor to go toe-to-toe with them, challenge their thinking, and stretch their imagination around the full potential such a transformation can deliver. The CIO viewed the transformation from a business lens rather than technology and fundamentally understood the business impact the transformation would bring. The relationship with business stakeholders was a true partnership and not that of a service provider.*
>
> **Joseph Edwin – Senior Partner, Bain & Company**

The strategic advisor will sharpen the strategic focus of the transformation, and their challenge will "pressure test" everything using evidence and logic. While these advisors are engaged it is likely that they will not have much interface with the proposed vendors. Their engagement with internal champions may also be limited. This is key context to bear in mind though, as it has a material impact on how you can influence this process.

> **Note**
>
> *In early conversations, what signals tell you a client is ready for a high-impact transformation versus one that is likely to stall, especially when major platform or cyber decisions are involved?*
>
> *From my experience, I typically look for the below signals. This is important for me to understand so that I can align the right solution for the client. Also, it tells me if the CIO/CISO is just doing a dipstick check in the market or if they are serious about the transformation journey:*
>
> - *Clear articulation of cyber risk and how the business plans to reduce that risk with this transformation. In absence of this, I am a little wary of the engagement. A red signal is when the client is asking for technical features. A green signal is when the client is able to articulate business pain and why they want to remediate the cyber risk.*
> - *Executive sponsorship. Any transformation engagement should be run at the right level. I seek engagement at the senior most level to judge if this is a serious project and*

> *the business is aligned to the cyber transformation. Many clients ask me to come and meet the board. That is a good sign that the client is ready!*
>
> - *Stakeholder engagements. This is what I call "Who is in the room" test. Are the right stakeholders in the room for the transformation program? E.g. if you only have the CISO in the room for an Identity Governance engagement, then we are missing something. Similarly, if we only have SAP IT product team members in the room for a large SAP Security project then it's a big red flag.*
>
> **Gautam Kapoor – Cybersecurity Lead, Accenture**

The interchange of different leaders engaged in the transformation is a dynamic that is not that well understood. In large enterprise transformation this is like a confluence of many rivers flowing together, with many executive peers all having similar but different objectives, each managing their own S-Curves.

Executive S-Curves in a transformation

While you have been focused on influencing the CIO and CISO to make this sale and your whole support structure, including the champion and other supporters, have been brought onside to support this goal, in the scenario of selling into a major transformation, there is now a new key stakeholder to be aware of: the CTO. This is often a peer of the CIO and while they work together closely, they have some very different thinking and motivators.

The CTO has a complex role that is measured by the ability to drive a planned future state of the business. Their success metric is radically different from that of CIOs and CISOs as they want to realize a brave new future that incorporates a new culture and way of working. In essence, they want to change the whole trajectory of the business curve and shift it upwards by breaking existing processes and behavior. (We look at how to sell to CTOs in the next section).

As I noted earlier in the book, in *Chapter 5*, CIO careers tend to operate within an S-Curve. (When we start our role, this progresses slowly as we build trust and get up to speed, then our impact on business performance increases. But at some stage of our career, this starts to slow down. The progress reaches a point that our success then drives more demand, and this is when our ability to take on more, with resource constraints, means that we reach a saturation point.) CISOs and CTOs also, of course, have their own curves.

The concept of S-curves can also be mapped to a transformation effort:

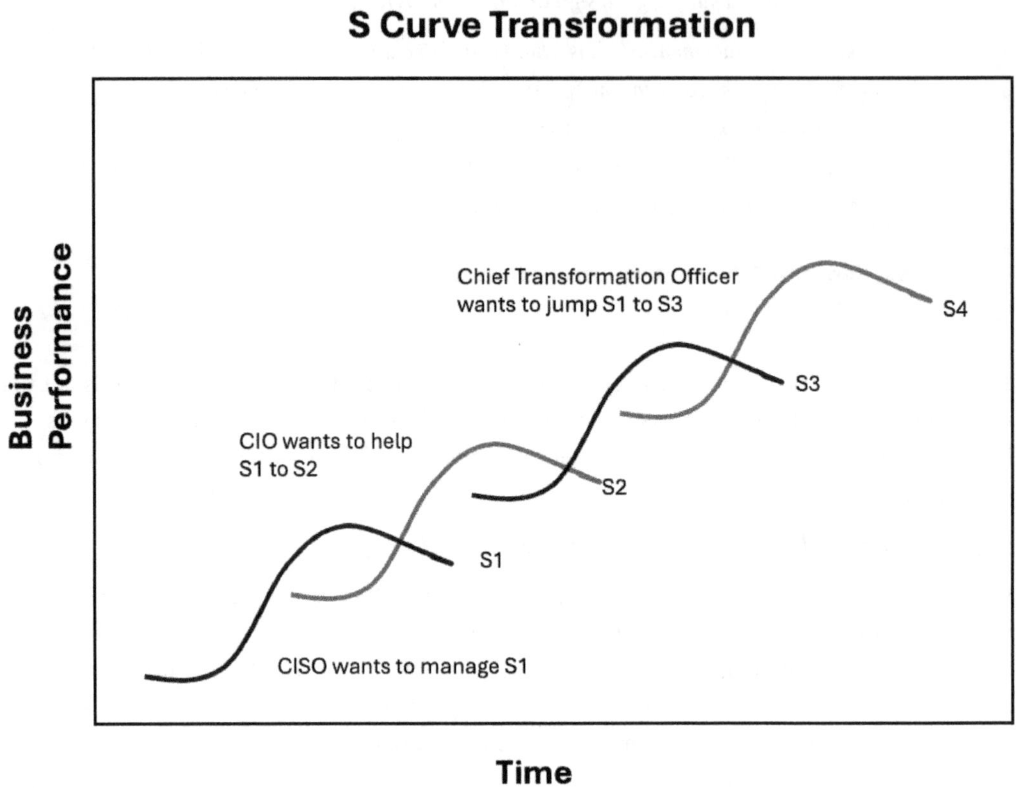

Figure 14.1 - Transformation S-Curve supported by CIO, CISO, and CTO

The CIO needs the CISO to move fast enough to govern the risk created by transformation without slowing the transformation itself, but the CISO's curve (S1) is shaped by external threat realities that do not care about the CIO's delivery timeline.

The CTO curves (S3 and S4) are shaped by long-term coherence decisions that can appear to obstruct short-term delivery. They are driving new business capability and innovation considerations that sometimes pull in the opposite direction.

All three are trying to improve business performance. The key difference is that the scope and degree of radical change are expected to be the highest for the CTO curves.

> **Note**
>
> Note that while CIOs may end up in the role for a few years, the CTO role is often not a permanent position. This role is there to deliver real, significant change (they then

> might expect to be rewarded with a larger responsibility at the successful end of the transformation project).

The three executives therefore have different motivators, which will drive their specific focus, and this is best illustrated by thinking of them all valuing different time horizons. While the CIO is aligned with their CEO and CTO in terms of the strategic direction, they will measure success fundamentally differently. When you stack up all three executives, there will be natural tension and likely some conflict that emanates from how their roles engage. The following table provides an overview of how each of these executives has slightly different motivations. On the surface, all will probably publicly support the major transformation; however, their day jobs can often create some conflict with this:

CTO 	Desires speed and tangible business outcomes that are aligned with the board's strategy.
CIO 	Delivering the IT strategy, they desire to drive digital change and manage any major risk.
CISO 	Desires to avoid major incidents in which data is lost or compromised.

Table 14.1 - Motivators by C-Suite Stakeholder

I would also add that during a transformation the role of the champion becomes amplified since there are many more stakeholders. They may feel that their contribution is watered down, but my own sense is that champions really matter even more for the CIO and CISO when there is a large-scale transformation underway.

This gaining of approval of a transformation is a significant C-Suite challenge and requires considerable effort. The CIO and CISO will need to really trust the solution that is being proposed for it. I spoke to Ram Kalyanasundaram, an impressive CIO who is on the rise in his career, about this.

> **Note**
>
> *I trust transformation solutions through three signals.*
>
> *First, reference customers I can speak to without the vendor controlling every word. I do not want the polished success story. I want to understand what nearly went wrong, how the vendor behaved, what the customer would do differently and whether the promised benefits survived contact with reality.*
>
> *Second, evidence of analogous complexity. The best reference is not always the biggest logo. It is the organization that had a similar operating model, similar constraints, similar risk profile, and a similar delivery challenge. I am less interested in perfection than in pattern recognition.*
>
> *Third, pre-mortem honesty. Every transformation has a difficult Tuesday morning when the steering committee is unhappy and the room is quiet. I trust vendors who are willing to talk about that Tuesday before the deal is signed, not after.*
>
> *AI will accelerate this process by lifting the standard of diligence. We are moving toward a world where proposals, contracts, reference transcripts, implementation plans, and public case studies can be compared quickly for consistency, gaps, and hidden assumptions. AI will not replace judgment, but it will make weak claims easier to detect.*
>
> *For vendors, the implication is clear. Make your pitch structured, evidenced, and defensible. Marketing language that survives a meeting may not survive machine-assisted diligence. The winners will be the vendors whose claims are still true when a human and a model both interrogate them.*
>
> **Ram Kalyanasundaram – Chief Information and Digital Officer, Harris Farm Markets**

Joseph Edwin, Senior Partner at Bain discussed with me what signals tell you a client is ready for a high-impact transformation versus one that is likely to stall, especially when major platform or cyber decisions are involved.

Note

The business ambition – or the "WHY" – is clear, and the c-suite is aligned to the broader group strategy.

They are approaching it as a business transformation—a once-in-a-generation opportunity to transform the business—and are willing to make tough business decisions in support of the same (e.g., willingness to radically simplify products and processes).

And they typically have a multi-faceted "case for change" that spans business, technology, and operations.

Joseph Edwin – Senior Partner, Bain & Company

The bright side

When your product starts to be repositioned as part of a larger transformation effort, then budget may no longer be a concern. The bright side is that you have this opportunity to sell more functionality than what was originally discussed. Potentially, you may be able to sell more professional services as there will be stronger risk-averse thinking from the change team.

Note that your pitch will probably be viewed more as a strategic partnership than a one-off relationship, and while being part of a broader effort could blow out the timelines, it can also increase the magnitude of the potential contract.

You can expect more stringent procurement and contracting processes as the deal will have the oversight of the board and management. Any calculations that you have shared in terms of ROI returns will also have to be refactored and most likely reduced for political reasons.

Note

The transformation will be aiming to achieve specific strategic outcomes. A salesperson/vendor needs to ensure their pitch and solution show specifically how they will help achieve the strategic outcomes, so they show relevance.

Tanya Graham – Group Executive, iCare, (former CIO)

Tip

Transformations usually speak about speed and change, but the reality can often appear to be contradictory and more governance is added. My advice is to keep it simple and be aligned with the key principles of the transformation.

> The complexity of the transformation often means that vendor partners who can take on implementation responsibility are valued.

If we adopt the same long-term time horizon as the CTO, then there are some other bright aspects to consider. Being adopted as part of the transformation can provide a "stickiness" for your solution as it will be integrated with this broader change. There is also a "halo" effect in that you will be associated with the large-scale enterprise change program, which will provide a great reference and whitepaper case study example.

> Note
>
> *Trust is built on evidence, not promises. The solutions that successfully drive transformation are backed by providers who invest beyond the transaction. They bring both business and technical expertise, commit resources throughout the journey, and tie success to measurable outcomes like productivity gains, not just deployment milestones.*
>
> *The best partners also have a track record of leading similar transformations and can clearly articulate how they improve your competitive position in addition to your compliance posture. They're accountable, adaptable, and focused on making your organization more effective and competitive. That's what ultimately earns executive trust.*
>
> **Bradon Rogers – Chief Customer Officer, Island**

If the program of change you are associated with has been incorporated into the larger transformation project, you effectively need to sell to the CTO. That leader may appear indifferent and perhaps say that they don't want to know all the fine details but bear in mind that they have the budget power to block or slow down your product implementation.

How to sell to the Chief Transformation Officer

At this point you understand that the CTO has a different time horizon than the CIO and CISO and wants to make significant organisational shifts that perhaps disrupt the business in the short term but re-position the firm for the long run.

> Note
>
> Large organisations often fire their CIO when expected transformation doesn't materialise, then find a business leader willing to take on that challenge. My first experience of this was at Pioneer International, where I was appointed Technical Program Director for a four-year, enterprise-wide transformation, tasked with

> reengineering 100% of business processes and finding systems to support the new future state.
>
> Working alongside Tony White, Program Director (later Chief Procurement Officer at Qantas), and inspired by Michael Hammer's *Reengineering the Corporation*, we redesigned the business from the ground up. The program "Pioneer 2000" reshaped structure, processes, and technology, including computers in trucks (in the 1980s) and centralised order and inventory management. The results were significant: a 20% reduction in the truck fleet and a competitive leap that took Pioneer from #3 to #1 in the field, overtaking CSR and Boral.
>
> Behind that mandate came a sobering reality, though. Having watched my boss, the CIO, be ceremonially fired, I stepped into the role with no budget and no staff— feeling exposed and alone. I share this because it illustrates something important: the CTO may project confidence and gravitas on the outside, while quietly knowing their days are numbered and that success ultimately means transforming themselves out of a job.

The CTO mindset is very different from that of other executives whom you sell to. All they care about is the organisational impact that your product or service will be able to provide. The time to business outcome really matters for them – they want to know how quickly new business revenue will commence and when "hard" cost savings can be realized.

> **Note**
>
> Note - The CTO is usually a business leader with a reputation for getting things done. They are often "tech-savvy", but do not generally have strong technical backgrounds.

The CTO can feel exposed, if you like, an "emperor with no clothes", and what I mean by that is that they don't have much to show until the transformation itself is completed. This means they will respond very positively to anything that gives them visible, communicable proof of progress before the transformation is complete.

Therefore, if you can provide them with specific metrics that help paint this picture of accomplishment, then the CTO will be your best friend. For example, the following metrics can be shared by the CTO with the board and CEO, who will always want to trust but verify that real progress has been made:

Metric	Explanation
Adoption Velocity	How fast can our customers adopt this new solution?
Speed of Deployment	How fast can new customer journey maps be deployed?
Milestone Compression	What time has been saved by this approach?
Process Improvements	Cycle time reductions (time to market, and so on)

Table 14.2 - Performance metrics for the Chief Transformation Officer

However, selling to the CTO is not simple. There is new complexity in the scale of the scenario, and the timing of approvals is likely to be much slower. The sales cycle you were worried about can be blown out, as you must navigate a multi-stage internal vetting process that usually occurs in sequence rather than in parallel.

Getting a transformation approved can be incredibly complex and difficult. I've seen many examples of this myself and have heard the same from other industry leaders too.

> **Note**
>
> *Trust in a transformation context is earned across three dimensions — technical credibility, organizational fit, and risk posture.*
>
> - *Technical credibility - Can the vendor demonstrate outcomes in environments similar to yours? Reference customers in your industry, at your scale, with your regulatory constraints carry far more weight than generic case studies.*
> - *Organizational fit - Does the vendor's implementation methodology align with how your organization actually changes? A technically superior solution with a poor change management approach will underdeliver.*
> - *Risk posture - Look at the vendor's own security practices, financial stability, and contractual commitments around service level agreements (SLAs), data sovereignty, and exit rights. A vendor unwilling to stand behind their product in contractual terms is signaling something important.*

> *For board and executive approval, frame the trust question around "what happens if this goes wrong"; having a clear mitigation and exit strategy is often more persuasive than the upside case alone.*
>
> **George Lee – Senior Vice President, Proofpoint**

I agree that addressing the worst-case scenario is very compelling, given that many CTOs think about the negative case as much as the positive one, as a personal "north star," if you will.

> **Tip**
>
> To sell to the CTO, speak their language and provide them with context on how this solution has been successful at other admired peer sites.

The CTO, CIO and CISO all operate within the organisational architecture and the constraints that this contains. It is often the case that new organizational structures are clumsy but necessary to enable the change that is required. As the CTO owns the new strategic vision and has committed to new business outcomes, they will likely not have the capacity to duplicate the existing resources with a brand-new team.

> **Note**
>
> *From a transformation perspective, it is important that a pitch from a vendor isn't just focused on the technology. Any new technology/tool/application also often requires changes in processes, potentially job design, and broader operating models. These are all in the domain of the CTO. So, the salesperson needs to consider all dimensions in any discussions. It's a full business perspective rather than technology.*
>
> **Tanya Graham – Group Executive iCare**

> **Note**
>
> *My most successful clients were the ones who did not view security platform transformation as a "tech" project but as a business enablement project.*
>
> *Many CISOs are obsessed with the capabilities of a security tool, like SIEM capabilities. Questions like "Does the SIEM support user and entity behavior analytics (UEBA)?" and "Does it have AI capabilities?" are common now. However, the questions that should be asked*

> *are, "How does this make us more secure?", "Can we detect attacks faster?", "Can we eliminate false positives?", etc.*
>
> *Clients which have the business interest and objectives in mind usually deliver a better output. The traditional method was when security teams were gatekeepers. The language used was "we can't do this because of policy x", or the focus was on compliance checklists and "acceptable risk" forms. The more transformative approach is to enable the business to achieve its objective securely. This also requires a strong capability to convert much of the tech jargon into business language. For example, converting high vulnerability counts for a platform into a resilience and return on investment (ROI) discussion. The language used is "How do we architect this securely without slowing down the development?"*
>
> *Vendors and partners who focus on the underlying business objective will do well to sell into organizations. The underlying truth should be: how can we add value to the client in achieving its business objective? Many vendors and sales professionals push for a certain product or solution because it aligns with their quota or portfolio, rather than the client's strategic priorities. The vendors who stand out are those who step back from the product pitch and instead ask: What problem are we solving? How does this solution accelerate your transformation journey?*
>
> *The difference lies in intent. Intent which truly comes from the heart and mind. It's an intent which is selfless. It tells the client that I am a genuine partner truly invested in your journey whether you give the work to me or not. This is even more true in the cyber security space where CISOs and teams are always struggling to show the business impact of their investments or jazzy tools.*
>
> **Gautam Kapoor – Cybersecurity Lead, Accenture**

I'd note that having business transformation and technology transformation aligned is the ultimate goal, but unfortunately these are not always designed in this manner. In some cases dotted line (indirect supervisor) reporting is the operating model between these teams. These structures are put in place to help drive accountability for the delivery of these outcomes. See the following examples:

Leader	Reporting relationship
Enterprise Architects	Direct report to the CIO and dotted to the CTO for the transformation roadmap

Leader	Reporting relationship
Cyber Architects	Direct report to the CISO, dotted to the CTO for this program of work
Platform Owners	Direct report to the CTO, dotted to the CIO
Data Leaders	Direct report to the CTO/CDO and dotted to the CIO

Table 14.3 - Matrix reporting to CTO

From my personal experience, these structures can cause some confusion to the lead staff involved, as they effectively now have two supervisors. These matrix management structures can also not be well defined in terms of managing decision rights and who has the final sign-off on strategic direction. These decision rights sign-offs may not be transparent to you, but certainly your champion will have this understanding or can find out for you.

Some confusion can also start to manifest as the CIO and CISO stakeholders will assume that their lobbying to the Chief Transformation office is also shared with the CIO office. I've again seen that it is hard to keep these two separate teams aligned despite governance structures and processes.

It is important to note that the CTO usually holds the budget, and the CIO maintains ownership of operational performance. Hence, you can imagine that the conflict of reconciling priority for this new transformation and business-as-usual (BAU) will always be top of mind for the CIO, but not at all a concern for this CTO. The largest impact here is that the champion that you have worked with is now having to listen to two bosses and may be less confident than before about the change that they are proposing and supporting you with.

Given all this complexity, you need to think about how to reconcile C-Suite members to maximize your opportunity for success.

How to reconcile the C-Suite

All three of these executives are now your customers, and you must attempt to make them happy with your proposed solution. In an ideal world, you would try to "divide and conquer", to have separate discussions with each, but that is often not practical.

In transformations, there will be winners and losers. It's important to understand each of the key stakeholders' expectations and concerns, and to exercise sensitivity in dealing with them.

What they all want is to be successful and to not have their own careers exposed by any change program being a failure. The key difference is that their individual risk appetites and tolerances will have a large variation.

> Note
>
> *You need to hold 2 time horizons simultaneously: a 10-year enterprise vision and the reality of where you are at right now.'*
>
> *If your organization is mid-transformation but sitting on shaky foundations, the foundation must come first. Period. The temptation is to chase the exciting strategic initiatives, but you can't build long-term capability on an unstable base.*
>
> *The harder question, and the one most get wrong, is ensuring whatever you build today is architecturally compatible with where you're heading. You can solve today's problem and create tomorrow's technical debt in the same investment. Sequencing isn't just about priority; it's about coherence.*
>
> **Jimmy Wong – Former AIA Australia CISO**

We would naturally expect that the CISO will have the lowest risk appetite and that their typical mindset is to avoid actions that create new major risks from moving too quickly when transformations require. The CIO is an active supporter of the strategic transformation efforts, if this does not jeopardize operational stability. The CTO likely has the highest risk tolerance (for innovation) and will always want to move faster than is currently the case. They will accept imperfection, provided there is speed to deliver the board-mandated strategic shifts.

As a vendor and champion, you are faced with three executives who are wired slightly differently, but to be successful, gaining alignment with them is critical. I'd argue that if you are unable to gain this position, then a positive outcome may not be the result.

It is important to modify how you support their business case with different artifacts. This will require you to provide each leader with specific deliverables that they each value:

- For the CTO: Quick wins and board metrics
- For the CIO: Operational technology governance
- For the CISO: Working security guardrails

To be successful in working with all three requires more concerted effort that recognizes that tension and conflict will naturally occur. You need to consider how you as a vendor can actively address all three stakeholders and their risk appetites but also work within a risk framework that acknowledges this shared ownership of accountability. At the end of the day, when outcomes are aligned then transformations proceed.

> Note
>
> *Transformation gets approved when outcomes are provable, not when vision is compelling.*
>
> **Mathias Bücherl – Group CISO, Heidelberg Materials**

My suggestion is that you design your interactions and address questions to the primary decision owner for any defined RACI model that has been agreed. (I discuss RACI models in the next chapter.) A RACI model specifies the defined role around any decision (either Responsible, Accountable, Consulted or Informed). The key here is to understand who is "Accountable" and that should be only one leader. This is a discussion for you to have with your champion.

It is possible that some of these will not be thought through in advance of any new transformation. But you can act in this fashion and then not be seen as taking sides or being biased.

Note that the timeline for transformation efforts is significantly political and invariably involves audacious dates, which have been committed to at the start and are often not met, often due to wrong assumptions, bad planning, or both factors. Therefore, while the CTO is the leader who sets the initial timelines for delivery, this timeline will have several iterations and a series of negotiations as the deadlines are reset. All three leaders will likely be consulted in resetting these timelines, but the accountability for this sits firmly with the CTO, while very strong responsibility sits with the CIO for delivering to this timeline.

Each of the C-Suite players has very clear decision rights when it comes to transformation programs:

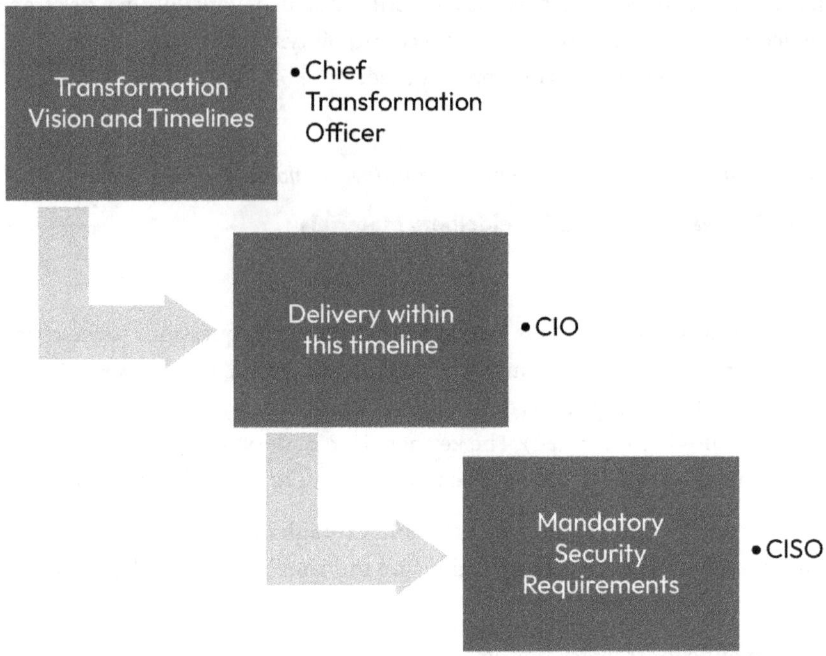

Figure 14.2 - Key Transformation Decisions by C-Suite

You are selling "business outcomes" to the CTO, then "acceleration" to the CIO, and "resilience" to the CISO. From my own experience, for any major enterprise transformation, the CISO is always the harder sell:

Chief Transformation Officer	**CIO**	**CISO**
Easiest They exist to accelerate change, and they get most of the credit for success.	**Medium** Have resource constraints and operational stability concerns.	**Hardest** Often concerned with downsides from the change and skeptical about accepting increased risks.

Table 14.4 - Easiest to hardest sell by C-suite stakeholder

Due to the magnitude of change and the expectation from board and management, I should note that none of the C-Suite is going to be an easy sell. They all have much to lose if this change goes poorly.

> **Tip**
>
> Always speak to the overall transformation strategic agenda, as this is mandated by the board. This alignment is always going to be the one that has the most natural support.
>
> Only when you have a private opportunity to speak with the CIO or CISO can you talk openly to address what you are aware of as their own personal concerns.

The CISO will always want to reduce complexity and manage change carefully. The very rationale for transformation is to quickly introduce new added complexity in the short term, attributes that the CISO will not favor.

We all want to be on a winning team; that is natural human behavior. But we must remember that transformations are by nature complex and difficult, and success is never guaranteed. Joseph Edwin provides some terrific insights on why they sometimes just don't work.

> **Note**
>
> *Transformations that struggle to achieve the ambition, or fail, are those that are unclear on the business ambition they are trying to achieve, have insufficient backing from senior decision makers or general misalignment on the direction (e.g., whether they should go with an enterprise platform or line-of-business specific ones and why), and almost always have very poor governance and oversight from key leaders (no business sponsor, unclear definition-of-done, unclear metrics for measuring progress and success, sponsors who cannot or do not inspect the progress deeply, etc.).*
>
> **Joseph Edwin – Senior Partner, Bain & Company**

I've noticed that package vendors (with larger integrated products) will often possess the commensurate support structures that will be able to support the scale and pace of transformations, while the nature of these programs may be hard for best of breed vendors to cope with, in terms of prolonged buying cycles.

Summary

In this chapter we covered the scenario of your solution being absorbed into a major enterprise transformation. In these cases, the rules of engagement change completely.

The CTO emerges as a new stakeholder, timelines can blow out, and budget politics intensify. Rewards can be greater however, but you will need to be patient. It is also possible however that while there is more governance, solutions that are aligned with the strategy can accelerate faster.

The CTO is a critical new buyer who cares only about speed to business outcome and board-visible metrics, which creates a three-way tension with the CIO (favouring operational stability) and CISO (focused on risk reduction).

Only vendors with patience, a structured stakeholder management strategy, and the ability to speak three different languages simultaneously will close a deal effectively.

The key learnings from this chapter are:

- **Three buyers, three languages** – sell "business outcomes" to the CTO, "acceleration with stability" to the CIO, and "resilience with minimal new risk" to the CISO (a single pitch to all three fails all three).
- **The CISO is always the hardest sell in a transformation** – they see only short-term complexity and new attack surface. The CIO is medium difficulty due to resource and operational constraints; the CTO is the easiest as they exist to drive change and claim the credit.
- **The Champion may get destabilised** – matrix reporting to two bosses (CIO and CTO) can create confusion over decision rights and reduce the champion's confidence and autonomy.
- **The upside is real but requires patience** – transformation deals can be 3x the revenue of standalone product sales, with long-term stickiness from deep integration. Furthermore, the "halo" effect of being part of a major transformation can be a career asset for your champion and a brand asset for your company.

15

Case Study – When Ownership Is Unclear

When you are selling your product or service to the C-suite, there are times when it is genuinely unclear who owns the decision you are trying to influence. In these situations, it creates a specific set of challenges for both you and the internal champion. Such misunderstandings are unfortunately common in large enterprises where different roles and positions have been established. I've personally seen this play out in my own career between different executives within IT.

Here is a very short example of the kind of dialogue I've seen:

CEO: *So, who owns cloud security architecture?*

CIO: *The CISO owns security.*

CEO: *Right, but who owns the cloud?*

CIO: *The CTO builds on the cloud.*

CEO: *Okay, so the CTO owns cloud security?*

CTO: *No, I own the applications. Infrastructure is the CIO's.*

CISO: *I don't own infrastructure. I own the security of the infrastructure.*

The whole dialogue can sound a bit circular and become akin to the Abbott and Costello skit, *Who's on First?* (`https://en.wikipedia.org/wiki/Who%27s_on_First%3F`). I've seen first-hand examples like this in different technology discussions. This happens more frequently than management would like to admit; we have this lack of clarity as each executive role is constantly changing.

The goal with this chapter is to provide some context to what a frustrating scenario this can be for you and the internal champion (when ownership is unclear then your efforts can be stifled and this can become a major source of friction), and what you can do if you find yourself in this scenario.

The key topics we will cover in this chapter are:

- Impact on the vendor
- Impact on the champion
- The RACI reality check
- Who owns the budget?

> **Note**
>
> John Taylor (Mimecast Field CTO and former CIO/CISO) highlighted to me that fractured ownership is a frequent point of failure; this can be where a business unit selects a vendor independently and then expects the technology team to implement the solution without having been part of the decision-making process. The selection of technology should be the CIO/CTO's role, as they are the ones tasked with the ultimate implementation.

Impact on the vendor

The immediate impact the scenario of unclear ownership can have on you is that there will be sales cycle friction. The deal that you have been chasing is suddenly stalled and you can't get a clear "yes" or "no." Now you start to observe that proposals get recycled through multiple stakeholders, each adding new requirements or objections that were not anticipated. Then as a result, time-to-close this contract can be extended significantly, distorting forecasts, and taking away free bandwidth.

There is likely to also be messaging dilution, as you end up tailoring pitches to multiple executives with different priorities, which can create contradictory or incoherent positioning. Unfortunately, when there is no clear decision-maker, you risk over-investing in the wrong executive, who later turns out not to have budget or authority. Your competitors with better political intelligence can then outmaneuver you by finding the real power center faster.

> **Tip**
>
> The most important question you can ask when you sense unclear ownership is not "Who is the decision maker?" as that question may not produce a useful answer. Instead, ask the question, "Who is the accountable owner for different parts of this

> change?" Asking who has been involved in similar decisions in the past may also be useful.
>
> Consider whether there is merit in reframing the conversation around shared executive outcomes rather than departmental wins to reduce turf dynamics.

Impact on the internal champion

In this scenario, internal champions can be at risk of losing credibility—the champion could look ineffective if they brought in a vendor but can't conjure a solution decision. As a result, they may be seen as having poor organizational read or weak executive relationships.

In this case, the champion may unwillingly enter a power vacuum, and this may force them to pick a side. This carries risk if the "wrong" executive eventually wins the authority battle, the danger then being that they can become collateral damage in a C-suite turf war they didn't start. The champion will need to spend disproportionate energy managing upward politics rather than building a business case; this can both lose them goodwill and chew up their bandwidth.

I'd add that the healthiest resolution to this scenario involves the champion working with the C-suite to help drive clarity. The core problem is that ambiguous ownership creates a situation where everyone can veto but no one can approve and this asymmetry almost always kills deals and demoralizes champions.

> **Tip**
>
> Champions could benefit from seeking "air cover" from a neutral C-suite member to help protect themselves as they try to gain clarity.

This is a higher trust level conversation that you cannot initiate prematurely as you are still building these foundations. From my experience, the most practical tool for structuring is the RACI model. (Unfortunately, in large enterprises I've often seen organizational charts obscure rather than clarify decision authority.)

The RACI reality check

Large enterprises have decisions that are usually made by more than one leader, and organizational charts do not always provide clarity. Instead, many decisions will require multiple levels of sign-off across the silos of different teams, even within IT.

We currently have many enterprises wanting to take advantage of the new AI era, not wanting to miss out on this window of opportunity. Each department will see that they have a role to play to enable this desired change. In the following example I've illustrated this scenario:

Who	**What**
CRO	Creates a new policy for AI Guardrails for Cloud
CISO	Creates a new standard to meet AI Guardrails for Cloud policy
Chief Technology Officer (CTO)	Evaluates new network layer tools to be able to comply with this policy and standard
CDO	Evaluates new data discovery tools that provide some of these requirements
CFO	Questions the ownership of the budget for this new initiative

Table 15.1 - AI roles example

In this example the policy exists but accountability doesn't follow it. A RACI chart can help. RACI charts are a widely used project management tool designed to bring clarity to decision rights and accountability. It is a simple way to record the stakeholders for every major decision, with an assigned level of ownership per task:

Letter	**Meaning**	**Description**
R	Responsible	Key stakeholders that help deliver this outcome
A	Accountable	The person ultimately responsible for success or failure
C	Consulted	People who provide opinions and input
I	Informed	People who are updated as progress is being made

Table 15.2 - RACI Responsibility Matrix

Note that this can get complex very quickly.

Let me present a mockup RACI for a decision on AI governance. I've highlighted the **A** for accountable and **R** for responsible, and note there are a few examples where one leader could be both **A** and **R**:

RACI Chart: The First 6 Critical AI Governance Decisions							
Decision	CEO	Board	CIO	CTO	CDO	CISO	CRO
1. Who has final decision authority for AI deployments	**A**	I	**R**	C	C	C	C
2. What defines "AI" for governance purposes?	I	I	**R**	C	C	C	**A**
3. Platform vs best-of-breed as default strategy?	I	I	**A**	**R**	C	C	C
4. How do we handle shadow AI discovery?	I	I	**A**	C	C	**R**	C
5. What's our AI risk appetite?	**R**	**A**	**R**	**R**	**R**	**R**	C
6. Who owns AI governance framework/tools?	C	I	**R**	C	C	C	**A**

Figure 15.1 - AI Governance RACI example

In theory, the RACI model requires there to be absolute certainty and there should be just one "accountable" role, although it is acceptable to have more than one "responsible" leader. It is also acceptable to have one leader take on both roles, as in this example.

As a champion working within the enterprise, a missing or incorrect RACI can be frustrating, as it means many more decision-makers must be engaged to conclude matters. For you as a vendor, I'd go so far as to say this is a nightmare that will hamper your progress. When this is absent, then you will certainly feel a sense of confusion and lack of clarity of decision rights.

> **Tip**
>
> Matrix reporting and conflicting decision rights reduce the ability of champions to moderate or accelerate. Recognize when your champion is stuck and help them by surfacing the governance question diplomatically rather than forcing a confrontation.

Having an unclear RACI can look like one of four different scenarios:

Scenario	**What can you do?**
No RACI	Suggest a workshop. This is dangerous territory, however, as your relationships are usually building, and this requires a gentle push to try to get clarity on key decision rights.

Scenario	What can you do?
Wrong RACI	Stakeholder management. Engage with all the parties (if possible) and ask them to help you understand who owns the decision.
Political RACI	Avoid taking sides. It's best to work with all key stakeholders in this scenario, and, where the opportunity arises, to ask about what you observe as potential barriers.
Ignored RACI	Ask the question yourself. If the current matrix is not being followed, you can ask if the RACI has been changed without being confrontational.

Table 15.3 - State of decision rights

In any of these scenarios, the CIO can feel that they are in the middle of a tricky situation to navigate, particularly when there are strong opinions. They would likely welcome you as a vendor partner to help steer the project to safety, as long as this is outcome-driven. I have seen instances of vendors being invited by their champion to join a RACI workshop (but assume that this was by invitation only).

When there is no owner, then we have a potential orphan project that will not be able to proceed. As a vendor you are not really in a position to do much, but your champion will be aware of the situation and may be able to take steps to help. Then you have just three choices: walk away, wait it out, or take some action to help move this decision along.

Walking away can sometimes be the right tactic which means that you disengage, as you feel that the project will not get off the ground. My own view is that waiting it out feels like a political move and I'm never going to be in favor of that.

If you still find yourself in a position of uncertainty, a useful clue is to look at the budget and ask, "who owns the budget?" While this may be a crude way to evaluate the situation, there will be a clear owner.

Who owns the budget?

Most technology budgets operate on a rolling basis, with financial planning teams providing a set percentage increase in year-on-year plans. If these budgets are reduced, then they typically are a flat figure amount to help fund other strategic priorities or support when there is a shortfall in planned revenue.

The CIO often controls the purse strings (with help from their finance team or Chief Operating Officer (COO)). It's important for you to understand what it takes for the CIO to commit to shifting budget from one bucket to another to fund your solution. When I reflect on the decisions I faced in this position, these factors consistently shaped my thinking:

- How confident did I feel about the new solution being a winner?
- Whether I thought there would be much resistance to this change from my key stakeholders
- Whether this could complicate my plans to simplify the architecture roadmap or support a board request
- Whether the benefits of this change would be relatively quick to deliver, and hence help my own short-term bonus rewards
- What new enterprise-level risks this would create

Budgets can often be fluid and structured at a corporate level to control the scarce resources that they are. Once the overall budget is approved, the CEO and CFO may then delegate parcels of this budget to different owners. The result is that the CIO "controls" this budget without truly "owning" these funds. In this example, the CEO or CFO is the budget owner and releases this money. The danger, therefore, is that funding for year 2 or the next stage may be reallocated if there is a change in management.

The CIO and CISO may, in this case, have "delegated authority" and not "delegated accountability." This may seem like a watered-down position to you, as these executives can only move as fast as the CEO and CFO allow them to operate. You probably prefer working with a decision-maker who has full ownership, as this has greater clarity, making the sales process smoother and more predictable, but this often isn't possible.

There can be complexity in the governance model that can be the root cause of ambiguity. In the following figure, I've outlined three of the different variances from full ownership of the budget:

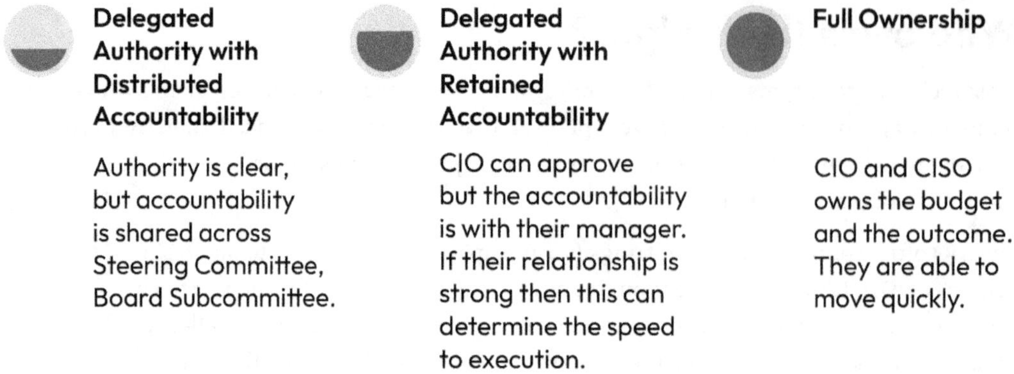

Figure 15.2 - Governance complexity

This complexity is not visible, nor is it shown on the organizational chart. Indeed, some of these nuances may not be fully understood by the champion, let alone by you as the vendor. Your path here is to ask the question about whether there is additional governance required in addition to budget ownership. This dialogue will help you to get more clarity.

When these models are in place, there can be some frustrations and blockages in making progress. You cannot simply change this governance structure but understanding it changes what you do next. Awareness of who truly owns the budget in this complex governance structure, and on what terms, can be the foundation of your next move.

If you can overcome these barriers—the political ambiguity, governance conversations, and the champion whose confidence needs rebuilding—then the deal that once felt stalled has come back to life. You have demonstrated under real pressure that you are the kind of vendor worth trusting with what comes next.

Third base is beckoning, and you have already earned the right to continue!

Summary

In this chapter, we evaluated how unclear ownership can impact the proposed change you are pitching. Unclear ownership is one of the most common and frustrating deal-killers in enterprise sales—and it's almost always invisible from the outside.

I've seen myself that when no single executive has full accountability projects become orphans, budgets get reallocated, and champions lose their ability to drive decisions. The RACI model exists to solve this, but in practice it's often absent, wrong, politicized, or simply ignored, leaving you navigating a governance maze with no clear path to a decision.

This chapter was designed to raise awareness of what is not often well established within enterprises and to empower you to trigger your champion to act in these scenarios.

The key learnings from this chapter are:

- **Lack of clarity will impact both you and your champion** – in both cases this is a potentially negative scenario.
- **Shared accountability means no accountability** – a RACI with multiple "A" owners is a warning sign that no one is truly on the hook; this is where orphan projects are born and your time gets wasted.
- **Package vendors have a structural advantage** – as existing relationships across multiple C-suite stakeholders mean incumbents are already navigating these ownership debates. Best-of-breed vendors with limited presence must work harder to engage all relevant decision-makers simultaneously.
- **Find the budget owner, not just the business owner** – the CIO may "control" budget, but the CEO or CFO might "own" it (delegated authority without delegated accountability means your deal can be stalled or defunded at any management change).

Part 3 (Third Base)

Solution Validation

In this third part of the book, you'll move into the critical work of solution validation. This is the stage where deals are won or lost, not on the strength of your product, but on the quality of your judgment, preparation, and relationships under pressure. I will explore the nuance of deepening executive relationships at the right moment, and why your "bench strength" is critical (this means you are bringing the right person to the right conversation at the right time). I then take you through the business case approval process. You will learn how to navigate Procurement, a late-stage gatekeeper with real veto power and incentives that are fundamentally misaligned with the CIO and CISO, and how to move through contracting without damaging the internal relationships you have worked so hard to build. By the end of this part, you'll have the frameworks to build a defensible business case, the composure to survive Procurement and Legal without losing momentum, and relationship depth across every level of the organization.

This part of the book includes the following chapters:

- *Chapter 16, Let's Go for Lunch*
- *Chapter 17, Show Your Bench Strength*
- *Chapter 18, Business Case Approval*
- *Chapter 19, The Procurement Playbook*
- *Chapter 20, Contracting*

16

Let's Go for Lunch

You have done the work, the business case is made, the key stakeholders are aligned, and everybody agrees that this initiative makes sense. Now you may want to enhance your relationship with the CIO and/or CISO. You may see your relationship with them as a strategic partnership, but the CIO and CISO may still see it as transaction-based.

How an invitation will be perceived by the CIO and CISO will often depend upon their personas. There will be leaders who will welcome these invitations, others who will prefer a more formal office-based meeting, and others who may decline. You should consider which persona your CIO and CISO are before making your invitation.

I should note that there are also strict governance protocols within enterprises which could potentially prevent the CIO and CISO from accepting your invitation. There is a geographical element to this; lunches with vendors are common practice in some regions, but not in others.

For this reason, the idea of going for lunch as a chapter is a polarizing one, but an invitation to lunch can be a significant milestone, carrying more weight than it appears. This can be the beginning of building a deeper personal relationship and trust with the CIO and/or CISO. I don't mean that you get their trust in return for buying them lunch, but that these events can provide an opportunity to speak more informally with them and understand them more holistically. I guide you through this in this chapter.

The key topics we will cover in this chapter are:

- Sliding into third base
- The CIOs and CISOs to target for lunch invitations
- Making the invitation
- Going for the lunch

- What you do if the invitation is declined
- Going for coffee

Sliding into third base

Returning to my baseball analogy, at this point you have found a champion to coach the players on the field and have reached first, second, and now third base yourself. As you have progressed through the bases, you have built credibility. Now, as you are sliding into third base, you are being seriously considered, and there will be strong scrutiny from a broader range of stakeholders including Legal, Procurement, and management.

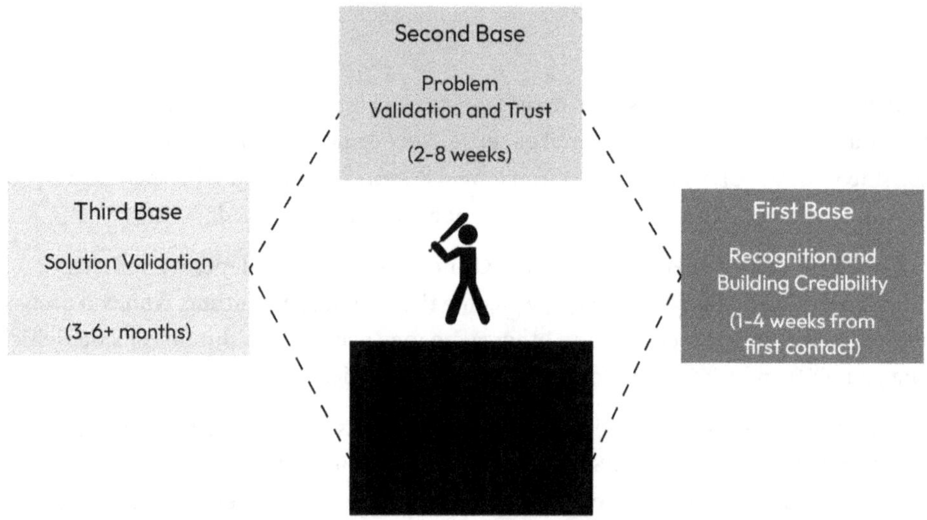

Figure 16.1 - Reaching third base

Be aware that your champion can only take you so far now, as they will not have direct authority or may not have political capital with some other C-Suite executives. There are more political silos to navigate with these stakeholders, and what comes with this territory is some degree of fatigue for the internal team.

On average, the solution validation exercise that this base encompasses can take 3-6 months. However, there are usually multiple strategic priorities all competing for resources, hence the time required to validate the solution can actually extend to years. Headwind economic events, leadership changes, mergers and acquisitions, resource constraints, strategy shifts, and budget cuts can all impact the timing of this. Unfortunately, all these factors are out of your own direct control. There are some things that your champion can help you with, however.

I've often thought that third base is when the champion is most critical. Having success with the proof of concept (POC) and/or proof of value (POV) is great, but you need a champion to fight for this funding and ensure that it is secured against other competing strategic initiatives.

Your internal champion will need to help you navigate procurement processes, particularly when there are internal politics at play. The champion has a unique perspective, as they have an inside view of what is going on and the barriers that exist. They have also bought into this strategic initiative and staked their own reputation on its being successful.

Here are some specific ways your champion can help you at this point:

- Inviting you to roadmap and planning sessions
- Inviting you to select internal strategy discussions
- Defending the proposal in internal discussions
- Letting you know who is likely to push back
- Asking you for benchmarks and metrics that show success

Each of these actions can help to maintain momentum, helping you push further into third base.

Issuing a lunch invitation to the CIO and/or CISO to discuss matters further often happens around this point. At this stage you are not selling the product features but wanting to understand if there are any residual concerns you can address.

> **Note**
>
> Going for a coffee can also work, and some CIOs and CISOs may prefer this to a lunch. I'll discuss this later in the chapter.

CIOs and CISOs to target for lunch invitations

Extending a lunch invitation is a classic approach that when executed well, can help to deepen relationships.

The size and scale of the contract with you, as well as the strategic relevance of your solution, will be a key factor for the CIO and CISO to decide if they will accept your invitation or not. There are also compliance considerations for them to consider, with many enterprises having very strict restrictions on attending vendor-funded events like lunches. Not paying attention to these nuances can backfire on you; therefore, issuing a lunch invitation and going for it must be treated with a level of sensitivity.

While going for a coffee with the CIO and/or CISO will likely still feel like a professional exchange, a lunch engagement is usually much longer, and this means that it can start to cross a threshold from professional exchange into what appears to be a social engagement. Clearly the costs are higher, and this is more likely to require formal disclosure under most enterprise compliance policies (for accepting hospitality from external parties), particularly in regulated industries such as financial services, government, and healthcare.

Timing of course is critical; any hospitality accepted during an active evaluation or procurement process carries the risk of perceived influence regardless of intent. The CIO or CISO who accepts a vendor lunch while at proposal stage also opens themselves up for intensive scrutiny. Even an invitation for lunch issued once a contract has been signed will likely still require compliance disclosure and approval.

> **Tip**
>
> Lunch invitations may be most likely accepted when you are no longer trying to win the business, and the executive is no longer evaluating you.

> **Note**
>
> *Sometimes people working on the projects do not understand the complexity. They have decided "IT will not help me and so I'm going to go talk to these two vendors." The vendor takes them to lunch and dinner and movies, plays, shows, and sports games. Then we get this request: put this product in. But it does not fit in any of the kits that we have internally and no one in security has evaluated this. Then, we get all the escalations, and IT just says "No".*
>
> **Anonymous – CIO, Large Financial Institution**

How the CIO and CISO think about a lunch invitation will also depend on their persona. Some are likely to readily accept, while others are more likely to decline. The following table explains how each of the CIO/CISO personas is likely to respond to this:

Persona of the CIO/CISO	Willingness to take lunch meetings
Transformation	These leaders value lunch meetings, but this comes with a caveat. They are seeking strategic partnerships and innovative ideas. If you have positioned this as a thought leadership briefing that fits their transformation agenda, they are more likely to accept.

Persona of the CIO/CISO	Willingness to take lunch meetings
Operational	As these leaders value efficiency, they tend to regard these events as a waste of time. Their reaction may be to say "no" (at least initially) and avoid lunch meetings. Their preference is for structured, data-driven meetings during business hours that share the essential facts that they seek.
Risk	These leaders worry about the perception of impropriety and that accepting your invitation may create personal risk for themselves. However, they do value lunch when this is planned to be a sharing best practices session rather than sales-y.
Business	These leaders are likely to say yes to an invitation as they value relationships and will use this opportunity to further assess you as a partner. Sharing a meal and breaking bread together gives them an avenue to understand your strategy better so that they can get more comfortable working with you.

Table 16.1 - CIO and CISO personas lunch invitation

I've always been a transformational leader, so I'm naturally more in favor of saying yes to a lunch invitation to further develop a relationship that I can call upon when things are not going so well later, but you will note from this analysis that only half of the leader personas may openly welcome an invitation, at least initially.

> Note
>
> *CISOs already run long days, and time outside work matters to our families. If you're an existing vendor, meet us in the office and focus on the work. If you're a new supplier, start with the architects; we'll meet once they recommend you. Please don't invite me to breakfasts, lunches, or dinners.*
>
> **Lee Barney – CISO, Ventia**

For the Operational and Risk CIO and CISO personas, it might be best to avoid lunch invitations altogether. Instead, consider offering them a quick coffee to discuss implementation risks and contingencies (more on this later). To these sessions, bring your industry collateral or perhaps a peer reference that can provide insights. You may then also suggest celebrating after the project is completed and the benefits have been delivered.

Once you have determined the persona of the CIO or CISO you are selling to and know how they are likely to consider and respond to a lunch invitation, you can plan your approach.

Making the invitation

So, you have done some analysis and checked with your champion on the notion of organizing a quick bite with the CIO and/or CISO to further explore their challenges and to better ensure alignment with their strategy.

As I mentioned in the previous section, the timing of this event is extremely sensitive. You will want to avoid offering a lunch too early, but you will struggle to have a lunch accepted when the contract is just about to be signed, too. Timing at that stage can send the wrong signals internally; the CIO and CISO will usually decline such invites.

The time is right, I'd argue, when you have built up a degree of trust with the CIO and CISO, perhaps you are at level 3 on the trust maturity model. Signing a contract with them may be best as a prerequisite to this, however, I'd note that this is not the industry practice I have observed.

The reality is that many vendors extend lunch invitations considerably earlier in the relationship, often during the active evaluation or around the procurement phase, and many executives accept them. That practice is not without risk to the CIO's and CISO's compliance obligations, however, and to the perception of their ethical independence.

Given this common practice, my advice is to aim for good food and ambiance, but not to go too luxurious. For instance, going for a nice hamburger at $25 is less likely to feel like you are trying to compromise a leader's ethics; however, a fancy steak dinner that costs $400-500 may look like you are trying to impose a sense of obligation on them.

Be sure to choose a restaurant that the CIO or CISO doesn't have to travel too far to get to, and one where they won't be embarrassed to be seen by other colleagues from their company.

Ideally your invitation should be verbally delivered in a meeting and not be made into too formal an event. By doing this casually, the CIO and CISO can feel more comfortable considering the invitation.

> **Note**
>
> When I received such invitations via email as a CIO and CISO, usually my Executive Assistants (EAs) would have read them first and could either block or decline them without my knowledge. The EA would also likely register the invitation on the

> enterprise's "Gifts Registry", which then requires approval, etc., from Compliance or their supervisor.

> Tip
>
> I personally accepted lunch invitations when I saw that they would be results-focused working sessions.

You may want to consider inviting a senior colleague of yours along to the lunch meeting as well—for example, the Executive Vice President. The CIO and CISO may see this as a good opportunity to develop their network, which can be helpful if they later need to escalate issues to management.

Five reasons why the CIO/CISO says "yes" to an invitation, prior to contract

As a former (transformation) CIO and CISO, I'd say there are five reasons that CIOs and CISOs would accept an invitation to lunch prior to contracting. In order of importance, these are:

1. They want to ensure that there is 100% **alignment** with what they want to achieve and your own objectives. Both CIOs and CISOs are aware that past this stage, their own reputation is on the line, as this implementation is coming with their endorsement.
2. They want to discuss **expectations** and any areas that are not clear in their mind on what good looks like. They may want you to provide assurances about extra support you can offer them from your extended team during the critical stages of the project.
3. Their realization that this project will require a strong commitment on their part, and anticipation that there will be some moments of strain on the **relationship** that they are building with you. Developing this further is therefore worthwhile as it can become a useful asset to them later.
4. They want this as a form of **insurance**, as they are encountering resistance to the business case. A private discussion provides an opportunity to gain more sound bites that can be used when they are challenged by their executive peers.
5. For **risk mitigation** purposes, to cover off any last-minute performance or security concerns that have not yet been addressed.

> **Tip**
>
> You can entice me to attend a lunch by addressing my agenda—my challenge or risk concern, but bring an expert or some information on a hot topic that I'm learning more about. Avoid making this a sales pitch with follow-up requests.

Why the CIO/CISO might say no

Some CIOs and CISOs may only find lunch invitations attractive when they are with vendors that they know and trust well, whom they consider partners.

> **Note**
>
> *Tech is not a 9-to-5 Monday through Friday job; there are only maybe one or two weekends when something isn't going on. I have had global scope roles covering 38 countries; there was not even one or two weekends free. So, your time is unbelievably precious.*
>
> *When we have a good partnership, then I'll make time for that.*
>
> **Scott Collary – Group CIO, Westpac Group**

Another reason a CIO or CISO may reject a lunch invitation is that there are many internal meetings in their enterprise calendar that can prohibit any window to meet. This can include board and operational committees, the annual reporting period, and other governance meetings that take priority.

I'd also add that celebrating a milestone like a new partnership beginning is not generally going to be attractive to the average CIO and CISO. That is a vendor-centric view and will not be convincing enough for the CIO and/or CISO to take time out of their day to join you. However, having said that, I'd always be happy to celebrate a successful completion of a project where the outcomes have met the expectations.

If you are in doubt about whether a lunch invitation will be appreciated, then ask your champion. These leaders will have insider knowledge of the personal preferences and perhaps the availability of the CIO and CISO.

> **Note**
>
> *The worst sales experience started with arrogance. The account representative pretended to know our environment needs and made us feel like we were an insignificant customer. They tried to win our business through social events and little substance. They never showed the tool in demos—only PowerPoint slides. Their product might have been useful, but the company*

> *approach felt wrong. Later we learned they had quarterly layoffs and a toxic workplace. That is not a partner we wanted, and I think we dodged a bullet by not working with them.*
>
> **Adam Palmer – CISO, First Hawaiian Bank**

They will also likely feel respected that you are asking them rather than feeling that you are only now focusing on the boss. Remember that the champion has used their own political capital to support you and they want this to work so that they get a slice of the glory.

You as a vendor may want to approach the champion this way:

I would value your advice. I want to build stronger relationships with the CIO and/or CISO, but I want to be respectful of timing and their preferences. Do you think I should wait, or would a working lunch or informal coffee be well received at this stage?

You should think carefully about inviting your champion to the lunch, as well as the CIO/CISO, however. Inviting the champion gives that leader some recognition but also may be awkward for them, as they may be seen as being too close to you, given the position they will already be taking on your behalf.

> **Tip**
>
> I would be more transparent and candid if you ask me for a 1:1 lunch, but I'm less likely to talk about sensitive concerns around fellow peer executive stakeholders with the champion at the table.

Be sure to loop back with the champion after your lunch meeting to give them credit and keep them informed about how it went.

Once you've leveraged your relationship with the champion to prepare for the lunch event, getting a refresh on the latest CIO and CISO hot topics, you are now ready for a productive lunch meeting.

Going for the lunch

So, the CIO or CISO has agreed to have lunch with you. How then should this go?

As I've mentioned, this should not be an occasion for celebration, but instead should be a focused discussion on implementation and how to make it successful (if the lunch is pre-contracting), and the opportunity to develop your partnership (if the lunch is post-contracting).

Either way, your mission for this lunch is to start to develop a deeper relationship with the CIO or CISO and use this opportunity to learn more about their agenda. Bear in mind that your own motivations to have this sit-down lunch, and those of the CIO or CISO, can be different. Both parties share several objectives however.

Here is an insight into what will be going on inside the brain of each party at that lunch:

Lunch Conversation goals		
CIO and CISO 	Stakeholder management	Benchmarking
Common 	Problem solving	Diagnostic
Vendor 	Relationship building	Injecting urgency

Table 16.2 - Lunch goals

They both are motivated by the opportunity for **problem solving;** for example, to discuss current internal issues, and perhaps constraints, and how together you can resolve these problems to reach a positive outcome. In this case, they will only share what they are comfortable sharing openly.

Where these parties differ is that the CIO and CISO will be evaluating if they would want their internal peers to engage or not engage with this vendor, going forward. This **"stakeholder**

management" is usually very sensitive to the C-Suite and only if they offer should any further contacts be made.

> **Note**
>
> I know from my own experience that when vendors use the "IBM approach," talking to the CEO and stakeholders at other levels at the same time, but separately, it always felt like a political maneuver. This is not something that I would encourage.

On the other hand, as the vendor you will have a desire for **relationship building** to make the CIO or CISO into a long-term customer and perhaps also sell them some additional services.

You may also want to **inject urgency**. You are motivated by your personal sales targets after all and aware that the CIO and CISO are managing many priorities. Your solution is just one of many, so you probably want to understand where this fits in that pecking order.

The lunch is all about gaining a better understanding of the CIO and/or CISO, and then delivering on that. That is how a CIO and CISO will recognize your capability and capacity to support their strategy and how trust will continue to be built with them.

> **Tip**
>
> I would advise against any alcohol consumption at your lunch meeting, bearing in mind that this would normally be arranged on a weekday afternoon.
>
> This is particularly important if your lunch with them is at an early stage in your relationship. Personally, when I've accepted an invitation with a vendor for the first time or at an early stage, I've been on guard and careful not to say anything that could hinder any future negotiations. In short, I've wanted to be fully present in the discussion. Alcohol can hinder that.

What can you do if the invitation is declined?

The CIO or CISO who declines a lunch invitation is signaling to you that either the relationship has not yet reached the level where they feel comfortable accepting, or that their enterprise policy prevents it, or that the timing is wrong.

I'd suggest you reflect on the decline, as it is an opportunity for an honest self-assessment of where your relationship with them currently sits in the trust maturity model.

> **Tip**
>
> Don't lobby the champion.

As I explained earlier, accepting vendor hospitality is tricky. I have seen every kind of event and much creativity in many of these invitations, with the intention of making them unique and distinct. Frankly, every CIO and CISO enjoys being treated; however, they will be very aware that accepting your hospitality can be viewed negatively by their boss and staff.

My sense is that if they aren't comfortable accepting a lunch invitation with you, there are lighter alternatives you could try. I'd suggest that you offer a lower-threshold alternative. Coffee is almost always still available as an option and, at the right trust level, it is genuinely valuable. (I discuss this in the next section.)

> **Note**
>
> I've seen vendors bring donuts and cakes to meetings within an office. This will likely always be welcomed and as everything is shared with them too, there is unlikely to be any suggestion of impropriety.

The following figure shows the full spectrum of vendor hospitality, from coffee, all the way up to international trips (rare):

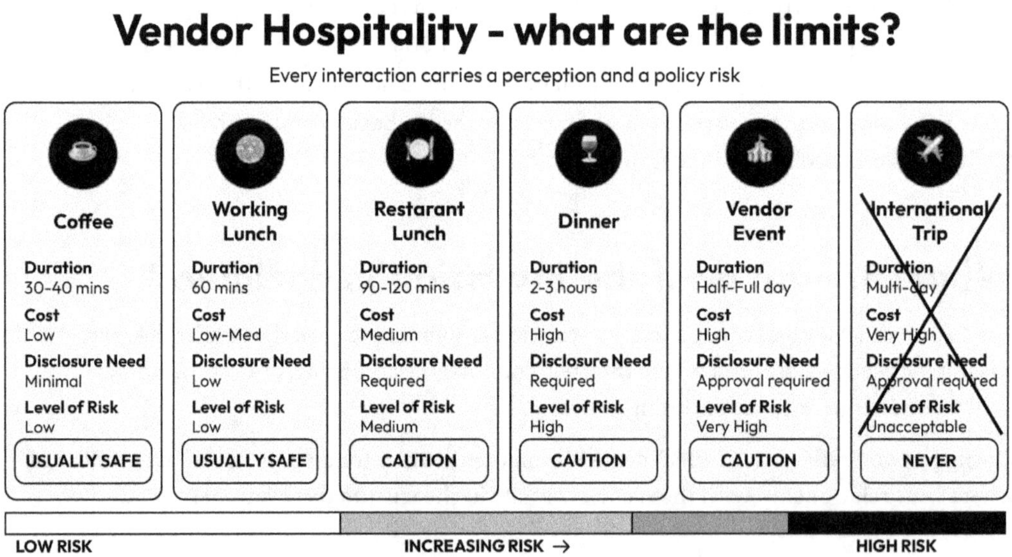

Figure 16.2 - Vendor Hospitality Risk Spectrum

Each event has different risk dimensions in terms of how they may be perceived, and therefore only a couple are safe bets that are sure not to offend.

> **Note**
>
> Having personally received all these types of invitations in my career, I'd argue there are scenarios where every type of invitation can be accepted (except perhaps international trips). However, I've also been in companies that have considered it a compliance issue that I've offered to buy lunch or coffee for a vendor.
>
> Sensitivity to these forms of hospitality can be very different from enterprise to enterprise and from industry to industry.

Note from the preceding figure that duration and cost are the two levers that drive both disclosure and perception risk. As each increases, the interaction moves from a professional exchange that requires no explanation to a social obligation that demands one and therefore makes it less likely that the CIO and CISO will accept.

Let's briefly look at why going for a coffee meeting may be a good option.

Going for coffee

An invitation to coffee is pretty normal for a business meeting and for the CIO, CISO, and champion these are probably standard practice for networking with colleagues in the industry.

I'd argue that coffee is an acceptable practice to the CIO and CISO as the meeting will likely be brief—typically 30-40 minutes. It is low cost and therefore sits comfortably within most enterprise gift and hospitality policies, perhaps without requiring formal disclosure.

The average executive may be open for a coffee, but they will need to feel that this is justified, in terms of it being of interest to their strategic agenda. Remember that their schedules are frantically busy so getting time to meet and have a casual chat is sometimes not feasible.

> **Note**
>
> *A coffee or a drink is my default: casual, balanced, and for anyone in a regulated environment, far less likely to trigger an internal compliance declaration. It keeps the relationship professional without the optics of a long lunch on someone else's tab.*
>
> *For strategic long-term partners, an occasional meal makes sense, not because you need the food, but because you need the depth. More time means more candor, more industry insight, and a better relationship. But even then, it's rare. There's no standing lunch calendar with vendors in my world.*

> *The moment it becomes routine, it becomes a problem.*
>
> **Jimmy Wong – Former AIA Australia CISO**

Importantly, as these meetings take place in a local coffee shop, they carry no implied obligation and create very little sense of reciprocity.

Summary

In this chapter, I explained the benefits of inviting the CIO or CISO to lunch but also explored why a simple lunch invitation can backfire. A lunch invitation carries significant political and relationship weight. Timing it wrong, pitching it to the wrong persona, or framing it as a celebration rather than a working session can damage the trust you've spent months building.

Transformation and Business CIO and CISO personas may welcome it. Operational and Risk CIO and CISO personas may see it as a waste of time or as a compliance risk.

If and when a lunch (or coffee) does happen, your goals (relationship building, urgency) and the CIO/CISO's goals (problem solving, diagnostics, stakeholder control) are only partially aligned and the executive knows it.

The key learnings from this chapter are:

- **The CIO or CISO's persona can determine the answer to your invitation** – consider asking your champion before extending an invitation to avoid an awkward rejection that signals misjudgment.
- **Frame the lunch as a working session** – celebrating a milestone signals your interests, not theirs, and your invitation may be declined or resented. Instead, aligning on implementation and discussing what good looks like are acceptable ways to approach the invitation.
- **Timing is everything** – your champion can advise you on this if you're uncertain. Avoid the window immediately before contract signing, as it reads as a last-minute relationship buy and can trigger compliance concerns.
- **The lunch is a diagnostic** – the CIO/CISO uses it to assess fit, surface implementation concerns, and to gather sound bites for internal defense, for example, while you want to deepen the relationship. Recognize the gap and don't oversell at the table.
- **Going for a coffee will generally always be acceptable to the CIO and CISO** – This is low cost and low effort.

17

Show Your Bench Strength

I've been in the room for the awkward moment that most vendors never see coming. The meeting is going well, the demo landed, and your champion is nodding. Then someone in the room asks a question you can't answer; not because your product can't do it, but because you brought the wrong person with you. CIOs and CISOs will notice this; they are looking for a comprehensive solution which includes human expertise.

By the time a deal reaches its serious stages (proof of concept (POC), business case, budgets) you have already made significant investments in time, relationships, and credibility. Everything that follows depends on whether that investment holds under scrutiny. All this time your champion is going out to bat for you. They are defending your solution at meetings that you are not invited to and they are handling objections from procurement and pushback from finance. But have you given them enough support?

For a CIO and CISO, vendor "bench strength" (the strength of your team) matters incredibly. CIOs and CISOs will tell you that they are unlikely to choose a superior technology solution if they have no faith in the support and responsiveness of the vendor when things don't go as planned. The enterprise will not just be buying a product on their recommendation but also buying the team that will stand behind it.

When a CIO or CISO evaluates a vendor's bench strength, they are asking what I believe is a fundamentally different set of questions than a procurement team. The stakes for them are higher and more personal because they are accountable when something breaks and this then becomes their problem.

I've never personally seen a vendor show up solo (just a single account executive) and without access to legal, security, or technical leads. In my experience, the quality, seniority, and responsiveness of your team is being evaluated just as closely as the terms of your contract. When there is a competitive deal, bench strength can be the deciding factor when the technology itself is roughly equal across vendors.

This chapter is ultimately about bench strength as the lived experience of every interaction a vendor has with a CIO or CISO and their teams. The vendors who win and retain enterprise relationships are not always the ones with the most advanced technology but the ones who consistently bring the right expertise to the right moment, who have leaders who can speak peer to peer with C-Suite, and who never leave a client feeling that the best people left the room after the deal was signed. In this chapter I will explore the following topics:

- Why the CIO cares about bench strength
- Why the CISO cares about bench strength
- Bringing the right people to the table
- The people behind the product
- A championship bench

Why the CIO cares about bench strength

The CIO needs to know that the vendor has depth across the delivery lifecycle, not just a strong sales team. Over my career I've seen many examples of poor delivery and a lack of technical expertise from vendors, with the vendor's bench contributing negatively to an outcome—I won't be naming and shaming, though.

The truth is that many IT teams lack great delivery expertise and they will rely on subject matter expertise from vendors to help them deliver. Hence the CIO and CISO want to be able to rely on the vendor to supplement their teams with expertise. That is always at the back of their mind.

Their nagging concern is whether the right expertise shows up after the contract is signed. I've learned that the impressive pre-sales technical team, that answered every question with confidence and turned up to every meeting, is frequently not the same team that arrives on day one of the implementation.

Vendors routinely deploy their best people to win the deal (their "A" team) and then hand the account to a less experienced delivery team (the "B" team) once the contract is signed; this bait and switch is one of the most common sources of early relationship breakdown.

In circumstances where there is a "bait and switch" tactic in play, and the "A" team is suddenly no longer available, that can instantly lose the CIO's (and CISO's) trust.

Tip

I learned that the smart move is to ask the vendor directly, during the negotiation, who specifically will be leading the implementation, perhaps request their CVs, and, if possible, make the retention of key personnel a contractual commitment. If the vendor is unwilling to name the post-sale team before signing, that reluctance itself is worth noting.

Note

The smart vendors I've worked with get key members of the delivery team involved in pre-sales. This helps with continuity and helps reduce the issue raised of getting the B or C team in delivery.

Tanya Graham – Former iCare Group Executive (former CIO)

I've also heard horror stories of a new deal being signed with a vendor only to find they then go and recruit from the market for the delivery team. Allowing the CIO early visibility of the critical members of your delivery team is therefore crucial.

The CIO thinks about your bench strength through the lens of operational continuity and delivery confidence. When evaluating a vendor, they want to know whether the team behind the contract is deep enough to scale, absorb turnover, and bring in specialists if needed, when the work gets complex.

There is an understanding that a vendor with a poor bench creates a huge dependency risk; if, for example, a key resource leaves or gets pulled to another account, the program stalls. In contrast, a busy, well-trained bench suggests a vendor who can grow with them. The CIO looks at bench strength in this way as a signal of your overall organizational health and investment in your practice.

Note

The CIO will be considering these questions:

- Who will support their integration?
- What is the escalation path when the project hits trouble?

- Does your internal team talk to each other?
- Are all the resources from the vendor available to meet the plan?

I'd note that CIOs who have been burned before will probe your bench and ask to meet your team, often before signing the final contract. They might want to make executive commitment to team continuity a non-negotiable in every subsequent procurement. A vendor that can only field a compelling sales executive but has resource gaps at the solution architect or delivery manager level will lose credibility fast.

Why the CISO cares about bench strength

The CISO's version of bench strength is more specific and more detail-oriented generally than the CIO's. The CISO wants particularly to know there is a credible technical counterpart on your side, a leader who understands their environment, speaks threat and risk language and can be trusted with sensitive information about vulnerabilities and architecture.

As a CISO, I considered vendor bench strength as a third-party risk variable. Every person on your bench who touches the environment is a potential threat surface, so depth cuts both ways.

> Note
>
> *The CISO can assess each vendor resource not just for competence but for access level, security training, and vetting status.*
>
> **Jimmy Wong – Former AIA Australia CISO**

For the CISO, relevance is everything. They may trust you as a person and respect your reputation as a vendor, but if the talented resources that you are touting have no immediate need at their enterprise then this will not have any credibility.

When it comes to the implementation team, the CISO's focus shifts quickly from capability to access: who has it, at what level, and whether those individuals have been formally security trained and vetted. A vendor who cannot answer those questions clearly and quickly creates a red flag in their mind.

The CISO also wants vendor resources who have operated in a similar environment to theirs, who understand regulatory exposure, and who will be reachable long after the contract has been signed.

Unlike the CIO, who is often focused on momentum and implementation, the CISO is trained to find the gaps, stress test the assumptions and ask the questions that nobody else in the room wants to raise. Any vendor who misreads this as obstruction is making a serious mistake. The CISO who asks the hardest questions before signing is the same person who will defend you internally when something goes wrong post-implementation. What can you do to take advantage of this dynamic? There are four specific action points that I would recommend:

- Welcome the hard questions explicitly and publicly. In the first key meeting with the CIO and CISO, signal clearly that their scrutiny is valued rather than tolerated (e.g. "we would rather you find the gaps now than discover them in production").
- Match the CISO's expertise with equivalent depth on your side. The vendor who brings a security architect, a compliance specialist, or a CISO-equivalent from their own organization signals immediately that they take the conversation as seriously.
- Provide a named post-sales security contact before the contract is signed. The vendor who names a specific, senior security resource who will remain accountable to the CISO throughout the implementation and puts that commitment in writing will be respected.
- Turn the gap analysis into a joint security roadmap. Rather than treating the CISO's pre-signing questions as obstacles to be managed, use them as the foundation for a joint security improvement plan that maps your remediation commitments to the CISO's own governance obligations.

Finally, CISOs also think about concentration risk. A vendor without enough qualified staff to respond to an incident at 1 a.m. is not truly a resilient partner, regardless of what the contract says.

Based on these concerns, how do you ensure that you bring the right talent to the table? Let's explore this further.

Bringing the right people to the table

As I have discussed, bench strength in this context means that you have a solid team on hand to support the enterprise on an ongoing basis.

In my view, getting the right people to the table is one of the simplest but most consistently mishandled decisions in enterprise technology sales. You need someone who can walk into a security architecture review, not just a boardroom, and it means your technical team is able to answer hard questions about topics such as data residency, incident response, service level agreements (SLAs), and integration security, without escalating to a product manager.

The vendor who over-indexes on seniority sends a team that impresses without engaging, and the one who under-indexes sends a team that engages but does not impress. Either case can leave the CIO or CISO feeling that the vendor does not quite understand what they are dealing with.

> **Tip**
>
> Match the expertise, seniority, and domain knowledge of your team to the specific stakeholder they will be dealing with. For instance, in addressing the Chief Financial Officer (CFO), you want resources that speak business outcomes rather than product features.

The following figure provides an overview of each layer of a bench that will support this partnership:

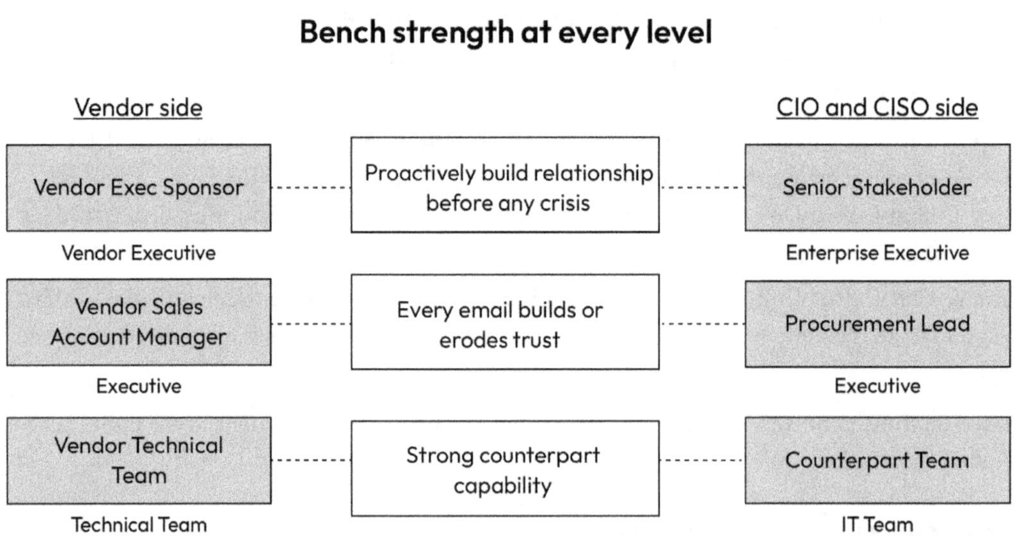

Figure 17.1 - A strong bench

As you can see, bench strength is comprised of a deliberate network of personal connections built across every level of both organizations. The sum of all these interactions is what ultimately determines whether you are seen as a partner or simply another supplier.

Note

Get the exec sponsor connection in place before you need it. It is very hard to build a new relationship while dealing with a thorny issue.

Gerard Florian – Former ANZ Bank Group Executive & CIO

Note

A common misinterpretation of "bench strength" is that this is about numbers, rather than the right level of seniority and expertise. In fact, when you try to bring in a large entourage to signal capability, this can in fact backfire. 'When I see a vendor bringing in a very large entourage of technical experts to deliver a tender presentation, it may seem like a good move to show strength in numbers, but it is also a very risky strategy. Over the years, I have seen many instances of inconsistent messaging and fumbles during the hand-offs between presenters. Very often, I would wonder why the most senior executive couldn't deliver most or the entire presentation and control the narrative himself. I would not fault him for not knowing all the intricate technical details and would instead respect him even more.

Alvin Ong – Former Nanyang Technological University CIO

I've seen many times that vendors that are very stretched will bring in some of the "A" team and sprinkle in "B" team members, as they are resource thin. This is exactly what the CIO and CISO do not want to witness. They expect the very best bench to be deployed to their account (the "A" team).

The right bench strength means that you are reading the room, knowing what the customer needs to see, and bringing precisely that capability to the table. Matt Boon, Senior Director of Strategic Research at Adapt, frames this as "homework."

Note

Vendors, in doing the homework, knowing who they're going to talk to, knowing the challenges they're facing... bring someone else along with you, bring along that subject matter expert. When a salesperson goes to a POC, bring the right subject matter capability with you. And for many right now, that's the architect.

Matt Boon – Senior Director, Strategic Research, Adapt

The pattern is clear - bring the right person at the right moment, prepared for the specific conversation happening in that room. The depth of the team that supports the product technically really matters; I will cover this further in the next section.

The people behind the product

Product superiority is where the team has been focused mainly up to this point. This has been front and center in how solutions have been evaluated. Beyond the individuals at the table, I want to reiterate here that buyers also weigh the character of the organization behind the product.

> Note
>
> *I place strong weight on believing in the people behind the company. A founder's vision, their ability to execute, and their genuine attitude toward partnership are strong indicators of where a vendor will take you over the long run.*
>
> **Yabing Wang – CIO & CISO, Justworks**

From my own experience, your organization's reputation usually precedes your actual meeting. How they have treated other customers, how they have handled a crisis, and whether their values align—these may not be on a formal evaluation scorecard, but matter enormously to the CIO and CISO who will have to live with their choice.

> Tip
>
> Your personal network will be able to provide anecdotes and data points about working with you that are both positive and negative.

When we are about to sign a contract, we start to worry more about who we are about to enter a long-term relationship with. This is not about a simple one-off transaction; the intention is that your solution will support the business strategy going forward, and the CIO and CISO need to be confident that this outcome will be achieved. It is for this reason that your bench strength really matters.

> Note
>
> *I recently approved a large software-as-a-service (SaaS) solution. All the vendors had similar capabilities, price, etc. They also all put up a large list of client referenceable logos. They all thought their technical solution was the paramount issue in the decision-making process.*

> *What the determining factors were in deciding on the vendor were the senior representation at the presentations, commitment from the executives that there would be no "bait and switch" from the proposed team to the actual team that would deliver the solution, and the client references were tailored to the industry and sector we operate in.*
>
> **Paul O'Rourke – former CISO, CRO and BCG Global Cyber Leader**

You can have the strongest executive relationship in the room, but if your technical team cannot build rapport with their technical counterparts in the enterprise, your deal is at risk. Your bench must perform at every level, not just at the top.

> Note
>
> *The relationship is key. If solutions are similar, will work, and the price is about the same, then the relationship (i.e., can we work with these people?) will sway it. Part of this assessment will be the reference call discussion.*
>
> *The bigger challenge for the selling organization is the support crew behind the sales leader. In my role, I may establish a great relationship with the sales leader and the executive level, but if the technical staff can't work with their counterparts on the vendor side, then that will sway me significantly.*
>
> **John Taylor – Field CTO, Mimecast (former CIO & CISO)**

There's one more dimension of bench strength that often gets overlooked: what happens between the meetings. The most important conversations in a deal are frequently not the formal presentations or the executive briefings, but the working-level exchanges between the vendor's technical team and the enterprise's IT staff. There will also be a backchannel of communications that the internal champion maintains with both sides. It is in these informal touchpoints that trust is either built or quietly eroded.

> Note
>
> *Vendors must invest in the right people. Account executives and customer success managers are the face of the company—and if they fail to demonstrate partnership, support, and care in day-to-day interactions, it undermines everything the product promises. Great technology means little if the people delivering it aren't fully invested in your success.*
>
> **Yabing Wang – CIO & CISO, Justworks**

Bear in mind that the champions you have been cultivating are watching everything, beyond your polished executive briefings. They also notice, for example, the afternoon email that didn't get a reply and the support ticket that bounced. These little moments accumulate into an opinion that becomes hardened over time.

Although I earlier referred to your bench strength as bringing the right people to the table for simplicity, it goes beyond that to encompass the entire cast of characters your customer interacts with over the lifetime of the relationship. The CIO and CISO particularly will not want to treat this as purely a transaction. If you can gain a long-term partnership with them, it means that your bench is championship level.

> **Tip**
>
> When I meet the technical staff from a vendor and engage with them, in the back of my mind is a nagging question: would I hire this leader for my own team? The CIO or CISO sitting across from you may be asking exactly that question about you right now, and they may not even be fully conscious that they are doing it.

A championship bench

The whole sales process has been an audition for full engagement, and the CIO and CISO have been watching how you handle pressure and whether the people you bring into the room match the people who you promised in your pitch.

> **Tip**
>
> The strongest vendors know that bench strength is about having the right person ready for the right moment and the organizational discipline to deploy them without being asked.

In larger transformations, the CIO and CISO often engage external senior advisors, as discussed in *Chapter 11*, to provide strategic counsel, challenge assumptions, and give the internal team confidence that the direction is sound. A vendor who recognizes this and knows how to earn credibility with both the decision-maker and their trusted advisors operates at a fundamentally different level. These advisors have the ear of the C-Suite; hence, my advice is to treat them as proxy client stakeholders.

> **Note**
>
> *Great clients treat advisors as thought-partners and seek their advice on some of the hardest problems; they create conditions that allow the advisor to challenge the client's thinking, even*

> *when the answer is not what they wish to hear. They use advisors to create alignment on difficult decisions while surfacing and resolving tensions/conflicts in the organization. They use the advisor to drive decisions and create value vs. overly focusing on deliverables; they assign their best people to work with the advisor, own the transformation, and are willing to move at pace and, most importantly, act on the advice given.*
>
> **Joseph Edwin – Senior Partner, Bain & Company**

A championship bench also means that you have strong ties to a broader set of stakeholders, not just day-to-day contacts. You need to build these broader connections with the enterprise before you need them. I'm not necessarily suggesting that you take this too deep but ask your internal champion for guidance on who is influential within the enterprise that you may want to extend your reach to.

From my own experience sitting in the CIO and CISO chair, it was rarely the formal presentation that formed my view of a vendor's team; it was instead the informal conversations that happened in the corridor or an unprompted comment from a technical lead in a session. These were the signals I used to judge whether a vendor had genuine depth or was simply well-rehearsed. My advice is to treat every interaction as an opportunity to demonstrate strategic bench strength, not just to the CIO or CISO directly, but to the advisors, staff, and peer executives whose opinions carry more weight than most vendors appreciate.

Personally, the deals I felt most confident signing were the ones where I had seen enough of the vendor's team, in enough different settings, to trust that the people behind the product were as strong as the product itself. They were earning their "Preferred Vendor" status on my trust maturity model. That status, once earned, goes beyond a commercial advantage to be the foundation on which everything that follows in the relationship is built. I discuss building a partnership of trust further in *Chapter 21*.

Summary

When solutions are comparable and pricing is similar, the people behind the product become the deciding factor, not just at the executive level, but also across every interaction your customer has with your organization.

Building the right relationships at the right levels must happen deliberately and early, long before a crisis forces the issue.

Your bench strength is the sum of every person your customer encounters, from the senior sponsor in the room to the account manager answering emails on a Friday afternoon.

The key learnings from this chapter are:

- **Build executive and cross-functional relationships before you need them** – a high-stakes moment is the worst time to be introducing yourself to a new stakeholder for the first time!
- **Bench strength is about precision, not presence** – bringing the right person with the right expertise to each conversation, rather than a large team that risks inconsistent messaging and loss of narrative control, is the way to go.
- **Technical relationships matter as much as the executive one** – if your teams can't work effectively with their counterparts at every level, even the strongest sales relationship won't save your deal.
- **Every interaction between meetings is a trust deposit or a withdrawal** – the emails, support tickets and handovers your customer experiences between the highlights are quietly shaping their verdict on whether you are a partner or just another vendor.

18

Business Case Approval

We are now at the pointy end of the sales process, the stage where the business case is formally appr18.5oved. We have shifted from technical validation to seeking executive and financial approval to proceed.

The intention behind a business case is to ensure that a proposal for new investment directly addresses a business problem. This is a key guardrail, preventing organizations from spending capital on features or technology without a clear, strategic purpose.

Everything that you have done with the internal champion so far has been to get to this stage. However, the reality is that business case approvals are not a "rubber stamp" for going ahead, even when the CIO and CISO have budget provisions. Often the strategic nature of the investment and scale of spend will trigger additional financial governance steps. This moves out of the direct control of the CIO and CISO, and new parties will have visibility of the proposal.

This is a moment that the CIO and/or CISO have been building toward too, an opportunity to demonstrate strategic credibility and sound judgment, to shine with their boss. However, it's likely (and considered best practice) that stakeholder engagement around the business case would have commenced some months prior to this milestone, with the intention of gathering support for the initiative at a strategic level.

The business case approval stage is where deals can stall. This is often not because the solution is wrong, but because the financial argument for it was not built in the language that the Chief Financial Officer (CFO), the board, and other key stakeholders can understand, in terms of why it should be approved.

In this chapter we cover the dynamics of the business case approval process, including the role of the CIO and CISO as internal advocates, the CFO's singular focus on hard savings, and the political dynamics of competing budget requests.

In short, the key topics we will cover in this chapter are:

- Business case outcomes
- The role of the CIO and CISO in the business case approval process
- The role of the CFO in the business case approval process
- The cost of inaction
- Obtaining approval
- What you can do

> Note
>
> *For a business case to be successful, the initiative must be aligned with and enable the business priorities.*
>
> **Sunil Varkey – CISO, Hexaware Technologies (Former HSBC CISO)**

Business case outcomes

There are new dynamics, now involving a significantly broader set of stakeholders, which will determine how smoothly business case approval proceeds. Scope ambiguity, competing priorities, and revision cycles, alongside the complexity that comes with new stakeholders, can significantly extend the time to sign off on a business case.

Because business cases of this nature are treated as extraordinary items (they are new and unique, sometimes non-recurring, investments), their approval cycles are sometimes unpredictable, as they often fall outside standard governance cycles and cannot be neatly scheduled into routine review windows.

> Note
>
> Ideally, to help mitigate extending approval processes, the CIO, CISO and champion would have engaged stakeholders early, pre-socializing the business case before formal submission and building sufficient buffer time into project plans to absorb potential delays.

Let's now start with the result in mind. After the business case approval process has played out, one of four outcomes will occur:

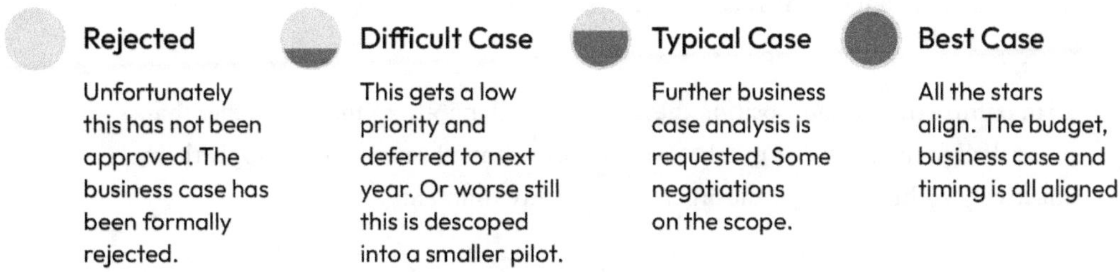

Figure 18.1 - Business case outcomes

We always plan for the "Best Case," but typical and difficult cases from my experience are more likely. By my estimates, based on my experience over the years, I've seen that the stars align perfectly in only about 15-20% of cases.

Even when the business case has been executed perfectly and the outcome is regarded as a "Best Case", the actual approval can be pending funding. I've seen examples where macroeconomic headwinds can delay the official approval and subsequent progress of the request.

Bear in mind that the number of capital requests always exceeds the actual available budget. I've seen many examples of demand exceeding supply by 3x. What this means is that at the start of the planning cycle, there are probably already requests from the prior year or two that did not get approved in the last year and are trying again for approval.

These are often hard to compare, where the return on investment (ROI) can be difficult to calculate. There may be, for example, operational projects to provide more office space or refit older buildings, competing with cost-saving initiatives that are designed to save on headcount via LLMs. These also compete with revenue-generating or regulatory compliance projects, which are always going to be aligned with the overarching strategy.

You can help get to the best-case outcome by providing practical templates (such as business case structures and stakeholder mapping tools) to share what best practice looks like with your champion. This can help them navigate what can otherwise be an inconsistent and time-consuming approval process.

> **Note**
>
> *You look at some of the big players, they've got so many great business case examples that they could bring to the table here, whether it's a template or whether it's a real example.*
>
> **Matt Boon – Senior Director, Strategic Research, Adapt**

The most effective templates are simple, tailored to the client's context, and introduced early before they are urgently needed, so that your clients can familiarize themselves with the format ahead of formal business case submission.

> **Tip**
>
> To maximize their value, position these tools as collaborative guidance rather than a prescribed process. Be sure to take time to walk clients through how to apply them effectively within their specific organizational environment.

Gaining approval of the business case the first time is always going to be a challenge, and this is due to the number of new players who have input into this process. These artifacts will often be rejected, and further analysis or optionality is required by the board for their endorsement.

The CIO will be held accountable for this spend to the board, CEO, CFO, Legal, and other peers:

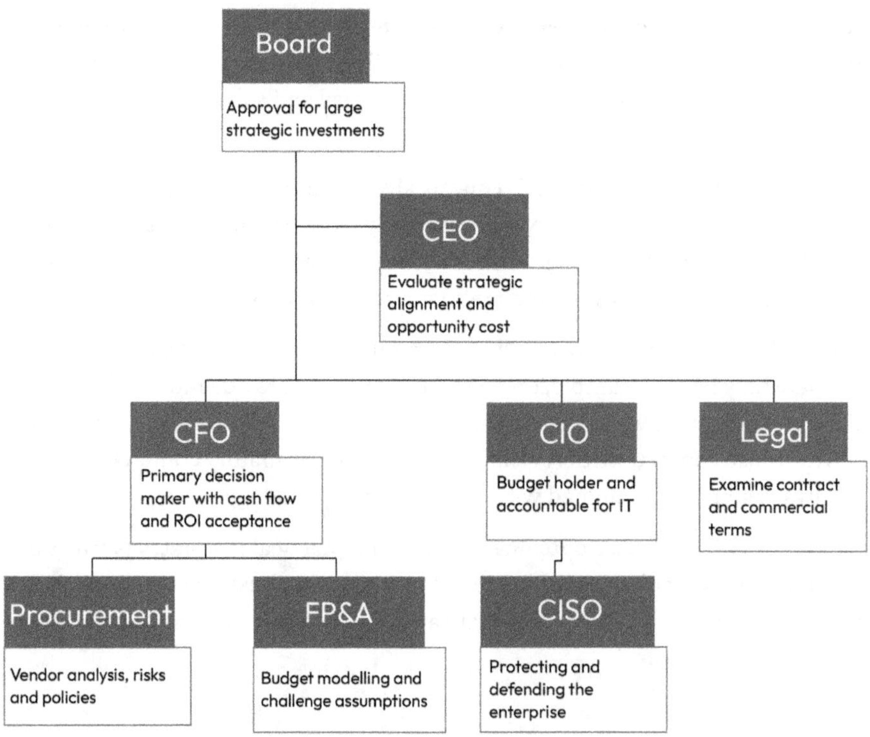

Figure 18.2 - Business case approval stakeholders

This becomes for the CIO a deadly serious matter. (Note, in most cases, the CIO will take forward for approval submissions for technology, and this includes the CISO's business case documents.)

> Note
>
> Note that, as I have mentioned in earlier chapters, there is always competition for funding between the C-Suite, as they all must get approval for this discretionary spend from the same CFO bucket. This is a critical reality that is not well understood unless you are operating at this level. On the surface, these roles are all collegial and encouraged to operate for the greater good of the enterprise; however, the CIO/CISO project now must compete with those from other peers.

For these business case approvals the CIO and CISO play distinct roles within enterprises. I'd note that the dynamic between these two roles is not always harmonious. The CIO has a natural urgency to move forward and the CISO's obligation is to hold the line on risk. This can create natural tension that the business case must resolve before it ever reaches the CFO or the board, which is why the vendor who helps both executives find a common narrative around risk-managed delivery is doing valuable work. I explore this further in the next section.

The role of the CIO and CISO in the business case approval process

The CIO typically serves as a primary sponsor or approver for technology-driven business cases, focused on strategic alignment, delivery feasibility, and personally sponsoring the case to senior leadership and the board.

> Note
>
> *My CIO role involves wearing a "business leader hat" to ensure initiatives align with business priorities.*
>
> **Charlie Bai – Vice President and CIO, Information and Digital Solutions, Eli Lilly China**

In many cases there may also be a business sponsor, if the benefits of the change are primarily operational improvements.

The CISO, in contrast, plays the role of risk gatekeeper, reviewing the business case through the lens of data security, compliance, and third-party vendor risk, and holds the authority to block or delay approval if those concerns are not adequately addressed.

> Note
>
> The role of the CISO is being elevated now and their exposure to board and management is growing; however, most still report to the CIO, with some exceptions that report to a Chief Operating Officer (COO).

Where the two roles intersect, your champion should ensure the business case explicitly speaks to both strategic value and risk mitigation. Misalignment between the CIO and CISO is a common source of delay in the approval process.

> Note
>
> *The most successful business case discussions, in my opinion, are those where they are co-presented by the business executive and CIO together. This shows a well-thought-through approach, role clarity, clear accountability, and acknowledgment of the outcomes to be delivered and how they will be achieved.*
>
> **Tanya Graham – Former iCare Group Executive**

Gaining approval is a challenging process. Personal capital (an individual's influence and goodwill) always ends up being expended to gain a positive outcome by all parties. Approval will need to be gained at the expense of another competing initiative. These are often owned and sponsored by the CIO/CISO's executive peers (this is why personal capital is expended).

The following illustration provides a visual representation of this dynamic, showing how a significant CIO and CISO-led program must compete for budget alongside multiple other strategic initiatives, each with its own sponsor, priority, and organizational weight. These competing projects also carry the personal hopes and ambitions of other champions within the business who have made efforts to push for change.

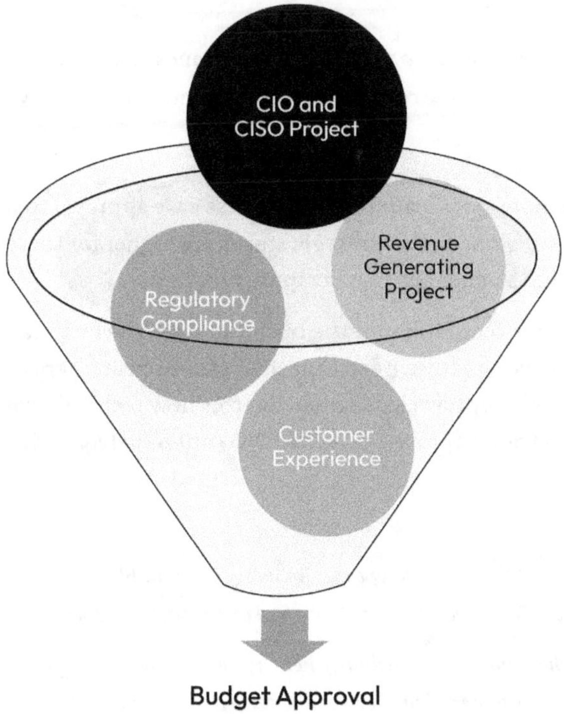

Figure 18.3 - The overall Business Case portfolio

The funnel here is a simple representation of the capacity of an enterprise; there will always be demand greater than the supply of funding to meet the requirements of different stakeholders.

The size of the bubbles in this figure is an example of the weight that different projects can carry. From my experience, technology projects tend to be on the larger side, hence get more scrutiny.

As a vendor, you will be excluded from these discussions. This may unfortunately also be the case for internal champions, too; they are not guaranteed to be at the decision table. This is just the reality of the logistics of these board and senior meetings, that usually only the executive sponsor/s is invited to present and argue the business case.

Tip

The champion can, however, help to promote the business case to other stakeholders and decision owners. Their role continues to drive momentum in this way.

The CIO plays a much more significant role in business case approval than the CISO. This is due to budget ownership and because the strategic stakes are higher for them given the stakeholders that need to be engaged to gain approval.

The CIO has a very specific set of roles for the business case. The fact that this is going forward at all means that they have already agreed that this makes sense (there is strategic alignment with their IT strategy and they have assurance that this new tech will work effectively with their existing tech stack) and approved this. The CIO cannot delegate this accountability to their staff.

Note

Talking to CIOs, most of them will accept they're not good at building business cases. They are technologists by trade. So, we've got a lot of internal competition happening around that.

I will then come to the vendor's responsibility here as well. I'm not saying they need to write the business case for their customers, but they need to have a business case-level conversation with their customers.

Matt Boon – Senior Director, Strategic Research, Adapt

Business benefits are important too, but the CIO will not want this overestimated, as the new solution may, for example, involve automation that eliminates existing full-time equivalent (FTE) staff roles. (In this example, this may require joint approval from both the CIO and line of business executive to commit to delivering these savings once the project is completed.)

Finally, the CIO will want to ensure that resources have been assigned that will help make this new project a success. Often, a key constraint will be a shortage of an internal role, such as a project manager, business analyst, or subject matter expert (SME), and this will halt the commencement of a new program of work.

The following diagram summarizes these CIO responsibilities in the business case approval process:

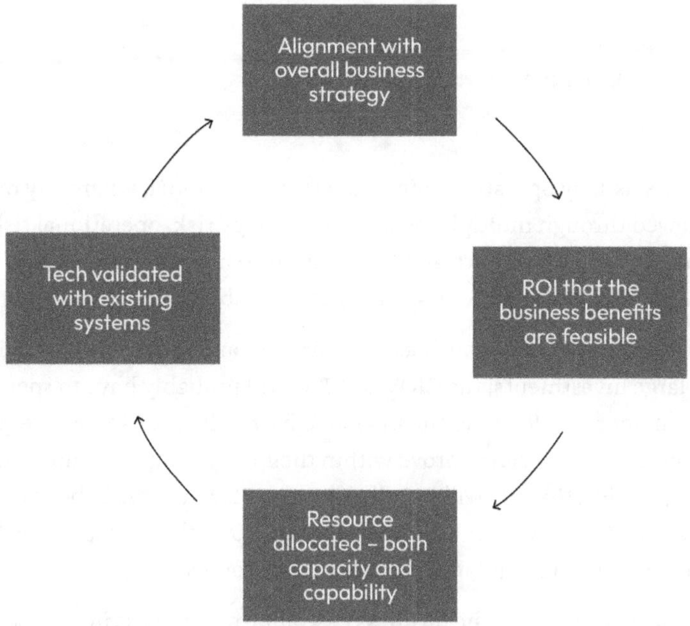

Figure 18.4 - The CIO's key role in business case approval

On the other hand, the CISO has a lesser role to play in the business case. The CISO has the power to veto and block, and/or request a change to the project if they're concerned, but they do not have the formal authority to approve the investment. That authority sits with the CIO and CFO. If the CISO is indeed concerned, I would, however, expect that their veto would have been exercised much earlier in the process.

> Note
>
> *You can help here by getting your own finance team to help build the financial business case. Many CISOs are not chartered accountants and might appreciate your help.*
>
> **Lee Barney – CISO, Ventia**

The CISO formally has a specific task to complete a security risk assessment, and they will need to assess which current and new controls will be necessary for this solution (identity and access management (IAM), privileged access management (PAM), multifactor authentication (MFA), etc.). This risk assessment is likely to have commenced prior to the business case, but governance approval will require this as a mandatory prerequisite now.

> Note
>
> *I don't just buy tools, but rather "outcomes" related to risk reduction, efficiency, and compliance.*
>
> **Adam Palmer – CISO, First Hawaiian Bank**

Management teams usually operate within a collective risk model, where any major investment is viewed through multiple lenses—technology risk, operational risk, legal risk, and reputational risk. What the board and CEO want is to have their executives feel that they have "skin in the game", and that there is shared accountability.

The CFO is a key stakeholder in the business case process and will likely be partially accountable for large investments; the CIO and CISO will probably have to spend some time with them at this point to understand their perspective on this. For some enterprises the CIO will have an amount that they can approve within their own budget, without reference to the CFO, although in practice, the CIO will usually keep the CFO informed about large projects. I've seen that the best way for the CIO or CISO to keep the CFO in the loop is to involve them early and give them regular monthly updates as evaluations progress.

Let's look at the role of the CFO in the business case approval process in more depth.

The role of the CFO in the business case approval process

A CFO's duty is to protect the organization's financial health, which means they will naturally approach any new business case with a healthy dose of analytical skepticism. They are constantly balancing current financials and cash flow, making them highly attuned to unbudgeted expenses.

The top-down perspective of the CFO is akin to having a balance sheet and a real-time running profit and loss statement. The CFO's purview is also broad, across the portfolio of investments; they are looking for the best financial return - the classic ROI. In comparing this across all the proposed projects, the CFO is not emotionally attached to any new initiative or project. Every CFO does, however, want to ensure that your proposal has a payback.

> Note
>
> *Internal pitches fail if they cannot connect to our strategy and show how they are reducing risk or improving a key business function.*
>
> **Adam Palmer – CISO, First Hawaiian Bank**

When they are presented with any project proposal, as they are mathematically inclined, they can understand without doubt that, for example, project *A* invests $2m to reduce operational cost by $1m each year, or project *B* introduces a $5m new channel that generates $2.5m in the first year and $7.5m over three years. In both cases, they only have implementation risk to consider in achieving that business outcome.

> **Tip**
>
> Revenue growth drives long-term enterprise value and market dominance, while operational cost reduction provides the predictable, near-term margin stability that boards demand during economic uncertainty.
>
> The executive team will prioritize whichever lever aligns with their immediate strategic horizon—cutting costs to survive a downturn or chasing revenue to capture a shifting market.

> **Note**
>
> *From a CFO perspective I have always attempted to identify the non-financial and critical elements that must be true or managed for a successful project outcome and then ensure these are measured and the right person is accountable.*
>
> **Geoff Stalley – Non-Executive Director & former CFO**

The CFO likes hearing about "hard" cost cutting measures like headcount reduction, license consolidation, and direct cost removal. Your IT investment proposal will generate benefits, but these are often not "hard" measures. The CFO may consider benefits like risk reduction, faster processing, or improved digital customer experience "soft" benefits, and usually does not pay much attention to these items.

> **Note**
>
> *ROI needs to be stronger than a spreadsheet. A robust ROI rationale connects business outcomes, operational metrics, cost drivers, risk reduction, and time to value. It should show where value comes from and how it will be measured. For example, reduced manual effort, faster onboarding, lower incident volumes, improved compliance evidence, better customer experience, reduced rework, faster product launch cycles, or lower dependency on legacy systems.*

> *The best ROI cases are built with the customer, not presented at the customer. They reflect the customer's baseline, constraints, assumptions, and internal benefit logic. A generic calculator may help start the conversation, but it rarely closes an enterprise deal. Senior buyers need a value story that can survive finance review, procurement challenge, architecture scrutiny, and executive sponsorship.*
>
> **Sundar Iyer – Managing Director, Emertel**

Rather than pushing for immediate, unconstrained sign-off, the CIO and CISO can help the CFO move forward by showcasing robust governance frameworks. In particular, how project risk is mitigated through stage-gated milestones and strict entry/exit criteria.

Note that there is usually also another level of financial analysis involved, before the CFO examines the business case: that done by the financial planning and analysis team (FP&A).

The financial planning and analysis team

Before the CFO sees your submission, the FP&A team will closely review the business case calculations on net present value (NPV) and ROI. For reference:

Metric	Full phrase	Definition
ROI	Return on Investment	A percentage showing the total efficiency or profitability of an investment, relative to its cost
NPV	Net Present Value	The current dollar value of all future cash flows (positive and negative) generated by the project, discounted back to today's money.

Table 18.1 - Useful financial metric definitions

Their job is to act as financial gatekeepers, which means they will stress-test every assumption with a highly critical eye. While this level of scrutiny can feel like an uphill battle when you are trying to drive change, this is simply their way of managing risk, meaning the best way forward is for the CIO and CISO to keep initial commitments conservative and defensible. They will likely challenge the numbers in the business case.

As a CIO and CISO, I treated FP&A as a partner to work with. This can translate into a regular monthly meeting to discuss budget vs. spend tracking and also having them in the loop on the strategic plans that are being progressed.

In discussions with FP&A, respected external sources of industry data will assist. They will generally trust customer references from your industry peers and analyst reports from Gartner®, Forrester®, IDC®, etc. (we discussed these in *Chapter 11*) and use these for benchmarking purposes.

> Note
>
> *Winning a competitive tender often depends on providing "evidence-based ROI" and linking technology investments to "measurable business outcomes."*
>
> **Linus Lai – Group Vice President, IDC**

If a project does not gain approval, another way forward is for the investment to piggyback as part of a regulatory compliance uplift (cybersecurity) or a digital transformation (technology, cyber, data and AI) initiative. However, in these scenarios there will be some further stakeholder engagement needed for the CIO and/or CISO to do, to align a few of their peers with this option. These efforts are usually not visible to you or your champion, but when you have a committed CIO and CISO, this path can be an option to consider.

Considering the cost of inaction

In any strategy we want to have firm clarity on what is to be done. I've always said that the essence of a strategy is about making choices. This choice is the basis for deciding how to move forward. The CIO and CISO will narrow the focus down as much as they can and try to avoid getting into a broad debate on options and alternatives. That would be a difficult dialogue to navigate and not good governance at the board and management level.

Having said that, part of the strategy around the business case is to consider the "status quo" – the cost of inaction. When presenting any business case, there is always the option to do nothing. This is rarely the preferred path, but the board and management will always want to have this analysis.

The business case must make a strong argument for taking on the change proposed and making the investment. The CIO and CISO will be assisted by their own team and an FP&A financial analyst for this. Here's an example:

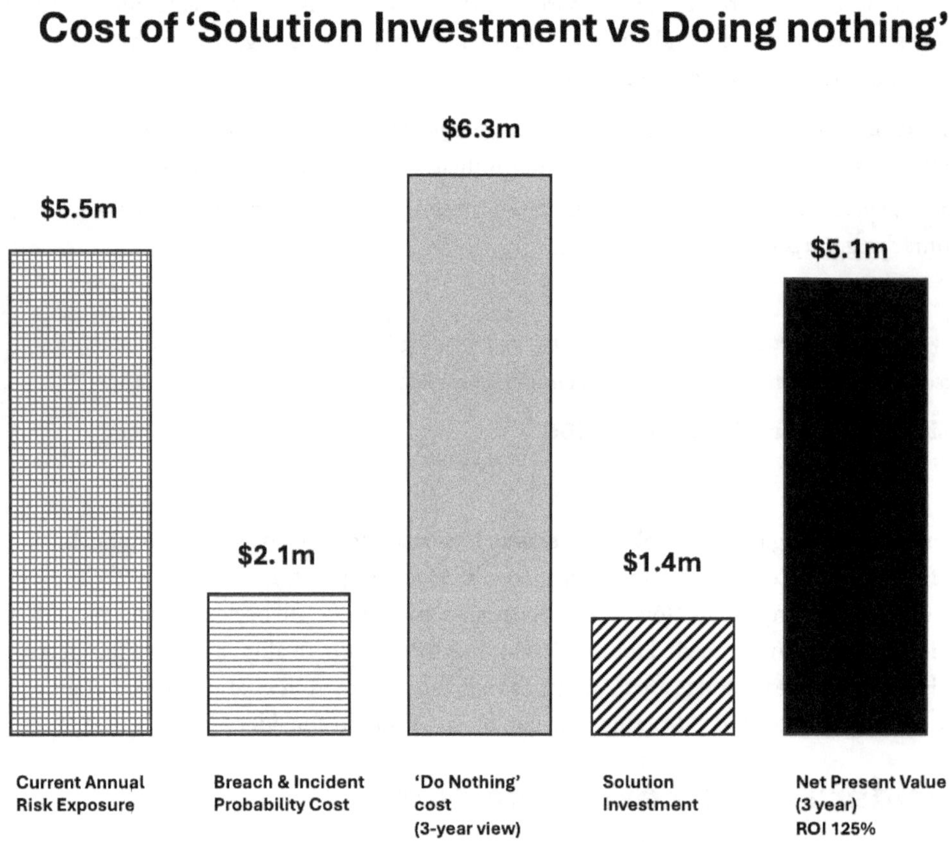

Figure 18.5 - Comparing the risk of inaction vs. the investment

This example establishes that while the organization faces a current annual risk exposure (calculated by Loss Event Frequency × Probable Loss) of $5.5m, the true "Do Nothing" cost (the cost of not making any decision, plus the cost of the technical debt that this adds) escalates to $6.3m when evaluated over a three-year view.

In contrast, deploying the proposed solution requires a comparatively low upfront investment of $1.4m, alongside an annualized breach and incident probability cost of $2.1m. Overall, in this example, opting for the solution delivers a substantial three-year NPV of $5.1m and an impressive ROI of 125%. This effectively reframes the conversation for the executive team from a simple cost request to a compelling exercise in risk mitigation and cost avoidance.

Note

When trying something new or testing it out, evaluation period or the pre-eval debate, these can be time killers. One of my good colleagues and friends dubbed this the "Washing Machine process". Things go in the process, and you see it going around and hope it comes out clean.

The biggest problem is getting a clear decision either way: are we pursuing or stopping? You need that answer as quickly as possible.

Scott Collary – Group CIO, Westpac Group

These arguments for the business case work well when this is a new initiative that the CIO and CISO are seeking approval for. However, when this is an approval for an ongoing transformation, this argument must be more nuanced.

Ongoing investment business case

When there is an ongoing investment, the CIO or CISO will need to tell a story of how this next funding will enable the journey of improved maturity. In these situations, the CIO and CISO may need to show how this ongoing investment can help improve the overall maturity of IT or cybersecurity.

Across technology there are numerous standard approaches (NIST, CMMI, and others) to evaluating and measuring relative maturity. I'll touch on NIST's here (`https://doi.org/10.6028/NIST.CSWP.29`).

The NIST Maturity Model illustrates an organization's progression from informal, ad-hoc risk management practices to a highly sophisticated cybersecurity posture. This model categorizes an organization's capabilities into four distinct implementation tiers, moving from Tier 1 (Partial) and Tier 2 (Risk Informed) up to Tier 3 (Repeatable) and Tier 4 (Adaptive), where cybersecurity processes continuously evolve and dynamically shift based on real-time threat intelligence and lessons learned.

Most enterprises operate in the middle zone of maturity and progress can be measured in fractions, rather than whole numbers.

The CIO and CISO will use this approach or an approach like it in their board paper that supports their strategic investment proposal, framed as a storyline which shows the bigger picture, including the risk of no action and quantifying this cost. This thus provides the context of how the ongoing investment will enable maturity uplift relative to the overall position.

I'd also argue that this approach provides an anchor for the CIO or CISO to strategically plan in a multi-year manner, to gain approval in principle for the overall journey, while also segmenting the approval for this current planning cycle.

Vendor-agnostic business cases

Business cases, by their nature, tend to articulate the need for capability uplift at a macro level, focusing on the strategic outcome, the problem being solved, and the organizational benefit, rather than advocating for a specific vendor or solution in detail.

While a vendor may have been instrumental in shaping the thinking behind the business case, their direct involvement, and value proposition, will rarely be visible in the formal approval document. This is a critical dynamic to understand: the business case is the client's document, not yours, and success depends on ensuring your solution is embedded in the capability narrative rather than presented as a commercial proposition.

All boards and management prefer a tranche-by-tranche approach. This is because some large-scale programs that scale multi-year should deliver the business benefits expected first. When you can articulate a phased value delivery then the actual benefits can be considered incrementally rather than seeing this as the alternative "big bang" approach.

They also usually don't want to talk about product specifics. The dialogue needs to be about addressing a business problem. When this drifts into a discussion about product features, then there is a significant risk that the board will be drifting into the management realm.

I know from my own experience that I always wanted the discussion to be about the level of maturity and how this could be accelerated. This is a strategic discussion, so staying vendor-agnostic is best practice. There is always the possibility, right up until contract signature, that a competitor could re-enter the picture, which is another reason CIOs tend to keep business cases vendor-agnostic.

Obtaining approval

Obtaining the board's approval is a great milestone to achieve. This means that the board recognizes that this problem is one that needs to be addressed. However, note that this does not guarantee that the exact investment proposal has been approved.

Gaining approval from each stakeholder is not easy. To take one example, Geoff Stalley outlined to me how, as Risk Committee Chairman, he evaluates a business case from the perspective of audit and risk.

> Note
>
> *As the Chair of the Audit and Risk Committee, I look for the risks that go beyond the traditional ones to ensure the organization understands what is involved and will embrace the new technology and changing processes, structures, and business models accordingly. Especially where the new environment will create risk for customer data and privacy that must be managed well.*
>
> **Geoff Stalley – Non-Executive Director and former CFO**

What satisfies one stakeholder may not satisfy another. The CIO may be focused on strategic fit and delivery feasibility, the CFO on return on investment and cost containment, and the Audit and Risk Committee on risk exposure and regulatory compliance. Navigating these differing criteria is one of the most demanding aspects of the approval process and precisely where personal capital, careful preparation, and a well-constructed business case become indispensable.

Even after the board endorses a business case, final operational approval is a separate step. The CFO and their finance team will often continue to ask probing questions regarding the specific details and quantum of the spend to ensure absolute alignment before funds are released. While navigating this multi-layered review process requires patience, anticipating this additional level of diligence is simply a standard part of corporate governance.

To navigate this phase successfully, it is best to anticipate:

- Scope optimization challenges, around whether specific project phases or deliverables can be deferred or rolled out incrementally
- Assumption validation - a rigorous final check of the core financial and operational hypotheses underpinning the case
- Timeline adjustments, perhaps minor programmatic pauses to accommodate additional compliance reviews and governance checkpoints

I've seen that CFOs often see the "pilot" approach as the best path forward, as this allows the CIO and CISO to build real-world proof points and demonstrate the solution's value before unlocking the capital required for a full-scale rollout.

Note

Especially for new things, I like to get line feedback on usability, see world scalability, have the cyber teams go after it ... You can do that in a more isolated pilot and roll out progressively. You might take a smaller subset, put 100 people on to try it and work out all the kinks. How it operates and things like usability.

Scott Collary – Group CIO, Westpac Group

What you can do

In my experience the relationship between the internal champion and the vendor is a critical factor for business case success.

Securing budget approval from skeptical gatekeepers like the CFO, Legal, and the board is rarely achieved by a vendor selling from the outside; it requires a tightly coordinated, strategic partnership with the champion acting as a bridge to facilitate this stage.

A best practice vendor serves as a strategic partner by supplying the internal champion with defensible financial models including NPV, ROI, and "Do Nothing" cost-of-inaction metrics. These need to be robust enough to withstand the rigorous stress-testing of a skeptical FP&A team.

You could also provide the political insulation boards require for major expenditure via external validation through peer case studies, analyst reports, and benchmarks showing how other clients have increased their maturity levels.

Offering flexible commercial frameworks that mitigate financial risk for the CFO will also help, as will structuring agreements that accommodate pilot programs, milestone-based stage gates, and tranche-by-tranche funding.

Congratulations! You have now had your solution signed off. On to the procurement process!

Summary

In this chapter, we explored how to gain business case approval—a vital step for all parties.

Business case approval is the moment the sale moves beyond the CIO and CISO's control into a web of CFO scrutiny, board politics, and competing budget requests, where I've seen demand routinely exceed available capital by 3x.

The CIO generally plays the primary advocacy role in this process whiletheCISOholdsvetopower; neither can fully shield the proposal from FP&A challenge, peer competition for the same discretionary pot, or a CFO who defaults to on soft benefits.

As a vendor, you are excluded from the room but can arm the CIO/CISO with the right financial language, maturity frameworks, and "doing nothing" cost analysis before they present the business case.

The key learnings from this chapter are:

- **There are four possible outcomes** – business case approval rarely goes smoothly on the first attempt. A best case where everything aligns accounts roughly for only 15-20% of situations.
- **The CFO only trusts hard savings** – they heavily prioritize tangible Type 1 hard savings like headcount reduction and license consolidation. They may dismiss intangible Type 2 efficiency and risk-reduction gains as soft metrics. To overcome this skepticism, consider using reputable external analyst data from firms like Gartner, Forrester, and IDC to provide objective credibility for their business case assumptions.
- **Doing nothing must be costed explicitly** – the business case as current risk exposure × breach probability + three-year cost of inaction versus NPV of the investment; this is the language that converts a CFO from a "defer" stance to approval.

19

The Procurement Playbook

In the technology and cyber buying journey, procurement is a formal, often lengthy, stage of the process that involves financial scrutiny and potentially, internal conflict among stakeholders.

Procurement is typically a late stage in the buying cycle, often after technical evaluations and business case approval are complete. They are key stakeholders and have a seat at the table for the final contract signoff. They may have been involved earlier in the sales process, but they generally wait for approval to engage with vendors. (The fact is that procurement is resource-thin. They are stretched across multiple projects, so they may not want to waste effort unless the initiative is already approved. By staying somewhat independent of the earlier project activities, they are also free to ask what may be seen as silly questions at this stage.)

You may feel at this point—once the business case has been approved—that the enterprise has committed this path to the board and management and will want to ramp up to implement your solution. You may now expect that this will go through, and that procurement can't now stop it. Unfortunately, this may not be the case.

Winning the technical and commercial argument with the CIO and CISO is only half of the battle. The other half is navigating the procurement process that follows. Procurement as a function operates independently, with its own risk thresholds and governance obligations. Sadly, no amount of CIO or CISO executive enthusiasm can insulate a deal from being refused at this stage.

I've found that procurement is one of the most misunderstood stages of the technology buying journey, but it is one of the most consequential. In this chapter, you'll learn how procurement teams think, what they are measured on, and why their priorities so often clash with those of the CIO and CISO. I will also share best practices in how to navigate the procurement process strategically from early engagement and fact-gathering through to contract negotiation, vendor viability assessment, and escalation when things stall.

In short, in this chapter we'll cover the following topics:

- The procurement process
- Procurement governance
- Contract negotiation
- Procurement escalation

The procurement process

The procurement stage is necessary for the operation of the business. Let's look at how the procurement process fits in the context of the whole sales process:

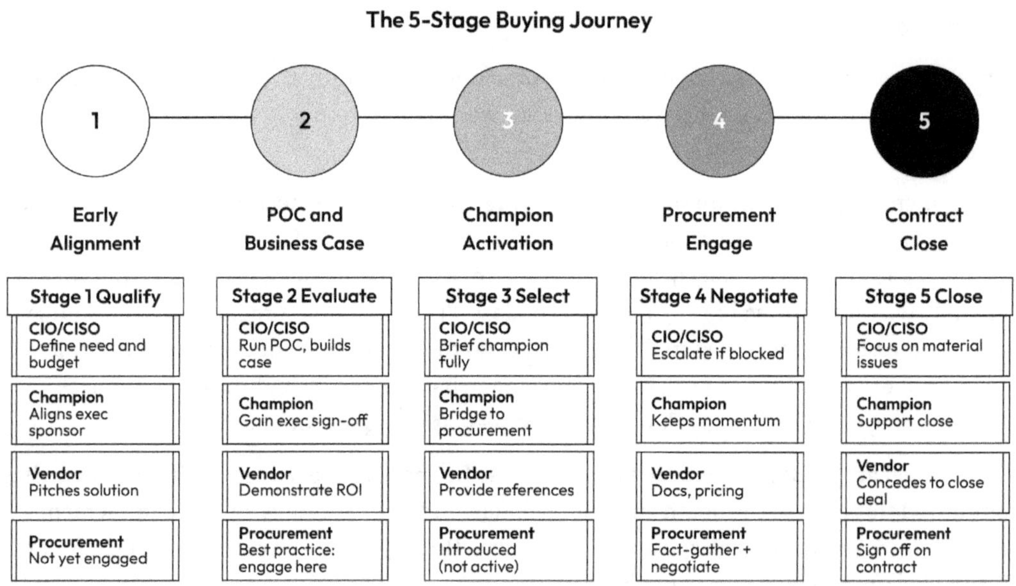

Figure 19.1 - 5 steps to buying a new solution

This provides a 10,000-foot view of the sales process and highlights that there is some depth required to fulfill the requirements at each stage. From the initial pitch and proof of concept through to executive sign-off and commercial negotiation, every stage requires a different kind of contribution from each party, with the relay baton passing between them as the deal matures.

In *Figure 19.1*, I've explained how each key stakeholder is aligned at each point of this process and what their impact is on this journey. As you can see here, best practice will be to try to have some engagement of the procurement team (usually driven by the internal champion) before the business case is approved, around the proof of concept (POC) stage ideally, or perhaps even earlier, if the proposal is very strategic and part of a large transformation.

The Procurement team may insist that a Request for Proposal (RFP) is run to create a genuine sense of market competition, and when they do, I'd argue that the rules of engagement change considerably for every vendor in the process.

An RFP introduces competitive tension and establishes a formal evaluation framework. At the end of the process there is an audit trail that demonstrates for internal governance that the organization explored the market before committing to a vendor. The objective of an RFP is to get proposals on price, performance, and alternate bids and therefore ensure that no single vendor can claim the business without demonstrating that their proposition holds up against comparable alternatives.

> **Tip**
>
> Some vendors proactively share analyst reports with benchmarking data to help provide a comparison of their product vs. other solutions, which positions their solution favorably against their competitors.

A well-run RFP can actually be an opportunity to demonstrate depth of preparation, contextual understanding, and genuine alignment with the organization's strategic priorities that a generic competitor simply cannot replicate in a document. The vendor who has done their homework will always write a better RFP response than the one who has not because the RFP will ask questions that the well-prepared vendor will have already answered in the room.

> **Note**
>
> *With very few exceptions, the initial engagement with vendors by (IT people) is a recipe for disaster. They are often too interested in the application and sometimes "shiny new possibilities" to do some normal negotiation check points, a.k.a. before we start, how do you charge and how much (– I am assuming this is not a charity?).*
>
> *In simple terms, procurement involvement very early on is essential for three reasons:*
>
> *Sales staff control is lacking in vendors of software – they like to sign a deal with CEOs early on before there is any idea of what the application does (sell the dream!!!).*
>
> *Procurement asks the uncomfortable question – why are we doing this and if we find a solution, will it actually do something that we will implement (if it works? – the answer is often "No").*

> *A full and comprehensive project process from day 1, with all stakeholders on board, is the only way to an effective business problem solution and business deployment.*
>
> **Tony White – Former Qantas Chief Procurement Officer**

If procurement only gets involved later in the process, the exercise becomes mostly just about pricing, and it may be too late to talk about options. It will often feel to the CIO and CISO that the decision has effectively already been made at that point. At this stage, Procurement's key sourcing levers—competition, specifications, flexibility, volume negotiation, and timing—have already been largely settled. This may result in a "ritualistic" negotiation (going through the motions) where the CIO or CISO's "friends" in procurement ask for a discount and, as the vendor, you offer them some relief. Then, quietly, both sides can declare victory. Involving procurement earlier in the sales process changes this formula.

The POC/proof of value (POV) provides a good bellwether of the product fit and therefore how successful the implementation will be. This can help inform how the contract should be structured.

> Note
>
> *If you're being given one solution that your people want to buy, you know you haven't got much choice, right? So, the old adage that an analyst is never only working with one vendor applies. Always have a minimum of three.*
>
> **Matt Boon – Senior Director, Strategic Research, Adapt**

> Note
>
> *At times, when looking at a technology that has no competitor product, it is then just a direct procurement exercise, and we would be required to go and get Gartner® to help us price what we should be paying for it. At several of my previous roles, we had someone in the department whose job was IT procurement, and he's the one who negotiated all the contracts.*
>
> *He would argue with vendors and work with firms like Gartner® or Forrester®. He had an idea of where they should be, price range-wise, so he would negotiate with them and get them within the price we could afford.*
>
> *The process would take a lot of effort; we would spend a lot of time making sure that we got all of the correct SKUs (stock keeping units) we wanted.*

> *We didn't want to go ahead and install it and then find out the best piece of the platform that we needed was not included.*
>
> **Gary Hayslip – CISO, Halcyon.ai, Board Director and Investor**

Many enterprise procurement functions subscribe directly to analyst pricing intelligence services, giving them access to benchmark pricing data, typical discount ranges, and deal structures for the exact categories they are buying in. This means that by the time you arrive at the negotiating table with a carefully constructed price, procurement may already have a well-informed view of what your solution should cost.

> **Tip**
>
> Should your solution be a new, novel solution, engaging procurement early in the process is particularly important, as traditional comparators or benchmarks will be much harder to collect.

The smartest approach is to treat procurement as an informed counterparty from the outset, and to build a commercial proposition that can withstand their scrutiny.

The CIO and CISO will usually try to maintain a positive working relationship with Procurement (and the CFO, who this function often reports to), but to be totally honest, in my experience they tend to see them as "blockers", who are often working on their own cost-saving agenda which puts them at odds with the CIO/CISO's plans. I've never heard a CIO and CISO describe their procurement function as a genuine strategic partner, and I doubt I ever will.

> **Note**
>
> *Finance processes tend to make everything more complicated. The internal financials are often the cause of the most conflict among teams within the organization.*
>
> **Anonymous Group CIO – Large financial institution**

CIOs and CISOs are typically operating on a business timeline and have staked their credibility on the outcome, while Procurement is measured on risk reduction and commercial savings.

A vendor that sides too visibly with the CIO or CISO risks alienating Procurement, which has veto power. However, on the other hand, note that a vendor that builds an independent channel to Procurement without the CIO/CISO's knowledge risks undermining the relationship that made the deal possible in the first place. The most effective approach is to give the CIO or CISO commercial framing that Procurement can work with - business cases written in Procurement's own language of risk, governance, and total cost of ownership.

I should add that the procurement process can be drawn out (I've never heard anyone rave about the exceptional speed of the process). In truth, the review cycle and legal contract work often overlap.

> **Note**
>
> When I was at Macquarie Group, we had an internal procurement workflow process that required all stakeholders to review and approve. As Global Head of Tech, Cyber, and Data Risk, I was the last or second-to-last approver. Before it was my turn in the queue, there were 30-50 other executives who were required to review and approve. As a result, the best-case approval was 3-4+ months, while worst-case approvals could extend for 6+ months. The process was frustrating for the CIO and CISO, as they had to wait to start their implementation and cool their heels while this process played out.
>
> When I shared this experience with Tony White, former Chief Procurement Officer at Qantas, he laughed and said that they did the same at Qantas but also held a physical meeting to get everyone on the same page, and this helped them accelerate the process.

Procurement is a key stakeholder; there is no doubt about that. In the next section I dive deeper into this discipline (that is an apt word to introduce this function, as they operate quite differently than any other team in an enterprise).

Understanding procurement

Understanding what procurement cares about starts with understanding what they are measured on.

In contrast to the CIO and CISO, they have absolutely zero interest in the "coolness" factor of the technology or the benefits that have been promised. They care about prices and risks. The outcome that they are rewarded for is getting savings on the contract, and this goes against an annual scorecard from the CFO. They likely also have these broader KPIs that will incentivize them:

- **Risk mitigation** – Procurement is accountable for ensuring that every vendor relationship is stress-tested for financial stability, contractual exposure, data security, and operational continuity. They also want to avoid vendor lock-in.

- **Process compliance** – They ensure that no purchase bypasses the enterprise governance frameworks.
- **Vendor consolidation** – Procurement is incentivised to question whether a new vendor is truly necessary or whether an existing relationship can be extended.
- **Payment terms** – Procurement is measured on its ability to negotiate terms that protect cash flow and align with the CFO's liquidity priorities.

These KPIs will drive the basic behavior of Procurement.

The CIO and CISO will also have some degree of responsibility for these elements as good corporate citizens, but none of these will likely feature in this way in their own personal objectives. (The most direct correlation for CIOs and CISOs is of course risk mitigation, but they will be more concerned about how this new technology may disrupt the current environment than legal and financial exposure.) Herein lies a large part of the alignment issues that exist when these two stakeholders talk. These benefits are all useful, but they just don't rise to the top for the CIO and CISO.

You and your champion can greatly assist Procurement with their risk management goal through fact-gathering.

Fact-gathering

Procurement will need to satisfy itself that any new vendor meets enterprise standards before they can be accepted onto the supplier's register, and that assessment requires evidence. This can include financial stability, security certifications, regulatory compliance, reference customers, insurance coverage, and contractual protections.

By anticipating these requirements and arriving prepared with a complete, well-organized due diligence package (rather than a collection of responses assembled under pressure) you can remove friction from the process and signal to procurement that you are a trustworthy counterparty.

> Note
>
> *Most procurement processes are similar, but the first step is to document the steps to understand what they are, how long each is expected to take, whether there is a specific owner, and, finally, the inputs/outputs of each step. Beyond that, show up prepared with the required information for each step ready for the customer.*
>
> **Dan Wheatley – Vice President of Sales, Gravwell**

The champion plays an equally important role here, acting as a guide who helps you understand the organization's risk framework and what the register approval process demands in practice.

Then comes the meat of the requests, which is all about pricing: what the breakdown of pricing is, including discount tiers, multi-year pricing, and whether they in procurement have heard from industry peers about other "best" prices they could obtain. In the next section, I will cover what is called pressure testing, where the actual price is established for the contract.

Pressure testing

Procurement is required to be commercially astute, across the financial details at a fine level. The CIO and CISO are more concerned about getting this solution implemented and are less concerned about costing models.

Procurement will forecast future costs and consider the different approaches, including per seat, per asset, site license, etc. These growth assumptions will be well understood by them.

They will pressure test the pricing models in terms of looking more broadly at the options available. What I mean is that they place an analytical lens over the pricing model. As they are impartial to the solution, they are able to be less parochial in their investigation.

In doing this, they can, for instance, ask questions around the *structure* of what is being proposed and what this means over time. For instance, at first glance, a perpetual license with a 15% annual maintenance fee might look cheaper than software as a service (SaaS) but modeled over five years with expected growth, this may be less attractive.

> Note
>
> Tony White, former Chief Procurement Officer at Qantas, kindly provided me with these key considerations/guidelines that procurement teams use when stress testing pricing models, to give you an insight into this process:
>
> ***Scenario modeling*** *- model costs under multiple growth, usage, and renewal scenarios. It is essential to include more unlikely cases, just in case the unexpected does happen. For example, rapid user number expansion, unusual seasonal spikes, or increased feature adoption (extra modules) driven by changing business circumstances. This, in turn, will drive contractual provisions to limit up-sell gouging.*
>
> ***Total cost analysis*** *- not all application options are equal when it comes to internal and other costs that are driven from the adoption of an individual vendor solution. Ensure the total costs are compared, not just the direct vendor payments. Include costs such as integration, data storage, comms bandwidth, training, support, costs of workarounds to cover functional*

> *shortfalls for special cases, and administrative overhead. Also, closely examine overage penalties, upgrade upsell costs, and escalation clauses.*
>
> ***Contractual protections*** *– negotiate caps on annual price increases (e.g., 3–5%) and other pricing protections required from the stress-testing analysis. Consider rights to obtain credits for inactive users, protect against higher charges for excess licensed users, and enforceable exit clauses.*
>
> ***Competitor and peer benchmarking*** *- compare pricing models across alternative vendors, as mentioned, ensuring that total cost of ownership (TCO) is being compared. Seek directional insights from consultants who have supported multiple procurement cycles in this vendor segment. While they may not share actual details of pricing other organizations have achieved, they can well express an opinion on the appropriateness of an offer and its structure and provide some guidance on concessions and protections that can be achieved. Where possible, conduct "should-cost" modeling to assess the reasonableness of support and service fees. Vendors can often give very deep discounts as the marginal cost of an additional client for software or a piece of equipment is under 20% of the normally achieved sale price. There are cases for both software and hardware in my own experience, when with a strong competitive environment, pricing of 85% discount or more on the benchmark pricing has been achieved, where the organization has leverage and the vendor wants the organization as a client badly.*
>
> ***Best practice*** *– stress-test pricing models before contract signature and at every renewal. Use TCO calculators, scenario modeling, and benchmarking to ensure transparency and predictability. Negotiate flexibility and futureproofing into the contract.*
>
> **Tony White – Former Qantas Chief Procurement Officer**

Vendors can often design subscription and consumption-based pricing to be very attractive at low volumes, but which then becomes more onerous as they scale upwards. This is where Procurement can add genuine value to the CIO and CISO.

> Note
>
> *Vendor pricing structures have grown increasingly complex. These models have significant implications for total cost of ownership (TCO), scalability, operational risk, and renewal leverage. A disciplined approach to stress-testing pricing models is essential to avoid cost surprises and ensure long-term commercial sustainability.*
>
> **Tony White – Former Qantas Chief Procurement Officer**

Pricing complexity can be a symptom of a deeper question that procurement must answer before any commercial terms are agreed: will this vendor still be here in three years? This is why vendor viability sits alongside pricing as one of procurement's most pressing concerns and why it deserves its own scrutiny before a contract is signed.

Vendor viability

In addition to cost concerns, procurement will have a focus on the business risk being taken with any new vendor. They will conduct a risk assessment, as they will want to be satisfied that the solution is going to be well supported in the long term by a strong potential partner.

They will assess the vendor's financial health and longevity; this is particularly important for smaller best-of-breed vendors. Where there is a natural risk that the vendor may be acquired or shut down, Procurement will be sure to consider how to protect the enterprise from this scenario.

Cybersecurity hygiene has become an equally critical dimension of vendor viability, and in many organizations, it now runs as a parallel workstream to the commercial assessment. In today's enterprise, third party vendor risk from a cyber resilience standpoint is usually one of the top 3 or 4 risks. The Verizon Data Breach Investigations (DBIR) report 2025 found third parties were involved in 30% of all the breaches they analyzed (`https://www.verizon.com/business/resources/Tea/reports/2025-dbir-data-breach-investigations-report.pdf?msockid=1030e0fb2e9b669e3338f40a2f7b6764`).

> **Note**
>
> *Vendors should anticipate and work with buyers to clearly define the procurement and security review demands upfront. SOC 2, ISO, DPA templates, sub-processor lists, AI usage disclosures, and pre-negotiated Master Services Agreement (MSA) redlines should be in a data room on day one, not promised in week six.*
>
> *The vendors that move fastest treat Legal and Security reviews as a sales motion, not an obstacle: dedicated deal desk, a named security governance, risk and compliance (GRC) contact, and a willingness to accept the customer's paper when the deal warrants it. Every week of friction here erodes the business case that got the project approved in the first place.*
>
> **Amir Kazemi – Senior Director, Product Marketing, Cycode**

Much of this viability assessment will come from reference checking. (In practice, the CIO and CISO may want to level set that a good reference is often not 100% proof positive.)

Note

Of course, we all do reference checking, and you must do that, but what I found after 38 years is that we have had so many who didn't work somewhere else but worked for us. And vice versa. This is not always the product; it could be the strategy situation, the complexity of the environment, or the expertise of the team.

Scott Collary – Group CIO, Westpac Group

I should note that a true backup plan is often not feasible when it comes to technology. This can mean an extra system would effectively need to be run in parallel, as manual processes cannot keep up with high volumes of data; manual processes are a poor substitute for an automated system.

Tip

If the procurement team pushes for consolidation to reduce contract risk, this can also reduce architecture complexity, which can be the wrong strategic decision when the architect looks at the overall roadmap. The best architects will be working toward a future state pattern of more desired technology and elimination of aging end-of-life platforms.

Note

I'm happy to share Tony White's checklist on how Procurement evaluates vendors, bringing a practitioner's rigor to the question of vendor evaluation. His framework is worth examining in detail because it reflects how sophisticated procurement functions actually make these decisions (rather than how you may assume they do):

Financial health:

- *Review audited financials, funding history, profitability, and burn rate.*
- *Assess customer base, retention rates, and revenue growth.*
- *Monitor mergers and acquisitions (M&A) activity, which may signal integration risk and the distraction that brings, along with significant changes in strategy and portfolio.*

Roadmap credibility:

- *Request detailed product roadmaps and historical release conformance performance to assess reliability.*
- *Validate claims through independent references and analyst reports.*
- *Investigate negative references thoroughly — issues may stem from the customer's own failures, not that of the vendor.*

Viability in M&A-heavy markets:

- *Consider market movements and potential for the vendor to be acquired and "integrated" – acquisitions can occur at times to simply eliminate a competitor leaving you with a "lame" supplier.*
- *If the vendor is an acquirer, evaluate acquisition history and integration outcomes. Specifically ask vendors about future M&A plans, they may not be able to disclose them but body language will usually indicate any possible activity, particularly in an informal setting.*
- *Review contractual protections such as change-of-control clauses, assignment rights, and data portability.*
- *Continuously monitor market activity that may affect vendor stability.*
- *Incorporate financial health and roadmap credibility into your vendor evaluation matrix. Red flags should be treated as absolute exclusion criteria, not averaged to a weighted score. For critical vendors, ensure periodic financial reviews and contractual audit rights.*

Best practice is to use a tiered evaluation model:

- *Analyst reports for broad market scanning and shortlisting*
- *Peer references to validate operational fit in your industry or application setting*
- *Internal testing/POCs as the decisive factor for functional and strategic alignment*

Document clearly the weighting and decision criteria:

- *Used to ensure transparency and visibility for all stakeholders*
- *Essential at decision time when you are asking for their sign-off and commitment to implement*

> - *Define non-negotiable "no-go" mandatory criteria (e.g., source code access, data ownership, portability in the event of acquisition)*
> - *Use a two-stage process – a solution must first pass all mandatory criteria to be even considered for further evaluation.*
>
> **Tony White – Former Qantas Chief Procurement Officer**

What is being judged by procurement is the financial health, roadmap credibility, and long-term viability of vendors. Of course, this no doubt provides some degree of bias toward established players rather than new entrants.

This bias toward incumbents creates its own category of risk, however, one that regulators have begun to take seriously. The more an enterprise consolidates its critical technology dependencies around a small number of established vendors, the more exposed it becomes to a systemic consequence of concentration itself. I will explore this in the next section.

Vendor concentration risk

Regulatory authorities in most major markets have begun specifically warning CIOs and CISOs about the systemic risks of vendor concentration. Procurement has its own overlapping concern with the same issue; however, their bias will be toward incumbent vendors. They are rewarded for group deals, but it is the CIO and CISO who will be asked by the regulator about concentration risks in their review sessions.

The reason for this bias is simple: they already operate and have a working contractual relationship with these vendors. For Procurement, one contract, rather than two, is easier to manage, and there is the potential to negotiate harder for larger scope. Package players (Microsoft, Google, etc.) have tended to price their products and services as bundle deals to gain a larger share of the wallet.

> **Note**
>
> There is real systemic risk when several industry players all rely on the same vendor for their critical infrastructure, such as data storage. This has less to do with financial difficulties being a risk and more to do with system availability, which can have a broader impact across many enterprises.

Packages, by being integrated "out of the box" can reduce the risk of integration and data interchange. This is a large advantage for the success of the solution but also creates "stickiness" and that can assist you in building a longer-term partnership.

As I noted earlier, the CIO and CISO will tend to favor best-of-breed solutions for critical business processes where genuine competitive differentiation is required — despite the well-understood risk of vendor concentration that comes with assembling a portfolio of specialized tools.

Their logic is straightforward: in the areas that matter most to the organization's competitive position, a purpose-built solution from a vendor whose entire business depends on being the best in that specific domain will almost always outperform a tool that performs generally across a broader scope. I'd argue that this case is particularly true in cybersecurity. The dedicated niche security tool is typically stronger and more innovative than a package equivalent.

A best of breed portfolio that delivers superior capability in each individual domain also delivers greater integration complexity however, as well as a larger governance surface area to attack, with more third-party relationships to manage and a higher probability of gaps at the integration points of separate systems. The package that delivers slightly less capability in each domain delivers considerably more coherence and integration out of the box.

At the end of the day, this is a decision for CIOs and CISOs; however, they will be pushed by Procurement toward fewer vendors, not more.

The fragmentation risk of managing too many vendors with all the overhead and integration burden that entails is well understood, but the risk of over-dependence on a single dominant platform is equally real and considerably less discussed. The mega-platform may appear attractive in the short term: one contract, one relationship, one throat to choke. But this very scale is also its limitation. With an installed base of thousands of enterprises, it will inevitably be slower to respond to specific requirements and less incentivized to innovate at the pace a dedicated best of breed must.

> **Note**
>
> *Vendors can accelerate procurement by treating assurance as part of selling, not as an obstacle after the verbal "yes."*
>
> *The fastest vendors come prepared with a trust pack: data residency and handling, security certifications, resilience and disaster recovery position, cyber insurance, privacy impact material, sub-processor list, breach notification commitments, AI governance position where relevant, and clear answers on who owns what risk. Do not make the buyer chase documents that your own security and legal teams already have.*
>
> *The second accelerator is a redline-friendly contract. If every standard clause becomes a bespoke escalation, the deal slows down and confidence drops. The best vendors know which*

> *clauses are genuinely load-bearing and which ones can be handled through sensible customer positions.*
>
> *The third accelerator is bringing the right people in early. My security, privacy, procurement, and legal teams do not want every answer filtered through the account executive. Give them access to your trust, legal, and operations leads. The cycle shortens when experts talk to experts.*
>
> *The fastest deal is not the one that avoids scrutiny. It is the one that respects it.*
>
> **Ram Kalyanasundaram – Chief Information and Digital Officer, Harris Farm Markets**

Let's now explore procurement governance (which the CIO may very much dislike, as suddenly they no longer have full control and Procurement has the power to slow down progress).

Procurement governance

In most organizations, there is a centralized function that has dedicated procurement professionals for technology. They therefore understand the lingo and the importance of strategic vendor management. As a result, they will be very process-driven and be much harder to negotiate with as they are experts in the field. While you will want to build a relationship with them, note that they will be wary about getting too close to vendors or accepting any gifts from them.

> **Tip**
>
> Procurement governance models are dictated by each enterprise's policy. Always be respectful of what is required.

In contrast, a more ad hoc procurement team will be harder to work with, as they are less knowledgeable about IT. They can be less process-driven, and it may be necessary to help them understand the tech domain.

There is also sometimes a hybrid procurement model, where a third-party consultant is assigned to help drive the negotiation. They care even less about the continuity of the relationship and can be the most aggressive on pricing as they need to justify their own fee. Often, they are in fact reimbursed from the percentage of savings that they can extract from the transaction.

The process that Procurement uses, though, will be the same in terms of fact gathering and contract negotiation. What can differ is the degree of intensity for each activity.

For you and your champion, understanding procurement governance matters enormously. Misreading the governance model, treating a centralized specialist team with the informality suited to an ad hoc function, can derail negotiations that were otherwise well positioned. The first task is to understand exactly who you are dealing with, what they are measured on, and what kind of engagement they are prepared to have with you. Then you will want to know the specific points you need to negotiate with them about.

In the next section, we explore contract negotiations. This is where the vendor, the champion, and Procurement discover just how well their interests actually align when the stakes are written down in black and white.

Contract negotiation

Contract negotiation can be an arm wrestle, a test of relative leverage.

When the vendor in question is a major enterprise package supplier, Procurement enters the negotiation with a clear understanding of where the power sits. These companies often have annual revenues and scale larger than those of the enterprises buying from them and are usually not flexible in terms of changing standard contract terms. Their contracts will have been engineered over decades to protect their interests and Procurement knows this. The experienced procurement professional won't walk into a negotiation expecting to rewrite the agreement from scratch.

> **Tip**
>
> Understanding this power imbalance in advance and building a negotiation strategy that works within it rather than against it is one of the most important things a champion can help Procurement do before the first commercial conversation begins.

Discussions are often about the amount of liability, such as caps relative to contract value. There may also be much discussion about data breach responsibility, IP ownership, and there is an emerging AI concern. Unfortunately, this leads to delays, as both legal and procurement teams have little incentive to move quickly.

> **Note**
>
> *Vendors who make procurement easy usually get the contract. The most impactful things a vendor can do are:*
>
> 1. *Pre-negotiate "standard terms" with common legal frameworks (GDPR, SOC 2, ISO 27001 addenda), so security and legal reviews start from a baseline rather than a blank page.*

> 2. *Remove the back-and-forth. Your team should proactively engage procurement teams with clear pricing structures, volume commitments, and multi-year options upfront.*
> 3. *Maintain a self-serve trust portal (security documentation, penetration test summaries, compliance certifications) so InfoSec teams can complete their review without waiting on sales cycles.*
>
> *The vendors who treat Procurement as a partnership rather than a hurdle consistently close deals faster and with stronger relationships.*
>
> **George Lee – Senior Vice President, Proofpoint**

In these instances, I've seen a few small clause negotiations drift for weeks or even months. Procurement sees it as a downside if this is rushed and some details are not managed. Time is not a key driver for them.

After all the discussions, both parties will likely have to make different concessions to proceed. This becomes an exercise in priority management, and an enterprise will only likely argue hard for showstoppers. (As a CIO and CISO, I'd always ask Procurement to be focused on material issues, and not all the "rats and mice" details.) The CIO and CISO have a business case that they have committed to, so undue delays will only serve to make this more difficult to achieve.

> Note
>
> *We went to request for proposal (RFP) for an offering. Technically, all vendors that were selected and responded were excellent. If the RFP had been a horse race, it would have been a finish-line photo with all the "horses" noses crossing the line at the same time.*
>
> *When we started to go through non-functional requirements like costs, the one that won made it very clear what the costs were, with products and SKUs in writing. This made it super clear what we were getting into. One of the other vendors, whose pricing was way off consideration, was trying to ask my RFP team to reveal pricing given by the other competitors.*
>
> **Nigel Hedges – Executive General Manager & CISO, Chemist Warehouse**

I've also seen Procurement use benchmark pricing; that is, intel from their peers, via a buying group or an analyst organization. Of course, the specifications and timing are always different, which can account for willingness to provide discounts or not.

I would add however that benchmark pricing is often not very accurate, and all the fine details matter for comparison purposes. Parameters such as contract duration, scope, volumes, bundles, quarterly cycles, etc. can all make a significant difference to the outcome you can achieve. I have personally used analysts to provide market intel on pricing however. This can be useful provided the data is not outdated. The more recent this intel, the more useful it is.

Note

A couple of years after the initial contract is signed, your contract will need to be renewed. My ex-colleague Tony White provided me with insight into this process, from Procurement's perspective:

- ***Early renewal planning****- it is essential to begin renewal discussions 6–12 months in advance and run competitive RFPs and POCs where feasible and make incumbents aware of this—without disclosing results.*
- ***Market benchmarking*** *- gather pricing and service benchmarks from peers, consultants in the field and analyst reports. Also consider using completive RFPs to announce your organization's serious considerations moving forward.*
- ***Switching cost transparency*** *- quantify both the hard costs (migration, retraining, integration) and soft costs (business disruption, relationship loss) and change management support required.*
- ***Contractual flexibility*** *- in preparation for a future switching scenario, it is important that all contracts have commitments to exit plans, including incumbent vendor support along with data portability facilitation in the contract.*
- ***Contract details*** *- if not in the original, then at renewal, negotiate or strengthen performance-based incentives and penalties. Also ensure that fee caps, renewal rights, and product modernization commitments are clearly defined (e.g. require that modernized or re-platformed versions are included in maintenance, not sold as new products).*
- ***Performance audits*** *- conduct regular performance reviews and track issue resolution, with clear and rigorous escalation of performance shortfalls. Use any poor performance as leverage to strengthen performance guarantees are renewal.*
- ***Executive engagement*** *- involve C-level sponsors in meetings with critical vendors to signal strategic importance and a strong willingness to change vendors if needed. Discuss the competitive product capabilities and shortfalls and ask the incumbents for their plans in detail to "catch-up". Also reinforce the expectation that application*

> *modernization and capability improvements will be included in the contracted maintenance releases should the organization renew.*
>
> **Tony White – Former Qantas Chief Procurement Officer**

Even the most disciplined negotiation, one where both parties have prioritized well, can reach a point where progress simply stops, perhaps on a term that neither side will move on, a risk position that procurement cannot accept, and your team will not agree to.

When negotiation hits a genuine impasse, the process does not end though; it should be escalated. Escalation, handled well, is not a sign of failure but a necessary mechanism for resolving the issues that negotiation alone cannot.

Procurement escalation

Unfortunately, procurement processes often become bogged down and progress too slowly, impacting the draft plan put forth in the business case. In these instances, an escalation to the CIO or CISO by you and your champion will be required. Once the CIO and CISO have been briefed, this will likely be an executive-to-executive discussion, either from the CIO or CISO to the Chief Procurement Officer or the CFO.

In escalating Procurement, my advice is to keep language non-emotional and focus on problem-solving to understand how the delay can be resolved. Indeed, the worst action to take is to outright blame them for delaying the project.

In the following table, I have summarized the best practices when an escalation is being considered:

Procurement Escalation	
Do	**Avoid**
Focus on problem solving	Never point the finger to blame others
Use neutral language	Avoid invoking the "nuclear option"
Quantify delay = *XYZ* lost value	Don't rush material contract issues
Propose compromise options	Avoid going around Procurement

Table 19.1 - Escalating procurement issues

Resolving issues will often require some degree of compromise by both parties. This compromise is usually about project risk acceptance and what changes to negotiated positions are required. My esteemed colleague Abbas Kudrati provided me with some gems of insight into his experience in these circumstances.

Note

Procurement delays are rarely about price alone; they stem from friction. This includes uncertainty about risk, opaque data-handling practices, and the heavy lifting required by internal teams to validate a new vendor.

The most effective vendors don't just sell technology; they help the buyer navigate their own internal complexity. They remove friction before it appears by being hyper-transparent:

- ***Pre-emptive clarity**: Providing detailed data-flow diagrams showing exactly what is accessed, stored, or processed.*
- ***Direct answers**: Offering straightforward documentation on sensitive topics like credential handling, data residency, and encryption standards.*
- ***Framework alignment**: Mapping security documentation directly to the frameworks the procurement team already uses (e.g., SOC2, ISO, or NIST).*

This shifts the conversation from "we need to investigate this vendor" to "this vendor has already addressed our requirements."

Furthermore, CISOs aren't just buying capability; they are accepting accountability. Vendors who offer structured pilots, phased rollouts, or flexible commercial terms make it easier for stakeholders to say "yes" without feeling exposed. When a vendor speaks the language of the business, focusing on blast radius reduction and operational relief rather than just "features," Procurement shifts from a defensive gatekeeper to a business enabler.

Abbas Kudrati – Chief Identity Security Advisor, Silverfort

The CIO and CISO will be very conscious that the business objective for digital change or for improved security is being directly impacted by any substantial delays. However, they will also want to note that the "nuclear option" remains on the table—when they can blow up the whole idea and walk away. I'd argue that neither executive will ever want to invoke the nuclear option, though, and that this is a last resort. Instead, they are more likely to be open to switching approval for a full contract into a smaller pilot.

> **Note**
>
> The nuclear option can be used to attempt to rebalance when the vendor is unwilling to amend or change clauses. When there is a significant enterprise size difference, this can be a leveler.

The pilot

Procurement will always be open to staging projects, which means, in effect, scaling back the implementation with a shorter pilot. This approach is very common in financial services, especially when the enterprise is working with a new vendor.

I've not seen a report on the percentage of pilots for new vendors but know from my own career, across a range of enterprise engagements, this occurred in 50-60% of all new projects that went via Procurement. There is often a natural institutional suspicion regarding new vendors and their product claims. The pilot approach allows some progress to be made while under Procurement gatekeeping. The CIO and CISO will usually be ok with this approach as this maintains their own momentum, while also reducing their own personal risk for endorsing the change. Often when a pilot is conducted, there will be findings and gaps identified during this process. These gaps then become prerequisites for the vendor to address prior to any contract.

From my own experience, only 30% of pilots are successful and proceed into implementation. What I have also noticed is that, if these pilots fail, this is usually for non-technical reasons, for example, because commercial teams were too ambiguous, or executive sponsorship lacked real commitment to drive the change.

Summary

There is a complex set of dynamics between technology leaders and procurement teams during the cyber buying journey. While CIOs and CISOs often view Procurement as a "blocker" focused on cost-saving, procurement teams act as a critical gate, focused on financial scrutiny and contract sign-off.

Procurement is a typically late-stage but high-stakes function that operates independently from the technical and business case process, with genuine veto power that neither executive enthusiasm nor prior approvals can override. I encourage champions, CIOs, and CISOs to engage with Procurement earlier and more frequently, however.

Vendors and champions who treat the outcome as decided before Procurement signs off are the ones most likely to be blindsided. The most effective vendors treat Procurement as an informed counterparty from the outset, arriving with complete due diligence packages, security documentation, and commercially flexible terms that make it easier for all stakeholders to say "yes" without feeling exposed.

The key learnings from this chapter are as follows:

- **Procurement's goals are fundamentally misaligned with the CIO and CISO** – while these leaders focus on capability and implementation speed, Procurement is measured on cost savings, vendor consolidation, risk mitigation, and process compliance, making early, structured engagement worthwhile, bridging this gap before conflict emerges.
- **Procurement evaluate pricing and vendor viability** – as well as the price on the table, Procurement are concerned with whether you will still be a viable partner in three to five years, and your cybersecurity resilience.
- **Vendors who treat assurance as a sales motion move significantly faster through procurement** – bringing a complete due diligence package, transparent data-handling documentation, and redline-ready contracts can help remove the friction that most commonly stalls deals.
- **When negotiations stall, they should be escalated** – in a non-emotional and solution-focused manner. A pilot allows both sides to make progress while managing risk, buying time for commercial terms to be resolved.

20

Contracting

The journey for you and your internal champion has not been easy. You have progressed through the proof of concept (POC) and/or proof of value (POV) stage, and the business case has been signed off. There is no time to celebrate a win however, as you have entered the realm of the procurement and legal teams.

Let me be direct: getting contracts finalized can be a pain. This may in fact be the least favorite stage for the CIO and CISO; speaking from my experience in these roles, it can feel like you are entering a dark hole with little light to shine the way forward. These leaders are accustomed to operating in a world of frameworks, controls, and measurable outcomes. They operate with much independence, with their teams and vendors responsible and held accountable. When a project enters the legal team's domain, it can feel like the rules of engagement change entirely. Creating and maintaining momentum is difficult and takes real energy, and during the contracting phase deals can stall. However, this is the very moment that the enterprise enters into a legal commitment, so this should not be purely a tick-the-box exercise.

When a project is handed to the legal team, planned timelines become unpredictable and outside of the CIO and CISO's direct control, and decisions that seemed straightforward, suddenly carry contractual, regulatory, or liability implications that no amount of technical expertise can resolve. The average CIO and CISO will usually have some experience with such matters but will have to defer to their legal team's expertise to move the process forward.

The legal team is generally well respected. Their voice carries weight within the corridors of the C-Suite, and their concerns must be taken seriously, no matter how much pressure exists to move quickly.

The legal team play by a different set of rules and they only care about one thing, and that is "consequence". They are less concerned about delivering business benefits or return on investment (ROI); instead, they are looking ahead to what could go wrong in the future. They want to avoid any negative compliance or reputation-related impacts.

At this stage you may feel like the sale goes into a black box and that there is little transparency. This can be frustrating; the aim of this chapter is to explain this part of the sales process to you, including the CIO and CISO's perspective on this, with insights on making this easier. In this chapter I will cover the following:

- A brief primer on contracts
- What do the CIO and CISO care about?
- Vendor legal teams
- Enterprise legal teams
- What cannot be negotiated?
- Contract pivots

Note

Lengthy procurement and legal reviews can delay critical security initiatives.

We proactively and collaboratively help prospects move efficiently while maintaining the appropriate level of diligence and risk management. We view procurement and legal review as important parts of establishing a trusted partnership. Our goal is to engage early, be responsive, transparent, and prepared, enabling prospects to complete their due diligence efficiently while accelerating their path to achieving their business outcomes.

Ryan Jones – Vice President, Cyera

A brief primer on contracts

I should note that I'm not a lawyer; I studied contract law in my first university degree and have been required to read and review many contracts in my career, however. The insights here come from my experience doing that (not from professional legal expertise).

Most vendor contracts are not a single document but four interconnected agreements, each covering a distinct layer of the relationship. This includes the Master Service Agreement (MSA), Data Processing Agreement (DPA), Service Level Agreement (SLA), and Statement of Work (SOW):

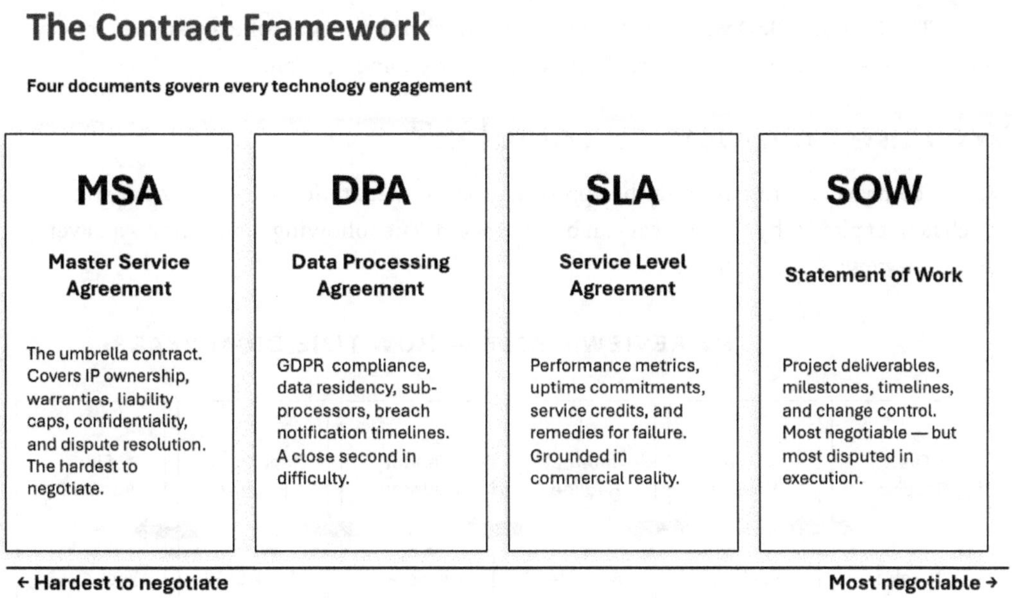

Figure 20.1 - Standard elements of the contract

I'd add that some large corporates or multi-national organisations will have multiple operating entities for contract signing. Therefore, they would also have Local Service Agreements (LSAs) for each of the local entities to consume the product/service being acquired. This extra layer can add more time to this step.

Of these documents, the MSA is the most contentious at this point, and this is likely where most delays in agreeing the contract will occur. The clauses in this agreement contain the key financial and legal exposure, that each legal team will prefer to transfer over to the other side.

Next comes the Data Processing Agreement (DPA), which governs how your data is handled. Then there is the Service Level Agreement (SLA), which holds you accountable to performance commitments. Finally, the Statement of Work (SOW) defines exactly what will be delivered, by when, and how changes will be managed, making it the most negotiable document but also the most contested once work begins.

> **Note**
>
> The CIO and CISO will have their own personal agendas where contracts are concerned and will want to ensure that security and privacy requirements are aligned with their own positions.

Weakness in any one of these documents can undermine the protections you negotiated in the others. The CIO and CISO will need to stay engaged with their legal colleagues; they may give you some pre-warning about where there is likely to be some friction.

Why are contracts so complex?

When a contract is going through the approval process, there tend to be six distinct stages, which help explain why the process can be protracted. The following figure shows an average contract review:

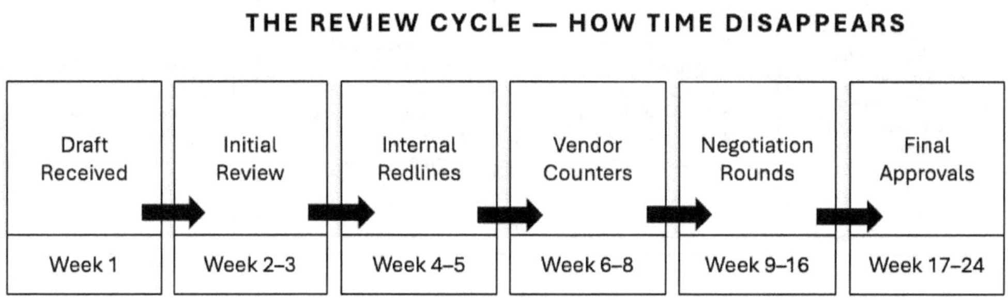

Figure 20.2 - The Contract Review Cycle

You will note that the final two stages are the longest. These final two stages are the longest because they involve the most stakeholders, with the most complexity. Each exchange of redlined drafts will trigger a series of internal review cycles across Legal, Finance, and executive teams, any one of which can stall progress entirely.

> **Note**
>
> There are also an increasing number of fourth parties that sit in supply chains (cloud providers, AI models, etc.), each with their own terms that may need to be considered.

There are generally 6 different parties involved in this review cycle; see Figure 20.3. Each of these parties operates independently, each examining a different slice of the agreement through their own lens, and only one team (IT/Security) reports to the CIO and CISO.

Figure 20.3 - Multi-level review of contract

When you consider that the initiation phase involved a small, trusted circle of stakeholders, it should not be a surprise that this stage now slows down to what can feel like a crawl for you and the CIO or CISO. Where things start to get more tangled is that each of the parties usually works in a sequential fashion and there may be little that occurs in parallel. Bear in mind that each of the stakeholders also has their own priorities that may not be aligned to the CIO and CISO. Then they will need to gain their own internal approvals from their line management. Senior executive sign-off also depends on their availability. This is partly why contracts take far longer than anyone expects and why structuring parallel workstreams from the outset is ideal. The CIO and/or CISO involving Legal early in the sales process will also help in this regard.

> **Tip**
>
> In enterprises, I've seen this legal contract step take 8+ months to complete. It's best to set a realistic expectation of required timing with all stakeholders.

Another part of the issue is the legal language and complexity of the actual contract. I know from experience that there can be 200-300 clauses in these documents. Typically, CIOs and CISOs will be asked by the legal team for their input on a few clauses, but the legal team will manage 80-90% of the details.

This is where I'd argue that your legal team needs to show up as collaborative problem solvers (rather than blockers). I cover this further later.

I've discussed how multi-party stakeholders can add complexity but there are other key factors that can too. Understanding why contracts are so complex is the first step to navigating them without losing months of momentum at the finish line:

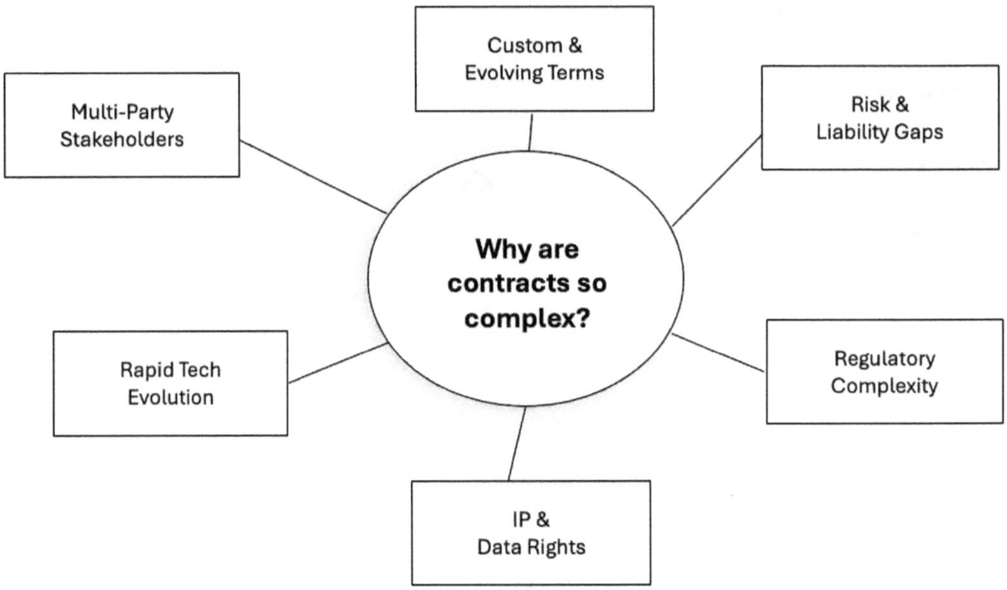

Figure 20.4 - Why getting a contract signed is so hard

Let me go through these, starting with custom and evolving terms. Every enterprise has unique operational requirements, regulatory obligations, and risk tolerances that mean no standard contract template ever arrives fit for purpose. And now, in the AI era, these terms are evolving faster than most legal teams are prepared for.

As technology solutions become more deeply embedded in critical business operations, the question of who is liable when something goes wrong arises. This is particularly difficult when the damage is difficult to quantify and there are perhaps multiple vendors including fourth parties.

Many enterprises operate across multiple geographical jurisdictions and therefore face regulatory complexity; often, a single contract must address different regulations and obligations. Furthermore, technology contracts are written at a point in time but must govern a relationship that will evolve continuously in light of advances in technology. How then can a contract effectively cater for rapid tech evolution when new product features and additions were never anticipated at the start of the contract?

IP and data rights is an increasing issue to address. The question of who owns the data generated within a vendor's platform, who can use it to train AI models, who retains rights to the insights derived from it, and what happens to it when the relationship ends are becoming more important and are contentious, particularly as this may become a future source of competitive value.

You can see why contracts can be a mood killer for the CIO and CISO. Let's look at the CIO and CISO perspective a little more here.

What do the CIO and CISO care about?

Simply put, the CIO and CISO do not want any speed bumps. They have committed to this project and want to achieve the outcomes promised. Speed is also a key metric that they will be measured on by the board. The contracting process is often viewed as an "overhead" to these leaders, as they have already approved the approach and made a commitment to get this done.

From my viewpoint, the CIO, CISO, and legal team are not working against each other; they are working toward genuinely different goals that the contract process forces into the same room at the same time. The friction that creates is structural rather than personal.

There are clearly misaligned goals when we look across Legal, Procurement, and what the CIO and CISO really care about. In short, here is what I believe each party wants to achieve:

- When I was a CIO, my goal was delivery. I was rewarded for getting the right technology into the organization at the right time to enable the strategic agenda. Every extra week a contract spends in negotiation is a week the implementation was delayed and my own commitments to the board were at risk.
- When I was a CISO, my goal was risk reduction. I wanted to ensure that every new technology was governed, secured, and compliant before it touched production systems.
- Legal's goal, I understand, is identifying and trying to mitigate every contractual risk before the organization is bound by terms it cannot meet.
- Procurement's goal, I understand, is value extraction and process compliance. They are measuring success on cost savings, vendor consolidation, and governance adherence.

These concerns are depicted in the following diagram:

Figure 20.5 - Legal, Procurement, and CIO/CISO perspectives

These are three different functions with three different scorecards. Hence, there is a clear misalignment. As you can see, these parties are, however, aligned in wanting to hold the vendor accountable, ensure that risks are allocated appropriately, and that the contract is governed to the appropriate standard.

Sitting on the other side of the table is your legal team whose appetite for negotiation, speed, and flexibility will depend almost entirely on the size and scale of your company.

Vendor legal teams

In my experience, CIOs and CISOs regard vendor legal teams with a mixture of frustration and resignation. They understand that legal review is a necessary part of the process, but they rarely see vendor lawyers as deal-enablers. More often, they are viewed as the last obstacle between a committed business decision and a signed contract.

I have found, in my experience, that the bigger the vendor, the more entrenched and inflexible their standard terms tend to be, and the CIO and CISO probably know from experience that arguing with a market leader's legal boilerplate terms is a battle rarely worth picking.

What they want is simple: a vendor legal team that has done this before, comes prepared, knows which clauses are genuinely load-bearing, and doesn't use every redline as an opportunity to relitigate the entire agreement from scratch.

At this point in your sales journey, you will have spent many months, perhaps even years, getting to this stage. Like the CIO and CISO, you will be keen for contracting to move ahead smoothly. Jayant Dave, CISO at Check Point Software, has some great tips on this.

Note

Contracts are where good deals go to die, especially inside heavily regulated, global organizations. Vendors often make a fatal assumption: they believe hitting one major compliance standard acts as a global hall pass. Assuming your product satisfies EU requirements does not mean you have addressed the hyper-local data protection laws in other geographies.

To accelerate a deal, you must understand the specific legal, compliance, and regulatory obligations across all operating regions long before the contract hits the legal department's desk. You also need to map out every key stakeholder in the decision-making process and be completely prepared to brief the non-technical ones in plain English.

Beyond regulatory homework, here's a tactical playbook for surviving the procurement gauntlet:

- ***Standardize the baseline**: Use short, clear templates for common contracts. Do not overcomplicate the starting point.*
- ***Align before drafting**: Agree on the major pillars like scope, price, SLAs, and liability before anyone touches a formal legal document.*
- ***Ban silent edits**: Track all changes and comments transparently. Sneaking in an undocumented edit destroys trust instantly.*
- ***Define the boundaries**: Keep a simple internal playbook of what is acceptable, what is negotiable, and what is an absolute no-go.*
- ***Stop the redline ping-pong**: Time-box your redline rounds. Give it two passes, then escalate directly to a quick, live close-out call to resolve the final hurdles.*

Jayant Dave – CISO, Check Point Software

In addition to what was suggested by Jayant, allow me to add another tip.

> **Tip**
>
> A briefing session before the formal contract process begins can provide a great starting point. In this session your legal team can share the overall contract structure and note areas where movement is possible and where it is not.
>
> This approach should compress the negotiation timeline significantly and tends to produce a better outcome for both parties than the traditional redline exchange of marked-up documents.

Legal teams operate with some known norms. An overarching assumption is that the size of the organization matters. I've seen many instances of large enterprises with significant purchasing power carrying weight that small or mid-sized customers simply do not, and with that weight, more easily dictate terms to you as the vendor.

On the other hand, there are also instances in which your organization may be larger than the enterprise buying your technology. In these cases, where your organization operates across global jurisdictions and doesn't like to make exceptions to standard contracts, you can wield enormous power. At the same time, though, all vendors must sell, and you will not want to lose a large contract. Thereby, your legal team understands that being too rigid can cost a business deal worth millions, which will not be popular.

In some classes of technology (such as hyperscale cloud providers, dominant software-as-a-service (SaaS) platforms, or niche or specialist vendors), vendors hold a degree of monopolistic power. These vendors, regardless of the customer's size, will not budge significantly on their standard terms. These cases can become a standoff between two legal teams not willing to move on wording, while the CIO and CISO watch the clock and the business case they fought so hard to build slowly loses momentum.

While this is being debated and discussed, the CIO and CISO will often be nonplussed about the level of detail and the legal risk that is being highlighted. However, they will perhaps be coached internally not to engage in this disagreement. I'd argue differently. This is precisely where the CIO and CISO can play a decisive role by applying executive pressure to both sides, to focus on what matters. Their most effective move is to call out the difference between material issues and insist that both teams stop arguing about clauses that will never be triggered in practice.

> **Tip**
>
> I'd recommend you set up a direct conversation between the CIO or CISO and their legal team with the legal team counterpart on your side. The message is simple: we have a business outcome we both want to achieve.

Enterprise legal teams operate under a fundamentally different mandate to the CIO (and, to some degree, the CISO); their job is to protect the organization from legal risk. What may feel like unnecessary caution to the CIO and CISO is, from Legal's perspective, simply doing their job, and that tension is rarely resolved without someone senior enough to force a decision. In the next section I talk about how to engage with the enterprise legal team.

Enterprise legal teams

There are some cases in which the enterprise will hold more power than you as the vendor, and in these instances their legal team may be able to reduce their level of risk by having this accepted by your legal side.

"Risk accepted" means your legal team agrees to take on a greater share of contractual liability than their standard terms would normally allow. This is usually because the commercial prize of winning that enterprise as a customer is large enough to justify carrying that risk for the lifetime of the contract.

Some other reasons why this may occur include:

- You as a vendor are a startup or at a growth stage and want a large enterprise logo on your client list to enable your ambitions
- There is some real competition, and you are competing against other similar solutions
- The enterprise has some history of repeat business, or a long-term relationship with you is already in place

It should be noted that even in these situations, legal negotiation takes time, skill, and patience. I've learned that the legal team's job is to push where it matters most. This means that they will want to protect the organization on the clauses that carry the greatest risk. The CIO and CISO will trust that process, even when it slows things down.

Even the most commercially motivated legal team, on both sides, has a line they will not cross, however, and understanding what is genuinely non-negotiable before the conversation starts will save everyone a great deal of time. I will cover this in the next section.

What cannot be negotiated?

There are some standard clauses that every vendor's legal team will not want to change, which can then become a sticking point in the two legal teams' discussions. The three most common clauses in this regard are:

- Liability caps (vendors rarely agree to uncapped liability)
- IP ownership (vendors will not transfer core IP)
- Governing law (vendors insist on their home jurisdiction)

Other standard clauses in contracts tend to be more negotiable. The CIO has a stronger interest in these three clauses:

- SLA terms and service credits (system performance and uptime are major concerns for the CIO's scorecard to the board)
- Termination rights and exit provisions (having clear data portability and exit clauses is important for the CIO)
- Payment and pricing terms (the CIO cares about their own budget and keeping the Chief Financial Officer (CFO) off their case)

On the other hand, the CISO has a stronger interest in these three clauses:

- Data processing and security obligations (data sovereignty and privacy are a personal accountability metric)
- Termination rights and exit provisions (data destruction at the end of the contract)
- Audit rights (these are non-negotiable for the CISO because they are the only mechanism that provides independent verification that a vendor is maintaining the security standards they committed to)

This last one requires a little more focus and is often hotly contested. Many large vendors will resist agreeing to direct audit rights; from their point of view, this would be unmanageable with the number of customers that they support and could add data security risk. Hence, vendors will often offer a compromise such as SOC2 or a third-party questionnaire-style report. The CIO and CISO will have seen many cases of this response and will not be surprised.

Most standard terms and conditions include audit rights as a baseline provision. Often the real contention sits with the depth of this; a Q&A style assurance review and a full technical audit with access to source code, security architecture etc. is a considerable commitment.

> **Note**
>
> Particularly in a regulatory environment, where the CISO carries personal accountability for third-party risk, the ability to demonstrate ongoing due diligence to a regulator or the board is not a nice-to-have but a professional and legal obligation.

Non-negotiable clauses are typically driven by regulatory obligation, board governance requirements, or personal liability exposure. I'd recommend that you identify the non-negotiables early and focus your negotiating energy on the clauses where genuine movement is possible.

Here are a few examples of commonly negotiable and non-negotiable clauses, with the CIO's and CISO's perspectives:

Contract clause	CIO priority	CISO priority	Commonly negotiable?
Data Sovereignty and Residency	Non-negotiable; data must remain within approved jurisdictions to satisfy regulatory obligations	Non-negotiable; cross-border data transfer creates unacceptable security and compliance exposure	No
Breach Notification Timeline	Non-negotiable; board, and regulatory reporting obligations require defined notification windows	Non-negotiable; incident response planning depends on contractually committed vendor notification timelines	No
Exit and Data Portability	Non-negotiable; the ability to exit without data loss is a mandatory requirement	Non-negotiable; data must be returned or destroyed at contract end	No
Liability Cap	Non-negotiable; floor must be proportionate to the value and risk of the contract	Non-negotiable; the cap must reflect the potential cost of a security incident, not just the contract value	No

Contract clause	CIO priority	CISO priority	Commonly negotiable?
AI Training	Non-negotiable; enterprise data cannot be used to train vendor AI without consent	Non-negotiable; use of sensitive data in model training creates regulatory and reputational exposure	No
Audit Rights Scope	Negotiable; frequency can flex provided minimum assurance standards are met	Partially negotiable; the right itself is non-negotiable, but depth and cadence can be agreed	Partially
SLA Commitment	Negotiable; targets, and remedy structures can be calibrated to the criticality of the system	Negotiable; security monitoring and incident response SLAs can be tiered by severity	Yes

Table 20.1 - Negotiable vs Non-Negotiable Clauses

> **Tip**
>
> Smaller vendors need to consider whether their operational capacity can absorb the audit obligations that large enterprise customers will ask for and if they can charge for assessments beyond what is commercially reasonable.

One further dimension that both you and your champion need to anticipate is the consequence of third-party security assessment. This security assessment is a due diligence exercise, but it can also be a trigger for non-negotiable remediation commitments that must be satisfied before the contract can proceed or be renewed.

I'd argue that the vendor who pushes back or attempts to keep remediation commitments outside the formal contract terms is sending a signal that the CIO and CISO will hear clearly and remember.

> **Tip**
>
> Understanding that this dynamic exists and preparing you is one of the most practically valuable contributions a champion can make to this process, which is already politically complex enough.

The IP and data rights conversation is the one that catches both vendors and champions most off guard as this sits at the intersection of what the enterprise believes it owns, and what the vendor believes creates their platform value:

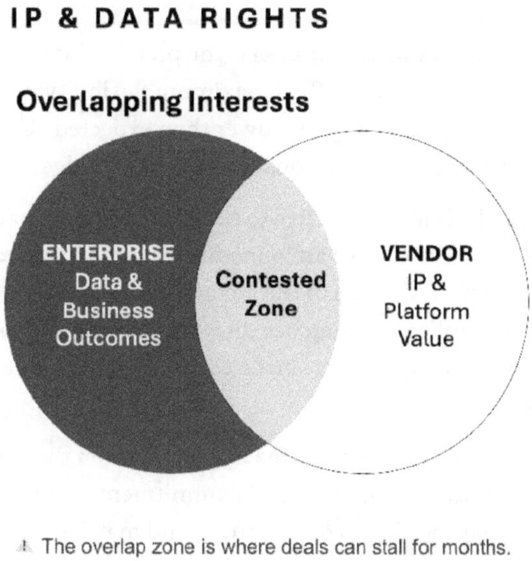

Figure 20.6 - Where negotiations can be problematic

What can appear to be a simple and standard term is anything but standard to the organization that just spent years generating the data their platform depends on.

The contract complexity explored throughout this chapter is about to become significantly more complex as the traditional per-seat pricing model that has governed technology contracts for a generation is now being disrupted by the AI era. This new shift from per-seat to consumption, interaction, and outcome-based pricing will require new contract wording.

Contract pivots

Much of what was discussed in this chapter about contract complexity assumes a pricing model that is rapidly becoming less relevant now with the shift from per-seat to consumption, interaction, and outcome-based pricing.

New approaches to payments are being proposed by vendors in an effort to ensure that they do not miss out on revenues as the AI era impacts the workforce. In particular, the **Pay-per-Work** model is emerging, which includes:

- **Consumption model:** This is the classic "AWS model" where you pay per transaction, such as API or some token of measure.

- **Digital employee model:** The customer pays for the cost of the digital employee per month. This is a fixed price cost.
- **Prepaid credit model:** The customer buys a set amount of credits, for example, 100,000, per month.

For the CIO and CISO, the **consumption model** is the preferred starting point when the use case is new or uncertain. This approach offers maximum flexibility; they only pay for what they use. Plus, there is no sunk cost if adoption is slower than expected. Remember that the CIO and CISO want to ensure that the CFO remains onside with their budget.

The **digital employee** model is also attractive to the CIO and CISO for one simple reason: it is very predictable. However, the CIO faces an immediate internal political problem in that the CFO will want to know whether this sits in the technology operating budget or the headcount budget. That question, by implication, touches on workforce strategy and HR policy. For the CIO and CISO, this is always tricky as they start a conversation about automation replacing or augmenting human roles.

The **prepaid credit** model is often the preferred approach when the solution is a mature, well-known use case. This offers the benefit of a fixed commitment that the CFO can understand. The CIO knows exactly what they have committed to and may be able to negotiate volume discounts.

I mention these models here as contracting is a key step, and from my own experience, cases with these pricing models always take more time and effort to obtain sign-off to proceed.

> **Note**
>
> Many large enterprises are actively trying to contain AI consumption costs by restricting unlimited staff access to AI tools, having discovered that uncapped token consumption can produce budget surprises that no CFO anticipated when the original agreement was signed.

Wrap-up

From my experience, the organizations that consistently close contracts faster are not the ones that bypass rigor; they are the ones that build it into the process from the start. The champion, CIO and CISO bring legal in early and agree on the non-negotiables upfront, then move with speed and discipline to progress this to a signed contract.

Note

John Taylor, a former CIO and CISO, now a CTO, gave me the following checklist for procurement and vendor negotiation. This serves as an excellent overview and is worth reviewing before entering any significant negotiation:

- ***Strategy*** *- create a negotiation strategy so your internal team is clear on the objective and what is important.*
- ***Negotiables*** *- what your non-negotiables are: what your red line is that you would be willing to walk away from the negotiations (this is very important, as often we can get fixated, which shifts the negotiation power).*
- ***Price*** *- price your solution yourself so you know what a good price/value is. (This will form part of your negotiation strategy).*
- ***Dedicated team*** *- put in place a dedicated negotiation team and let them run with the initial negotiations, driven by the strategy. (Executive sponsors, at this stage, should stay at "arm's length" with regular updates).*
- ***Strong exec sponsor*** *– be heavily involved once you get them to the down-selection of the final 2 or 3. This will ensure that the more "trivial" items are done and you are focusing on the important areas.*
- ***Negotiation approach*** *- it is important to negotiate professionally and "friendly". You need to assume that the relationship has started at the interaction. Your behavior at this stage will dictate the relationship going forward.*
- ***T&C's*** *- start the legal conversation early. Agree on the non-negotiables of the contract upfront as best you can and make sure that your procurement person/legal area are joined together. Depending on how your internal budgets work, include funding for a dedicated procurement and legal person in your budget.*
- ***Context*** *- agree on as much as possible and write those things down. If they don't end up in the contract, those notes will provide clarity later. This ensures that the context of the discussion is maintained.*

John Taylor – Field CTO, Mimecast (former CIO & CISO)

Summary

In this chapter I explored the often-dreaded topic of contracting which can be one of the most frustrating stages of any technology procurement because it shifts control away from you and the CIO and CISO and into the hands of teams that operate by entirely different rules. Legal teams are focused on legal consequence and risk rather than delivery and outcomes.

The contracting process involves multiple documents, with the Master Service Agreement (MSA) being the most contentious, and the balance of negotiating power depending heavily on the size and leverage of each party.

Today, there are new emerging AI-driven pricing models that further complicate contracts, requiring CIOs and CISOs to think carefully about how consumption, digital employee, and prepaid credit structures align with their budgets and use cases.

The key learnings from this chapter are:

- **Legal teams play by different rules** – the CIO and CISO are focused on speed and delivery, while legal is focused on future consequences and liability. Understanding and respecting this difference, rather than fighting it, is essential to moving the process forward without damaging internal relationships.
- **Know what is and isn't negotiable before you start** – you may not be able to shift on certain clauses, such as liability caps, IP ownership, and governing law. Instead, focus energy on clauses where movement is possible, such as SLAs, audit rights, and exit provisions.
- **Negotiating power depends on context** – often large enterprises can sometimes dictate terms, but dominant vendors like cloud and niche specialists hold significant power and won't budge on standard contracts. Recognizing your own position before entering negotiations is ideal so that you know how hard the contract negotiation may be.
- **Preparation and internal alignment are critical** – having a clear negotiation strategy, defined non-negotiables, a dedicated team, and early engagement with legal and procurement through your CIO, CISO, or champion dramatically reduces delays and misalignment once the formal process begins.

Part 4 (Home Base)

Closed Deal and Partnership

In this fourth and final part of the book, you have rounded third base and are heading home. But I argue that home base is not the finish line, it is the start of something harder and more valuable than the deal itself. I will explore what it truly means to build a partnership of trust with the CIO and CISO. This is where transparency, reliability, and alignment are demonstrated repeatedly under pressure. The final chapter brings the entire journey together, defining what it means to be a vendor MVP in the AI era. By the end of this final part, you will understand that the vendors who endure are those who can engage both the machine and the human and who never confuse closing the deal with earning the partnership.

This part of the book includes the following chapters:

- *Chapter 21, Building a Partnership of Trust*
- *Chapter 22, Book of Secrets*
- *Chapter 23, How to Be an MVP*

21

Building a Partnership of Trust

Let me start by reminding you that the CIO and CISO tend to begin discussions with new vendors based on a degree of trust that what the champion is proposing is a good idea and fits into their strategic vision. Vendors begin this relationship being seen as "noise" and build trust over time, proceeding through the stages of being known -> credible -> preferred -> strategic (you may recall I discussed this in *Chapter 2*). Now that you have a signed contract, you will want to continue building trust and cement your position as a strategic partner to the CIO and CISO.

I've seen that the strategic alignment between a vendor and the organization they are selling to is the foundation on which any meaningful partnership is built. Without it, the incentives of each party will eventually pull in different directions, and the relationship will fracture under the pressure of competing priorities.

Trust is what sits at the center of this and what holds it together. Trust is demonstrated through decisions made under pressure, how you handle problems when they are inconvenient, and whether your behavior in year two looks anything like the promises you made in year one. It is about doing the right thing, even when the deal is done and contracts are signed.

When trust is operating at the right level, this partnership fundamentally changes in character. I've seen some great examples of this, where shared goals replace competing agendas and decisions that once required weeks of justification start to move faster all because that foundation of trust has already been laid.

Trust, in this sense, is a currency. It compounds when handled well, with consistent performance and commitment, and depletes quickly when it isn't. Every vendor who wants to build something lasting with a CIO, CISO, and champion will need to figure out how they can be a trusted advisor and not seen just as a vendor. In this chapter I will explore trust as that currency and how it is built, what threatens it, and how the best vendors make it the defining characteristic of every engagement. This will include:

- The vendor-champion partnership
- Four trust behaviours that matter
- How trust is destroyed
- Making it a win-win

The vendor-champion partnership

Building a partnership of trust begins with the internal champion. In our analogy of a baseball game, you are the batter, stepping up to the plate, working to advance from first to second to third base, with the end goal of a home run. In this game, the champion could be seen as a coach, reading the field, signaling the plays, and creating the conditions for you to score.

Let me note here that champions and vendors are not friends. They begin as two parties with overlapping but distinct interests; the champion needs a solution that works and makes them look good internally, and the vendor needs support within the enterprise for their solution. This is a working engagement only and there is nothing wrong with calling it what it is. The vendor contributes by delivering solutions and expertise, providing resources and support, sharing market insights, and enabling customer success, while the champion contributes by advocating internally for them, providing context and access, aligning stakeholders, and driving adoption.

> Note
>
> *In the vendor's defense, one of the difficulties they face is that it's difficult to be a partner when you're selling a product. It's easier to be a partner when you're selling outcomes. If you want to be seen as a partner, you need to be focused on the outcomes of your customer. You need to have skin in the game, and a lot of the big players will do this.*
>
> **Matt Boon – Senior Director, Strategic Research, Adapt**

In order to create a partnership with the internal champion, and thus with the CIO, CISO, and enterprise overall, there needs to be trust between you and the champion. This is the connective tissue that holds the partnership together.

Industry veteran Benny Porat, a serial entrepreneur, has strong experience in building this trust with his customers. His perspective captures the reality that actually adding real value for your customer is the foundation for this trust. It goes way beyond just showing them something interesting; it must deliver!

> **Note**
>
> *One of my early lessons as co-founder and CTO at Claroty was the difference between showing your customer something and doing something for your customer.*
>
> *Showing gives them information.*
>
> *Doing gives them back their time.*
>
> **Benny Porat – Co-Founder & CEO, Twine Security, and Co-Founder & Board Member, Claroty**

Building trust is a critical activity for the internal champion within the enterprise too. They must first earn the confidence of their CIO and CISO before they can effectively advocate for any vendor or initiative. This is a high bar. As I have explained previously, senior technology leaders operate in an environment of constant inbound pressure: vendors, internal champions, and analysts are all competing for the same finite attention. The real challenge for a CIO or CISO is developing a reliable filter for which pitches deserve their serious consideration. An internal champion who understands this dynamic, and who has invested time in building genuine credibility with leadership, becomes a force multiplier.

> **Note**
>
> *Selling internally is very different. There is obviously an established relationship and an alignment, as we work for the same company. But often this introduces complacency, and the internal team does not work as hard as external vendors do and often this results in choosing to go external rather than use internal resources.*
>
> **Paul O'Rourke – CRO, CISO and BCG Global Cyber Leader**

When all sides are fulfilling their roles and trust is operating at the right level, the partnership produces four measurable outcomes: faster decisions, shared goals, mutual growth, and the potential for long-term value. I've depicted the partnership between the vendor and champion, and the crucial role that trust plays within this in the following model:

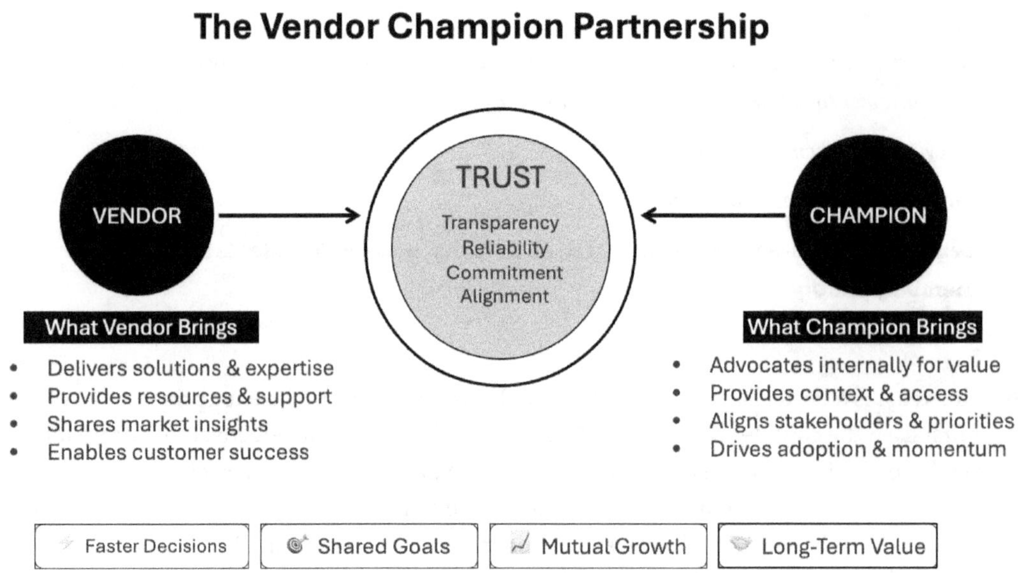

Figure 21.1 - The Champion and Vendor Partnership

As you can see, for this partnership to function, trust must flow in both directions. The vendor must equip the champion with the right intelligence and tools, and the champion must be willing to stake their reputation on the recommendation. You are unable to be truly effective in an organization where this mutual trust is not in place. You and your champion need to be able to speak plainly with each other on concerns and issues.

This model makes it clear that neither party can achieve the partnership outcomes alone, it is the quality of the trust in the middle, between the parties, that determines whether the potential on both sides is ever fully realized.

Each of us operates slightly differently when it comes to trust. I personally will trust a stranger when their actions remain consistent even in what may be difficult moments, although some perhaps wouldn't.

> **Note**
>
> *Trust depends on how the vendor behaves during the sales process. Senior buyers watch for signals. Does the vendor listen properly? Do they understand enterprise constraints? Are they realistic about implementation? Do they respect architecture and security teams? Do they bring useful insight without overclaiming? Do they follow through? Do they make it easier for the buyer to build internal alignment?*

For emerging vendors, the goal is to reduce perceived risk at every stage. That does not mean acting like a large incumbent. It means being clear, prepared, commercially mature, and easy to sponsor. A scaleup can be innovative and still enterprise-ready. In fact, that combination is often exactly what buyers want.

The vendors that establish themselves as trusted partners usually do five things well: They bring a strong point of view. They align to the customer's architecture and standards. They shape the category without confusing the buyer. They make differentiation simple and defensible. They prove value in a way that supports a real investment decision.

Enterprise buyers are open to emerging technology when the value is clear and the risk is managed. The opportunity for scaleups is to move beyond selling capability and start helping customers make confident decisions.

Sundar Iyer – Managing Director, Emertel

Note

Trust follows three things in order: evidence the vendor has done this at your scale and in your regulatory context, the quality of the people you'll actually work with post-signature (not the ones in the pitch), and a deployment path that produces a measurable win in the first 90 days. Regardless of platform depth, the vendors worth trusting can immediately land in a single high-pain workflow, prove ROI, and earn the next expansion. References are necessary but dig deep with a customer who won with the vendor and understand what materially changed.

Amir Kazemi – Senior Director, Product Marketing, Cycode

Building trust with your champion requires transparency, reliability, commitment, and alignment. I will outline these four behaviors in the next section.

Four trust behaviors that matter

Trust itself is defined by four behaviours: transparency, reliability, commitment, and alignment, which must be demonstrated by both parties. These are earned through repeated actions and are tested under pressure.

A vendor who is transparent when the news is bad, reliable when the timeline is tight, committed when the contract doesn't require it, and aligned when the client's priorities change becomes someone that the champion will defend internally, advocate for publicly, and return to when the next problem needs solving for the CIO and CISO. The same is also true in reverse. A champion who is honest about internal resistance and genuinely invested in the outcome is not only a buyer but starts to become your partner.

Trust is the outcome of this process, not the starting point, and there are no shortcuts to it. Let's look at the four trust-building behavior attributes in more detail.

Transparency builds trust

Transparency means always speaking plainly. It means surfacing a delivery risk before the client notices it, being honest about what the product can and can't do.

For the champion, transparency means keeping the vendor informed about the internal dynamics that affect the engagement, including the politics, the shifting priorities, and the stakeholders who are quietly unsupportive. When both parties are transparent with each other, this starts being a genuine working partnership.

> Note
>
> *Some of the better relationships that I've had are built on trust, honesty, and transparency, and with that we agree to adopt their different way of doing things and have been successful.*
>
> **Scott Collary – Group CIO, Westpac Group**

For the CIO, a transparent vendor is one they can bring into difficult conversations without fear of being embarrassed. For the CISO transparency is particularly important; a vendor who downplays a vulnerability or manages perception instead of managing risk will lose their trust quickly and permanently.

Reliability builds trust

Reliability is doing what you said you would do. For you, this is particularly regarding defined quality and the time committed. This sounds simple I know, but it is where most vendor-customer relationships quietly erode. When I've personally seen missed deadlines or scope changes getting renegotiated from vendors, then I've stopped believing that their commitments mean anything.

For the champion, reliability means being a consistent internal advocate not only when the relationship is easy, but also when there is pressure from above to question the investment or change direction.

For the CIO and CISO, reliability means that the vendor is doing what they committed to, to the agreed standard, repeatedly and predictably. As a CIO, I measured reliability in delivery terms—does the vendor show up the same way in year 2 as they did in the first month? How one performs over time is how I judge my own staff, and vendors have this same bar to reach every day.

> **Note**
>
> *The separator is trust under pressure. I have a barometer: will the partner/vendor double down when things get hard?*
>
> *In every shortlist, I run a simple mental simulation: It is Friday evening. A critical service is down. The CEO wants to know when we will be back. Customers or frontline teams are being impacted. Which vendor do I want on the call? Which account leader will tell me the truth before the message has been polished? Which engineer will stay with the problem until it is fixed?*
>
> *Price matters. Features matter. Relationship matters. But they matter in different ways. Price has to be defensible. Features have to meet the threshold. The relationship has to be real enough to survive a bad day. Past that point, I am choosing the team I want beside me when something breaks.*
>
> *I do not only buy the software; I buy the behavior of the people when it fails.*
>
> **Ram Kalyanasundaram – Chief Information and Digital Officer, Harris Farm Markets**

Real diamonds are forged by the pressures of the earth over more than one million years. The example that Ram refers to here made me reflect on this, comparing these to 'fake diamonds' (cubic zirconia), which are lab-grown with chemicals and high heat over 10 weeks. In a similar way, trust under pressure is the only trust that counts. The vendor who maintains their transparency and commitment to the customer's outcome when something goes wrong earns the kind of trust that is not easily lost.

When I was a CISO, I measured this trust slightly differently, in terms of response time—when something goes wrong, how fast does the vendor remediate this?

> **Note**
>
> *CISOs trust what they can defend. Customer stories matter when they're specific and operational, not polished. They care about details such as:*
>
> - *Incident outcomes: what changed during/after an event*
> - *Measurable metrics: mean time to detect (MTTD)/mean time to repair (MTTR), recovery time, false positives, coverage*

- *Peer validation: not logos—"someone like me" references*
- *Audit-ready evidence: what the auditor will accept, not marketing claims*

Sam Ghebranious – Director, Axcelerate / Senior Advisor, Frost & Sullivan

Commitment builds trust

Commitment means treating the client's outcome as genuinely important, something worth caring about. This shows up in your organization's willingness to go beyond the contract when the situation demands it and to stay engaged with them through difficult phases. This kind of commitment is what separates a transactional vendor from a true partner.

Note

It doesn't matter if it was in a contract or said across a table, a commitment is a commitment. When implementation timelines slip, especially on critical path milestones, the damage isn't just to the project. It ripples.

My promises to management, to the board, to key stakeholders—those were built on your promise to me. A missed deadline isn't just about losing face. It delays other programs with dependencies, affects enterprise key performance indicators (KPIs), and sometimes hits personal performance outcomes.

The vendor may think they're managing a timeline. I'm managing trust, both internally and externally. You get one or two of those before the relationship changes fundamentally. The vendors who last are the ones who treat their word as a deliverable.

Jimmy Wong – Former AIA Australia CISO

Then for the champion, commitment means continuing to sponsor the relationship internally even when there are competing priorities.

When I've been the CIO, I always wanted to see commitment expressed through ongoing continuity. What I mean is the same senior people staying engaged, the same energy being applied to the account as I saw at the start of the engagement. Linus Lai, Vice President at IDC, captured commitment in a broader scope.

Note

Focus on delivering measurable business outcomes and maintaining strong governance practices. Be transparent, responsive, and open to feedback. Position your organization as a

> *strategic partner, not just a vendor, and this means going beyond the contract at times or leaning into more innovative engagement models. Thought leadership, evidence-based claims, and willingness to engage in peer forums (e.g., IDC events, councils) build credibility.*
>
> **Linus Lai – Vice President, IDC**

The CIO and CISO both want to see it expressed through investment; they want a vendor who will proactively update their practices and bring new thinking to the relationship without being asked.

I'd note that in enterprise security especially, credibility is not built linearly in a step-by-step fashion. A track record of honesty and follow-through compounds in your favor. A single failure to deliver, or worse, a deliberate evasion, can undo years of goodwill however.

> Note
>
> *Trust is built on actions, not words. If you promise something and then try to wriggle your way out of it because you didn't read the contract properly, then trust will be hard to rebuild.*
>
> **Lee Barney – CISO, Ventia**

Remember what you see as incredibly strategic is not necessarily seen in the same light by the CIO and CISO. Your own priorities are different from theirs. The CIO and CISO have strategic priorities that are shaped by board pressure, regulatory obligation, and internal politics. The vendor who leads in discussion by focusing on what matters to the CIO and CISO is demonstrating commitment that will be both noted and appreciated.

Alignment builds trust

Alignment means genuinely understanding what the CIO and CISO are trying to achieve and making sure that every roadmap conversation and every commercial discussion serves this goal rather than just your own growth targets.

For the champion, alignment means ensuring that the vendor's work is consistently connected to these strategic priorities and that when those priorities shift, the vendor is brought into that conversation early rather than left to discover it late.

From my experience as a CIO, alignment is what separates a strategic partner from a supplier. I've always valued the partner who is thinking through my lens and bringing ideas forward that can assist my vision.

Note

Strong strategic alignment with technology vendors is critical, especially for applications that underpin strategic advantage, market differentiation, or core business performance excellence. It is essential that key technology partners have organizational objectives, values, regulatory compliance, and long-term resilience capabilities that are consistent and supportive of your organisation's requirements.

Vendors that withhold roadmap visibility, shift significant priorities regularly, have unclear financial funding, are takeover-prone, or fail to invest in capabilities can force organisations into unnecessary customisations, redundant integrations, or costly workarounds. These issues of misalignment over time compound, resulting in wasted spend, stalled innovation, missed market opportunities, and operational inefficiency.

Tony White – Former Qantas Chief Procurement Officer

Wearing my CISO hat, I looked for alignment of the vendor's security roadmap with my own plans. I'd argue that there is also a degree of realism required. No vendor will ever offer the perfectly matched product, and expecting perfection is a poor foundation for any relationship. What matters is whether the vendor was genuinely invested in my success.

Note

A CIO doesn't need another vendor pushing products; they need a trusted advisor who understands their architecture, constraints, politics, and risk. The strongest partnerships are built by those who invest the time to see the problem through the CIO's lens, bring context instead of features, and help leaders navigate difficult trade-offs with confidence. Credibility is earned not through selling technology, but through preparation, insight, and the ability to guide decisions the organization can stand behind.

Martin Dube – Head of Enterprise Applications Solutions, Data & AI, NTT Data

Note

No product will ever be a perfect fit—every solution comes with trade-offs. What ultimately matters is whether a vendor takes your needs seriously, continuously improves their product, and commits to growing with you as a true partner.

Yabing Wang – CIO & CISO, Justworks

We have explored how transparency, reliability, commitment, and alignment create the conditions for trust to grow. But unfortunately, trust can be destroyed in a single moment, and no amount of prior good behavior means that it can fully recover from it.

Factors that destroy trust are often the opposite of the four attributes I have discussed here, but there are other factors that can erode this trust too. I will explore these in the next section.

How trust is destroyed

I wanted to write about this topic because trust is the foundation on which everything else in this book sits. I have seen what great trust looks like between a vendor and a champion, and I have also seen what happens when it is broken—sometimes slowly, sometimes in a single moment.

Trust that develops between a vendor and an enterprise over years of delivery, transparency, and shared challenge, with many difficult conversations experienced, can be strong, but even this has limits.

> Note
>
> *Trust takes time and effort to build but once it's built, it will not be broken easily.*
>
> **Frankie Shuai – Vice President of Information Security, Bitdeer**

In my experience, trust is not a permanent asset but something that must be actively maintained. Bad examples, where trust has been eroded, have stayed with me and I want to share a few vignettes, so you do not have to learn the same lessons the hard way. Allow me to share one personal story that springs to mind to illustrate this.

A long-standing vendor provided our loan management system, a solution deeply integrated into our core banking infrastructure. This was a legacy technology, and we were well established in the relationship. The vendor had a well-known reputation internally for applying heavy charges to any change request.

We were in the middle of a major banking transformation, exactly the kind of inflection point where a vendor with genuine strategic ambition would have recognized an opportunity to reposition themselves as an indispensable partner in what came next. I requested a one-to-one meeting with their CEO specifically to explore that possibility, to have an honest conversation about our current relationship, what the transformation might mean for both parties, and whether there was appetite on their side to reconsider their commercial posture in light of the potential to play a genuinely strategic role in our future architecture.

The conversation that followed was disappointing as I found myself talking to someone who was defending the existing commercial model rather than being open about what an alternative one might look like. I felt like the trust that had been built over years was damaged in a single conversation—not because of a delivery failure or a technical gap, but because the CEO revealed that their priority was revenue protection rather than partnership.

Independent of the four behaviours discussed earlier, there are other events that can quickly erode trust, for example:

- A security breach
- A failed implementation
- A change in leadership on either side
- A competitor who reframes how the client sees the value they have been receiving

These moments do not always signal bad faith, but they test whether the foundation that you have built with the CIO, CISO, and champion, is strong enough to survive them.

This is why you cannot treat trust as a milestone that gets reached and then only manage it passively. It requires active maintenance and honest conversation from you when things go wrong, and the willingness of both parties to repair rather than retreat when the relationship is under strain.

Ethics is the attribute that can erode trust the fastest, I would argue. Of all the factors that can erode trust, ethics operates fastest and cuts deepest. While missed deadlines can be explained, a product gap can be road mapped, and a difficult conversation can be had and recovered from, ethical concerns bring your organization's character into question.

Ethical issues can show up in different ways. Concerns could be about values, associations, and conduct, and whether these are compatible with the enterprise's own brand and ethical standards (for instance, energy usage concerns, poor working conditions and treatment of staff, and nation state sanctions). It could be where a vendor is discovered to have acted in their own interest at the direct expense of clients.

When I saw this kind of ethical erosion as a CIO, it showed up as a creeping sense that the vendor's advice couldn't be fully trusted. Then in my career as a CISO, if a vendor wasn't fully transparent about a security issue with me, that was the end of our association.

Now, let's talk about the more positive topic of attaining a win-win. We understand what destroys trust, but the real goal of this chapter is why and how you build a partnership of trust.

Making it a win-win

A win-win partnership does not happen by accident. It requires a deliberate shift in how both you and the CIO or CISO and champion think about the relationship, moving away from the transactional event of winning a contract and toward the longer view of a sustained operational alliance.

A win-win relationship between an enterprise and a vendor is one where the values, ethical positioning, and public associations of each party actively reinforce, rather than merely tolerate, each other. This is when the relationship itself creates positive value for both sides on the values and reputational dimensions, not just the commercial one.

There will always be sales targets and quarterly numbers to meet. But the vendors and CIO or CISO and champions who resist that pressure, who keep one eye on the immediate deliverable and one eye on the relationship they are building are the ones who end up with something sustainable: a win-win for all parties—the CIO, CISO, champion, vendor and CFO. This is a complex web of relationships and getting all parties to be ok with the outcome is not easy.

> Note
>
> *The key elements for success in juggling the tension between the need for stellar performance and functionality (CIO and Operations), and cost and risk (CFO and CRO):*
>
> - *A clear problem definition of a business issue that all stakeholders agree is worth solving and that they are ALL committed to allocating resources to achieve a strong outcome.*
> - *All stakeholders sign-off the version 1 business case: This business case must be updated as the project progressed and re-signed-off at regular project reviews e.g. monthly. This avoids "flogging a dead horse" (continuity to progress and fund a project even when it is clear to most stakeholders that it is a waste of time. This will not solve the problem and/or is too costly).*
> - *Conduct a rigorous proof of concept (POC) and review outcomes at regular project reviews with a "go" or "no-go" sign-off by all stakeholders.*
>
> **Tony White – Former Qantas Chief Procurement Officer**

From a longer-term perspective, to create a win-win partnership with the CIO and CISO, focus must shift from being a transaction to win the contract, to sustaining a long-term operational alliance that balances the CIO's need for speed with the CISO's requirement for stability.

I recall in the past, making the CIO happy often meant making the CISO nervous. Innovation moved faster than governance could follow, security was treated as a constraint on delivery rather than a component of it, and the tension between the two roles was structural and largely accepted as the cost of moving quickly in a complex environment.

The AI era is changing that dynamic in a way that no previous technology wave quite managed and this represents a genuine window of opportunity for the vendor who understands what is actually shifting. The reason the dynamic is changing comes down to the nature of AI itself. Unlike previous technology waves where security could reasonably be crudely added on after the fact, AI introduces risks so fundamental that security governance must be established at the start.

This means the CISO can no longer be positioned as a brake on the CIO's innovation agenda, because the CIO who moves fast without embedding AI governance is accumulating risk at a pace that will eventually result in a serious incident.

I'd argue that AI is pulling both roles toward a common goal. The CIO needs the CISO to make AI safe enough to deploy at scale. The CISO needs the CIO to move fast enough that the organisation's AI governance capability keeps pace with the threat landscape.

The vendor who can speak credibly to both sides of that equation, whose solution demonstrably accelerates innovation while treating security and governance at the start, will be popular.

> Note
>
> *The modern CISO is no longer just a technical gatekeeper. Across technology choices, procurement, and cultural change, the role has evolved into one of orchestration. The goal is to balance simplicity with depth, remove friction without compromising rigor, and leverage AI without losing human judgment. The CISOs who succeed are those who move beyond being "defenders" to becoming enablers of better, faster, and more informed decision-making.*
>
> **Abbas Kudrati – Chief Identity Security Advisor, Silverfort**

Now, for the partnership to be seen as a win-win, your relationship with the CIO and CISO must prioritize operational stability, providing tools that are consistent rather than adding unnecessary technical complexity. Predictable performance is the baseline the CIO and CISO will both expect. No one will want to buy a fancy tool that creates "firefighting" work.

Indeed, true partnership requires you to subordinate short-term sales pressure to long-term client value. Gerard Florian, former Group Executive and CIO at ANZ Bank, describes what this looks like from the buyer's side well.

> Note
>
> *The single biggest factor is genuinely wanting the right thing for the client—even if that does not mean a sale this time. Trusted partnerships have genuine "win-win" for both parties. But that will occur around a real need. When the client has a need that the partner can address*

> *well, great things happen. When the partner simply has a new solution looking for a problem, trust is eroded.*
>
> *In order to find this need, the best partners I have had took the time to understand the business context, became students of the industry, and brought me relevant and timely information – e.g. case studies that were similar to my situation.*
>
> **Gerard Florian – former ANZ Bank Group Executive & CIO**

At the core of the matter, a win-win is not a negotiation where both sides calculate what they are willing to concede to get to a deal; that is only a transaction dressed up as a partnership. A genuine win-win starts with a different instinct entirely: the willingness to give, *without* expecting a favor in return.

> Note
>
> *Too many people approach a CIO or CISO thinking about what they want to gain, when the real opportunity starts with what you are willing to give.*
>
> *Real relationships are built on curiosity and the discipline of truly listening. Understand what keeps them awake at night, what they are trying to achieve, and where they need genuine support.*
>
> *Sometimes the most powerful thing you can do is help without expecting anything in return. Those moments plant seeds of credibility that grow over time.*
>
> *When the relationship is real and the value is consistent, opportunities come back in ways you never anticipated. If you want to stand out, stop trying to sell first. Start by becoming the trusted partner they are glad to hear from.*
>
> **Shamane Tan – Founder & Growth Strategist, AMBA**

I've seen many instances of new emerging vendors arrive with genuinely clever technology and cannot understand why deals move slowly or stall altogether. The answer is rarely the technology; it is most commonly (as I explain throughout this book) the case that the CIO and the CISO have not yet been given a reason to believe that this vendor understands their world. When you can provide them with this, they feel comfortable supporting you. This is truly a win-win scenario in practice.

Note

Emerging technology vendors do not win large enterprise deals just because the technology is clever. They win when senior buyers believe the vendor understands their world, can reduce risk, and can create measurable value without making the enterprise feel like an experiment.

For scaleups with real customer references, the challenge is not proving that the product works somewhere. It is proving that it can work here, in this customer's environment, with their architecture, their risk profile, their operating model, and their business priorities. That requires an investment in a local presence and patience.

It's about creating customer pull rather than being pushy. That is where trust is built.

Sundar Iyer – Managing Director, Emertel

The spirit of true win-win is thus teaming together for a joint purpose. Matt Boon, Senior Director of Strategic Research at Adapt, shared this in terms of a simple high school adage.

Note

A lot of the time when we were getting our reports in high school, it wasn't always about the grades you got. It was about the effort you put in to get that grade, right? So, a true partnership is having that ongoing effort working together to strive for that outcome together.

Matt Boon – Senior Director, Strategic Research, Adapt

A genuinely good vendor deal is not simply one that favours the enterprise; it is one that works for both parties over time.

As a CIO I observed a large regional contract with a vendor who was losing money in some markets while remaining profitable in others. This felt like a win on paper but was never truly sustainable in the long-term. Your commercial health within the relationship is itself a risk dimension which can affect CIO and CISO trust. A deal that doesn't work for you will eventually stop working for the enterprise too. CISO Lee's Barney's perspective is aligned with this thinking.

Note

I always leave something on the table for the vendor. If you've cut the costs to the bone then they have nothing left to protect; service quality often suffers.

Business should be mutually beneficial. We should pay a fair price for good service, and the vendor should want to keep our business. It still amazes me how many people negotiate as if

> *they're in an episode of* Suits, *trying to win the moment rather than build a strong partnership based on trust and maintained by fair compensation.*
>
> **Lee Barney – CISO, Ventia**

The vendor who understands this rhythm, and who is willing to walk alongside the CIO and CISO, rather than push ahead of them, is the one who earns the partnership that makes the win-win possible.

But don't be under any illusion that this is easy. If you ask any CIO or CISO they will tell you that they have a trusted partnership with only a handful of vendors. However, it's possible and well worth the investment.

Everything that I have covered in this chapter has been about the behaviors and the mindset that separate vendors who earn lasting trust from those who remain permanently transactional.

I'm aware that many of my CIO and CISO peers are frustrated by the current sales process, but at the same time they can all quote examples of building trust and creating genuine partnerships. There are practices that are both good and bad. The next chapter is my attempt to change this for the better. It's a chapter full of perspectives and quotations from the CIO, CISO, champion, vendor, and advisor community. These are all candid and offered in the genuine belief that these thoughts are more valuable shared than kept to themselves.

Summary

In this chapter I've argued that a strong vendor–organization partnership is built on deep strategic alignment and sustained by trust. From my own scar tissue, I've learned that trust is not given but needs to be earned through consistent behavior across four dimensions: transparency, reliability, commitment, and alignment.

When both parties hold themselves to these standards, something important shifts, and the relationship moves from transactional toward a solid partnership. Positive conditions for mutual growth and a win-win partnership benefit both sides.

The key learnings from this chapter are:

- **Trust is the foundation of every partnership** – it is not a milestone to be reached but a currency that compounds through consistent behavior and depletes quickly when your conduct falls short.
- **The vendor-champion relationship is the connective tissue of the partnership** – the champion advocates internally and provides context and access, while the vendor

delivers expertise and enables success, but neither can achieve lasting outcomes without genuine mutual trust.

- **Trust is built through four behaviours: transparency, reliability, commitment, and alignment** – each must be demonstrated repeatedly and under pressure, because it is how both parties behave when things are difficult that matters.
- **Trust can be destroyed faster than it is built** – ethical failures in particular cut deepest and recover slowest, because they cause the CIO and CISO to question not just the vendor's performance but their character.
- **A genuine win-win requires both parties to prioritise the long-term relationship over short-term gain** – a deal that doesn't work commercially for the vendor will eventually stop working for the enterprise too.

22

Book of Secrets

Reaching home base takes persistence, problem-solving, and knowing a few things most vendors never figure out and that most internal champions learn the hard way.

This chapter is a collection of hard-won secrets and pearls of wisdom gathered directly from CIOs, CISOs, advisors, and tech vendors who've seen both sides of the table. Whether you are an external salesperson trying to break through or perhaps an internal champion building the case from the inside, these insights are worthy of your reflection.

If you reflect on these perspectives and change how you show up with the CIO and CISO then the net effect will be significant. If not, then you are only going through the motions without considering how you can improve. Going back to the baseball analogy, we go to practice to get better at our craft. If we just play the game and skip practice, then it is much harder to make these improvements.

It is clear from the insights in this chapter that the current sales process is frustrating for most, and most are willing to share advice and tips that work personally for them. I'd like to acknowledge the various contributors of these quotations here for their generous willingness to provide these perspectives.

The insights in this chapter are organized around the following sections:

- Home run secrets
- First base secrets
- Second base secrets
- Third base secrets

Home run secrets

Let's start with the end in mind: getting ourselves a positive outcome with a winning home run! Getting to home base means we have closed the deal and have the start of a successful (hopefully) partnership.

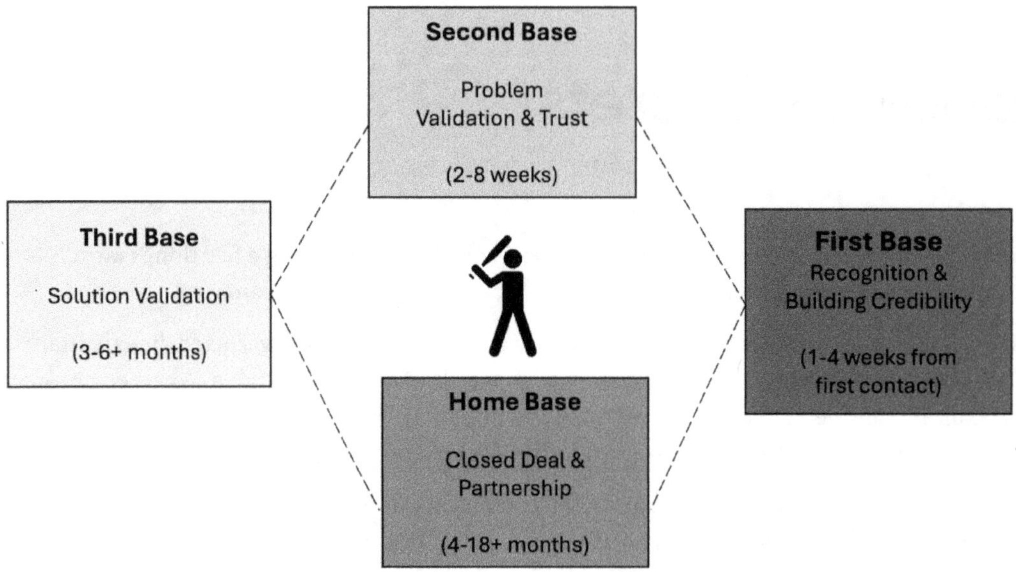

Figure 22.1 - Reaching home base

Some of the most valuable insights in this industry are hiding in plain sight, known to practitioners but never written down. These are not necessarily all diamonds and precious gems, as this will depend on your own progress; however, this buried treasure shouldn't remain a secret—it deserves to be recognized as industry truth.

Before I share secrets from industry leaders, I'd like to first sum up some of my own secrets from my own personal learnings.

The CIO and CISO are also selling (help them internally)

One of the least understood realities of these roles is that the CIO and CISO are constantly selling themselves internally for budget, for resources, for organizational support, and sometimes simply for their seat at the table.

Your job as a vendor and that of your champion therefore is not to sell to them but to "sell with them", providing the benchmark data, business cases, peer comparisons, and structured insights that make their internal case easier to build and harder to reject. The sales executive who genuinely understands this dynamic starts feeling like a partner. This shift in perception is worth more than any pitch deck.

Careers are at risk

The typical CIO or CISO spends somewhere between two and four years in any given executive role. That tenure is not always a reflection of performance; these are positions filled with political tension, competing agendas, and decisions that carry personal as well as organizational consequences.

Every significant technology investment is, in some sense, a career bet. Your job is to understand that reality and speak to how your solution reduces business risk and their personal risk exposure. A vendor who helps a CIO or CISO look smart and in control of their environment is one they will remember and return to.

Budget timing is everything

Technology budgets rarely follow a straight line. The CIO and CISO are subject to business headwinds that can reduce their budgets without warning, and they will often find themselves with unspent funds late in the financial year that need to be surrendered back to the CFO.

Your job is to be trusted enough that when that window opens, you are the first call they make. That level of trust is not built in the final weeks of the financial year; it is built over months of consistent, credible engagement so that asking for your assistance is natural to the CIO and CISO.

Uncover the actual root cause

Not everything that matters can be stated openly in a meeting room. CIOs and CISOs are frequently carrying awareness of unmitigated risks and regulatory pressures that they cannot always surface plainly in front of a vendor.

The root cause is lack of trust. This is obvious but the role that you play as a vendor is to create enough trust and psychological safety in the relationship that they feel comfortable sharing real issues with you. I'd argue that the vendors who get to this layer of the conversation are the ones who become genuinely indispensable.

Peer cheat codes

I've always felt that CIOs and CISOs have limited time to network, but the peers with whom they do maintain relationships are among their most trusted voices. These are often more trusted than any analyst report, case study, or reference call you can arrange through official channels.

I know from my own experience that an unsolicited endorsement from one of these peers carries a weight that no formal sales process can replicate. A quiet word of endorsement from a trusted peer is the cheat code that shortcuts years of trust-building in a single moment.

That shared, the rest of this section is comprised of a series of insights that I've gained from asking an incredible range of CIOs, CISOs, and other executives targeted questions about how to achieve a "home run".

Q: What one piece of advice would you give vendors who want to work with you?

Get to know the buyer. Use your contacts, do research, etc., and spend time building a trusted relationship. I do not expect perfection from vendors; I expect mutual trust and those that go out of their way to build a relationship and are not just transactional usually win far more work.

Paul O'Rourke – former CISO, CRO and BCG Global Cyber Leader

Approach the relationship as a partner, not a transaction. Be prepared to share responsibility for outcomes, not just deliver a product. Understand our environment, be honest about fit, and stay engaged beyond the contract signature. Vendors who commit to customer success over quarterly targets are the ones who earn long-term relationships—and long-term business.

Sunil Varkey – CISO, Hexaware Technologies (Former HSBC CISO)

Do your homework—understand what I do, what my priorities probably are, what I probably know or don't know, and how you can genuinely help as a partner, not just to make money.

Dr Maria Milosavljevic – former ANZ Bank CISO

I'm the CISO for our group, and I feel it's a waste of time when vendors explain trends in cyber threats —which I'm already well aware of—as if they're teaching me something I don't know. It's astonishing how many vendors adopt this attitude.

Group CISO – Large Japanese bank

If I had one secret to share with buyers it would be this: stop selling a product and start understanding the environment in which the buyer operates. Walk in their shoes. There is nothing more powerful than backing your team and transferring risk from buyer to seller in the commercial agreement.

John Sutherland – Chief Digital Information Officer, Calvary Health Care

Q: What's a common misconception or approach that tech vendors get wrong when selling to CIOs and CISOs?

Tech vendors often overemphasize product features or price, neglecting alignment with business culture, technical support, and strategic outcomes. CIOs and CISOs prioritize security, compliance, and measurable impact. Adjust your strategy by focusing on business value, integration, and support, and by addressing pain points such as talent shortages and regulatory requirements. In this age of agentic AI, it's imperative that vendors match the AI maturity of their intended audience to chart a path forward that is feasible and gains the buy-in of the audience.

Linus Lai – Group Vice President, IDC

Price and quality scores are part and parcel of the evaluation scorecard. What will clinch it is whether we envisage that the initial relationship will progress from purely transactional, based on a service level agreement (SLA), to a long-term strategic partnership based on win-win outcomes.

Alvin Ong – Former CIO, Nanyang Technological University CIO

Successful vendors come prepared with real customer context and are specific about the risk or value gap they are addressing. They tailor their narrative to the stakeholder, not just the product. Those who fail often deliver generic decks or struggle to articulate how their solution integrates into existing IT and risk frameworks. Consistency, credibility, and case relevance drive early trust.

Michael Kazantzis – CEO, Cyborium

Vendors often underestimate how critical trust and long-term viability are in enterprise decisions. Overselling features, bundling unnecessary licenses, or applying pressure through executive escalation erodes confidence. Technology leaders are accountable for operational resilience, risk reduction, and measurable outcomes. If a vendor's strategy relies more on sales tactics than on demonstrable value, it raises immediate red flags.

Sunil Varkey – CISO, Hexaware Technologies (Former HSBC CISO)

As a bank CISO, if I see comparable tools, I don't just look at the tool you sell me. I look at how you treat your people. Vendor reputation matters. Constant layoffs? High turnover? Abusive managers? If that's your culture, I don't want to work with you.

A less-than-perfect product from a company that respects its employees will outperform the "best" product from a toxic workplace. Why? Because good people support their customers better, innovate faster, and make better partners. This factors into CISO purchase decisions. The formula for success is simple: Great Product + Kindness for your team = Success. It's not just what you do—it's how you do it.

Adam Palmer – CISO, First Hawaiian Bank

A vendor approached us to introduce their AI solution for business intelligence with a good understanding of industry and business needs, but the product was not mature yet (the vendor thought it was good enough, but it was not). We decided not to procure their AI product. After being informed, the vendor provided regular updates about their deeper understanding related to the business's unmet needs and value proposition, as well as the progress made in their product. After a while, we gave them another chance to share the proposal, which was satisfactory. The vendor offered a free proof of concept (POC) to prove the value. After confirming the outputs, we decided to contract with them.

Charlie Bai – Vice President and CIO, Information and Digital Solutions, Eli Lilly China

Q: Walk me through your sales process for a recent major deal with a CIO or CISO

The first critical moment was establishing agreement on the need to change, the timelines, and the vision of what good looks like. This first meeting was a casual one at a tradeshow, and I knew what was on the CISO's mind from his people. At that time, he was not clear who on his team could drive the change, but he wanted the change. We agreed the timing was off and that once he had someone onboard, we could reconnect. He did encourage us to continue working on getting people excited about the technology capabilities.

The second meeting was the second critical moment, when he had assigned someone. He remembered our first meeting and was open to hearing how we could make his assigned person successful, what the change process, timeline, and costs would look like.

Then a budget challenge was surfaced by the CISO and in the meeting we committed to find a creative financial structure that aligned to his budget constraints. The next critical moment was getting alignment on the structure (week later over the phone) and using that meeting to agree the process to close and program to start...throughout the engagement, we listened, and worked with the exec timelines and gaps and the critical stages allowed us to be in constant alignment rather than pushing a one sided agenda and timeline, focusing on mutual benefits and being open on needs and challenges on both sides.

Yigal Elstein – Chief Revenue Officer, Checkmarx

First base secrets

Achieving first base means we have gained some recognition and started the steep process of building credibility. But, as we have seen, getting to first base is not simple.

The sheer volume of vendors that are also trying to contact the CIO and CISO is overwhelming to the recipient. The multi-channel approaches of email, LinkedIn and phone calls are well trodden. What secrets can I share with you here? Allow me to provide some of the responses I received from key parties in the ecosystem on this.

Q: What do vendors do wrong in those first critical contact points?

Where vendors often go wrong is they go straight to detailed content and forget about the context of the need of the buyer. For C-Suite buyers, the content is less relevant, as others will make that call, but surety of who they are working with, trust, price, and other similar factors are key elements in the decision-making process.

Paul O'Rourke – former CISO, CRO and BCG Global Cyber Leader

Geez, this list is very long. Here you go:

- *STARTING a presentation with a bio of the founders.*
- *A slide of customer logos.*
- *A chart where your colors are all green and your competitors are a variation of yellow, red, and green.*
- *Complicated slides with lots of lines and boxes going in many directions.*
- *Asking a CISO if they're concerned with a certain aspect of security.*
- *Quoting research that your company funded to validate the existence of your business.*

And on, and on, and on.

Best ones just jump into a demo and explain the problem their company solves.

David Spark – Producer, Managing Editor, Co-Host at CISO Series

How not to annoy the CIO and CISO – respect their time and attention by proving relevance. Understand their priorities before pitching replacement ideas. Too many managed security service providers (MSSPs) or managed service providers (MSPs) lead with "let us replace your security operations center (SOC)" instead of first showing reliability through smaller proof points like a pen test or gap assessment. Earn permission before expansion.

Michael Kazantzis – CEO, Cyborium

I had a (very well known) vendor ask to speak to me and I agreed because of their reputation. They turned up and knew nothing of what we did or what our challenges might be. They essentially just asked me to spend time educating them because they could not be bothered doing their homework. The meeting lasted less than 10 minutes as I asked them to come back once they had done some research as I wasn't being paid to do their jobs for them. They were gobsmacked.

Dr Maria Miloslavljevic – former ANZ Bank CISO

The best opening is simple: Here is what we think you are trying to solve, here is why we think it matters, and here is where we may be wrong.

That tells me three things immediately. They have done some homework. They have formed a view. And they are willing to be corrected. That combination earns attention because it turns the meeting into a useful working conversation rather than a performance.

The worst opening is the company history slide, followed by a generic logo wall and a scripted product tour. (Happens more often than you want!) I do not need to know what year you were founded. I need to know whether you understand my constraints, my operating model, my risk appetite, and the business outcome I am trying to create.

If the first 10 minutes are about the seller, the next 50 usually are too. If the first 10 minutes are about the problem, I lean in.

Ram Kalyanasundaram – Chief Information and Digital Officer, Harris Farm Markets

I know lots of executives who don't make time to meet with, or curate relationships with vendors: "They always want to sell me something!". In my experience, good partnerships look very different. Selling me something I don't need or not fit for purpose is usually a one-time deal...I'm not buying from you again! But many sellers who partner with me have sold to me multiple times at multiple vendors. Of course, product is key—but knowing it's backed by someone who has taken the time in invest in my problem space and has had the patience to work with me is priceless. Similarly, I have had long term relationships with sellers who may have never sold me anything—the value of meeting once every 6 months to hear what their customers are doing and keeping in touch across the radially evolving landscape is worth the time.

Andrew Dell – General Manager, Microsoft, and CISO

The biggest mistake is assuming I am buying technology. I am not. I am buying business confidence. That confidence can take different forms: a better customer experience, faster operating rhythm, lower risk, more resilient service, cleaner data, better decisions, or the ability to scale without adding complexity. The technology matters, but only because it enables those outcomes.

Vendors also underestimate the consequence of a bad fit in lean operating environments. In very large enterprises, a poor solution may be absorbed by layers of process, specialist teams, and governance. In a leaner organization, the consequences are felt personally and quickly by the executive team, the frontline, and the customer. That changes the trust bar.

Features get you into the room. Confidence keeps you there. The seller who understands that will spend less time telling me what the product can do and more time showing me how the organization will be better after we adopt it.

Ram Kalyanasundaram – Chief Information and Digital Officer, Harris Farm Markets

I always make my decisions based on how well the solution addresses our company's challenges, its compatibility with our technology stack, cost, and operational feasibility. Vendors seem to assume that if they cite the names of my peers as references, I will adopt their solution, but that is merely a supplementary factor—it is not the primary determinant of my decision.

Group CISO – Large Japanese bank

Q: What advice would you offer technology and cyber vendors who want to be taken seriously by CIOs and CISOs?

Do the research, lead with outcomes, and behave like you'll be there on their worst day. Because after all these years, the principle hasn't changed: people buy from people they trust.

Show you understand their world before the first call.

Make the value defensible to the board.

Don't sell a tool—sell a capability with a measurable delta.

Tell the truth about trade-offs.

Sam Ghebranious – Director, Axcelerate / Senior Advisor, Frost & Sullivan

Stop selling. Start being useful. Tell me you've researched my business and understand our problems. Then pick a problem you want to talk to me about.

The sellers I remember are the ones who helped before there was a deal. They shared an article I had not seen. They introduced me to someone credible. They challenged a piece of my thinking in a way that made the strategy better. They told me when their product was not the right fit. None of that is "sales activity" in the narrow sense, but all of it creates trust.

The winning message is simple: "I have walked in your shoes, I understand the operational friction you face, and I am here to support your broader strategy, not just pitch a tool."

Jayant Dave – CISO, Check Point Software

Useful is not a tactic. It is a posture. If the relationship only comes alive in the quarter where you need a signature, I can feel that. If the relationship has been useful over time, the first commercial conversation is much easier because credibility has already been built. The relationship begins long before a deal, and it is proven when there is no deal on the table.

Ram Kalyanasundaram – Chief Information and Digital Officer, Harris Farm Markets

A top successful engagement with a CISO was one that had several key points aligned:

- *Personal chemistry – execs want to be reassured that the person they deal with is capable and empowered to make them and their teams successful. They know that not all journeys are smooth and knowing someone is on the hook to make them successful, in conversation with the CISO I was able to establish some common past experiences that made my customers successful that he was able to identify with, that created an environment of trust as I spoke about a customer that he knows, the execs that I operated with.*
- *Excellent prep ahead of the meeting and knowing what is important to the CISO, such that the meeting is focused more, and validation and establishing a relationship of trust. My team was able to find a champion/change agent that wanted to drive new technology in and fix several issues where there was a security concern. This change was in alignment with what the CISO wanted to see from an outcome standpoint in the coming 12 months, meaning there was vision, needs and timing alignment.*

- *Being clear and data driven, factual and to the point, with no use of big words—just simple, plain English. Be realistic and talk about our experience making other customers (with the same profile, size, and industry) successful with our technology.*
- *Agreeing to a cadence that will ensure success and asking for early escalation rather than sticking to protocol, so handing them my mobile number should anything go wrong between reviews.*

Yigal Elstein – Chief Revenue Officer, Checkmarx

Q: What's something you got wrong early in your career selling to CIOs and CISOs?

Early days showing up with your company agenda to the meeting rather the agenda that is of top interest for the CxO, talking about your company rather than the CxO's, and only after talking about your company, referencing why what you are sharing is relevant to the CxO, and what they are trying to achieve. No sufficient prep, not enough thought on the desired outcome, thinking an extra future meeting is a good outcome.

You learn quickly that execs have no time to waste. If you can start by agreeing on what a good outcome for the meeting is and drive the meeting toward it while being sensitive to time, you will have great outcomes. If you are done before time is up, give them time back—they will be super appreciative.

Yigal Elstein – Chief Revenue Officer, Checkmarx

Q: What are the most common reasons for CIOs or CISOs disengaging from vendors early in the buying process

Allow me to paraphrase Michael Porter. He said that the essence of a good strategy is not what you choose to do, but what you choose not to do. So, if your strategy is not clear, it makes it hard to distinguish what to focus on, what cold calls to respond to, etc. You might wonder if you should return one of these 50 cold calls. Do you get on the phone, email, or LinkedIn?

Scott Collary – Group CIO, Westpac Group

Disengagement usually comes from misalignment of timing and tone. If a vendor leads with "why we're different" instead of "how we help you succeed given your stage of maturity," it breaks trust. Credibility gaps, for instance, overstating AI capabilities, or lacking proof of integration, are another factor. Often, vendors lose traction because they don't simplify complexity or respect the buyer's limited time.

Michael Kazantzis – CEO, Cyborium

Disengagement happens when the vendor doesn't move the CISO's objective. If the vendor can't tie value to the customer's current reality, the CISO cuts it early.

They didn't do the homework, so the first call becomes discovery theater.

They sell a tool, but the customer needs a capability (workflow, ownership, evidence).

They introduce operational cost (more alerts, more integrations, more admin) without reducing risk.

They can't answer "What improves in 90 days?"

They talk prevention only and ignore response and recovery (CISOs live in the "what if it happens" world).

Sam Ghebranious – Director, Axcelerate / Senior Advisor, Frost & Sullivan

Q: Vendors want to know your future strategy but that is confidential and perhaps not yet approved. How then do vendors learn about your plans so that they can better match your needs?

Future strategy is, by definition, confidential, and often not yet approved internally. A vendor who expects a CIO or CISO to hand it over, even a trusted one, has misread the relationship. The most a trusted partner should expect is a glimpse, and even that is earned. So, the real question is not how to extract the strategy, but how to infer it responsibly without ever asking the CISO to breach a confidence.

The answer, again, is context. A genuine partner should understand the maturity journey the CIO or CISO has been on—and the easiest, most willingly shared part of that journey is the past. Executives talk far more freely about what they have already done, what worked, and why. Listen to that and you learn where they have built strong foundations. From there, the forward view assembles itself in three layers:

Where they will fortify—the good foundations they will want to strengthen further.

Where they will build—the next problem they are likely to solve, or the next iteration of maturity they are anticipating.

Where they are quiet—the areas they mention only in passing. Sometimes that silence means it is simply not a focus. But sometimes it is something they are still wrestling with and are hesitant to surface in full. A true partner will usually have heard it raised more than once, even obliquely, and recognize the pattern.

Layer your own industry insight on top of this—what you have seen their peers do, what is emerging in adjacent markets, where maturity curves typically head next—and you can gauge their likely next moves with real accuracy. You arrive at a credible view of their strategy not because they told you, but because you understood where they came from, where they are now, and what usually comes next. That is the difference between a vendor fishing for confidential information and a partner who already understands the direction of travel.

Jimmy Wong – Former AIA Australia CISO

Having a few key trusted partners aligned with you, they sometimes will have a better view of what's coming next and how that may apply. Working with them on future capability opens what's possible to achieve better and faster in the strategy and frankly has allowed us to adjust strategy at times.

Scott Collary – Group CIO, Westpac Group

Q: Tell me about the best vendor interaction you've ever had?

The vendor had come in very prepared and knew our environment, our challenges, and tabled a one-page perspective on how others had addressed the challenges we were facing in our industry. They were engaged immediately.

Paul O'Rourke – former CISO, CRO and BCG Global Cyber Leader

The best vendor interaction I've had started with understanding and value, not a sales pitch. A former CISO and senior leader gave an expert presentation at a conference. Later, he advised me at no cost and even presented to my team with good practical advice. That earned instant credibility. He brought leadership depth and experience to the discussion. Instead of overpromising, he admitted what their product couldn't do and advised us on other solutions for solving part of our problem. That honesty built long-term trust. They eventually won the deal—and have remained a valued partner.

Adam Palmer – CISO, First Hawaiian Bank

When the vendor wants to show you this new product and explain its functionality with no expectation of selling it to you.

Debra Baker – CEO, trusted CISO

The best vendor engagements feel less like a sales cycle and more like the beginning of a long-term partnership. What stood out was the vendor's ability to bring the right people to the table early—technical leadership, product experts, customer success, and even executive sponsorship. That demonstrated organizational commitment, not just individual sales effort.

More importantly, they focused on solving our problems, not showcasing their full product catalog. They were transparent about where their solution fit, where it didn't, and how it would evolve. That level of honesty builds trust—and trust is what ultimately accelerates decisions.

Sunil Varkey – CISO, Hexaware Technologies (Former HSBC CISO)

After over a decade evaluating tech at a massive scale for Citi and now advising on the other side as a Field CISO for Check Point Software, I see one constant point of failure. Vendors pitch products, but buyers need controls. The best interactions happen when a vendor understands specific business dynamics, risk appetite, and existing investments before they even open their mouth. The technology is secondary to the business context.

But let's be fair, this goes both ways. As a buyer, you have an obligation to ensure your vendor understands your pain points. Staying quiet during (in fact, this should be done prior to the meeting) a pitch helps no one.

Jayant Dave – CISO, Check Point Software

The best vendor interaction I have had was with a seller who told me not to buy what they were selling. We were in the middle of a major transformation and looking at how our future architecture should work. This vendor had every commercial reason to push for a larger footprint. Instead, they came to the meeting and said, in effect, "You should not extend this product into the new environment. The use case has moved on." They had done the work, understood where we were going, and were prepared to reduce their own revenue because it was the right answer for us.

That meeting stayed with me because trust was created at the exact point where most trust is lost. They separated their sales target from my long-term outcome. They also said it openly, in front of their own senior leadership, which told me it was not theater.

They left that meeting with less revenue and more trust. The next time I had a problem in their space, they were one of the first people I called. That is what good selling looks like at the executive level: useful honesty before commercial convenience.

Ram Kalyanasundaram – Chief Information and Digital Officer, Harris Farm Markets

The best vendor interactions come from a deep understanding of my operational context, risk landscape, and business priorities. When the conversation focuses on real gaps and outcomes, it stops feeling like a sales discussion and becomes a collaborative dialogue.

Franco Marconcini – Group CISO, Electrolux Professional

The best interaction with a vendor was in around 2010/11 when I engaged with vendor XYZ. At the time, XYZ was still a relatively new company and had only recently begun to enter Australia. So, from the outset, they needed some referenceable customers to succeed in the market, and they had a lot of skin in the game. That means they were open to investing and building relationships that worked. Too often this is not the case, but it often is for smaller or newer companies and that is often a good place to start. It can come with risk, of course, because they may fail, but there's a golden window of opportunity with startups and scaleups.

The main thing that I initially found good about their interaction was that (at least at that time) they didn't send salespeople who had no technical clue, but they sent real engineers. I cannot stand a vacuous sales pitch and so this got my attention. I could ask serious engineering and design questions and get answers on the spot, not having to wait and then getting a "glossy" answer. I was looking for an open platform which was flexible enough (in terms of data architecture) for us to integrate highly disparate data and run security models across this data quickly and seamlessly. At the time, XYZ's data platform was immature, but its user interface was excellent and highly adaptable. So, I also wanted to be able to design and plug in a more sophisticated data layer (nearer the bottom of the stack) as well as building AI/analytics models on top, with the tool providing the integration and orchestration layer in between.

I had a very small data science and engineering team at the time, and I knew that as we developed new analytics models, we would not have the capacity to continue to support and sustain them all while allowing time to continue to build new ones solving more and more challenges. So most importantly, we were able to negotiate an arrangement which was a genuine win-win, akin to what now might be called a public-private partnership. In essence, the deal was that as we developed our data platform, tools, and new models, XYZ would take all the IP (as we were a government agency without our own commercialization interests) and then build it into their platform and return updates to their application with these now fully supported by them. This allowed my team to remain flexible and move from solving one problem to the next.

Another standout of this experience was that XYZ embedded engineers and data scientists into my team, and the camaraderie was excellent. We even had competitions to see which team could solve major challenges first, and this really helped build a seamless relationship.

Dr Maria Miloslavljevic – former ANZ Bank CISO

Q: Now the flip side—what's the worst sales experience you've had recently?

The sales team came in for a proposal presentation and were totally unprepared. The material they presented was highly generic, it had references to another client on their slides, and they had obviously put no effort into understanding either the content or who they were presenting to.

Paul O'Rourke – former CISO, CRO and BCG Global Cyber Leader

The worst experiences usually involve trying to force-fit a solution through executive relationships or procurement bundling, despite clear misalignment with our environment. When a vendor pushes a "strategic add-on" that does not address a real operational need, it signals short-term quota pressure over long-term partnership.

These tactics may win a deal on paper, but they damage credibility and rarely survive renewal cycles. Technology leaders remember when they were sold something they didn't need.

Sunil Varkey – CISO, Hexaware Technologies (former HSBC CISO)

My worst sales experience recently would be being harassed on LinkedIn by an overseas startup. When I didn't respond in time, they sent a message saying, "clearly cybersecurity is not important to you." I mean, who says that to a CISO? Fortunately, it didn't get any worse, because I blocked the sender and will not work with that startup.

Nigel Hedges – Executive General Manager & CISO, Chemist Warehouse

Selling to the wrong exec, assuming they are in power to make the decision, and realizing after the fact that the decision was made by someone else. Not all security decisions are made by the CISO. For example, we are seeing more and more application security testing decisions being made by the CTO and CIO.

We had a deal with great alignment with the CISO. We met, and the meetings seemed very good and positive. He then said he would take the offer for final approval to his boss, the CTO, and this is where it all went wrong. The competition was selling to the CTO and won the deal.

Yigal Elstein – Chief Revenue Officer, Checkmarx

Most vendors simply do not understand that I don't have time to meet with everyone. Unless I have a burning issue that I know a vendor can assist with, I usually ask vendors to meet with my direct reports first, who will then help to prioritize whom I meet with. On multiple occasions, vendors have escalated if they don't get time with me. In government, this is often to a minister and in the private sector, the CIO, CEO or board members. This only annoys me—it doesn't make me think more highly of them.

Dr Maria Miloslavljevic – former ANZ Bank CISO

The absolute worst experiences happen when a vendor ignores a specific problem and tries to sell their entire catalog. A CIO calls a vendor to solve a specific Zero Trust use case. That is the mandate. When the salesperson immediately pivots to a broad discovery phase, asking for user counts, assets, and global locations just to pitch their entire platform, they lose all credibility.

Jayant Dave – CISO, Check Point Software

It is striking how unprepared some vendors are when meeting a potential customer. I had recently the case of one of them that got our company name wrong, showed no understanding of our business, and he did not know who he was speaking to. These are all signals of lack of professionalism. Meetings with vendors that are not properly prepared add no value and waste everyone's time.

Franco Marconcini – Group CISO, Electrolux Professional

The worst sales experience is rarely bad because the product is weak. They are bad because the seller has not listened.

A recent example was a long proposal (90 pages!) that clearly came from a previous conversation, a previous problem and, frankly, a previous buyer. We had already spent time explaining what we were trying to solve. The response came back as if none of that context had landed. It was polished, but it was not relevant. That is worse than an imperfect proposal that shows real understanding.

The issue was the assumption behind it: that the buyer is a checkpoint in a sales process that has already been designed somewhere else. When I see that before contract signature, I assume I will see it again during delivery.

The other behavior that damages trust quickly is bypassing the accountable buyer after a clear "not now". Escalation is sometimes appropriate, but only when it is transparent and grounded in a genuine business risk or missed context. Going around the person who owns the decision may create a short-term meeting. It usually destroys the long-term relationship.

Ram Kalyanasundaram – Chief Information and Digital Officer, Harris Farm Markets

Second base secrets

To make it to second base we must have engaged in problem validation and in that process started to build a degree of trust. This is where most vendors will mess up and assume that as they now understand the problem, that in pitching harder they can only secure the deal.

In truth, second base is about building more trust from your starter level base. These relationships will be mandatory to get to home base, and this can't be rushed. I would add any trust that you have built with the CIO and CISO is still fragile and needs to continue to be earned.

Q: What makes a great POC?

A great POC doesn't validate features. Rather, it proves business value. If the outcome is just "the tech works," you missed the point. The best POCs measure real impact such as time saved, quicker response times, improved customer experience, and enabling new competitive differentiators. That means testing with real workflows and involving the teams whose productivity actually drives the business.

Just as important, a strong POC evaluates the vendor as a partner in driving that value. How quickly can they help you realize outcomes? Do they understand your business pressures and demonstrate success with similar organizations? The goal is to walk away with a clear, quantified case for change that executives and line-of-business leaders can stand behind with confidence.

Bradon Rogers – Chief Customer Officer, Island

Q: How can I encourage architects and champions to bring great new ideas forward?

Part of the architect's job is to figure out and suggest new ideas.

Scott Collary – Group CIO, Westpac Group

As a technology executive, I was always hunting for creative ways of doing things, and I learned that some of the best disruption comes from within. So, the first thing I'd say to any CIO or CISO is: make it clear to your architect or champion that bold ideas are wanted. The enterprise that encourages internal disruption is the one that grows from strength to strength over the long term.

But encouragement must be a two-way trust. I extended trust to my architects and champions, and in return I asked them to trust me with their thinking, to be brave enough to put their best ideas on the table, knowing I would see them as emerging leaders in their own right. A true leader never holds back their people's brightest ideas; you treasure them like jewels, and you let the hidden gems be exposed and shine. You want your team to be successful, and these are exactly the moments that reveal who your future leaders are—your successors, your right and left hands.

And I'll be honest; there's a more self-interested reason too. When your architect or champion succeeds, even if they hold the credit, it's the surest evidence that you've built a genuinely high-performing team. Their boldness becomes your reputation.

Jimmy Wong – Former AIA Australia CISO

To encourage internal champions/architects to bring great new ideas forward, I first identify and agree on the problems to solve, establish a psychologically safe environment, encourage divergent thinking and just listen.

Hackathons can be a great catalyst for this.

Jason Poley – Former Macquarie Group Head of Engineering

Q: What patterns do you see among vendors that successfully make it onto early consideration lists vs. those that never get past the initial screening?

A vendor who understands the problem will first speak the language of outcomes, not features. They'll reference the business context behind the challenge, showing familiarity with the industry environment. They don't rush into demos; they validate compatibility and assumptions collaboratively. By contrast, a "marketed" vendor often leads with accolades and product slides, ignoring whether the solution would even fit the organization at a basic level.

Michael Kazantzis – CEO, Cyborium

Lead with understanding and value, not features. Don't tell me your product is special—show me you understand how to solve my specific problem. At the end of the day, I don't buy tools, I buy outcomes. Solve my pain points in risk reduction, efficiency, and compliance.

Adam Palmer – CISO, First Hawaiian Bank

Winners demonstrate clarity of purpose: they solve a specific problem better than others, integrate cleanly into the environment, and reduce operational complexity rather than add to it.

They also show partnership behaviors—roadmap transparency, responsiveness, strong customer references, and a willingness to adapt commercially and technically. Features may open the door, but alignment and execution close the deal.

Sunil Varkey – CISO, Hexaware Technologies (former HSBC CISO)

Being on early lists is about confidence, not features. The winners usually do three things early: they pick a real wedge (a painful gap) and solve it cleanly, or bring a point of view based on patterns they've seen (not a generic pitch), or can show day-two reality: who does what, what changes, what gets measured.

While the ones that fail try to be everything to everyone, hide the operational load until later, or cannot articulate what changes after an incident.

Sam Ghebranious – Director, Axcelerate / Senior Advisor, Frost & Sullivan

Q: How do vendors ensure that their technology is best positioned with the research analyst in terms of capabilities and market position?

The best organizations ensure accuracy by providing transparent, evidence-based information, facilitating access to customer references, and proactively correcting misconceptions. They engage in regular briefings, share product roadmaps, and encourage analyst feedback. This builds trust and ensures research reflects true capabilities and market position.

Linus Lai – Group Vice President, IDC

Q: If you could give one piece of advice to technology and cyber vendors who want to work more effectively alongside firms like yours and genuinely help CIOs and CISOs succeed, what would it be?

My simple advice to technology and cyber vendors who want to work more effectively with firms like us would be:

- *Be genuine. Don't push your product or agenda.*

- *Align to the strategic priorities of the client rather than your own narrative.*
- *Embrace interoperability: clients don't want point solutions; they want ecosystems.*
- *Listen first. Invest time in understanding the client's business drivers and goals.*
- *Speak in business terms rather than tool language;*
- *Lastly, don't let your sales target drive your behavior.*

Gautam Kapoor – Cybersecurity Lead, Accenture

Third base secrets

Securing third base requires your proposed solution to be validated as the real deal. This is indeed the stage that is showtime—your solution will get more scrutiny and be exposed to a broader range of stakeholders in detail.

This is where I've seen organizational politics, slow procurement processes, and tempers tested. The CIO and CISO are on center stage and will be more exposed, with this proposal often being one that must use political capital to gain business case approval.

From my own internal perspective, this is the hardest part, and the internal champion who has been a source of strength and energy in driving this proposal also has their credibility on the line. Perfect solutions can and do fail to get past this base, and I'm certain this will continue to be the reality. Let me share the insights I have gained from my industry peers on this stage.

Q: How can vendors facilitate procurement and legal at this stage?

The key is early engagement with both teams, so they understand the broader vision and strategy. Equally, there should be strong executive engagement between client and vendor so that any legal or commercial issues can be talked through at the right levels and quickly resolved.

Gerard Florian – Former ANZ Bank Group Executive & CIO

Q: How do you evaluate the true total cost of ownership?

As a CFO or Risk Committee Chair, I am looking for a true understanding of the costs of adapting to the new technology. Yes, there are the traditional components, but more than that:

- *What will be the impact on the clients/customers?*
- *Will the revenue suffer?*
- *Will the business attract more customers?*

- *Does this help us differentiate our business (model) from the competition?*
- *Now turn this into items in a business case that can be measured for accountability, as well as what the other costs are that we haven't considered:*
- *How will we now manage data?*
- *What would the cost of a breach be to our data or privacy?*
- *Do we have privacy factored in?*
- *What would a misstep do to our revenue?*

Factor these also into the overall business case (not just costs) so that they can be measured for accountability.

Geoff Stalley – Non-Executive Director and former CFO

The decision came down to how well the solution addressed a defined pain point, how smoothly it could be deployed, and how well it integrated into our existing ecosystem. Flexibility in licensing and professional services, a credible product roadmap, and executive commitment were also key factors.

What mattered less than vendors expected was headline pricing. Cost is important, but it does not outweigh operational fit, risk reduction, and long-term sustainability.

Sunil Varkey – CISO, Hexaware Technologies (former HSBC CISO)

Q: What market trends or shifts are CIOs and CISOs talking about now that vendors are still ignoring?

Vendors still underestimate the shift from tools to outcomes. The market is punishing vendors who add complexity without measurable uplift.

Control effectiveness as evidence, not assumptions.

Resilience under stress: response and recovery, not just prevention.

Consolidation pressure: fewer vendors, deeper trust, clearer outcomes.

Third-party and platform dependency: ecosystem risk is now a core risk.

Staffing reality: automation that reduces load, not creates it.

Sam Ghebranious – Director, Axcelerate / Senior Advisor, Frost & Sullivan

Q: When you're competing against other vendors for the same account, what gives you the edge?

Competing and winning requires you to align to the customer technical needs and desired outcomes, everything you mention forms part of this equation. One point you are missing is honesty; prospects and customers rely on you to achieve important outcomes, if you are not honest and win, you will later churn and damage your reputation, not just with the one account and few people in the account, but with more people you actually appreciate. The world is a very small place, execs are well connected to validate and get backdoor references. If you are not honest and do not deliver on what you said you will do, the market will know and it will work against you in more than one deal, one area, or one region.

The important part is to orchestrate all the points above when you understand the client needs, timeline, and challenges, and you align your sales campaign to them. Surely you can influence some of it, but you need to earn the right to do so. Trying to influence too early, too aggressively, will only backfire on you and your business.

Yigal Elstein – Chief Revenue Officer, Checkmarx

Q: How do you encourage your own internal vendor team talent to work with CIO and CISO internal champions?

When working hands-on with enterprise clients, it's crucial to engage the CxOs, the CxOs' teams, and pay attention to who actively supports initiatives, communicates openly, and is trusted by their peers. These champions often demonstrate a willingness to bridge gaps between departments and act as the voice of their colleagues, making it easier for outside experts to understand the nuances of the organizations. By fostering relationships through regular training, coaching, and mentoring, I encourage my top talent to prioritize innovation, trust, and collaboration. This approach helps them become natural extensions of the CxOs' team, aligning their goals with those of the leadership and making them invaluable assets to both their company and ours.

Martin Dube – Head of Enterprise Applications Solutions, Data & AI, NTT Data

Q: What is something vendors consistently get wrong about selling to someone in your role?

Many (vendors) consistently fail to separate hype from reality, especially in heavily regulated industries like financial services. They drop generic compliance acronyms like NIST, ISO, and PCI-DSS, thinking that checks the box. Those are baselines, not the primary risks the business is dealing with.

You must understand the specific regulatory, geopolitical, and data protection dynamics of the exact environment you are selling into. Deploying SASE for an online banking platform requires a completely different architecture than deploying it for a low-latency trading environment. Context is everything.

Jayant Dave – CISO, Check Point Software

In competitive tenders, winners are typically determined by product capabilities, alignment with business goals, technical support, and cultural fit, while price remains a contributing factor. Existing relationships and implementation approach matter, but evidence-based ROI and strategic alignment are decisive.

Linus Lai – Group Vice President, IDC

A recent decision involved selecting a platform to help accelerate AI adoption safely across the organization. What actually influenced the decision was not the longest feature list or the most impressive benchmark.

Four things mattered. First, could I build trust with the named person who would own the relationship locally? At our scale, vendor relationships are still human relationships. Second, did the privacy, security, and data handling position stand up in writing, not just in a sales conversation? Third, could a capable non-technical user create something useful quickly without needing a central technology team to translate every idea? Fourth, was the commercial model transparent enough that success would not create a pricing surprise in year two?

What vendors thought mattered, but mattered less, were generic benchmarks, overseas logos, and future roadmap promises. Those inputs are not irrelevant, but they are not decisive. A benchmark does not tell me whether my people will use the tool. A logo does not tell me whether the vendor will understand our context. A roadmap is useful only after the product in front of me already works.

The deciding question was: can this help real people do real work safely, quickly, and repeatedly?

Ram Kalyanasundaram – Chief Information and Digital Officer, Harris Farm Markets

Believing they can force a procurement to happen because they know someone important.

Dr Maria Miloslavljevic – former ANZ Bank CISO

Q: What behaviors consistently separate "great" clients from average ones when it comes to maximising value from strategic advisors during large-scale technology and cyber transformations?

In my mind great clients:

- *Engage at all levels and make it a collective priority for success. Average clients dump the responsibility on advisors.*
- *Co-own the journey. Treat advisors as partners, trusted advisors. Average clients want advisors to own everything.*
- *Bring advisors into decision making process and empower advisors. Average clients create bottlenecks in decision making process.*
- *Perceive success is co-owned. Average clients believe success is only theirs.*
- *Know the strength of the advisors and play to the strength. Average clients only find flaws and faults.*
- *Invite challenge. Average clients only seek rubber-stamps.*
- *Measure outcomes; average clients measure outputs.*
- *Build long term relationships; average clients treat it as a transaction.*

Gautam Kapoor – Cybersecurity Lead, Accenture

Summary

This chapter compiles candid wisdom from CIOs, CISOs, vendors, and advisors on what really works when selling technology solutions to senior executives in a crowded, competitive market.

The central theme is that successful vendors shift from transactional selling to genuine partnership—doing deep research, speaking the language of business outcomes, and helping executives navigate internal politics and budget cycles.

Trust is the ultimate currency across every stage of the sales process, from first contact to closing, and it is both hard-won and easily lost.

The key learnings from this chapter are:

- **Help them sell internally** – CIOs and CISOs are always selling upward for budget and resources. Vendors who provide benchmarks, business cases, and data to support that internal selling become trusted partners, not just vendors.

- **Do your homework** – CIOs and CISOs do not appreciate vendors that have not prepared well before speaking with them.
- **Sell outcomes, not features** – executives don't buy tools, they buy risk reduction, efficiency, and compliance. Lead with measurable outcomes and demonstrate how you solve a specific, real problem in their environment.
- **Earn trust incrementally** – trust built at each stage is fragile and must be continuously reinforced. Pushing too hard too early can destroy what little credibility you have established.
- **Align all stakeholders, not just the champion** – deals fail when vendors over-invest in one relationship and miss key decision-makers, whether that's the CFO, CTO, or procurement. Map the full stakeholder landscape early.
- **Be honest about fit and trade-offs** – overpromising, overselling, or hiding operational complexity destroys long-term credibility. This can come back to haunt you—executives remember, and the industry is smaller than it appears.
- **Behave like a long-term partner from day one** – the vendors who win and retain business show up with commitment, transparency, and a genuine interest in the customer's success, not just their own quarterly targets.

23

How to Be an MVP

The most valuable player (MVP), whether vendor or champion, is defined by a consistent standard of conduct, judgment, and ambition that compounds over time. They are the people that CIOs and CISOs call when they have a problem they have not yet told anyone else about. These are the select few established vendors that Procurement might wave through more easily because the trust has already been built. And they are the internal champions who get promoted into a new challenging role because they have proved to be a leader that gets great results consistently.

Throughout this book, we have examined the mechanics of the tech buying journey, including the stakeholders, the politics, and the friction inherent in this process. We have explored what it takes to earn the trust of a CIO or CISO who has seen every vendor pitch and heard every promise, navigate Procurement, and help build a business case that succeeds. But these mechanics alone will not make your career; they do not build a reputation that precedes you into a room or create the kind of relationships that survive a failed implementation or a missed deadline. That is what this final chapter is about.

This chapter is all about how to succeed in the long term and be a most valuable player (MVP) to the CIO and CISO. But allow me a moment to acknowledge the coincidence that this chapter (23) is about MVPs. The absolute greatest player in the world in my opinion is Michael Jordan, #23 for the Chicago Bulls. Michael Jordan (MJ) is the epitome of an MVP—he was a winner who dominated the game of basketball, winning six NBA championships and being a five-time MVP. (Michael Jordan also tried his hand at baseball with the Chicago White Sox and ended up playing one season with their minor league team. This just goes to show that even the greatest player, when they move to a different game, must start at the beginning and re-learn. This book has been designed with this in mind).

The CIO and CISO dearly want to play with winners that deliver results for their organization and at the same time, make them look good. As you know by this point, the average CIO and CISO has a difficult role, filled with navigating the politics of their enterprise.

In this final chapter I will round out the book by explaining why you should aspire to be an MVP and what this means for you. I will cover the following:

- The vendor MVP
- The MVP vendor in the AI era
- Using AI to buy new products

The standard we are reaching for in this chapter is not perfection, but it *is* the relentless, deliberate pursuit of being genuinely excellent at something that matters and doing it with enough consistency that the market notices. Home base is not the finish line. It is where the real game begins.

The vendor MVP

The journey from being a "Credible", then "Preferred", then "Strategic" vendor has not been easy (see the following table as a reminder of this). I would encourage you to aspire to greatness, to become that "Trusted Advisor" that has the ear of the CIO and CISO.

Level	Vendor persona	Attributes from the CIO/CISO's perspective
0	Noise	*This vendor is a commodity, and I took a meeting with them by mistake*
1	Known Quantity	*I know this company and will take a meeting if my schedule allows*
2	Credible Vendor	*I rate your product and you talk straight to me*
3	Preferred Vendor	*I'm happy to talk to you as you have helped me*
4	Strategic Vendor	*I ask your opinion on things outside your product scope*
5	Trusted Advisor	*You have earned my full trust*

Table 23.1 - Vendor Trust Maturity Model

True vendor MVPs are not "valuable" because they invite the CIO/CISO to sports events or fancy restaurants. Earning respect and trust is much more important to becoming MVPs. They are partners (not just in commercial terms, but in themselves) that the CIO and CISO will continue to engage throughout their careers. And when those leaders change roles after a few years, they may be among the first people they call to ask for intel on the new company they are moving to, as these vendors have great networks that the CIO and CISO are not afraid to tap into.

> Note
>
> *In my 38-year career, I have worked with many vendors. The ones I worked with repeatedly are the ones I trusted—I have had great relationships with so many partners... you create a team with common goals.*
>
> **Scott Collary – Group CIO, Westpac Group**

Personally, I've experienced this only a few times in my career. MVPs are not that common. I'd argue that MVPs share some personal characteristics that resonate:

- They bring real integrity and honesty
- They respect your time, so don't attempt to sell you what you don't care about
- As they have an excellent understanding of your problems, they can anticipate what you would be interested in hearing about
- They get your strategic agenda and how you think
- Because they are tuned into your environment and strategic challenges, they operate like an "insider"

Essentially, they are partners that go above and beyond.

If and when they do make a mistake, these vendors own up to this proactively, taking full accountability, and facing the consequences. Once the dust has settled, then they demonstrate how they have learned from this and repay your trust through their consistency.

The shared trust that the CIO and CISO have with the MVP has come from their being able to deliver great outcomes over a sustained period.

> Note
>
> *Demonstrate that you understand my business—not just your product. Respect my time, respect the process, and focus on real outcomes.*
>
> **Franco Marconcini – Group CISO, Electrolux Professional**

Note

The winner is the one who acts like a specialist doctor. They actually understand your specific pain before prescribing the medicine.

Jayant Dave – CISO, Check Point Software

Throughout this book I've used the baseball diamond as an analogy for achieving your goal of selling to the CIO and CISO. However, to be a true MVP vendor, you will need to play this more strategically:

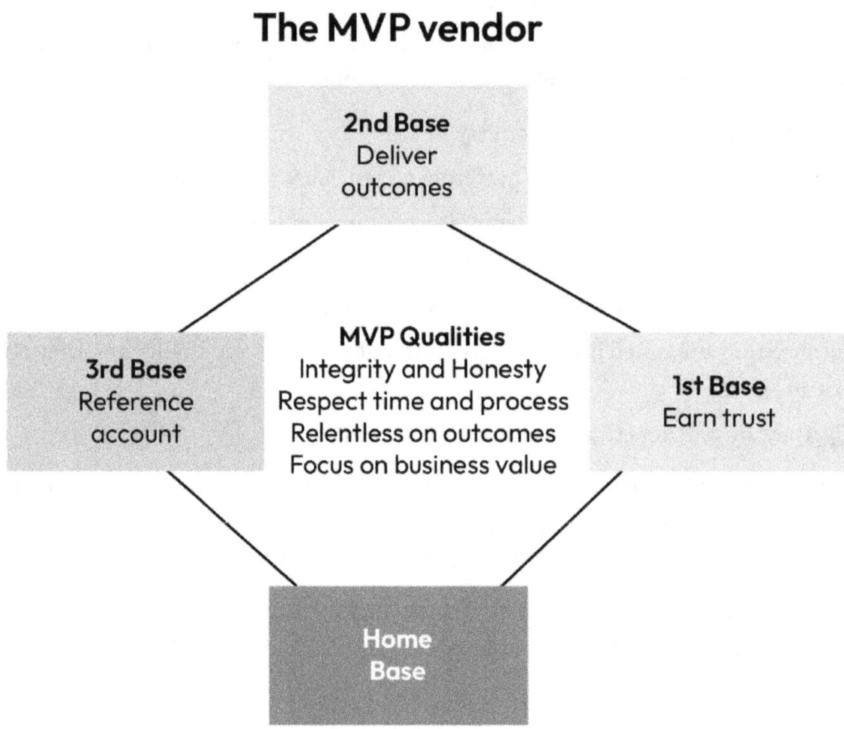

Figure 23.1 - Home run for MVPs

Note

This is a game within a game. Every vendor wants to secure the contract and get their solution installed. However, there is a larger play with the objective being to establish a dominant position, not just a foothold.

At the center of this diagram, sit the four core qualities that drive progression around the bases: integrity and honesty, respect for time and process, being relentless on outcomes, and focus on business value. I'd argue that these qualities are what separate the select few vendors who have reached level 5, "Trusted Advisor", in the Trust Maturity Model. These are qualities that are particularly welcomed by every CIO and CISO:

Integrity & Honesty	**Respect for time & process**
This is the foundation; without this, the other three qualities are meaningless. Honesty is what makes vendor advocacy credible.	This is where well-intentioned vendors can slip. You need to show up prepared, demonstrating that you're there to help. Respect their processes rather than seeking shortcuts.
Relentless on outcomes	**Business value focus**
This means staying accountable past the handoff to your client, pushing back when something won't work and measuring results rather than activity.	An MVP vendor frames everything through a business value lens so that your clients are clear on what you are offering and how it addresses their problems and will meet their needs.

Table 23.2 - MVP qualities

These four qualities can serve as your "north stars" when you are trying to become an MVP. These will also give your own team something to orient toward when things get hard.

True MVP status is cemented by consistently demonstrating these qualities across the entire post-sale journey until your customer becomes an advocate. Everything that came before was about earning the right to be here; everything that comes after is about proving that right was deserved.

The CIO and CISO have made their personal commitments to their board and management based on what you promised. The clock has started ticking and the MVP vendor knows that this is the time to deliver (not just to celebrate). While you can celebrate winning the contract, these leaders only care about the promised outcomes being delivered.

> Note
>
> *I've heard vendors talk about putting skin into the game, and that's beautiful when everything goes right. But if things go off the rails a little bit, then they suddenly cannot invest anymore—then that was never a partnership.*
>
> **Scott Collary – Group CIO, Westpac Group**

Being seen as an MVP often has the additional benefit of the CIO or CISO agreeing for their enterprise's implementation of your solution to be used by you as a "reference account". Having a reference account is, perhaps, the most powerful tool for you to have, as it means that now you have the CIO or CISO willing to speak for the positive experience they had in working with your solution. This testimony will be especially valued by their peers as it provides them credible evidence, particularly given how skeptical these C-suite buyers can be (considering the degree of spam marketing they receive).

Allow me to provide some further insights into this.

The strong reference account

I know from personal experience that not all reference accounts are the same. The person sharing the information as well as the company that provides this are both important.

The most credible reference accounts share several characteristics:

- They are from a comparable enterprise in terms of size and industry
- They are from a peer-level reference contact (i.e. CISO to CISO, CIO to CIO)
- References from well-known or respected organizations carry a halo effect
- Stage and duration are important, so that they can accurately speak to the post-implementation reality

> Note
>
> I recall my own experience of being a reference for TATA TCS (which was anticipated during a transformation when I was the CIO). I recognized that as this program provided a platform for them to refresh their core banking system, successful delivery could be a "win-win" for both of us.
>
> I knew that us having a referenceable account status would help facilitate stronger commitment by TATA TCS for the transformation program. Therefore, in this case I referred to this intention during the transformation program to signal the medium-

> term objective, which was aligned with what TCS as a vendor desired. Indeed, this enabled both of us to have "skin in the game".

Asking a CIO or CISO to allow you to use them as a reference account is a delicate request, even as an MVP. There are several factors that make this easier, though:

- Pick your timing well. The best moment to make your request is shortly after a successful implementation milestone or a moment when you resolved a difficult incident well (the customer's goodwill is highest and the experience is fresh).
- Make it reciprocal. Offering something of value to them in return, such as early access to new product features or inclusion on an advisory board, means they might be more inclined to accept.
- Consider their time. The CIO and CISO will agree more readily when the time investment required is defined and manageable.
- If you do not feel confident, let the champion broker it. In many cases the most natural path is for your internal champion to suggest the reference account status, rather than you asking directly.

If they agree, this signals that the CIO and CISO are willing to put their own name and reputation behind yours. That is not a small thing. I know from my own experience, for the CIO or CISO, agreeing to be a reference is a professional act of endorsement. It will not be extended lightly. The CIO or CISO who agree to participate can however find this an opportunity to build their own industry profile too.

> Tip
>
> The reference account relationship, when managed well, can become one of the most durable assets in your go-to-market strategy.

In the next section I will cover the journey from vendor to MVP.

Vendor to MVP

Once the solution implementation is completed successfully, you and your customer are in that real honeymoon period. Now that you've been successful in getting to this milestone, how can you build a long-term partnership with the CIO and CISO? At this point, the CIO and CISO may still not be ready to openly take on an advocate position for you.

You will be valued for your positive commitments (although it's possible there may still be some negative "noise" that remains). There will be a transition at this point from project to business as usual (BAU) governance. This transition can sometimes see the disappearance of the CIO and CISO, as this is now operational and not a strategic initiative that requires their effort.

Having said that, this is the time that you will want to move into a cadence of quarterly business reviews that retain the interest of the CIO and CISO by focusing on strategic alignment rather than support tickets. (But this does not mean, of course, that the basics of managing support tickets effectively and efficiently are not expected. The MVP vendor has to do both the strategic and operational well.)

Maintaining this interest is key to being an MVP. You want them to keep speaking to you about their strategy and how you can help, and you want to become the first call they make when things go wrong. And in normal business, of course, there will always be times when things don't work out as expected.

> **Tip**
>
> This is *not* the time to start introducing new products and services.

> **Note**
>
> *We used to say WYSIWYG (What You See Is What You Get). That was the internet age. In the AI era, I'd challenge vendors to go further.*
>
> *Stop showing me slide decks and demo environments that look nothing like my world.*
>
> *Give me a digital twin or the like. Simulate my environment. Show me what your product does in context—my architecture, my threat landscape, my constraints. AI makes this possible. If you can't show me, don't tell me.*
>
> *The vendors who will win are the ones who turn "trust us" into "see for yourself."*
>
> **Jimmy Wong – Former AIA Australia CISO**

Shifting from being seen as purely a vendor to being seen as a trusted advisor will require the relationship to move to one where there are mutual benefits, based on trust and collaboration. These words do sound flowery, so what this means in simple language is:

- Demonstrating a commitment to ongoing innovation
- Understanding customer needs and where continuous improvement is needed

> **Note**
>
> *The product is the product—it's the relationship that makes it a partnership. Understanding my strategy, my environment, and my priorities is essential to a mutually beneficial*

> *partnership. I don't want to hear what's bad about or wrong with incumbent vendors or competitors; I need to know how your product is going to accelerate my goals.*
>
> *I expect partners to understand that even if they are the market leader, sometimes an incumbent is "good enough", or from a sequencing or resourcing perspective, I can live with it for another funding cycle. MVPs listen, understand, maintain a relationship, and partner on my timeframe, not their financial year or targets.*
>
> **Andrew Dell – General Manager, Microsoft (former CISO)**

Caring about each other's success is crucial to the ongoing partnership. This is a big statement, and a long way from your initial first meeting. But this is the guide stick that you need to run by when you want to be an MVP.

> Note
>
> *If you are connecting with the people who are working with you, forming a good team, a trusted, open, transparent relationship, and anyone can call out things that are not right early, you can have everyone kind of circle up, then get moving in the right direction.*
>
> *You know that everyone you partner with has a profit and loss (P&L), and you also have a P&L—they don't always align at the same time. The good relationships are the ones where you care about each other's success.*
>
> **Scott Collary – Group CIO, Westpac Group**

To achieve the level of MVP takes real sustained commitment and execution. My own basketball idol, Michael Jordan, earned his MVP reputation by repeating his performance over many years of his career, for example. This is very difficult and increasingly rare.

With all this said, the world is undergoing an earthquake. The era of AI is changing how everyone is thinking about partnerships and what a vendor needs to do. This is shifting the requirements of what being the greatest player means.

The MVP vendor in the AI era

Being an MVP vendor to the CIO and CISO in the AI era is harder and much more difficult. AI has shifted the plates under the playing field. It's changed what CIOs and CISOs buy, but more importantly, it's changed how they think about vendors, what they expect from them, and how quickly they can detect when someone is wasting their time.

I asked several executives for their thoughts on this massive AI shift. Bradon Rogers and Gary Hayslip provided particularly insightful perspectives.

> **Note**
>
> *AI is shifting every knowledge worker from task execution to outcome ownership, supported by intelligent agents. But that only works if AI operates in an environment where security, data governance, and identity controls are built in and not layered on. The vibe-coded AI applications that will make companies more competitive and accelerate entire industries need to feel native and frictionless. Otherwise, the friction undermines the very productivity gains AI promises.*
>
> *At Island, we see AI accelerating transformation by enabling safe adoption at scale and improving customer outcomes in real time. When security becomes intelligent enough to enable speed, organizations can unlock 20–40% productivity gains while maintaining control. That's when decision-making accelerates and transformation moves from weeks to real time.*
>
> **Bradon Rogers – Chief Customer Officer, Island**

> **Note**
>
> *Honestly, I think cyber is still going to be cyber. You're still going to have to do hygiene. You still must do the basics all the time, continuously, and where I think things will change, especially with AI, is that security teams just aren't going to be humans.*
>
> *I'm talking to a lot of CISOs about this; we're not talking years from now—we're talking within the next 6 months we expect to have some type of digital employee or agent operating on our teams. This will cause us to review our stacks to discuss how we are going to monitor these agents.*
>
> *Questions we will need to ask include: Are they provisioned correctly? Can we see what data they're accessing? Truly, many of the same questions we ask for managing current employees and their access to corporate assets and services. I feel right now we are seeing pieces of that process flow and many security practitioners know they will have to either purchase or build some type of security tool where they can monitor everything that the agent is doing. Just like a CISO would do with human employees, focus on issues like insider threat and data exfiltration.*
>
> *A lot of the basics are still going to need to be there. I think humans are going to be using AI quite a lot. And so, I think you're going to have to go in and be monitoring and getting to know your bots and getting to know what they're doing.*

> *And when you start seeing the stuff that's an outlier, you flag it, sandbox it, and run your process to review the flagged activity, whether it's a human doing it or an agent—cyber is still cyber.*
>
> **Gary Hayslip – CISO, Halcyon.ai, Board Director and Investor**

In the AI era, the CIO and CISO must operate at an accelerated pace of change. They are fearful of major incidents but are being encouraged by the board to go quicker on new AI initiatives. At the same time, their regulators are fearful of new AI risks, and this pressure is only increasing.

I've seen fatigue in the eyes of my peers as they operate while trying to rationalize a sprawling AI toolset nobody fully governs yet. The AI era has brought an explosion of new point solutions, platform sprawl, and integration debt.

To a CIO and CISO in this new AI era, an MVP vendor is one who reduces complexity, not one who just adds capability. The vendor who wins is the one who makes the CIO and CISO's environment *simpler to govern*, not just more powerful. Let me take you through a few recommendations to help you do that.

Start selling in the moment

My sense is that all CIOs and CISOs are operating under a specific kind of pressure that AI has intensified. Every boardroom is asking "why can't we go faster?" They are not asking "can we be more careful not to have any AI incidents?"

In today's business environment, the CIO and CISO own the execution risk of transformation programs they didn't fully commission (delegated authority without delegated accountability). AI has compressed their tolerance for vendor noise. They can themselves also use AI to do pre-call due diligence on you, your claims, and your competitors. Information is more readily available; it may be subject to hallucinations, but that risk is often ignored and details are often not checked.

> Note
>
> *The board demands speed, regulators demand caution, and the CISO owns the incident if something goes wrong. The MVP vendor who names this tension directly and positions their solution as a bridge across it will resonate immediately.*
>
> **Jimmy Wong – Former AIA Australia CISO**

Note

Operational plans may change, the assumptions we make may be wrong, and we're treading water to sort out what to do next. I've done that with boards, and I never really talk about "we've got these threats." It is more about risks that are focused on specific business operations or focus on these specific portfolio companies, and we know from intelligence that we've gathered, they're being targeted, and this is my recommendation for us as a team to manage it.

Gary Hayslip – CISO, Halcyon.ai, Board Director and Investor

The MVP vendor needs now more than ever to read the *moment* the executive is in. Are they mid-transformation? Post-incident? Preparing for a regulatory review? Pre-budget cycle? Your positioning should reflect that, not just be a generic value prop.

Earn your base

I've seen that most vendors try to skip to third base (business case, commercial proposal) without having earned first base (genuine problem acknowledgment from the buyer). In the AI era, this is even more costly because the executive's time is now explicitly competed for by AI tools that can do research, synthesis, and analysis faster than a junior vendor team.

The MVP vendor cannot afford to skip bases because their entire value proposition is built on understanding the executive's environment more deeply than anyone else. The moment they show up with a generic business case before demonstrating genuine problem acknowledgment, they lose the trust that separates them from other vendors.

Reframe your product as a governance asset

CIOs and CISOs in regulated industries are evaluated on governance outcomes, not just technical outcomes. Your product may do extraordinary things technically, but if you can't articulate how it reduces audit exposure, maps to regulatory obligations, and helps with board-level reporting, then you are just competing on price. The MVP vendor translates their product into *governance language* without being asked.

These vendors also provide data that helps CIOs and CISOs explain risk to the board. There is a significant difference between having a risk framework and being able to stand in front of a board risk committee and speak to it with conviction.

I've seen that the CIO and CISO who walk into that boardroom unprepared are exposed. The vendor who helped them prepare, giving them the language, the evidence, and the confidence to own the conversation, can be seen as indispensable.

AI wisdom is scarce

Executives are increasingly taking the time to learn about AI and how to utilize it. I'd note that, from my own experience, CIOs and CISOs are becoming expert at spotting "clip-on" AI. By this I mean a feature layer applied to a legacy architecture after the fact, with no native integration into the model's core logic; something attached, not embedded.

Vendors often lack experience in AI, or AI in their products is underdeveloped. A vendor, therefore, who can demonstrate general and product knowledge in this area differentiates themselves. We are all deeply skeptical of vendors who cannot answer hard questions about model drift, data sovereignty, and supply chain exposure. The honest conversation here is where your AI creates risk, and how you manage it.

Bring real insight

This is the hardest shift for most vendor-side professionals. CIOs and CISOs want to engage with someone who has a perspective, challenges their assumptions respectfully, and brings external intelligence they can't access themselves.

In the AI era, this means providing information about their regulatory or threat environment they didn't already know. This may also be sharing insights from other industry peers without breaching confidentiality. Bringing a perspective as to where the industry is going is appreciated too—critical thinking is valued by the CIO and CISO as they always want to challenge their own views on emerging strategies. This approach may require you to work with other parties in the ecosystem to bring forward some innovative pairing of ideas that are synergistic.

> Note
>
> *Build alliances with similar vendors and partners who complement your solution. There is power in teamwork and executives will appreciate seeing you lead the collaboration to advance their strategic security and business goals.*
>
> **Mark Trumble – Cyber Sales & Solutions leader**

> Tip
>
> I'd expect that the MVP vendor will be an early adopter of new approaches, not just for the sake of innovation, but because eliminating friction in the buying process is something the CIO and CISO will notice and appreciate.

I'd like now to close this chapter with a discussion on use of AI to buy products, which is going to be increasingly prevalent. My view is that the current buying process has never needed more help. The MVP vendor understands this and recognizes that they have nothing to lose from a more informed, more rigorous, more efficiently run evaluation process.

Using AI to buy new products

How do CIO and CISO charged with ownership of the IT, Cybersecurity, Data/AI strategies know which products to consider for the future? Currently, navigating the technology and security market is like trying to map a coastline during a tsunami—by the time you've drawn the map, the landscape has already shifted. There are new entrants and new AI features being added to every platform and best of breed product continually.

CIO and CISO often go to industry conferences, such as RSAC (the world's largest and most influential annual cybersecurity event), for insight into available product offerings, as well as learning and networking opportunities.

Taking RSAC as an example, 43,000 leaders attend each year. They face 600+ companies exhibiting, with each vendor usually having 2–5 core products or service lines. Let me do the math for you: I estimate there are roughly 1,500 to 2,500 distinct cybersecurity products on display at any RSAC conference.

The RSAC marketplace organizes these thousands of products into roughly 25–30 high-level categories. Based on listings at the time of writing, the distribution of solutions looks something like this:

- Cloud Security: 120+ solutions
- Data Security: 100+ solutions
- Application Security: 80+ solutions
- Endpoint Security: 55+ solutions
- Identity Access Management: 45+ solutions
- AI/ML Security: over 130 AI-focused solutions

Then there are brand new and newish best-of-breed products spotlighted in a series of new startup sessions, including:

- **Innovation Sandbox**: 10 finalist products are selected as "top innovations"
- **Launch Pad**: Features 3 startup products that are often so new they haven't even hit the general market yet
- **Early-Stage Expo**: Features roughly 50–80 kiosks for emerging companies, often showcasing their first or flagship product

Note

Even the most seasoned CIOs and CISOs are struggling to keep their heads above this rising tide of new technology. About 10% of the industry changes hands every year, with 300 to 400 acquisitions and a similar number of new fundings annually. Meanwhile, roughly 160 to 200 vendors disappear each year. These failed startups often leave behind "ghost" websites while the founders have moved on to new roles, such as positions at major firms.

This (fractal nature) of the business makes it nearly impossible for a CISO to stay current through manual research alone. I spent 4,000 hours just building a database of what these vendors actually do. For a CISO, relying on manual vetting is no longer a viable strategy; you are effectively trying to drink from a firehose that is doubling in pressure every year.

Richard Stiennon – CEO, IT-Harvest

In this environment perhaps the only way to try to have coverage is for the CIO and CISO to bring their own AI bot to the table to fundamentally change how they scan the market. Operating in this new AI era, CIOs and CISOs need to work at the speed of a GPU.

This may sound cold-hearted and perhaps dehumanized (it feels to me like it strips something essentially human from a process that has always depended on relationships and judgment), but the reality is that the market has already made that choice on behalf of the buyer. Vendors are using AI to prospect and pursue at a scale and speed no human sales team could match. The asymmetry is already there.

Agent to agent

Imagine a future where the CIO and CISO have an AI agent that is constantly scanning the market for new emerging trends. What I'm describing is an autonomous buying process. This may sound like science fiction but parts of this already exist.

Note

AI impacts the sales process by leveling the playing field and allowing customers to gain deeper understanding faster and ask the hard questions. Magic quadrants will lose value and proving products with demos and trials will gain value. AI can also help provide last mile customizations to help close deals.

Jason Poley – Former Macquarie Group Head of Engineering

Note

AI transforms B2B sales through automated routine tasks, improved forecast accuracy, and scalable coaching using generative and agentic AI. Key improvements include AI role-play platforms that generate realistic buyer scenarios with instant feedback, predictive forecasts with time-series analysis for better pipeline management, automated coaching triggers that detect performance gaps, demo automation that delivers personalized experiences, and enhanced content generation that frees seller time for customer interactions. AI should augment rather than replace sellers, with successful organizations focused on both efficiency gains and effectiveness improvements.

Charlie Dai – Vice President and Principal Analyst, Forrester

I'd argue that pieces of technology that are currently in place include:

- Threat intel platforms that ingest, correlate, and prioritize signals
- Cyber Attack Surface Management (CASM)
- Cloud Security Posture Management (CSPM) tools, which map the current stack
- Automated proof of concept (POC) environments (sandboxed cloud tenancies)
- Red team automation, which already exists in mature security programs
- AI-to-AI negotiation, which has already been demonstrated in procurement contexts

These existing parts can plug into the early parts of this new process. Here's my theory of how this could evolve:

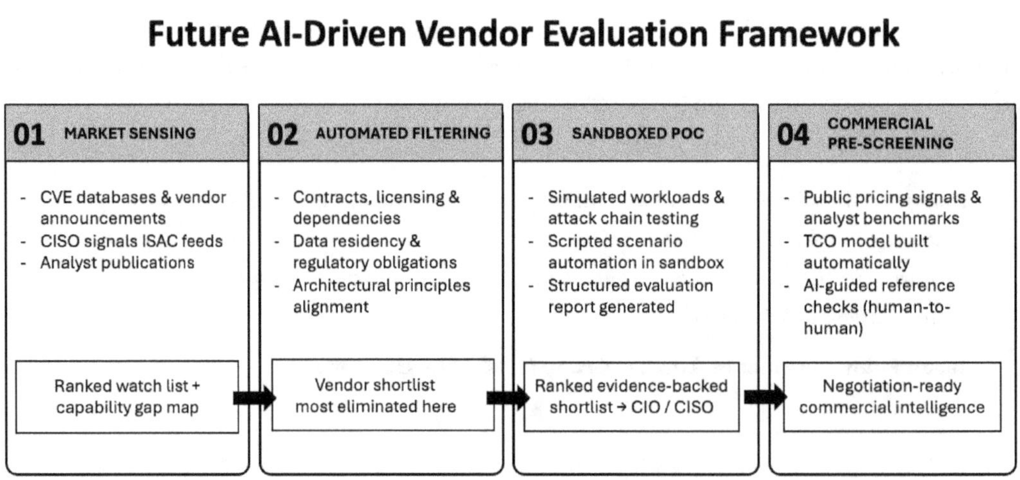

Figure 23.2 - How AI Agents could operate in the sales process

Let me explain each of these steps.

1. **Market sensing**: An AI agent continuously monitors vendor announcements, Common Vulnerabilities and Exposure (CVE) databases, analyst publications, peer network signals (CISOs talking on LinkedIn, ISAC threat feeds etc) and funding rounds. The agent builds a ranked watchlist of emerging vendors and the CIO or CISO's capability gaps. (Note that ISAC Information and Sharing Analysis Centers share cyber intelligence across industry communities).

> **Note**
>
> *AI is collapsing the timeline on every stage of the cycle, from discovery and due diligence to POC and even contract review, but it's also raising the stakes on what CISOs need to run diligence on in the first place. The vendors who win over the next five years will be the ones using AI to remove work from the buyer's plate (pre-filled security questionnaires, automated POC instrumentation, exploitability analysis that prioritizes the 2% of findings that actually matter) rather than the ones using AI as a feature checkbox.*
>
> **Amir Kazemi – Senior Director, Product Marketing, Cycode**

2. **Filtering:** Before any vendor gets human attention, the agent stress-tests it against the current environment, i.e. existing contracts, integration dependencies, data residency requirements, regulatory obligations, licensing models, and architectural principles. At this point, most vendors will likely be eliminated due to poor fit.

3. **Automated POC**: Vendors who pass step 2 are invited into a sandboxed environment. The agent runs scripted test scenarios—simulated workloads, attack chains, etc.—and produces a structured evaluation report. A human CIO or CISO then would see a ranked shortlist with evidence.

Note

It would be good to see validated proof-of-concept results from virtual environments that help to model the potential value of products tailored to organizational context. It would obviously need to be compliant with governance, risk, and privacy requirements.

Dan Chesterman – CIO, Teachers Mutual Bank

4. **Commercial pre-screening**: The AI agent pulls publicly available pricing signals, analyst reports, and benchmarks; it can then create a model of total cost of ownership (TCO).

   Reference checking, I believe, would still be human-to-human, but this of course would be guided by AI evaluation rather than being at the discretion of the leader.

Note

AI is already beginning to compress procurement and transformation timelines in meaningful ways, and this will accelerate even more in the near future.

- *AI-assisted RFP and vendor evaluation – Tools that can ingest vendor documentation, security questionnaires, and contract terms and surface risk flags or capability gaps in hours rather than weeks.*
- *Automated compliance mapping – AI that continuously maps vendor capabilities against regulatory frameworks, reducing the manual burden on legal and InfoSec teams during due diligence.*
- *AI driven procurement workflows – Soon, AI agents will handle the iterative back-and-forth of commercial negotiation, surfacing deal terms, flagging anomalies, and routing approvals—reducing what today takes weeks to days.*

George Lee – Senior Vice President, Proofpoint

A radical new approach?

Now, this is theoretical, but this model could radically change how the dynamic of the sales process works with much of the early stages automated with these AI agents working with other AI agents from the vendor side.

Theoretically these could be activities that are completed anonymously, with AI agents not disclosing who their human (watcher) is. CIOs and CISOs would likely prefer to operate and evaluate in private in this way, without any additional contact points from salespeople.

> Note
>
> *AI is already beginning to compress the evaluation cycle through automated request for proposal (RFP) responses and real-time security posture scoring to contract analysis tools. The bigger shift will be AI acting as a continuous procurement advisor, helping CIOs and CISOs. The winners on both sides of the table will be those who use AI to bring clarity and speed to a process historically defined by information asymmetry.*
>
> **Dan Wheatley – Vice President of Sales, Gravwell**

This will accelerate the process by a matter of months. But at the point of having a few pre-screened alternatives, I'd argue that the current processes revert to a manual one, to allow for relationships to be established as trust will remain an important part of the engagement going forward.

At later stages, procurement, and contracting, with all the complexity that I outlined in *chapters 19* and *20*, could also be accelerated with the use of AI agents to automate some tasks I imagine.

This potential change would eliminate cold calling and reduce the current focus on getting a demo, as the AI bots would run POC (and/or proof of value (POV)) exercises. This would remove much of the relationship-building that is the foundation of the traditional MVP approach.

> Note
>
> *All of a sudden, I have a research partner that can very quickly help me understand the vendor landscape, what advances have occurred, what features exist, and any key considerations. Understanding this means I expect to have shorter, more hi-fidelity conversations and fewer educational conversations. I also have access to non-traditional tools (agents) that may displace legacy vendors.*
>
> **Andrew Dell – General Manager, Microsoft, and former CISO**

Do you want to be open to this new potential shift and have MCP and API gateways to allow your solution to be discovered and evaluated by AI? Or would you rather be invisible to the buying organizations that are early adopters of this approach?

The traditional sales skills that made great enterprise sellers successful in the relationship era will not be obsolete, but they will be re-sequenced. Peer-level credibility and trust now operate at the *end* of a process that has been radically compressed and automated at the front. The sellers who will survive are the ones who can talk to both the agent and the executive—and know which conversation they're in.

> Note
>
> *I see AI as a force multiplier for sales teams, enabling them to spend less time on administrative tasks and more time delivering value to customers. In sales, AI is not replacing human interactions or relationships; it is enhancing the ability of sales professionals to understand customer needs, personalize engagement, and drive better value-based outcomes. As a beneficiary of AI, future sales teams will be more informed, more personalized, and as a result, more customer-centric. The teams that combine AI-driven efficiency with strong human relationships will be best positioned to deliver exceptional customer experiences and results.*
>
> **Ryan Jones – Vice President, Cyera**

Being an MVP in the AI era means enabling the CIO and CISO to be seen as successful in the eyes of their key stakeholder, the board. That requires speaking their language: translating your work into the governance, risk, and strategic outcomes that boards care about. The moment you confuse their objective with your own personal goals you stop being a trusted partner and become just another vendor competing for attention.

In this new era of AI, how will you help drive the change and uplift that the CIO and CISO really care about? This is the time to change how you show up to the table. As leaders, we can be guilty of not seeing gaps that need to be addressed and can also be negligent in not acting on those insights. I'd argue that in today's fast-paced AI era it is not hard to miss things. We all need to be very mindful and do our best to look around corners.

> Note
>
> *We are entering an era of intelligent acceleration, where AI agents will augment—and eventually execute—much of the security validation and procurement process.*
>
> *In the near future, AI agents will handle the cognitive "heavy lifting" that currently stalls organizations. When a vendor submits a bid, an AI system will:*
>
> 1. *Parse and map: Automatically ingest security certifications and architecture diagrams.*

> 2. *Gap analysis: Map vendor capabilities against internal compliance frameworks and risk appetites.*
> 3. *Risk modelling: Identify specific legal or security clauses that require human intervention.*
>
> *Processes that currently take weeks of back-and-forth will happen in hours. However, this shift introduces a "checkbox compliance" risk. If decisions are reduced purely to algorithmic scores, the nuance of organizational context can be lost.*
>
> **Abbas Kudrati – Chief Identity Security Advisor, Silverfort**

The implications for humans in the AI era and in AI-enabled buying processes are still being worked out and will be over the next decade+. I'm certain that there will be mistakes given the degree of possible change we are facing. I'd argue that it will still be important for us to focus on the human element.

> Note
>
> *The role of security and procurement teams will shift from manual evaluation to strategic curation. Humans will focus on exceptions, edge cases, and high-level risk trade-offs.*
>
> *AI will inform the decision, but the judgment and the relationship will remain human-centric. The organizations that thrive will treat AI as a force multiplier, not a substitute for critical thinking.*
>
> **Abbas Kudrati – Chief Identity Security Advisor, Silverfort**

Summary

Michael Jordan didn't become the greatest by winning one NBA championship; he became the greatest by being the player that every basketball team wanted on their side without question! The MVP vendor earns the same status through sustained trust and performance that makes the CIO and CISO look good, repeatedly, over the course of their career.

In an era where AI is, or soon will be, automating the front end of the buying process, the bar for what it means to be truly valuable has never been higher.

The key highlights from this chapter include:

- **Be a career partner** – the MVP vendor earns a place in the CIO and CISO's professional network that survives role changes. When the executive moves to a new organization, you may be one of the first calls they make. This partnership is built on integrity, honest counsel, and deep understanding of their strategic agenda.

- **Home base is the start line, not the finish** – winning the contract simply puts you on the clock. The CIO and CISO now expect the promised outcomes to be delivered. A key goal, one that being seen as an MVP enables, is for the CIO and CISO to agree to become a reference account for you, where they are willing to speak to the implementation experience, support quality, and results achieved together.
- **The AI era means reducing complexity is vital** – AI has compressed executive tolerance for vendor positioning that doesn't immediately connect to their operating reality. The MVP vendor translates their product into governance language and helps the CIO and CISO manage risk; they are honest about where AI creates risk including their own product's AI-related limitations.
- **AI will talk to AI** – the autonomous buying process may automate up to the first three bases of the selling process. AI agents are emerging that will scan the market, filter vendors against integration and regulatory fit, and run automated POCs in enterprise-owned sandbox environments before any human attention is given. Vendors who are not discoverable and evaluable by these systems will be invisible to early adopters.
- **Despite this, relationships still matter** – the relationship, peer credibility, and trust that defined MVP vendor status in the traditional model still matter, but they now operate at the end of a process that will likely be radically compressed and automated at the front. The sellers who survive are those who can engage both the AI buying agent and the executive decision-maker, always understanding which conversation they are in.

Wrap-up

The technology buying journey, as it stands today, is imperfect by design; shaped as it is by misaligned incentives, organizational complexity, and a sales culture that has historically rewarded velocity over value. This book was written in the belief that it does not have to stay that way.

This book has been designed to help you succeed in selling to CIOs and CISOs, reflecting on how this vital process can be improved. I've shared my own thoughts throughout, alongside many perspectives and insights from global leaders from all industries. Note that included in this are many leaders who have worn multiple hats as CIOs, CISOs and vendors.

I would like to thank all the leaders who have kindly contributed their thoughts to this book. They have added highly valuable depth from their own experiences and unique perspectives. My best wishes to you all on this next journey of success!

The practices, models, and insights shared across the pages of this book form something more than a playbook. I've tried to convey a different philosophy, one where the vendor shows up as a genuine partner, where the champion leads with conviction rather than politics, and where the CIO and CISO are served by a process that respects both their time and their accountability.

Allow me to reinforce how important the role of the champion is to supporting the strategic agenda of the CIO and CISO. In the absence of their drive, the CIO and CISO's ability to transform and create impactful change is more limited. The champion's leadership is so vital for this to work!

Every vendor who chooses transparency over spin, every champion who builds a business case with integrity, and every procurement team that is engaged early rather than managed late moves the whole ecosystem forward.

The next five to ten years will bring more disruption, more complexity, and more opportunity, arguably, than any other period that has come before. AI will reshape how solutions are bought, sold, and evaluated. The bar for what it means to be a trusted advisor will rise further, and the gap between those who adapt and those who do not will widen considerably.

But the fundamentals that matter will remain. Trust and outcomes will always be valued by the CIO and CISO.

Good luck with taking on the challenge.

Best regards,

David J. Gee

24

Unlock Your Exclusive Benefits

Your copy of this book includes the following exclusive benefits:

EPUB PDF

DRM-Free PDF Version

Download DRM-free PDF and ePub copies of this book.

7-Day Packt Library Access

Get 7-day unlimited access to 8,000+ books and videos. No credit card required.

Available for first-time Packt+ trial users only.

Next-Gen Reader Access

Read this book on Packt Reader with progress sync, dark mode and note-taking.

Follow the guide below to unlock them. The process takes only a few minutes and needs to be completed once.

Unlock this book's free benefits in 3 easy steps

Step 1

Keep your purchase invoice ready for *Step 3*. If you have a physical copy, scan it using your phone and save it as a PDF, JPG, or PNG.

For more help on finding your invoice, visit `https://www.packtpub.com/en-us/unlock?step=1`.

> Note
>
> **Note**: If you bought this book directly from Packt, no invoice is required. After *Step 2*, you can access your exclusive content right away.

Step 2

Scan the QR code or go to `packtpub.com/unlock`.

On the page that opens (similar to *Figure 24.1* on desktop), search for this book by name and select the correct edition.

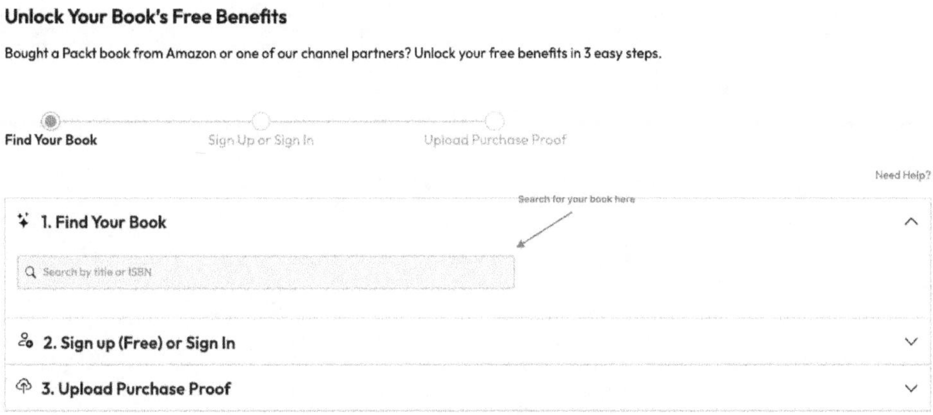

Figure 24.1: Packt unlock landing page on desktop

Step 3

After selecting your book, sign in to your Packt account or create one for free. Then upload your invoice (PDF, PNG, or JPG, up to 10 MB). Follow the on-screen instructions to finish the process.

Need help?

If you get stuck and need help, visit `https://www.packtpub.com/unlock-benefits/help` for a detailed FAQ on how to find your invoices and more. This QR code will take you to the help page.

Note

Note: If you are still facing issues, reach out to `customercare@packt.com`.

packtpub.com

Subscribe to our online digital library for full access to over 7,000 books and videos, as well as industry leading tools to help you plan your personal development and advance your career. For more information, please visit our website.

Why subscribe?

- Spend less time learning and more time coding with practical eBooks and Videos from over 4,000 industry professionals
- Improve your learning with Skill Plans built especially for you
- Get a free eBook or video every month
- Fully searchable for easy access to vital information
- Copy and paste, print, and bookmark content

At `www.packtpub.com`, you can also read a collection of free technical articles, sign up for a range of free newsletters, and receive exclusive discounts and offers on Packt books and eBooks.

Other Books You May Enjoy

If you enjoyed this book, you may be interested in these other books by Packt:

A Day in the Life of a CISO

David J. Gee

ISBN: 978-1-80611-069-8

- Adapt security strategies to manage emerging threats, including AI-driven risks
- Build and execute cyber strategies while balancing business needs and budget constraints
- Discover effective leadership and communication techniques critical for CISOs
- Implement talent development strategies for building a resilient cybersecurity team
- Learn from real-world incidents, including how to recover after breaches
- Explore career development pathways for cybersecurity professionals, including alternative and non-traditional paths to CISO roles

The Aspiring CIO and CISO

David J. Gee

ISBN: 978-1-83546-919-4

- Develop a compelling personal brand for CIO and CISO roles
- Gain mentorship through expert tips, techniques, and proven strategies to navigate executive leadership
- Be well prepared for interviews, with insights into interview questions as well as questions you can ask
- Gain insights into managing high-stakes situations and leading your organization through crises
- Practice leadership through real-life CISO and CIO scenarios
- Find out how to establish and leverage professional networks crucial for your advancement to CIO or CISO roles

Packt is searching for authors like you

If you're interested in becoming an author for Packt, please visit `authors.packtpub.com` and apply today. We have worked with thousands of developers and tech professionals, just like you, to help them share their insight with the global tech community. You can make a general application, apply for a specific hot topic that we are recruiting an author for, or submit your own idea.

Share your thoughts

Now you've finished *How to Sell to the CIO and CISO*, we'd love to hear your thoughts! Scan the QR code below to go straight to the Amazon review page for this book and share your feedback or leave a review on the site that you purchased it from.

https://packt.link/r/180730079X

Your review is important to us and the tech community and will help us make sure we're delivering excellent quality content.

Index

Symbols

A

B

C

D

www.ingramcontent.com/pod-product-compliance
Lightning Source LLC
LaVergne TN
LVHW060014210926
848481LV00013B/3706
9781807300791